STERLING
Test Prep

SAT
World History

Complete
Content Review

3rd edition

www.Sterling–Prep.com

3   2   1

ISBN-13: 978-1-9475565-9-1

Sterling Test Prep products are available at special quantity discounts for sales, promotions, academic counseling offices and other educational purposes.

Contact our sales department at: info@sterling–prep.com

Sterling Test Prep
6 Liberty Square #11
Boston, MA 02109

© 2021 Sterling Test Prep

Published by Sterling Test Prep

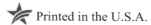 Printed in the U.S.A.

Congratulations on joining thousands of students using our study aids to achieve high test scores!

Scoring well on the SAT Subject Tests is essential for admission into a competitive college, which will position you for a successful future. This book prepares you to achieve a high score on the SAT World History Subject Test by developing the ability to apply your knowledge and quickly choose the correct answer. Understanding key concepts, developing historical thinking skills to properly analyze historical evidence and quickly respond to the exam's questions are more effective skills than merely memorizing events.

This book provides a thorough review of all topics tested on the SAT World History Subject Test. The content covers the foundational principles and theories necessary to answer test questions. History instructors with years of teaching experience prepared this material by analyzing the SAT World History test content and developing preparation material that builds your knowledge and skills crucial for success on the test. Our editorial team reviewed and systematized the content to ensure adherence to the current College Board SAT World History requirements. Our editors are experts on preparing students for standardized tests and have coached thousands of undergraduate and graduate school applicants on test preparation and admission strategies.

The review content is clearly presented and systematically organized to provide you with a targeted preparation for SAT World History test. You will learn the underpinnings and outcomes of essential historical events needed to answer exam questions. By reading these review chapters thoroughly, you will learn to apply chronological reasoning, draw comparisons and contextualization, and analyze historical evidence. This will prepare you for the test and significantly improve your SAT II score.

We wish you great success in your academics and look forward to being an important part of your successful test preparation!

Visit www.sterling-prep.com for more test prep resources.

210102gDx

SAT Subject Test prep books by Sterling Test Prep

- SAT Biology Practice Questions

- SAT Biology Review

- SAT Chemistry Practice Questions

- SAT Chemistry Review

- SAT Physics Practice Questions

- SAT Physics Review

- SAT U.S. History

Table of Contents

SAT Biology, Chemistry and Physics online practice tests

at www.Sterling–Prep.com

Our advanced online testing platform allows you to take SAT II science practice questions on your computer to generate a Diagnostic Report for each test.

By using our online tests and Diagnostic Reports, you will:

- Assess your knowledge of topics tested on the SAT Subject Test
- Identify your areas of strength and weakness
- Learn important scientific topics and concepts
- Improve your test-taking skills

Book owners

Check the last page for special pricing access
to our online resources

We want to hear from you

Your feedback is important to us because we strive to provide the highest quality prep materials. Email us any comments or suggestions.

info@sterling–prep.com

Customer Satisfaction Guarantee

Contact us to resolve any issues to your satisfaction.

*We reply to all emails – **check your spam folder***

Thank you for choosing our products to achieve your educational goals!

SAT World History Preparation and Test-Taking Strategies

To prepare for the SAT World History Subject Test, focus on the autodidactic study of relevant historical topics and periods to acquire and retain a capable understanding of the major trends within each historical period.

During preparation, it is essential to develop and perfect the following skills:

- Understanding the historical terms, concepts and information, cause-and-effect relationships, chronology, geography and other data necessary for understanding significant historical developments and historical analysis.

- Competence in interpreting data in maps, graphs, charts or cartoons using historical knowledge.

- Ability to analyze, interpret, and evaluate (primary) sources.

Work with the content of this review book to improve your performance. Take available practice tests (e.g., the free practice offered by the College Board), well before your test date. Using practice test results, identify areas of weakness, and readjust your study plan accordingly.

Every question on the SAT World History Subject Test is weighed the same regardless of difficulty. Answering challenging questions correctly does not result in more points. For every correct question answered you receive one point. You lose ¼ of a point for every incorrect answer. Skipped questions (where the answer is left blank) result in no points gained or subtracted. The sum of your points represents your *raw score*.

There are three major types of questions on the SAT World History test: *fact questions*, *trend questions*, and *graphic questions*. In the sample questions below, the correct answer will be underlined.

Fact questions

To succeed in answering factual questions, you must possess and be able to recall specific knowledge about names, definitions, dates, events, participants involved, and the significance of each. The sample question below (released by the College Board) is an excellent example of a fact question.

Differences between which two religions contributed to violent conflicts in India during and after the struggle for independence in 1947?

(A) Hinduism and Buddhism
(B) Islam and Christianity
(C) Hinduism and Islam *(correct answer)*
(D) Islam and Buddhism
(E) Hinduism and Jainism

Trend questions

Trend questions assess your depth of understanding of historical relationships, your ability to draw connections between facts and events within general themes and periods. These questions may include quotations that require the test taker to recognize the speaker's attitude and its possible association with relevant political or social movements and to frame the quotation with a larger historical context. Others may require the identification of key issues connected with a certain historical period. The sample question below (released by the College Board) is an excellent example of a trend question.

> "Where it is an absolute question of the welfare of our country, we must admit of no considerations of justice or injustice, or mercy or cruelty, or praise or ignominy, but putting all else aside must adopt whatever course will save its existence and preserve its liberty."

The statement above expresses the viewpoint of which of the following?

(A) Niccolò Machiavelli (*correct answer*)
(B) Sir Thomas More
(C) Desiderius Erasmus
(D) Dante Alighieri
(E) John Calvin

Graphics questions

To correctly answer graphic questions, you must be able to interpret the presented visual, which is commonly a map or artifact image. Before analyzing the graphic, read the question first, since the question might give you a clue for what to look for in the image. The sample question below (released by the College Board) is an excellent example of a graphics question.

The ancient Chinese symbol of the universe shown above represented

(A) the theory that everything consists of opposite but complementary elements (*correct answer*)
(B) the Zen concept of unity in artistic expression
(C) Buddha's vision of the perfect shape
(D) a dualism in which everything conflicts and nothing can be resolved
(E) the moral principles of Confucius

Setting a Target Score

As you prepare for your SAT World History Subject Test, you can set a target score you wish to achieve. Of course, you should strive for the maximum 800 score, but you should also know the range that would be acceptable for your objectives. Depending on the colleges you are applying to, the desired scores can vary. You can find this by utilizing the data available to you, such as reading college guidebooks, contacting college admissions offices, and talking to your guidance counselor. Once you know the average score for incoming students, set your target score above that. If you reach this target score, you will be above average.

The SAT World History Subject Test questions reflect topics covered in most high schools. However, since high school curricula vary from school to school, you may encounter questions on topics that are unfamiliar to you. When this happens, answer such questions as best as you can and try to avoid wild guessing. You don't have to answer every single question correctly to get a high score. You can even achieve the maximum 800 points providing wrong answers to a few questions and skipping some. For example, you could score:[*]

- 800 by answering 87 correct, 4 wrong and skipping 4 ($87 - 4 \times \frac{1}{4} = 86$ raw points)
- 780 by answering 77 correct, 8 wrong and skipping 10 ($77 - 8 \times \frac{1}{4} = 75$ raw points)
- 740 by answering 71 correct, 12 wrong and skipping 12 ($71 - 12 \times \frac{1}{4} = 68$ raw points)
- 700 by answering 66 correct, 16 wrong and skipping 13 ($66 - 16 \times \frac{1}{4} = 62$ raw points)
- 660 by answering 60 correct, 20 wrong and skipping 15 ($60 - 20 \times \frac{1}{4} = 55$ raw points)

[*] This is an approximation only. The actual score will depend on the conversion curve used by the ETS for your particular test administration.

No Wild Guessing

Since every question answered incorrectly results in a bigger penalty ($-\frac{1}{4}$ point) than unanswered questions (0 points gained or lost), guessing wildly is not beneficial and may reduce your potential score. A better strategy is to go through the entire test first and answer the questions you know with a high degree of confidence. Then, use the remainder of your time to go through the questions you skipped and analyze them more closely. By using this strategy, you will ensure that you see each question at least once and have the opportunity of answering them.

Do not allocate too much time to challenging questions. If you cannot make an educated guess for a particularly difficult question, it is better to leave it unanswered. While this may seem counterproductive, this strategy works the best with the scoring system of the SAT World History Subject Test (and all other SAT subject tests).

For SAT subject tests, educated guessing should take place when at least one (better two) answer can be eliminated. This is the application of probability: if a test taker guesses among four choices (instead of the original five), on average, they will get a single question right for every three they get wrong (25% chance). For the three incorrect answers, they would lose a $\frac{3}{4}$ point, but for the one correct answer, they would gain 1 point, which is $\frac{1}{4}$ point net gain.

If you can eliminate two choices and guess among the remaining three, your probability of correct guessing goes to 33.3%, meaning that out of three questions, you would guess one right and two wrong, and your net gain goes up to the ½ point. Therefore, if you encounter a question where you can safely eliminate one or two answer choices, ponder the remaining choices and take a guess. If you have no clue about the question and all answer choices look viable to you, skip this question and move on.

Managing Your Pace

Establishing a steady pace is one important component of your success that cannot be overstated. This skill can be acquired by taking timed practice exams to (re)familiarize yourself to testing with a time limit. If you do not pace yourself appropriately, you may not have the time needed to read every question. If you find yourself puzzled and stuck on a question, move on. Getting bogged down eats up valuable seconds. You can always revisit difficult questions later.

Memorization vs. Context

The SAT World History Subject Test assesses students' understanding of how facts fit within a larger historical context, rather than their ability to recall dates, names, and events. It is a common misconception that all you need to do to get a great score on the test is to memorize facts. Fact memorization is important and useful, but analytical intelligence and a wider contextual understanding are essential.

Thinking about history in unifying contextual categories, such as epochs, eras, movements, and trends (the "big picture") helps in organizing facts into unifying understandings, rather than leaving them as discrete bits of information. Placing facts into a common framework of a broader historical context will also help you recall information when needed.

For example, take a look at the sample question below (released by the College Board).

A major change brought about by Franklin D. Roosevelt's New Deal, 1933-1939, was the

- (A) creation of machinery for maintaining full employment
- (B) transformation of a business-dominated society into a labor-dominated one
- (C) redistribution of the population from urban centers to rural areas
- (D) development of new attitudes about the role and function of government
- (E) destruction of machine politics at the state and city levels

This question does not ask for specific names or dates. Instead, it asks the test taker to identify the correct major change. Contextual knowledge of the Great Depression period and the broad intent of the New Deal programs and initiatives are needed to answer this question correctly.

Having a healthy grasp of historical context, rather than just facts, can help you identify wrong answers, raising your chances of selecting the correct one.

Verify Your Answers

Since a machine, not a person, scores your test, it is very important to carefully and neatly fill in the proper ovals on your answer sheet, so that the grading machine reads it as you intended. Pay close attention to avoiding mistakes when marking your answer sheet. When you skip a question to revisit it later, be sure to fill out the grid correctly. For example, if you skipped question 57, you want to avoid the mistake of marking your answer to question 58 in row 57. Errors like this can have a domino effect and potentially ruin your whole test. To prevent this, develop the mental habit of double-checking question numbers and answers before marking the sheet.

Overconfidence and Lack of Confidence

Overconfidence and lack of confidence are polar opposite reactions test-takers can experience and it can hurt your score. Overconfidence may cause you to speed through the exam, miss important details when reading the questions, and not utilize the remaining time to double-check your answers adequately. Test-taking is not a race to the finish, and you will not get any extra points for finishing early.

Conversely, a lack of confidence can sabotage an otherwise well-prepared test taker. This defeatist response can lead to a sense of panic when difficult questions are encountered. When anxiety begins to become a distraction, remember: breathe fully, approach the exam methodically, concentrate on the question presented, and recall the test-taking strategies provided earlier.

Notes for active learning

Period 1

Prehistory and Civilizations
to the year 500 C.E.

Small, scattered populations coalesce into emergent civilizations

Nearly 2.6 million years ago, humankind began to develop and use primitive stone tools, marking the beginning of the Paleolithic Period. This newly acquired ability, along with other factors, enabled increased survivability, reproduction, and eventual mass migrations. Throughout this period, waves of populations migrated from Africa to neighboring Eurasia, Oceania, and the Americas.

At the end of the Paleolithic Period nearly 12,000 years ago (c. 10,000 B.C.E.), a severe shift in worldwide climate (marking the end of the Little Ice Age) influenced many populations to shift from hunter-gatherer society to semi-permanent pastoralist or permanent agricultural societies. This shift allowed a more settled way of life and significantly increased food production, which stimulated more population growth. Larger populations, in turn, led to the development of more socially-stratified societies.

Eventually, when large enough levels of agricultural surplus were achieved, urban societies emerged. These urban centers marked the advent of civilizations capable of supporting increasingly diversified specializations of labor and complex institutions, such as political bureaucracies, armies, and religious hierarchies. Long-distance trade routes were established, connecting these early civilizations. This connectivity and increases in wealth spurred swelling warfare as civilizations fought for territories, resources, and power.

The victorious states, obtaining increasingly diverse populations under their reign, developed methods of incorporating and governing these new subjects. Overexpansion often resulted in empires too large and riddled with too many political, cultural, or administrative difficulties to sustain them.

Global Comparative

Major historical events of the period:

15,000 B.C.E.:	Lascaux cave paintings
12,000 B.C.E.:	Paleolithic era (end of the Stone Age)
10,000 B.C.E.:	Neolithic Revolution
4,000 B.C.E.:	Yellow and Nile River Valley civilizations emerge
4,000 B.C.E.:	Rice cultivation begins in India and China
3,500–3,000 B.C.E.:	Cuneiform widely used among numerous Mesopotamian civilizations
3,000 B.C.E.:	Egyptians create hieroglyphs
1,200–1,050 B.C.E.:	Chinese writing system emerges
1,000 B.C.E.:	First notable alphabet originates in Phoenicia
600 B.C.E.–600 C.E.:	Confucianism. Taoism, Buddhism, the Greco-Roman religion, Christianity and Islam emerged
1 B.C.E.:	Trade along the Silk Road begins
200s C.E.:	Tea is introduced to China from India
161 C.E.:	Bubonic Plague devastates China
540 C.E.:	Bubonic (Justinian) Plague first arrives in Europe

PERIOD 1: Prehistory and Civilizations to the year 500 C.E.

GLOBAL COMPARATIVE

Archeological evidence indicates that during the Paleolithic era, hunting-foraging bands of humans gradually migrated from their origin in East Africa to Eurasia, Australia, and the Americas, adapting their technology and cultures to new climate regions.

The Paleolithic era refers to the end of the Stone Age (typically 12,000 B.C.E.) and is used to describe a period in time where people were nomadic and on the cusp of transitioning into a period of agricultural production, surplus, and more urban existence, dominated by never-before-seen social structures and societal norms.

Between the period of 8000 and 3500 B.C.E., small kin-based social groups were able to undertake new technologies, agricultural practices, and social expectations, laying the groundwork for later classical civilizations. Some academics have argued that all life stems from a so-called cradle of life, which, according to most scholars, is on the African continent. Recently evidence has emerged to support the *Out of Africa* scenario, which implies that the main human populations of today and ancient times derive from the same source in Africa and share a smaller DNA pool than previously thought.

The earlier theory of isolated human evolution in Australia was refuted by genotyping research of aboriginal Australians, New Guineans, Southeast Asians, and Indians conducted in 2013. It showed a close genetic relationship between these groups, with the time of divergence estimated at 36,000 years ago. Additionally, substantial gene flow detected between the Indian populations, and aboriginal Australians indicates an early "southern route" migration out of Africa to the region with the subsequent dispersal.

Results similar to the DNA findings of the *Out of Africa* model have been found regarding the settling of the Americas, which most argue was done by a single group of migrants who traveled across the Bering Strait. Current genetic evidence indicates that Native American populations are initially from East Asia, which would seem to be confirmed by the small DNA pool shared among those who initially settled in these regions. There is, however, evidence that there was also a second migratory line from Oceania, also based on DNA evidence. There is a continuing academic debate about when and how this second group got to North America.

Regardless of their place of origin, the early kin-based bands of immigrants evolved to live in regions of the world previously unknown to them, including, but not limited to, Mesoamerica, the Middle East, and Australia. These migrations have had undeniable impacts on the social systems and civilizations seen today, as it is easy to assume that life as we know it would not exist without these migrations. Migrants from the cradles of civilization explored the global system and eventually settled in the regions most capable of providing a stable existence. These migrations and adaptations proved instrumental in the later periods of settlement, as early humans were forced to continually adapt and evolve to sustain life within the global system.

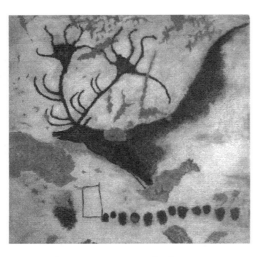

Lascaux cave paintings

It is worth noting that the existence of the global system was already noticeable at this point in history; migrants settled in various locations but originated from connected sources, evoking the concept that all life is interconnected in some capacity. Furthermore, while many in the academic community agree that migration occurred during this period, they disagree on the locations and the human species undertaking these migrations. Some academics also question the validity of climate change being a determining factor in these migrations. However, given the history of the Paleolithic era, it is reasonable to assume that climate change played a role in determining migration patterns.

The Lascaux cave paintings, found in modern France and dated to approximately 15,000 B.C.E., showcase the creative human spirit of the Stone Age leading into the Paleolithic era. These paintings, which depict over 2,000 different figures, are the earliest recorded examples of such art. Some academics have labeled the Lascaux cave paintings as the most famous and influential art of the Paleolithic era. This is a key example of art before the emergence of religion. They illustrate the behaviors and roles of everyday life, particularly hunting and gathering. Fossil evidence found in the caves supports the existence of many of the animals depicted in the wall art.

Humans used fire in new ways: to aid hunting and foraging, to protect against predators, and to adapt to cold environments.

As early humans continued to evolve and adapt, one innovation would drastically improve their means of survival: the use and mastery of fire. The most accepted date for the use of human-controlled fire is approximately 125,000 years ago, with other approximations ranging from 1.7 million to 500,000 years ago. The earliest archeological evidence of human-controlled fire was found in modern-day Israel north of the Dead Sea Valley and dated to approximately 790,000 years ago. This particular location is a fire site and contains evidence of meats and plants eaten during this period.

Humans were using fire as a means of heating to adapt to colder climates and temperatures as a result of climate change and migration. This adaptation was especially important because the European climate was much colder during this period, and mastery of fire may have allowed habitation by group settlements, which would have been otherwise unable to survive in this region.

In addition to adaptation for climate change and migration, the use of fire against predators provided an additional resource to early humans, who needed the ability to protect themselves beyond bare-handed self-defense. As hunting and gathering practices evolved and later translated into pastoralism and agrarianism, it became essential to use new means of locating and obtaining food.

The use of fire allowed early humans more access to resources necessary for creating a stable living environment because fire and the adaptive qualities it provided for early humans allowed for the settlement of more diverse and untouched lands, culminating in the current global system seen today. The use of fire also created a sense of human companionship and community. Early records show that, for small bands of nomads, this sense of belonging or connection would become a vital human emotion. Such connections would be explored more fully in early civilizations, where communities became dependent on their inhabitants and neighbors.

Without the advanced use of fire, early humans would have been unable to cope with climate change or the predators of the period. Fire gave early humans the ability to settle continental Europe, which was experiencing a decrease in overall temperature during this period.

Humans developed a wider range of tools that were specially adapted for different environments, such as tropics or tundra.

As early human groups migrated to their respective regions and attempted to adapt to the changing landscapes and surroundings, a technological revolution took place. Evidence of this revolution is seen in attempts to create new, stronger, more dependable tools out of better quality materials. In the initial years of this period, tools had been made of bone, wood, and stone, appropriate to a lifestyle of hunting and gathering. Archeological evidence found in southern Africa's Lesotho site and dating to the Middle Stone Age supports the construction of stone tools.

However, as more settled communities emerged, better tools were needed. The simpler tools of the Paleolithic period, such as spears and axes, would not do for these new communities. As a result, early humans began developing new technologies, which allowed for the production of tools from bronze, and later iron, molds. These early tools were not only used for agriculture, but also as a form of protection from invasions and outside threats.

Paleolithic tools

Plows were also developed during this period and would be used to kick-start the agricultural movement seen in later periods. This allowed for the population expansion that created the need and desire for urban dwellings. Initial urban settlements proved to be a success and showed the influence metal tools could have on various civilizations.

The use of tools during this period was as important as the advances made regarding fire. These tools were the precursor to the metal tools that would arrive in the Bronze Age and the Iron Age. Some of these new tools had precise cutting abilities, and soon hunting, and domestic tools emerged. Some of the sharper, more precise tools were used to sew clothing: an adaptation necessary for colder climates. Barbed wires were used for fishing, and grindstones were further adapted to create new plant-based meals. Projectiles were invented during this period, allowing the bands to hunt faster, more agile prey.

Bronze Age axes

These advances would eventually allow small bands to evolve into semi-permanent and, eventually, permanent settlements following the Neolithic Revolution. The continuous introduction of new tools shows the ability of these small sects to continue to evolve and adapt, qualities that were critical for survival in this period. Technological advances would continue to spur the feeling of exploration and adaptation seen during this period and cause early humans to experiment with metals and other resources in the hope of creating the most durable and reliable tools possible. This pursuit would eventually bring about the Bronze Age and the Iron Age.

Economic structures focused on small kinship groups of hunting and foraging bands that could make what they needed to survive. However, not all groups were self-sufficient; they exchanged people, ideas, and goods.

There is abundant evidence from this period that small, kin-based groups were migrating and settling throughout the Middle East, Southeast Asia, and the European continent, creating typically self-sufficient communities. While some of these groups may have been isolated, similar to the early humans of Australia, evidence has emerged that others interacted with various neighboring communities.

These small bands were not always comprised of close kin. Sometimes various members of hunter-gatherer communities would be incorporated into these tight-knit bands. A sense of cooperation emerged as early humans began to associate more extensively with others. While these small bands were supportive, they were incapable of developing any leadership roles, bureaucracies or artisans, as all available time was devoted to the collection of food and other resources. During this period, the roles of work within the band were evenly distributed. The idea of a ruling or elite class was unheard of, and slavery was nonexistent, although it would later become common in almost all early civilizations. Both women and men shared foraging responsibilities. Distribution of responsibilities led to many distinct roles within bands, creating a further sense of community.

The exchange of ideas, goods, and people during this period was common. Various bands embodied different social traditions depending on their kinship and place of origin, which were typically shared with other bands. These relationships were extremely important during periods of drought or adverse climate change, as many early humans sought other living situations during times of environmental uncertainty and resource scarcity.

Women moved between groups more easily, as they attempted to find mates outside of their kinship band. However, this would not always be the case, and incestuous breeding sometimes occurred. This became less prevalent as Indo-European migrations transferred populations, and the emergence of agrarian communities created new social expectations.

The long-term implications of such social customs can be seen as the foundation of community and connection apparent in the later period of agrarian and pastoral communities. The spread of knowledge, tradition, and culture is important because it shows a trend of inclusion and sharing among early humans—a tradition continuing today. Without these periods of migration and interaction, it seems likely that many small kin-based bands would have continued to pursue hunting and gathering as they migrated. Instead, the emergence of early civilizations was the result of Paleolithic migrations and transitions.

Beginning about 10,000 years ago, the Neolithic Revolution led to the development of new and more complex economic and social systems.

The Neolithic Revolution was a major turning point in early human and world history. The period is typically defined as beginning in 10,000 B.C.E. and would eventually lead to the construction of permanent agrarian and pastoral communities. This period saw the domestication of animals, such as cats, goats, and pigs, as well as the cultivation of crops like barley, wheat, maize, rice, and potatoes. The social transitions of this period were instrumental in creating what we understand today as a civilization.

The largest result of the Neolithic Revolution was the creation of permanent settlements. These would grow into small states, empires, and eventually, world-renowned ancient civilizations such as Egypt, Mesopotamia, and China. In addition to permanent settlements, the early humans experiencing this Neolithic Revolution began to modify their social systems. In hunter-gatherer groups, women had maintained an equal status and role to that of men. This changed during this period, as women were seen as domestic caretakers rather than equals. From this period forward, women would experience a gradual decline in status, in both political and civic life.

The initial villages of this period were typically headed by a council of elders, comprised of several prominent families in the village, or a chief elder, who maintained power over the structure and leadership of the village. This was important during times of crisis or war when these same leaders would assume leadership on the battlefield. New technologies developed during this period included calendars, tools, and weapons (made of bronze, iron, and copper), plows, and wheeled transports used for farming. Record-keeping systems used in farming show the increased level of organization by the population.

This period also saw the emergence of a new social class, due to its large populations and skilled workers. This new elite group included priests, civic workers, artisans, and warriors, all of whom were now able to pursue vocations previously unobtainable or unknown. Additionally, the emergence of patriarchal systems would influence the social structure of life following the Neolithic Revolution. These changes included a decline in the status and roles available to women within familial and political structures and the emergence of slavery in various cultures, most notably that of Egypt.

The major effects of the Neolithic Revolution can be seen in the social structures of village life following this period and the implementation of various agricultural practices. New understanding of agricultural resources culminated in the settling of fertile river valleys, such as the Indus, Tigris-Euphrates, Yellow, and Nile Rivers. These settlements paved the way for future civilizations, such as Egypt and Mesopotamia.

This rise in social or caste classes, along with the emergence of civilizations as we currently know them, can be labeled one of the most significant human transition periods to date. Without advances like agriculture, early humans would have remained hunter-gatherers, lacking the resources to develop stable communities and existing in continuous cycles of population increase and decrease similar to those experienced by the early humans during the Neolithic Revolution. Instead, early humans were able to make this transition, eventually to be followed by others in the Americas and Australia.

Caste and social systems also harmed some cultures which previously had none, but later instituted slavery and the oppression of women. These oppressive systems continued into modernity and certainly influenced the treatment of various demographic groups throughout world history.

Permanent agricultural villages emerged first in the lands of the eastern Mediterranean, likely in response to climatic change.

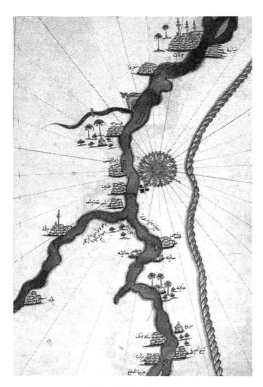

The Nile River

As early humans adjusted to the changing climate and landscape of this period, new settlements began to emerge that would later become the foundation of both Western and Eastern civilizations. The Phoenicians are one of a few early groups to form permanent settlements. As a result of limited resources, they settled colonies throughout the Mediterranean, such as the cities of Carthage and Cyprus. This trade-based civilization would be the foundation of the later empires of this period, including the Egyptian, Mesopotamian, Chinese, and Indian cultures.

These great empires would influence both regional and transregional matters of trade, religion, and legal codes. The idea of a culture dominated by social structure first emerged during this period and influenced later European traditions. The gender roles that emerged from this period would have long-lasting implications for both women and men. Additionally, the scientific technology of this period, such as the developments of calendars and mathematics, would greatly influence the academics of Greece, Rome, and—by default—Western Europe. Written record-keeping, mathematics, astrology, and early philosophy all stem from this period and can be seen in various cultures from the Shang dynasty to the Babylonians, from the Minoans to the Egyptians. Such advances were only possible because of the achievements of the early civilizations of this period.

Pastoralism developed at various sites in the grasslands of Afro-Eurasia.

The pastoral settlements and societies that emerged during this period can be defined as communities who moved with the migration patterns of their livestock, typically horses, sheep, and oxen. While these settlements may sound less stable than their permanent agrarian counterparts, pastoralists experienced greater flexibility in many areas of life, including climate concerns, invasions by enemy forces, and concerns regarding water scarcity experienced by urban and agrarian settlements. Its ancient hunter-gatherer roots typically overshadowed the emergence of pastoralism, but these populations were typically successful and powerful entities during their period. One example is the Hyksos, who invaded and ruled Egypt.

Different pastoralist sites produced various tools and weapons, including, but not limited to, handheld weapons such as daggers, flint points, axes, and spears. These were typically used for working with animals and hunting, though in times of turmoil, these weapons were also used in warfare. Other examples of warfare tools were chariots, which were extremely effective in waging war against rivals and neighbors, such as those between the Egyptians, the Hittites, and the Hyksos. The domestication of horses began in Central Asia around 4300 B.C.E. and was an integral part of the pastoralist communities.

Egyptian king on his chariot

Notable pastoralist sites during this period are typically labeled as Indo-European. Around 3000 B.C.E., the pastoralist communities began migrating through the continent, encountering permanent settlements along the way. While many of these interactions were peaceful and involved the sharing of knowledge, language, and traditions, not all migrations were peaceful. Some pastoral tribes of this group were forced to migrate as a result of drought, disease, population increases, and prolonged climate changes. These tribes often conquered or plundered permanent settlements, displacing people, and violating family structures.

Pastoralist communities also embodied different values than those of agrarians, whose values centered on limited material possessions but a rich tradition and culture of the family group. The social standards within pastoralist groups were also different; women were able to maintain equal status as in the Paleolithic periods and were even able to attain a type of warrior status in certain clans or tribes.

The long-term implications of pastoralist societies were significant. The emergence of this style of living would influence later cultures, such as the Mongol hordes that dominated Central Asia in later periods. The juxtaposition between settled agrarian communities and pastoralists exemplified a cultural rivalry that continued for many years as a source of tension between the two groups. Pastoralists were also crucial to the spreading of Indo-European cultures throughout Eurasia, as their migratory patterns allowed them to interact with permanent settlements. Typically, such interactions were tense, though sometimes they shared a sense of shared values and traditions.

Different crops or animals were domesticated in the various core regions, depending on available flora and fauna.

Early civilizations explored their paths to cultivating crops and domesticating animals; a result of various trends of agricultural progress and different capacities of leadership. Mesopotamia shows evidence of goats, pigs, and sheep were domesticated between 7000 and 6000 B.C.E. During this same period in Egypt; they had domesticated cats. Archeologists have found further evidence of the importance of domestic animals in the Harappan communities.

Dogs were the first animal to be domesticated by the human species (up to 12,000 years ago). No other animals were able to bond with the human species like the domesticated dog, which would eventually lead to greatly expanded breeding and human companionship in later periods. Throughout human history, though, peasants would sleep indoors with cattle, goats or other animals—a practice pervasive in feudal Europe, ancient India, and other Asian civilizations.

Agricultural production was also a direct result of the various climates throughout the global system. In the Indus Valley, there is vast evidence of the cultivation of many plants and the domestication of many animals. Between 6000 and 5000 B.C.E., the Indus River Valley saw the cultivation of cotton, wheat, barley, mustard, and rice. Evidence of horse bones causes some academics to conclude that horses were used in some capacity, possibly as food. However, a typical diet of this period would have included wheat, barley, milk products, fruits, vegetables, and fish or meat.

Other notable crops included strawberries in the Americas, soybeans in northern China, apples, and almonds in the Middle East, sugarcane, rice, and oranges in Southeast Asia. Civilizations in Africa cultivated sorghum, barley, wheat, and rye. The variety of cultivation speaks to various types of river valley civilizations of the period. Depending on the climate and the existing plant and animal life, many civilizations had to adopt the appropriate plant and animal cultivating practices.

The long-term impacts of domestic animal and plant cultivations can be seen throughout world history and into the contemporary period. Advances in plant and animal cultivation allowed early civilizations to have surpluses of food for the first time in history. With this agricultural surplus, communities were able to grow at unprecedented rates. This was a necessity for the evolution of early settlements into large civilizations and sprawling empires.

Agricultural communities had to work cooperatively to clear land and create the water control systems needed for crop production.

As communities developed and expanded during this period, new concerns emerged regarding the use and conservation of water, a resource crucial to the success of agricultural communities, and the lifeblood of these newly formed civilizations. People began to understand water as a means of survival and expansion with a limited supply. The emergence of irrigation systems allowed for the settlement of areas previously uninhabitable or considered difficult to develop. Some of the first irrigation systems can still be seen in present-day Iran.

These systems, called qanats, were a series of shallow slopes and wells dug into the foothills of a mountain to allow water to drain from the underground aquifer; many are still used in some capacity today. These revolutionary irrigation systems allowed for the transportation of water from a source outside the community, a source that could be increasingly farther away as technology developed.

Ancient Syrian water wheel pump for irrigation

During this period, the size of civilization was dependent on the resources available to sustain it, most notably water. It is because of this necessity that early humans were always adapting and inventing new ways of extracting and maintaining water levels. Some of the earliest permanent water wells were dug in approximately 6500 B.C.E. in the Jezreel Valley. Other examples of water innovations from this period can be found in the Mohenjo-Daro ruins: shadoofs, or sakias, which used a bucket attached to a large lever to lift water to ground level, allowing for the extraction or pumping to irrigation systems.

These undertakings were required to promote an agrarian society, and without the cooperative efforts of all those involved, agricultural development would not have been possible during this period. While many civilizations desired to maintain power, all early civilizations faced similar challenges that unified some cultures in the exchange of ideas, goods, and people. Such cooperation would be seen throughout later periods of world history. These irrigation systems and cooperative practices were hugely important to the period as well as in future agricultural endeavors. They were also pivotal to Western European history; without the technologies of aqueducts, wells, and irrigation channels, urban agrarian communities would not have been sustainable.

These new agricultural practices drastically impacted environmental diversity. Pastoralists also affected the environment by grazing large numbers of animals on fragile grasslands, leading to overgrazing and erosion.

Slash-and-burn practices were employed to clear adequate agricultural lands. Typically used in forests or areas of heavy vegetation, slash and burn is an agricultural technique in which old crops or existing vegetation are burned to make room for new crops. It was used for centuries and initially created fertile soil as a result of the burning process. However, with time this practice would lead to overuse and deforestation of the land.

The agricultural practices of the period allowed for the cultivation of various plants that greatly diversified the environment and agricultural capabilities of the people. Examples of diversity can be seen in the various types of domesticated plant life during this period, including maize, rice, tomatoes, wheat, barley, and potatoes. Although this diversification meant humans were developing various plants that otherwise might not have been cultivated, it did not result in a more widely diverse diet.

Although many saw the increased agricultural production and larger populations as progress, there was cause for concern. Overgrazing of fertile land and erosion threatened to reverse the advances of previous periods. Overgrazing is defined as the extensive exposure of plants to intensive grazing practices, without adequate recovery periods for the land involved. This is typically caused by livestock; however, overgrazing can also occur in strictly agricultural settings where there is no crop rotation or crops are poorly managed. To address these concerns, both pastoral and agrarian settlements were forced to reevaluate certain practices in hopes of returning the fragile grasslands to their original states.

When land has been overgrazed or overproduced, the productivity and biodiversity of the soil are compromised, and desertification and erosion can occur. Both desertification and erosion were detrimental to agrarian cultures but had less effect on pastoralists, which could relocate in such conditions. The increase in population seen during this period arguably led to overgrazing and overproduction. The overgrazing led to soil erosion, which could have had damaging effects on the entire ecosystem of the region. However, truly extensive overgrazing or overproduction was seen in minimal amounts and provided little resistance to the agricultural movements.

The lasting environmental implications of these agricultural practices are debatable. Because pastoralists typically grazed an area and moved on to another, the environmental damage was not concentrated in any one particular place. No long-term environmental impact was seen as a result of overgrazing by pastoralists during this period, but it anticipated its later agricultural impact on the environment. Although early humans learned the pitfalls of overgrazing and soil erosion, this did not stop future generations from making similar mistakes, leading to the development of safer agricultural practices. Examples of later advancement in this area include crop rotation to rest the soil and produce quality agriculture.

Agriculture and pastoralism began to transform human societies.

The emergence of agrarian and pastoral settlements marked the transition period between nomadic practices and the classical civilizations associated with Western civilization, such as those of Rome and Greece. Many pastoralists came into contact with agrarian settlements as part of their migration patterns. Without both pastoralist and agrarian settlements, we would not have seen populations increase as they did, and technological advancements in warfare and agriculture might not have been developed without these communities. The spreading of ideas, religions, and cultures was also greatly facilitated by the pastoralist communities who transported goods, ideas, and people throughout Eurasia.

These two early systems of organizing society, agrarian and pastoral, eventually evolved into the contemporary social system. As they gave way to newer ones, the social structures of cities and families changed. Agriculture and pastoralism were the transitions between the Stone Age and the classical period, which produced the advanced art and culture of Greco-Roman civilization. Greece and Rome were greatly influenced by the societies that preceded them and would not have developed without the achievements of both agrarian and pastoral communities.

Pastoralism and agriculture led to more reliable and abundant food supplies, causing an increase in population.

Due to the agricultural and technological advances of the period, both agrarian and pastoral settlements flourished and experienced greater food security, leading to an agricultural surplus and a massive increase in population. Economic and agricultural stability commonly produce an increase in population as the quality of life improves, and diseases are less rampant.

Some of the positive attributes of this increase in food production and population can be seen in greater quality and duration of life, the social stability produced as a result of food security and the increase in skilled laborers and other vocations that expanded the social structure of many early empires to include additional classes or castes. Traditionally, as long as the water source supporting an agricultural transition continues, stability and prosperity will continue; however, when the water supply runs out or becomes limited, instability and chaos results.

Some of the negative attributes of the agricultural and population booms can be seen in the lack of resources necessary to sustain and provide for an increased population. As cities and populations grew, states were concerned about their ability to sustain such populations. A drought or unexpected flood could decimate food production, and lapses in production could prove detrimental to the entire community.

Additionally, the increased population and its presence within the ecosystem could also inflict damage on the environment, as is with overgrazing and overproduction of soil, which could have a long-term impact on the viability of the soil and future crops. This boom in agricultural production and population size can be seen as an accomplishment of the early civilizations and certainly as a form of progress. However, it is important to note both the advantages and disadvantages associated with this increase in size and production capacity.

Important regions to remember, regarding the food production increase and population booms, include the Mesoamerican civilizations (home to the Olmec, the Mayans and the Aztecs), the Andean region (home to the Inca civilization), the Nile River Valley and the Egyptians, the Mesopotamian region between the Euphrates and Tigris Rivers, the Indus River Valley (home of the Harappa communities) and the Huang Ho River Valley (home of the Chinese Shang and Zhuo dynasties).

The cultivation of a stable food source was influential in creating the cities of this and later periods. Without such production, these developments would have been less abundant or nonexistent, depending on the severity of the region regarding climate, precipitation, and water resources. The early human settlers had a supplicant relationship with the gods who governed the weather, resulting in religious rituals designated for agriculture, weather, and the cosmos.

Surpluses of food and other goods led to the specialization of labor, including new classes of artisans and warriors and the development of elites.

As cities and pastoral communities began experiencing greater successes, an abundance of food and other resources presented itself for the first time. As a society obtains a food surplus, that society will invariably experience growth in specialization, as all of the ancient civilizations being discussed here did. In the seminal work, "The Division of Labor in Society," the nineteenth-century economist Emile Durkheim described specialization as the phenomenon of workers increasingly diversifying what they do, continually over time.

The two significant benefits of specialization to a whole society are that society can produce a greater variety of goods and produce them more efficiently as well. For ancient civilizations, this

Emile Durkheim, economist

division or specialization of labor meant that they could produce the weapons of war (which enabled them to conquer) and the elaborate trade goods (which made them tremendously wealthy). This could not have happened if they remained in a state in which each member of society had to spend all of his or her time foraging for food; in other words, a subsistence level society.

In the Neolithic period, early humans had never maintained a surplus of food; no archeological evidence of storage facilities or texts can be found to support the existence of prior surpluses. However, during later periods, architectural projects were being undertaken to house surplus agriculture or other resources. Examples of these projects are the use of ziggurats, large pyramid-like structures meant to serve as civic centers, but also as storage facilities for the entire community; individuals could not store surplus foods or goods in their homes due to limited space.

As a result of these expansions in population, cities began developing agricultural resources through rural areas directly adjacent to the community, to ensure adequate food supplies to all inhabitants. As the issue of food security was addressed, it became clear that a more efficient food system required fewer agricultural laborers, causing more and more people to search for work in other areas such as trade, warfare, and government. The creation of additional vocational opportunities, such as the positions of scribes, engineers, civic workers and craftsmen, greatly expanded economic opportunity. However, these new opportunities were not available to all classes. This led to the social transitions which took place during this period.

Terracotta jug from Mesopotamia

As these early civilizations developed and acquired new levels of wealth, crime and warfare also increased. Outside forces were attracted to the opportunity of plundering, and the proliferation of urban dwellings allowed individuals to commit crimes more easily. Expansion of wealth, war, and war technologies led to a rise in crime, as seen in pastoralist and nomadic communities. Organized and structured warfare created a mechanism for plundering and looting, which seemed appropriate, given the expansionist attitudes of the period. This was most notably seen in the interactions between permanent agrarian settlements and the raids undertaken by pastoralists, who were able to develop more extensive warfare technologies than their agrarian counterparts. The pastoralists did not necessarily experience a widening of an elite class. Many of the pastoral traditions of the period were spurred by culture and prosperity rather than empire building.

The creation of a new elite class perpetuated the social structures of the period and caused many lower-class citizens to seek better treatment or better employment; however, given the limited social mobility, such transitions were difficult. The social structure created and enforced by this class would create tension and rivalry among social stations, a trend that would continue into later and contemporary periods. Eventually, such social distinctions and oppression would result in rebellions and revolutions, but such events did little to alter the social structures seen during this period.

Ornate vessel of Shang Dynasty

This new elite class was also instrumental in promoting the bureaucratic institutions of early civilizations and the expansion of various religions using priests, seers, and oracles. Without civic workers or government stations, many of the newly formed civilizations would have struggled to maintain order and structure within their cities. Examples of this type of leadership can be seen in the Shang dynasty of China. The Chinese had a governor appointed by the emperor, who could be replaced at any time in instances of political rivalry or corruption. The flaw in this system demonstrated numerous times throughout history, was that the emperors who rendered judgment on their appointed governors, were also human and themselves prone to corruption.

Technological innovations led to improvements in agricultural production, trade, and transportation.

The superiority and successes of the early empires were largely due to technological advancements like the plow, the wheel, and wheeled vehicles, developments in pottery and textiles, and an explosion in metallurgy. Mesopotamia was the original center for these technological advances. In approximately 8000–7000 B.C.E., the first textiles using flax were produced, and the wheel was introduced. By 6000–5000 B.C.E., Mesopotamia was the first to use irrigation systems. Irrigation was crucial for maintaining new, agriculturally based communities in the river valleys of the Nile, Euphrates and Indus Rivers.

This period also saw the emergence of the Bronze Age in Mesopotamia. Bronze allowed for much better weaponry than copper. Until the emergence of the Iron Age, these new metallurgy skills were widely used, from the Huang Ho River Valley in China to the Mesoamerican settlements. In China, advancements in metallurgy were far more sophisticated than in other regions. By approximately 7000–6000 B.C.E., copper smelting was fully practiced. While these copper tools were ineffective in warfare, they were important stepping-stones to the Bronze Age and the Iron Age, which would produce great weaponry and transform warfare. For example, the Hittites' use of iron ore in weaponry allowed them to conquer Anatolia, also known as Asia Minor easily, and to threaten Egypt.

Ornate pottery was also characteristic of the Shang dynasty and would continue into later dynasties, including the Zhuo. By approximately 2000–1000 B.C.E., Chinese engineers had created and perfected the use of war chariots, giving them greater opportunities for continued expansion. By the end of this period, chariots were also being used for sport and leisure, most notably in the Greek and Egyptian spectacles of chariot racing. The Roman Empire would later adopt this practice. Chariot racing was the centerpiece of the first recorded Olympic Games, which took place in 776 B.C.E.

In addition to metallurgy, pottery, and wheeled vehicles, the introduction of linen and woven textiles was also significant in this period. The earliest example of textiles incorporating flax was seen in Mesopotamia in approximately 8000–7000 B.C.E. Similar advancements were also seen in Egypt in 7000–6000 B.C.E., where new uses for linen were found and expanded.

These technological advancements allowed early civilizations, which had previously been partly or totally unsuccessful, to thrive and prosper. Without agricultural advancements such as irrigation systems and the plow, permanent agrarian settlements may not have been possible, and early humans might have continued their tradition of hunting and gathering indefinitely.

Additionally, the expansion of metallurgy greatly influenced this period and subsequent periods by creating durable and reliable tools. These agricultural and war-related advances allowed early civilizations to influence and wield power within their territories and abroad. These advances are also important in later periods, as this perception of power and influence would eventually lead to the great empires of the classical period and European expansion, in many ways emulating the practices of the river valley civilizations.

In both pastoralist and agrarian societies, elite groups accumulated wealth, creating more hierarchical social structures and promoting patriarchal forms of social organization.

As agrarian and pastoralist communities experienced stability and success, it was quickly discovered that outside entities and rival groups were capable of and interested in acquiring the status and wealth of these societies. Notable examples include Egyptian invasions and the continued rise and fall of Mesopotamian settlements. To repel invasions and outside threats, a center of power had to be established in the community. This was typically a ruling class that allowed the early civilizations to create social organization and standards.

Social structures evolved from gender equality and the equal distribution of work (e.g., gathering food and managing the household) to patriarchal dominance. As cities were established and ruling structures were formed, the male gender was given ample opportunity for growth and expansion within the culture's understood and accepted hierarchical social structures. Such social norms would continue to develop until a new class of elites had been created as a result of urban development and the introduction of early empires.

Social organization, using government or religious institutions, also emerged during this period and would eventually become the norm in most Western civilizations. Examples of this can be seen in early Egyptian texts discussing the ethical and moral obligations of the population to maintain a life free of crime, dishonesty, and immorality. The social norms and organizations introduced during this period had varying consequences, as many groups, such as women, were now considered less than equal. This perception would continue into later periods, causing social tension and unrest in modern periods.

The new classes of elites and workers which emerged as a result of the social reorganization provided structure and organization. These social changes made the transition to urban living and the transformation of agricultural practices more effective, with little room for dissent among the lower class. It is possible that without the social pressures created by these stratifications, the populace might have opted to revert to a form of hunting and gathering or pastoralism, which is less demanding than agrarianism.

Core and foundational civilizations developed in a variety of geographical and environmental settings where agriculture flourished.

During this period of transition, many civilizations developed regions that had differences, but also shared an abundance of similarities. It is because of these similarities, as well as later interactions between populations, that many of these civilizations began to develop and transition in similar patterns of cultural development, agricultural and technological achievement, and the expansion of newly emerging empires.

Code of Hammurabi

All of these early civilizations had distinct characteristics but shared several commonalities, including very fertile soil (in most cases loess or alluvial soil) and the establishment of complex irrigation systems. They also implemented legal codes, such as the Code of Hammurabi, and eventually developed currency, either used together with a barter system or replacing it altogether. These civilizations all saw the development of art, culture, and literature, which was personified and supported by newly emerging elite classes. They developed and applied scientific knowledge, such as calendars based on astronomical observation, numbering and recording systems, and the applications of mathematics by the Phoenicians and Chinese. Finally, they all engaged in an escalation of inequalities (especially in gender roles) compared to the Neolithic and Paleolithic periods.

The first states emerged within core civilizations.

As previously mentioned, many of the first states seen in history, such as the Egyptian state, the Mesopotamian states, and the Aegean states, evolved from core civilizations that had emerged during this period. Many of the river valleys mentioned are known among academics as centers of civilization, or cradles of life, that led early humans to develop more prosperous and stable living conditions. Such evolution led to increased production of resources, most notably agricultural, that in turn caused a population increase. As this cycle continued, new states like Egypt were beginning to understand how to utilize new forms of agriculture as well as to develop new vocations such as the warrior and merchant classes. These cultural changes allowed states to be formed from the core civilizations, like those seen in the Nile River Valley. The same can be said of the newer states seen in Mesopotamia, such as Sumeria, Babylon, and Assyria.

These early states are important within the scheme of world history and global systems. Had these early states failed early in their emergence, further expansion and development might not have been pursued, completely altering the historical landscape as we know it. These cultures provide the precedents for social and political structures, economic practices, religion, mathematics, language, and science.

States were powerful new systems of rule that mobilized surplus labor and resources over large areas. Early states were often led by a ruler who was supported by the military or whose source of power was believed to be divine or divinely supported.

As early civilizations grew and became more established, many rulers looked to harness the new workforce for warfare and production. This was the first time such an explosion in population had been seen. Many successful civilizations, such as Egypt, Mesopotamia, and China, extensively employed manpower to expand their power base and territorial holdings.

In addition to military power and resources, expansion and the security of kinship was intensified by the belief that many rulers had a divine right to rule or were, in some sense, divine themselves. This was most visible in the Egyptian and Mesopotamian cultures, where pharaohs and kings claimed divine birth, giving them a direct line of communication with their gods and an unchallenged position of authority. Similar claims are also seen in Chinese cultures. The Zhou Dynasty followed the Zhou Mandate of Heaven, which promulgated the divine status of the ruling elite and the "son of the gods." Women were not allowed to hold ruling positions during this period. This is another example of the use of the divine right or divine authority to rule various peoples successfully.

This idea of divine authority or a divine right would have monumental effects on future empires, most notably the European monarchies who called upon this theology as a way of limiting pushback to their reign. From the 17th century onwards, popular rejection of such ideas would result in the removal of absolute or divine monarchies in Europe and cause revolutions throughout the continent. Not all early civilizations used this idea of a divine right to rule. One notable exception was the later Sumerian city-states: Although initially ruled by leader-priests, this gave way to warrior leaders who ruled their cities by codes and laws transcribed from the gods with the approbation of the priests.

As a result of this expansion of power and influence, many river valley civilizations were able to maintain influence on colonies abroad or in land conquered as a result of their military conquests. Before this period, such imperialism would have been impossible. However, as a result of the global system coupled with technological advancements in the

Phoenician, Egyptian, Chinese, and Mesopotamian Empires, vast military and political influence was now possible. This force greatly influenced the Macedonian, Persian, Greek, and Roman Empires of the classical period. Such philosophies of influence and power have persisted into recent centuries as the justification for European colonialism.

As states grew and competed for land and resources, the more favorably situated—including the Hittites, who had access to iron—had greater access to resources, produced a greater surplus of food, and experienced growing populations. These states were able to undertake territorial expansion and conquer the surrounding states.

As newly emerging civilizations competed for status and power, it quickly became clear that some, such as the Hittites and Hyksos, were better able to successfully invade their neighbors. Such pastoral communities were better equipped to deal with the evolving climate and social changes of this period and expanded their communities using military force, trade agreements, or assimilation.

This spirit of expansion was important both to its specific period and to the grand scheme of world history, as it was the foundation for future empires, including Macedonia, Persia, Greece, and Rome. This expansionist spirit would continue into much later periods of Europe, with expansion and colonialism being crucial components of their foreign policies.

Culture played a significant role in unifying states through laws, language, literature, religion, myths, and monumental art.

As early civilizations emerged during this period, commonalities among populations can be seen in the development of common languages, the establishment of systems of order and laws within the urban setting, the desire to create monumental art and architecture and the influence of religion on all social levels—from the ruling class to the lowest classes.

One of the largest unifying factors of this period is the emergence of regional and transregional languages such as cuneiform, which was used by various civilizations and adapted to facilitate trade and commerce. An example of this was seen in Phoenicia where avid seafarers and traders modified cuneiform into a smaller, more easily understood language. This exemplifies an important characteristic of the period, the spreading of knowledge, histories, and languages, emphasizing the importance of analyzing world history from a global perspective.

The language was also crucial in implementing and enforcing the idea of laws and codes within urban and pastoral settings, employed most notably through the Code of Hammurabi. For a king or ruler to hold absolute power as prescribed by the divine right ruling, he or she must be able to enforce laws and structure, imposing societal institutions on all subjects. Typically only the elites gained any real benefit from the ruling class. The introduction of the Code of Hammurabi and later legal codes shows the desire for rules and government protection within the early civilizations. Such codes would influence later civilizations, most notably the bureaucratic institutions adopted and exported by the Roman Empire.

As civilizations expanded and shared knowledge with their neighbors, independent cultures were emerging within their populations, expressing themselves through literature and art. This was a new concept for many early peoples, who had previously worked tirelessly to maintain a semi-stable existence. Earlier art was focused primarily on day-to-day experiences such as agriculture or hunting and gathering. This period, however, saw an explosion of art focused on religious themes or depictions of divine rulers, who were typically seen as an extension of these deities. Such a transition in monumental artisan work shows the new idea of divine kingship, a concept that would continue for centuries and would finally lead to the revolutions of Europe. For millions of people, the idea that their ruler was divine was a readily accepted tenet of their culture, certainly so in Egyptian culture.

Phoenician art depicting religious figure Baal

Mythology also played an important role in the lives of both the common and elite classes. These tales, typically passed down orally, were the foundations of culture within society and provided great insight into each early culture. The idea that the gods reside in the heavens or the stars was typically embraced, as was the need to build earthly "homes" for them in the form of temples, was also evident in all cultures. Additionally, burial rituals emphasized the transition from the physical world to the afterlife and were seen in various religions of the period, including those of China, Egypt, and Mesoamerican civilizations.

By understanding the cultural backgrounds of each civilization, one can begin to see their influence within the global view of world history and also the impact such practices had on contemporary society, such as the development of law codes and the practice of creating monumental architectural projects as a visible signifier of political and military power and prestige. These early civilizations transformed the political, military, and domestic landscape and set the tone for the further evolution of culture, economics, politics, and the expansion of the Greek and Roman Empires.

Early civilizations developed monumental architecture and urban planning.

To continue the advancement of early civilizations, many rulers sought to create urban centers with breathtaking monuments to their gods. The function of these monuments was to instill fear and awe of the gods to maintain a sense of law and order, regulated by an elite class.

In addition to the ritualistic and religious needs of urban centers, the government and elite populations also faced practical issues such as water management, pollution of the city, and increases in crime due to a higher population density. As these populations increased and many citizens were able to pursue jobs outside of food and production, a new, more efficient city could be developed. The expansion of vocations included engineers, who began to create more ambitious architectural projects and more efficient irrigation systems.

This tendency can be seen in the construction of defensive walls that date back as far as 8000 B.C.E., in the Mesopotamian city of Ur and the city of Jericho. In East Asia, we see one of the most notable and world-renowned examples of defensive walls, the Great Wall of China. It was built during the Zhou Dynasty, in approximately 3500 B.C.E. Other notable examples of defensive walls can be seen in the city of Mundinak, in present-day Afghanistan, which was recorded as erecting a vast defensive wall around 2500 B.C.E. Additionally, Assyrian stone carvings depicted assaults on towns and cities with defensive wall fortifications. Images of this type were seen around 900 B.C.E.

The Los Millares site in modern Spain is the largest fortified Neolithic settlement, dating from 3200–2300 B.C.E. This complex settlement is made up of three walls with an inner citadel and elaborate fortifications, tombs and passages. Defensive walls and fortifications were necessary for all early civilizations and were the precursor to the castles and other defensive measures later seen in Europe. Other examples of defensive fortifications can be seen in Egypt throughout the Old, Middle, and New Kingdoms. Fortresses were built along the border regions to the south, east, and west in hopes of deterring invaders and monitoring the flow of goods and people throughout the region. These fortresses were surrounded by defensive walls similar to those seen in Los Millares. They kept the majority of invaders out, excluding the successful campaigns of the Hyksos, Hittites, and Kush Empires.

Sewage and water systems allowed for a new quality of urban life, one previously unknown. Some of the first water systems of this period are seen in the qanats of Iran, early forms of the systems widely used later in the Common Era. Qanats and aqueducts were responsible for the water flow into urban areas, which in some settlements was also used to supplement irrigation. By about 1000 B.C.E., water filtration systems were being used in Greece and Crete, using clay pipe systems with inverted siphons similar to those in today's modern systems.

Other notable cites with advanced engineering include those of the Minoan civilization, particularly Knossos, which by 2700 B.C.E. had developed sewage systems with flushing toilets. Additionally, Minoans created early baths and drainage systems that ran from homes into a community reservoir or other body of water. This was also the case in the cities of Harappa and Mohenjo-Daro, which archeological excavations have shown had both sewage and water systems in use by about 2600 B.C.E. These included outdoor flushing toilets and sanitation systems that were quite advanced for the period.

Addressing water and water management within the city setting was key to establishing a thriving urban site and would continue to be important in future urban endeavors. These water management systems are still in use, in some form, across most of the regions in which they were discovered. These early inventions were improved drastically by the Romans, who created vast aqueducts and reservoirs to meet the needs of their urban populations. The most notable examples were seen in Rome.

Palace of Knossos

Like agriculture and political life, the rate of development for roads varied from region to region. However, all successful early civilizations maintained some roadway. In Egypt, the first paved road dates to approximately 2400 B.C.E. Other stone-paved roads were seen in the city of Ur in the Middle East, around 4000 B.C.E. Roads made of wood were found in Glastonbury, England, during this same period. Brick paved roadways were seen in India, beginning in about 3000 B.C.E. The first paved roads in the Minoan civilization date to the Neopalatial period (1700–1400 B.C.E.), connecting villages and palaces throughout Crete.

Other notable transportation projects of this period include the Sweet Track causeway, made of oak planks, and found in the Somerset Levels, England. Until recently, many historians believed this to be the oldest road, as it dates back to 3806–3807 B.C.E. However, there is some debate surrounding this claim, as similarly dated roads have since been found in England. These early roads were expanded by the Roman engineers who constructed a vast network of roadways, many of which survive today, to connect the Italian peninsula to new territories.

Elites, both political and religious, promoted arts and artisanship.

As civilizations progressed, the opportunity to focus on more than the day-to-day struggle of survival presented itself in various cultures, by different means. While some individuals found opportunities in trade and warfare, others were able to pursue craftsmanship and artisanship, creating the foundation of Western art. Many saw sculpture as embodying the culture of their people and felt honored or blessed to participate in the creation of deity carvings, funerary complexes, or tributes to their rulers. Such a sentiment shows how devoted early populations were to their religions and what a pivotal role the leadership and ruling classes played in that relationship. It is easy to understand how these rulers quickly gained power, given their claim of relationship to the gods and their divine right to rule.

The type of art seen in the early Neolithic period focused on the daily activities of its creators, such as agriculture or hunting and gathering. By the Metal Age, many people were beginning to produce art that highlighted religious devotion, possibly a ruler or dynasty, with other examples focusing on the human image.

The art from this period shows a population in social and physical transition. Art no longer solely depicted daily struggles, such as food gathering or laboring; it began to show new classes—even working classes—experiencing more leisure time and expanding their spheres of interest to include, or even be dominated by religion. Not all art from this period has a religious context—decorative vases were not meant for the religious ceremony—but many forms of art do depict the importance of religion to early civilizations. This art would go on to influence the role of religion in later periods.

The artisan works of this period were important in molding the later classical civilizations that would continue to thrive and expand into core civilizations. The idea that governments and elites should support artisan pursuits is also important, as this concept would eventually propel the architectural advances of the Greek and Roman Empires, and later the European Renaissance. Such support provided the resources previously unavailable for the construction of great works.

Systems of record-keeping arose independently in all early civilizations and were subsequently diffused.

The emergence of written records and record-keeping during this period was instrumental in creating future urban settlements and dominant civilizations that came out of this period. Arguably the most important form of written record and record-keeping from this period is cuneiform, a wedge-shaped system of writing that came from Sumerian civilization. By approximately 3500–3000 B.C.E., cuneiform was widely used.

Initially, it was used as an accounting system to manage the supplies and resources housed in ziggurats. Records indicate that cuneiform was typically written on wet clay tablets with the use of a stylus. Eventually, this form of writing became a means of transcribing and sharing Sumerian literature, histories, and epic poems. The most important Mesopotamian civilizations, such as the Sumerians, Akkadians, Babylonians, Hittites, and Assyrians, used cuneiform. Only small classes of scribes were able to read and write in the language, not shared among other strata of society. Hieroglyphics were also extremely important systems of writing and record-keeping during this period and, like cuneiform, helped to unify the various populations under the banner of Egypt.

The use of Cuneiform declined by the beginning of the Common Era. However, other cultures—including the Phoenicians—would evolve and adapt the language into a condensed system containing twenty-two characters, making it easier to learn and share. This would become the basic alphabet for the language systems of Greece and Rome, which greatly influenced present-day languages, most notably the romance languages, such as French and Italian.

Egyptian pyramid hieroglyphs

Adaptations of Egyptian hieroglyphs, similar to the Phoenician adaptations of cuneiform, also emerged, including adaptations to the Minoan language. Examples of this similar style can be seen in the Phaistos Disk, dated 1700 B.C.E., which some scholars argue is a prayer to a Minoan goddess. Pictographs were also important to the evolution of the written record and record-keeping during this period; pictographs predated many of these languages. Some of the most notable examples of pictographs can be seen in the ancient Chinese book *Han Zei Zei*, written by a Chinese philosopher in approximately 300 B.C.E. Pictographs were also widely seen during the Paleolithic era.

After using symbols, using cuneiform, hieroglyphs, and pictographs, people began experimenting with alphabets. The first notable alphabet came from the Phoenicians in approximately 1000 B.C.E. and evolved from the Proto-Canaanite alphabet. This alphabet was most likely created as a means to facilitate and expand trade, something that Phoenicians were extremely concerned with, as they held few resources within their native lands.

The importance of written language and record-keeping cannot be overstated, as this was the first step in creating modern communications and also allows historians to understand the periods of the Sumerian and Egyptian cultures better. The sharing of language—and, by extension, the knowledge, religions, and ideas which could be recorded and communicated with writing—allowed for communication between distant civilizations and created unifying economic and cultural bonds. Such relationships would continue to be maintained in later periods and would serve as the basis of early civilizations. Many academics believe the use of written language to be the first step toward civilization. It should be noted that these forms of writing were read and transcribed by small sects of elites and not the general populace, as most people were uneducated and illiterate.

New religious beliefs developed in this period continued to have strong influences in later periods.

Many religions developed during this period as a result of polytheistic beliefs, with emphasis on deities who monitored agriculture, the weather, and the sun, as well as deities symbolizing morality and truth. However, very few of these religions would maintain their popularity into the Common Era, like Christianity, Judaism, and Islam became the dominant global religions.

Additionally, ancient religions had a great cultural influence on their respective regions; this period, for the first time, saw active religious rituals, shrines, oracles, and temples. People would come to use religion as a centerpiece of their lives, whether they embraced the increasingly popular monotheistic faiths, such as Judaism, or the more traditional polytheistic theology of the Vedic and Egyptian religions.

Trade expanded throughout this period from local to regional and transregional, with civilizations exchanging goods, cultural ideas, and technology.

This movement of both physical and cultural goods again highlights the concept of a global system beginning during this period and leading into the future. Future empires would measure their success against those of Egypt, Mesopotamia, and the Middle East in terms of trade, expansion, and diplomatic successes. Such concepts of communication, regional and transregional trade, and exploratory and military campaigns would all become key features of European traditions and are still evident in contemporary international relations. Due to these various interactions, world history should be explored through the perspective of global affairs and relations.

Social and gender hierarchies intensified as states expanded, and cities multiplied.

In the early Neolithic and Paleolithic periods, women experienced a status of equality not seen again for thousands of years. As civilization developed, the role of women became one of subservient, domesticated wives and mothers. This is not to say that women during this period had no rights—this was not the case—but there was a marked change in the status and role of women when urbanization began and hunting and gathering movements faded away.

The expectations of women during this period included housework, domestic chores, and childbearing, while men pursued work in urban and agricultural settings. Despite domestication, women held substantial legal rights in the legal codes of Egypt, including the rights to seek a divorce, buy and sell property, file lawsuits, and serve as a witness in court. While most women did not seek a divorce, that they were able to do so speaks to the social standing of women in the Egyptian culture during this period.

As patriarchal systems were embraced, women and slaves were considered among the lesser inhabitants of their respective regions. However, there are always exceptions to such a generalization; for example, women in pastoral communities were able to maintain warrior-like status within the clan.

The emergence of new elites such as merchants, priests, and civil or government workers also created new positions of influence and power within the culture and ruling structure. Social mobility was a new phenomenon, and it did not last, as later governments put in place rigid social constraints to keep the social classes fixed and the elite and ruling classes small. The structure governments created to instill law and order into a previously chaotic social system also caused urban problems, including the oppression of certain demographic groups under the increasingly stratified class structure. The social constraints of the period required parents to teach their children their trade or craft, and such vocational traditions were carried on from generation to generation.

Further evidence of social hierarchies can be seen in all early civilizations of this period, including the Chinese and Indian caste systems. Slavery was also a component of society, with slaves holding little status or legal means except for the ability to purchase and own land.

These social structures have had vast implications for western European history as well as world history in its entirety. The idea that women are responsible for domestic concerns emerges extensively for the first time during this later period; it had not been emphasized in the earlier Neolithic and Paleolithic periods. These restrictive social customs would remain standard for thousands of years to come, limiting women in most societies to secondary or nonexistent roles in politics and government.

The rigid social class structure that came into being in this period would have great implications for thousands of lower-class laborers, peasants, and farmers. Social mobility would become less and less obtainable, limiting the elite and ruling classes to a smaller pool of members. The policies and social standards explored and expanded during this period would eventually culminate in revolutionary movements throughout Europe, and this pushback would greatly influence the gender roles and social standards of later periods.

Literature was a reflection of culture.

Like other arts of the period, literature flourished with the introduction of written language; examples include the Mesopotamian, Egyptian, and Chinese civilizations. Early literature would continue to facilitate the sharing of knowledge and culture between foreign peoples and inspire the epic literary works of the Greek and Roman Empires.

These literary works influenced the regional and transregional affairs of this period and impacted later works and even present-day ideals and literary stances. *The Epic of Gilgamesh* was the first of its kind, later followed by the transcriptions of *The Iliad* and *The Odyssey,* composed by Homer, and the works of Ovid in the Roman period. The significance of *The Epic of Gilgamesh* has caused many historians to call this text the first great work of Western literature.

Homer, author of The Odyssey

However, it should be remembered that other important texts also influenced Western literature. The cultural insight gained by the reading of the *Rig-Veda*, the Egyptian *Book of the Dead,* and the Chinese *Book of Songs* allows one to begin to understand the early civilizations that set the tone for future Western and Eastern cultures. Such works shed light on the daily lives of many of the lower and working classes, which otherwise might have remained unknown, as many of the surviving literary works of the period only describe the ruling families or the elites.

Codifications and further developments of existing religious traditions provided a bond among the people and an ethical code by which to live.

Religion has been a dominant cultural, ethical, and political force throughout both recent and ancient human history. It has served as both a science and an asylum for many generations by uniting people in their common faith. Temples were built for people to pray and perform sacrifices, which gave them a common cause for which to live and form personal relationships. A unique feature of ancient religions was that they were all polytheistic, meaning that they recognized many gods instead of one main god. In ancient history, before the invention of writing, nothing was documented; stories and laws were passed down verbally. Writing was a difficult task for ancient people, and they gave great respect to those who were able to write because written beliefs are easier to spread and harder to forget. Written religious and political texts have greatly facilitated religion's diffusion throughout the globe and, consequently, have worked to bring together and tear apart many religious peoples and governments.

Sitting Buddha temple

The success of major modern religions was determined by incorporation of previous faiths.

A key factor that helped currently popular and dominant religions spread was that most of them built upon the religious beliefs already accepted by the societies in which the religions developed. For example, Christianity was built upon the already existing beliefs of Judaism and the Hebrew God, Hinduism was built upon the ancient Aryan religion and the Vedas, Buddhism was partly built upon Hinduism and Islam was built upon Christianity (and to a certain extent Judaism). Pharaoh Akhenaten created the first monotheistic religion known, but it did not survive the short reign of his son. The first monotheistic religion to become a major religion was Judaism. The most influential religion in Western society was Christianity.

Emergence and spread of new belief systems and cultural traditions that asserted universal truths.

There are many religions in the world, and the most helpful unifying characteristic of the great faiths such as Christianity, Buddhism, Hinduism, and Islam is their ability to spread their unifying questions. Religions may differ in their definition of what divine power exists, and they may differ in promises of an afterlife. However, all of them attempt to answer several fundamental questions of existence that are common to all human beings.

One question raised by all human beings and addressed by practically all great religions in their teachings is the idea of the self, as seen in the human personality, consciousness, feelings, emotions, thought, and psychology. The Christian religion believes in a soul – an immaterial spirit given to humans by God – through which people have a sense of self. Islam also believes in a similar concept of the soul. Hinduism has the Jiva, a concept that Westerners might equate with the concept of a soul, for it is similarly immaterial and demonstrates the consequences of life on Earth. From 600 B.C.E. to 600 C.E., Confucianism, Taoism, Buddhism, the Greco-Roman religion, Christianity, and Islam emerged and spread universal truths about ethical behavior is the way to a better life. Overall, the new religions often had similar beliefs.

Belief systems affected gender roles. Buddhism and Christianity encouraged monastic life.

The newly founded religions, such as Christianity and Buddhism, had a great effect on the gender roles of that time. In Europe, for example, religious practices were limited to men. The Greeks had only male preachers, and in Hinduism, most of the Brahmins were male. Christianity opened its doors to women who were allowed to participate in religious practices. For example, women were allowed to become nuns, which allowed them to dedicate themselves to living a religious life outlined by the core tenants of the Church. This undoubtedly increased women's rights and authority in society since religion was a dominant force in Europe. However, the male population of the Church still tended to have more power, as men traditionally were popes and the highest echelons of power in the Church.

Other religious and cultural traditions continued parallel to the codified, written belief systems in core civilizations.

While the great religions spread far and wide, traditional religions such as animism and shamanism also shaped the lives of people throughout the entire world. Places like Mongolia, the Americas, Japan and parts of Eastern Russia continued practicing their traditional faiths. The most common faiths of people who weren't introduced to monotheism or Hinduism were shamanistic or animistic. When Mongolia conquered nearly half of the world in the 13th century C.E., it was a very religiously tolerant state. Mongolians believed that there were spirits tied to their homeland, and since the people they assimilated lived on different lands, those spirits were not present there. Hence, it made no sense to convert them.

Shamanism and animism continued to shape the lives of people within and outside of core civilizations because of their daily reliance on the natural world.

Shamanism is a type of faith in spirits and in a human's ability to interact with them. Shamanists believe such interaction would be generally impossible for a regular human and therefore, must be conducted by a person who is an expert in spiritual communication. This communicator is the shaman, hence the name "shamanism." These communications were used for many different reasons, including praying for help from the spirits or for healing. If the shaman is properly prepared, communication could happen that might achieve the desired result. Often, shamanistic spiritual healing was the only medical treatment available.

Animistic religion is similar to Taoism, for it also professes a belief that everything in nature has a spirit of its own and is living in harmony with nature. Animism affected larger societies through Taoism. This sort of religion was prominent among ancient Turks, Mongols, Northern, and Eastern Russia's indigenous population and Native American tribes. Some people who decided to carry on the traditions and culture of the indigenous populations of Eastern Russia, Mongolia, and the Americas are still practicing animism and shamanism to this day.

The number and size of key states and empires grew dramatically by imposing political unity in areas where previously there had been competing states.

By 600 B.C.E., the world had seen the rise of civilizations, organized societies, and major empires. However, it was still highly decentralized, as many different civilizations and nomadic people were competing for land and resources in the same area. Europe had Germanic tribes, Greek city-states, small Italian kingdoms, and native Spanish tribes. Mesopotamia, Babylon, the Median Empire, Egypt, and the nomadic peoples of Arabia were all near Europe. India was decentralized for a long period with competing city-states and kingdoms, along with nomadic people in the North. China was not yet united but contained the Han kingdom and several rival kingdoms around it. The world did not stay fragmented in this way. Very soon, it saw the rise and fall of many great empires. The following is a breakdown of these empires and civilizations, organized by their general region.

Empires and states developed new techniques of imperial administration based, in part, on the success of earlier political forms.

Empires were extensive political units and often contained many different ethnic, religious, and cultural groups. Empires had the task of keeping these groups together under their realms, so they could continue to exist. To do this, empires used a variety of techniques. First and foremost, almost all empires that remained intact for a long period realized they had to answer the demands of their people on some level. Athens created a system of democracy in which some of the people voted on the laws and policies under which they lived (or at least that was the illusion because sometimes—such as under the Athenian Empire—Athenians had a government leader).

Bureaucrats were often corrupt and made things better for themselves but not for the people. That is why, for example, Roman emperors built the Colosseum, promoted gladiator sports, chariot, and horse racing, and other entertainment to keep the population occupied and happy. Many emperors promoted their military and rewarded people for their military successes. Some trading-post empires or economically successful empires allowed people to become rich, to trade, to keep a profession, and to have a successful career. Often people did not want to rebel against a government that allowed such freedoms. Some states, like the Parthian state, promoted national patriotism, and people were loyal to one state or the other because of the national religion or culture that the state promoted.

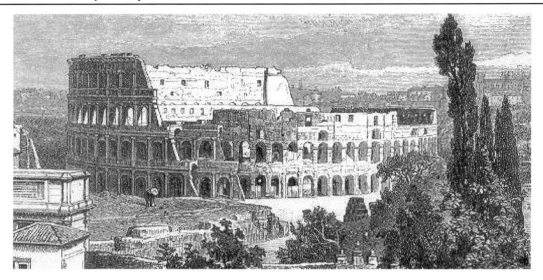

Colosseum

Many more states used the military to suppress those who did not obey or were unhappy with the system. Rome, an extensive and cosmopolitan empire, not only gave out free bread and entertainment but also built fortifications, dug roads for the military, and established garrisons for cities. This was so that existing rebellions could be suppressed, and future rebellions would be prevented. Future revolutionaries would see that opposition to their rebellion would come from the Roman army. Persia and China also used this method. For leaders, it was very important to suppress revolutions because the legitimacy of their rule depended on their reputation among their people.

To organize their subjects, the rulers created administrative institutions in many regions.

The key to holding onto an empire or a state lay not only in the economic and cultural realms but also in the political realm. Political institutions and systems kept the regions of which they were in charge stable; they organized the people in such a way that work would be done so that the economy would develop, and the people would serve the government's needs. The government would serve the people's needs.

Imperial governments projected military power over larger areas using a variety of techniques.

Throughout history, military power was projected by several strategies that were very different and yet complementary. When the war was inevitable, the use of engineering and good systems of supply and communication were the most decisive strategies. The most successful conquering empires took these to brilliant new levels. If war could be avoided by intimidation or moral coercion, then the wisest conquerors used many types of diplomacy, and some of them made an art out of eliciting collaboration from conquered peoples. When neither conquest nor cooperation was possible, the construction of defensive walls was a frequent last resort.

One of the pivotal ingredients in Rome's successful expansion was its famous engineering. The two engineering achievements which were most important to Rome's expansion were its road system and its ability to make freshwater portable. In Rome's early history, it needed to defeat rivals throughout the Mediterranean, which entailed naval conflict. After the Carthaginians, Illyrian pirates, Greece and Egypt had been subdued, and Rome controlled all of the Mediterranean and North Africa, Rome needed to defeat the Germanic tribes in central Europe. To transport and supply the large and heavily equipped armies that Rome sent thousands of miles deep into Europe, it needed roads and reliable sources of freshwater. Two thousand years ago, neither of these existed in Europe, which was mostly forest, plains land, and small Germanic villages at the time.

As Rome conquered one territory, it linked two things to it: aqueducts, which would bring a steady supply of freshwater to the Roman frontier and stone roads, which made it easy to bring everything else (e.g., armies, supplies, weapons, goods needed to establish civilization there). The Romans then built fortresses which could be supplied by the roads and aqueducts. These frontier fortresses were the seeds of many cities, including London, which exist in Europe today.

Many conquerors were brutal and massacred the people they defeated; however, some of the most successful conquerors adopted the smart technique of turning their defeated enemies into allies by allowing them to participate in the administration of the conquered territories. Alexander the Great and Genghis Khan are two of the most successful conquerors in human history. Each of these men rapidly conquered an area which, when their empires were at their peaks, included most of Asia and half of Europe.

However, neither could have done so without the help of people whom they conquered. Each of these men used a similar strategy: when invading a new territory they would make it clear that they were the overwhelming force and then give the targeted enemy an ultimatum: they could surrender and be treated as members of the empire and benefit from the empire's protection, or they could resist, in which case they would be annihilated and their settlements demolished.

Eliciting collaboration was a wise strategy that usually worked for these conquerors. This rendered thousands of effective fighters and farmers as allies instead of the empire expending soldiers and supplies to destroy the enemy. Another strategy of collaboration, which was used masterfully by Alexander the Great and innumerable other conquerors throughout world history, was to become the champion of groups who were oppressed by their enemies and to unite smaller groups against a common enemy.

Bust of Alexander the Great

After conquering and subjugating a city, Alexander the Great would allow the defeated people to maintain their own culture and continue to govern themselves in alliance with him. Thus, most of Alexander the Great's armies were not from his home of Macedonia. They were allies whom he liberated from the Persians or other oppressors, or they were former enemies who were given a reprieve and allowed to rule their lands in return for contributing soldiers and wealth to Alexander's campaign.

Alexander loved to learn about foreign cultures and adopted many of the customs of the people he conquered – particularly the Egyptians. This diplomacy of collaboration should not be mistaken for altruism. Alexander was shrewd enough to realize that his force was not the dominant side in his fight against Persia – or for that matter, against most of the large empires he confronted. Alliances were pivotal to his surprising success.

When all else failed, walls were built by imperial governments to keep un-subjugated enemies from attacking the empire. The most extensive ever built was the Great Wall of China, a large barrier of broad walls and fortresses which was constructed to wall all of China off from the Mongols. It was never totally completed, but the walls which were built (including many extensions) extended for almost thirteen thousand miles.

At roughly the same point in history, the Roman emperor Hadrian constructed a defensive wall in the province of Britannia to cut the northern portion of the island – inhabited by a barbarian group known as the Picts – off from the Roman Empire. This was a network of stone walls and large fortresses, which extended for seventy miles. When military force could not be projected outwards, many emperors believed it could be projected defensively to establish an impassible boundary limit to the empire. Walls never worked for very long, though, because they were tremendously expensive to maintain and – as they are immobile – walls are extremely susceptible to siege attacks.

Much of the success of the empires rested on their promotion of trade and economic integration by building and maintaining roads and issuing currencies.

The success of ancient empires was based heavily on trade and their control of trade routes. Many of the economies of the classical age civilizations were based on farming. Creating a food surplus so that more and more people would be able to live without needing to farm was pivotal to creating an empire. All states are limited by their geography and will lack something for which they want to trade. For example, Mesopotamia lacked wood and traded clay to obtain it.

As regions and empires grew, their economies grew and fewer people needed to farm to sustain the population's need for food. This enabled specialization – where members of a society focused on types of work other than producing food. The implication of this was that all of the things which an empire needs can be produced. Demand rose for other goods, including luxury goods, craft materials, military provisions and weaponry, and construction and industry needs. In other words, people needed lots of things, so they imported goods and services they lacked and exported goods and services they had in abundance. Money was constantly changing hands, and to support that trade, the government not only provided subsidies but also built roads to facilitate not only military movement but also civilian movement. None of this would have been possible without food surpluses that resulted in the specialization.

Currency was also vital for empire growth because of the efficiency it created. Before the invention of money, people traded goods and services. Eventually, they concluded that that would not work because there was no universal standard for the value of any good. People started using gold, bronze, silver, and other precious metals as a means of exchange. When governments saw this, they started issuing currency, which meant traders did not need weights to weigh gold—instead, they could use the currency. One of the first governments to issue currency was China, and all the rest followed its example: Persia, Rome, Greece, India, and some civilizations in Africa started issuing currency and exchanging goods and services more easily.

Constantinople

Currency was not only a good way to exchange goods and services, but it was also a good way to collect taxes. Trading routes were often extensive. Rarely did someone travel all the way down the Silk Road, so goods and services were exchanged along the way and to foreign states where there was demand. Every time money changed hands; there was a tax paid, so governments had a special interest in keeping the flow of trade going. Large empires often controlled the most trade, which is partially why they were so successful.

The Byzantine Empire controlled Byzantium, or as it was later called Constantinople. It is a port located on a strait that goes from the Black Sea to the Mediterranean Sea. It connects Anatolia with the Balkans, linking these two seas and two continents, Europe and Asia, who traded constantly. Europeans mostly used the Silk Road, which went through the Persian Empire into China. China was the only producer of silk, which was the cloth used in royal apparel for centuries.

China made china, iron, textiles, dyes, and many other goods, while Europe exported olive oil, marble, and more. Empires that were situated on the Silk Road, such as the Persian Empires, controlled much of the trade. India, China, and West Africa were involved in the Indian Ocean Trade, which Islamic empires also joined once they rose to power. Overland trade was preferable to sea trade because of the extremely dangerous conditions that shipping faced in the earliest ages of seaborne travel.

Unique social and economic dimensions developed in imperial societies in Afro-Eurasia and the Americas.

The period from 600 B.C.E. to 600 C.E. saw the rise of the socioeconomic dimensions present today. New concepts and new social, political, and economic orders came to dominate the world and changed lives. Those orders progressed in complexity and development for generations to come.

Cities served as centers of trade, public performance of religious rituals, and political administration for states and empires.

The first of these orders was the rise of cities. Cities had been major centers of life before, but now their importance was increasing. Cities became the capitals of new, much larger empires. To satisfy the needs of these empires, cities needed to create complex bureaucracies, and new cities were built to become centers of life, economy, and government on a smaller scale as empires continued to expand. These new cities were built with the idea of hosting complex bureaucracies, developing culture, fostering economic growth and promoting smaller, local level governance—all so that the empire could continue to expand successfully.

In the Han dynasty of China, every province had a new capital with everything needed to sustain its political life: barracks, treasuries, and tax-collecting institutions. Education was provided in major learning centers in the cities, be it in Rome in the Roman Empire, Athens in Greece, Babylon or Pasargadae in Persia, Pataliputra in India or Chang'an in Han China. Religious ceremonies were also undertaken in cities, as churches and other places of worship were located in cities. Some examples of this are the Mayan cities and Teotihuacán, with religious monuments located in their respective centers.

Cities became the centers of trade, a vital activity of any state during this period. Farmers working on the outskirts traded their goods in the city, and blacksmiths, artisans, artists, and merchants traded on major trade routes such as the Silk Road or the Indian Ocean Trade. Roads were built through cities so that all trade which flowed along them would also go through cities. This made it easier for merchants to trade and for consumers to buy. It also facilitated trade and communication throughout empires, states and among people. Cities created not only the fundamentals of today's economic and political life, but also cultural diffusion, the importance of which is hard to overestimate.

The social structures of empires displayed hierarchies that included cultivators, laborers, slaves, artisans, merchants, elites or caste groups.

Social hierarchies existed in the pre-classical and early classical civilizations, and as time went on their importance increased, peaking in the period of 600 B.C.E. to 600 C.E. Politics became dependent on social classes, thereby affecting economics, education and everyday life.

People of the Silk Road

Some things were accessible only to those who had wealth. Education and high-level political roles were accessible only to the rich, even where there was no absolute monarchy, such as in Greece or Rome.

In the democracies of that time, the social divisions, such as those between the patricians and the plebeians, became critical to one's political life. Only the patricians could hold office in the Senate and become consul. At the same time, the plebeians were only allowed to become members of the State Assembly and act as representatives of their group.

Hierarchies also played a major role in religion. Hinduism was one of the earliest religions to establish a social hierarchy. The caste system deemed people as "destined" to be in a profession, and each profession, be it a Brahmin (priest), Kshatriya (warrior), or anything else, found its place somewhere in the hierarchal structure. Buddhism's rise was largely due to the existing hierarchies because, in India, Hinduism completely limited social mobility for its believers. Buddhism allowed its believers to escape that hierarchy. Confucianism proposed to solve the problem of social ills by recognizing existing hierarchies, thereby reinforcing them, and creating new ones. Christianity did not actively support a hierarchy, but some interpreted it as supporting slavery.

The growing importance of social status impacted societies all over the world for generations to come. It would ultimately only be altered by modern industrial capitalism, which was based on merit, i.e., one's effort, and abilities. Social hierarchies of all types continued to exist from that point to the present.

Imperial societies relied on a range of methods to maintain the production of food and provide rewards for the loyalty of the elites.

As empires grew, so did their populations. The Persian Achaemenid Empire, for example, contained nearly 40 percent of the world's population at the height of its power. Growth in the territory of an empire guaranteed the growth of its bureaucracy, which made for the growth of the nobility. The nobility, or those who were wealthy and owned land, wielded power and needed to be pleased so they would not use that power against their governments. The nobility may have come from the conquered territories, as in Persia's satrap system, or from growing systems of bureaucracies like in China. Since the elites wielded power, their respective governments had to please them through the current social order by issuing or allowing them to own free laborers like corvées and slaves, cut their taxes and/or lower their rents.

The issues of an expanding population were explored by scientists, engineers, and political officials of the times. Officials implemented land reforms by organizing farmers into communities and holding bureaucrats responsible for collecting taxes and competing for provincial administration. Nobles' governing of the land developed into what is now known as feudalism. To solve the problem of growing populations, farming was subsidized, and every empire attempted to improve its farming technology. Persia implemented new irrigation techniques in which they used rainwater to help irrigate the soil, transporting it by using gravity. The Romans transported water into cities and farms via aqueducts. Many technological advances in farming around the world were made by better irrigation technology.

Patriarchy continued to shape gender and family relations in all imperial societies of this period.

Engraving of Cleopatra, Egyptian Pharaoh

As social hierarchies became more rigid, so did patriarchy, another form of social division. Patriarchy was practiced throughout the world, although some places gave women more rights than others. In Sparta, women were not allowed to hold office in the council of elders or be king, yet they could own property. In Athens and Rome, women were not allowed to vote, hold political office, or own property.

Many empires and civilizations oppressed or marginalized women, so there is little documentation about the lives of women who lived during the period. Rarely did women become powerful rulers. One exception is the last Pharaoh of Egypt, Cleopatra. Although some societies gave women more rights than others, only Germanic, Celtic, African, Siberian and Mongolian tribes show evidence of egalitarian or semi-egalitarian societies where women had equal rights and responsibilities to those of men. As societies progressed into modern civilization and more tribes were brought under Roman civilization, African merchants, and other empires and powerful states, the two genders were only rarely treated equally.

Empires created political, cultural, and administrative difficulties that they could not manage, which eventually led to their decline, collapse, and transformation into successor empires or states. External problems resulted from security issues along frontiers, including the threat of invasions.

The fall of great empires is always far more complex than it seems. Many empires fell because they were involved in wars they could not sustain, which drained their economies and made them less able to defend themselves. Most of the time, the fall of empires resulted from systematic problems, such as governmental corruption, weak leaders or a decline in trade. Identifying the causes of decline is complicated, and it is easier to point out some specific problems and lost battles rather than identifying the systematic issues.

Many great empires declined because of conquest, but most of the time, conquest was merely the final step of the fall. Usually, corruption in the government and socioeconomic problems cost an empire much more than mere military strength, and further examination of such problems is one of the reasons for the study of history. It is important to the understanding of present and future problems.

Through the excessive mobilization of resources, imperial governments caused environmental damage and generated social tensions and economic difficulties by concentrating too much wealth in the hands of elites.

The seeds of future problems were often planted in ancient times by how humans interacted with their environment. By building better irrigation, humans learned to shape the environment to suit them, while other animals adapted to the environment around them. Large amounts of cattle may have caused the Sahara to grow, and all the animals ate the jungles of Africa humans had domesticated, and the farming has done to feed them. As the human population grew, there was not only the need for more food but also more space. Forests were chopped down to create more space for human villages, cities, and farmland.

In the period 600 B.C.E. to 600 C.E., the concept that nature was for human consumption grew in popularity. The level of deforestation increased, and environmental problems occurred as a result. The Neolithic Revolution caused people to start settling and building. At this time, humans developed industries based on natural resources. Mismanagement of these by authoritarian governments became a threat to human existence later in human history.

Trade has had an extremely important effect on the world. It formed the markets and international trading relations that developed and grew into those of the present day. Goods were not the only—and maybe not even the most important—things that traveled along the major international trade routes. The much more important things that traveled along the Silk Road and the Indian Ocean Trade routes were ideas.

Ideas inspired people to act and change the fate of entire civilizations, and their value is hard to overestimate. People from different cultures that possessed different ideas met and conversed, which often facilitated cultural diffusion by introducing merchants to a new faith or tradition or making them aware of technological advancements and other perspectives on the world.

Land and water routes became the basis for transregional trade, communication, and exchange networks in the Eastern Hemisphere.

As previously discussed, trade was very important for people and governments of the classical age as they could obtain goods that they lacked in exchange for the goods that they had in abundance. Regular people could make a living by trading goods. Any major empire either controlled some trade or wanted to.

China controlled the Silk Roads. Rome traded with China via the Silk Roads and controlled Mediterranean trade after it conquered Carthage. The Persian Empires were the connecting link between Chinese and Roman trade. India controlled Indian Ocean Trade, in which China was also heavily involved. The Islamic countries that rose after the classical age also greatly benefited from Mediterranean trade routes and Indian Ocean Trade. Egypt had great economic ties to Nubia, trading gold, and agricultural products along the Nile River. In short, trade was very important in classical and postclassical history.

Tradesmen of the Tang dynasty

Many factors, including the climate and location of the routes, the typical trade goods, and the ethnicity of people involved, shaped the distinctive features of a variety of trade routes.

Probably the most famous of the trading routes were the Silk Roads. The Silk Road, as it is usually called, was not just one road; it was a network of different roads that went from China through the Kushan Empire in Central Asia to the Persian and Roman Empires. Its routes spread to Arabia, the Caucasus, Afghanistan, and all over Asia, including India. Trade along the Silk Roads began around 1 B.C.E. and skyrocketed during the 2nd-century C.E, alongside the long-term and large-scale trade taking place between the Roman Empire and Han China.

Rome exported such goods as marble, wine, grapes, olives, and olive oil, while the Chinese exported silk, iron, silver, china, and other precious goods. During the Qin and Han dynasties, Chinese goods were produced by Chinese governmental industries and exported via merchants, very few of whom traveled all the way from China to Rome or Persia. It was a trade of people rather than a trade of countries; the merchants brought goods from the Chinese government, traveled a certain number of miles, and then sold them to other merchants for a higher price than they bought them for. This happened again and again until the goods reached their destination.

Sometimes merchants would get rich from this, which led to increased taxes on trade. The Silk Roads were noted for uniting the people of Asia, Rome, and China in the pursuit of wealth. The lion's share of China's wealth came from the silk trade. Silk had many functions, including use as a cloth for sails, the material on which to write, fabric for clothing, and as a commonly accepted trade currency. The prominence of silk on this network of roads is how the Silk Road received its name. China also became the biggest producer of iron and silver in the world, exporting it along the Silk Road, which shaped the nature and the legacy of this famous trading route.

Mediterranean Sea Lanes were very important trade routes that were established by the Phoenicians, Egyptians, and Greeks who traded with each other, forming colonies all across the Mediterranean to support this practice. These lanes dramatically rose in importance once Rome stepped onto the stage. Rome had been a major market for Carthaginian goods before the Punic Wars, spreading Phoenician culture and goods. Rome was growing in size dramatically and eventually had to feed a much larger population, which made them seek large amounts of grain and other food from Egypt. Greece traded ceramics, marble, and other goods in between its divided states, Persia and Rome until the Romans conquered it.

New technologies facilitated long-distance communication and exchange. New technologies permitted the use of domesticated pack animals to transport goods across longer routes.

The most widespread tool used in trade was animal labor. Animal labor was used worldwide, from the early domestication of animals thousands of years ago to the Industrial Revolution. Technologies appeared in the classical period that allowed for animal labor to be more effectively harnessed for trade. Two of the most important inventions were the saddle and the stirrup. These allowed people to both mount and control horses very well, which allowed for much better riding and carriage.

Not only were horses used for cavalry in warfare, but they were also extensively used in trade to carry goods and help merchants perform more efficiently, which greatly facilitated trade across the globe. In addition to horses, other animals were used to facilitate trade. Camels were vital in trans-Saharan and sub-Saharan trade. The saddle and other modifications for camels allowed Africans to use them as trading caravans consisting of one thousand camels strong. In Persia, the mail was delivered by donkeys, which included military and government commands and messages as well. Historians describe this as being mail that could not be stopped or anyhow prevented from reaching its destination.

In Asia, oxen were used as beasts of burden and for farming, with the development of the technology of ox yokes. Many more inventions came to be that would facilitate trade and let humans use animals for labor. Without such inventions as the saddle, long trade routes like the Silk Road would not have been as effective. These trade routes established foreign relations and goods exchanges, which proved extremely beneficial to human development.

Alongside the trade in goods, the exchange of people, technology, religious and cultural beliefs, food crops, domesticated animals, and disease pathogens developed across far-flung networks of communication and exchange. The spread of crops, including rice and cotton from South Asia to the Middle East, encouraged changes in farming and irrigation techniques.

Grain staple foods—rice in Asia, corn in the American hemisphere, and grains like wheat, barley, and rye in Europe and North Africa—were pivotal to the development of civilization and great empires. The amount of grain that could be produced per unit of cultivated land was a far more efficient food source than raising animals or plucking fruit off trees. The abundance of food which could be produced by uniting deliberate agriculture with staple grains enabled early civilizations to liberate a huge part of their population to do work other than producing food. When only a portion of the population was required to grow food, others were free to become the armies that conquered, the skilled people who created their weapons or the merchants who brought wealth to the country with which to pay the warriors—the craftsmen and the farmers.

Around ten thousand years ago, agriculture began in Asia. Rice cultivation began in both India and China at around the same time, roughly 4,000 B.C.E. There are two competing theories about how Asia began to produce food crops. The theory which is broadly accepted by historians and anthropologists today is that agriculture developed in different places independently; however, a competing theory, known as "diffusion theory," suggests that it may have developed in one region and then spread to other human populations when they came into contact.

An Ab Anbar, a component of the Qanat

Irrigation techniques led to a surplus of food and specialization of labor and triggered a trade in tools with other nations who wanted to adopt agriculture. Growing rice requires intense flooding of a plantation for part of the year. This could only be done by digging trenches to divert water from rivers or to catch rainwater. Other grains cultivated around the world also required irrigation in some form. Early irrigation techniques generally included canals or the watering of crops by hand with pots of water. These techniques required entrenching tools and pottery.

In India, there is archaeological evidence for sophisticated granaries, animal husbandry, and bronze tools from 3,000 years B.C.E. Canals and irrigation methods were well established in China by at least 1,000 B.C.E. The iron plow was invented in China in roughly the 6th century B.C.E. The "qanat" system used by the Persians eventually spread to China and Rome. The qanat system was an irrigation method that utilized tunnels built in such a way as to use gravity to transport water from underground supplies into villages. Without these inventions and the domestication of animals, widespread agriculture would have been impossible.

Tools were also tradable goods, and iron tools and pottery were traded extensively by nations like India and China to civilizations which did not know how to produce their tools. Wealth from this trade empowered the dominant civilizations.

Cotton has been grown in many places, on a small scale, for thousands of years. It became commonly known and grown around the world by about the year 1500 C.E. India was producing cotton as early as 5,000 B.C.E. Evidence has established that there was cotton production all over the Americas more than five thousand years ago. Cotton was developed by many civilizations independently of one another, as were the tools they needed to process it – combs, spindles, and eventually simple looms. The cotton trade was an important part of a major change caused by the diffusion of knowledge from India to other human civilizations.

Tea was introduced to China, most likely from India, in the 3rd century C.E. This good was pivotal in the 18th and 19th centuries when the British Empire dominated the entire globe. Before that happened, though it became popular in China. Techniques for cultivating tea were brought to China from India.

Religious and cultural traditions were transformed as they spread.

Religions, especially those faiths with missionaries, spread rapidly via trade. Two large missionary religions that spread over different parts of the world during that time were Christianity and Buddhism. Buddhism arose 600 years earlier than Christianity, so it had more time to become a prevalent philosophy. Christianity was the fastest growing religion of its time—spreading to Africa, North Africa, Italy, Greece, Spain, France, Britain, Germanic lands, Eastern Europe, Russia, and Anatolia— and did not see as drastic a change as Buddhism until the Photian Schism.

While Christianity had not seen such radical change yet, it rose later with the rise of Islam. Islam, also a branch proceeding from Judaism, was seen as such a different entity altogether by the European Christians; their society considered it a completely different religion, demonstrating how drastically a religion can change when it spreads into different areas via trade routes and mixes with the culture of the region.

The spread of disease pathogens diminished urban populations and contributed to the decline of some empires.

Another major effect trade had on the world was the spread of disease. As quickly as cultures and ideas diffused throughout populations via trade, diseases did so too – using the same process of simple human contact. Animals brought diseases with them via ships; for example, the rats aboard inbound ships introduced smallpox to Europe. Smallpox, measles, and the Bubonic Plague originated somewhere in Asia and could theoretically not have affected many people; but thanks to the Silk Road, they made their way into China and Rome, devastating their societies and populations. Disease even killed two Roman emperors: Marcus Aurelius died of smallpox during the Antonine Plague in the 2nd century C.E. and Claudius II died of smallpox during the Plague of Cyprian in the 3rd century C.E.

Marcus Aurelius, Roman emperor

The Bubonic Plague's first known outbreak (also known as the Justinian Plague) arrived in Europe in 540 C.E., killing almost one-fourth of Eastern Europe's population. China was devastated as well, facing outbreaks in 161, 310, and 322 C.E. All of these plagues would not have occurred without the large-scale international trade taking place between Rome and China at the time.

These plagues are argued to have played a major role in people questioning their old faiths and converting them to new ones. It has been said that the Cyprian Plague facilitated the spread of Christianity into Rome, and the devastating outbreaks in China drove Buddhism to appear there. People were not sure if their gods were there to help in times of trouble like the plague, so they turned to other religions. This was very important to the political order of both countries, as it shaped their political policies for centuries to come. All of this shows just how important trade was to world history: by spreading culture, goods, and disease, it shaped future generations.

Notes for active learning

Notes for active learning

Major historical events of the period:

800–700 B.C.E.: Homer writes *The Iliad* and *The Odyssey*

509 B.C.E.: The Roman Republic emerges after the overthrow of Etruscans

431–404 B.C.E.: The Peloponnesian War rages, Athens and its allies eventually being defeated by Sparta and allies

400s B.C.E.: Rationalism emerges in Greece

300 B.C.E.: Alexander the Great begins the conquest of the Persian Empire

44 B.C.E.: Gaius Julius Caesar is assassinated, plunging the Republic into civil war

29 B.C.E.: Gaius Octavius, nephew of Caesar, becomes the first Roman emperor

395 C.E.: The Byzantine Empire (Eastern Roman Empire) and Western Roman Empire are established upon Emperor Theodosius I's death, marking the definitive division of the Roman Empire

476 C.E.: Western Roman Empire falls to Germanic Barbarians

PERIOD 1: Prehistory and Civilizations to the year 500 C.E.

EUROPE

Eastern Mediterranean civilizations fostered the arts.

Examples of various forms of sculpture existed in Minoan civilization during this period. Minoans produced small sculptures in contrast to the monumental sculptures seen in Egypt or Mesoamerican civilizations. Many of the recovered Minoan sculptures are dedicated to deities and kings, highlighting the idea of divine rulers and their grip on political and social power in this period. The most notable example of sculpture from another civilization is the monumental Sphinx, which is thought to have been constructed under the Old Kingdom (2686–2181 B.C.E.).

Christianity, based on core beliefs about the teachings and divinity of Jesus of Nazareth as recorded by his disciples, drew on Judaism and initially rejected Roman and Hellenistic influences. Despite initial Roman imperial hostility, Christianity spread through the efforts of missionaries and merchants through many parts of Afro-Eurasia. Eventually, it gained Roman imperial support by the time of Emperor Constantine.

Christianity is one of the foremost examples of religions spreading in the West. Christianity began as a sect of Judaism founded around 15 C.E. by Jesus of Nazareth. Jesus was a preacher who was born in the Roman province of Judea. Jesus was one of many Jewish reactionary preachers at the time, but he was distinguished from the others by his more radical view on love, peace, and justice; along with his claim to be the son of God. The Roman emperors were also said to have been related to gods but the difference between Jesus and Emperor Augustus, the first Roman Emperor, was that Jesus was a poor Jew who did not have any socially-expected prerequisites, such as wealth, fame or power, to be a Son of God.

The word "Christianity" derives from the "following of Christ" or "being like Christ" ("Christ" means "Messiah"). It emphasizes the divinity of Jesus of Nazareth and the following of his teachings, which generally emphasize monotheism, obedience to God, peaceful and ethical behavior and love for thy neighbor. A Jewish prophecy foretold that a Savior would come in times of trouble. The time of Jesus' birth was a representation of this prophecy, for it saw the rise of King Herod and his son (also named Herod), both of whom were famous for being brutal to the Jews.

Jesus was seen as the Messiah, who sought to bring back the rule of Jerusalem. He promised the Jews another kingdom, the Kingdom of Heaven, and to get there, one had to follow the covenant made with God. At the time of Jesus's death, he had a small but very loyal and devoted group of followers. Those with whom Jesus was closest were known as apostles, and after his death, they recorded his teachings and spread the Word of God across Judea and the Roman Empire.

Engraving of Adam and Eve

Christianity was different from other Asian religions of that time because it was not based so much on understanding how to achieve greater peace in oneself (e.g., Nirvana, moksha, or going to heaven), but rather on a narrative and one's analysis of the narrative. The covenant that Jesus spread was one of belief in only one true God, the God of the Bible, in exchange for forgiveness of the inherited sin in oneself. However, if one does not follow the covenant and lives in sin, one will be sent to hell and burn there for eternity. Therefore, what the Bible or the Church considered sinful is discouraged, and in this way, Christianity tries to form social order.

The Christian belief is rooted in the idea of creation (i.e., that everything came to be because God willed it to be) and the idea that the first humans (Adam and Eve) lived in paradise before Eve ate the forbidden apple from the Garden of Eden. God sent them to live on earth with an "original sin" that all of their predecessors would inherit from them. In Christianity, Jesus was the one who came to save humans from that original inherited sin of Adam and Eve so that people would not go to hell, but rather achieve forgiveness.

The Roman government saw this rising sect of Judaism as a threat. Though at first the religion was banned, it appealed to many commoners in the Roman Empire because it promised an afterlife (something the Roman religion did not emphasize) and because they believed that Christ was, in fact, a Messiah. The teachings of Jesus were so influential that the Roman authorities had Jesus tried and crucified because the Roman government saw Jesus and his followers as a threat to Roman authority. They were afraid that if Jesus were the Messiah, he would lead an uprising and restore the Kingdom of Jerusalem. To avoid such a challenge to their authority, the Roman government tried and crucified Jesus, which was a normal way of executing Rome's enemies at the time.

Christ on the cross with the Virgin and St. John

Christianity was open to everyone, whether they were Jews or not. The followers of the Christian religion did not have to be circumcised, and there were new ethical rules by which they had to live. One of the most influential missionaries of the young religion was the apostle Saul of Tarsus, later known as Paul, who facilitated the building of churches devoted to the worship of Jesus throughout the Roman Empire. Another apostle, Peter, who lived in 30 C.E., is considered by Catholics to be the first Pope of the Roman Catholic Church.

Saint Peter's repentance

The religion grew slowly but steadily. When Western Rome fell, and Emperor Constantine rose in the Byzantine Empire, the Edict of Milan was issued, making it legal to practice Christianity. This meant that missionaries who had been preaching illegally would be able to profess their faith openly. There were now more missionaries preaching the Word of God, and it was legal to convert via those missionaries.

There was also a rumor that Emperor Constantine converted to Christianity himself, a story that dramatically increased the spread of Christianity. Christianity later spread across Europe, and the Christian faith became such a dominant force in Europe that the Church had more authority and power than many of the continent's monarchs.

After Jesus's death, the religion became commonly known as Christianity, and it was spread by many of his followers, including apostles, missionaries, and even regular people who shared their beliefs. Later, Christianity would become one of the most practiced and influential religions in the world. Its moral code was the foundation of peasant and rural everyday life in the European Middle Ages. Christianity was used to legitimize the rule of European monarchs, and it was the driving force behind the Crusades.

Most of all, Christianity became a uniting force among the many peoples of Europe and other Christian countries and empires throughout history. In the centuries since the Edict of Milan, Christianity has been spread throughout Africa and Asia by various conquerors and traders who settled in different parts of the empires. It was also spread by the conversion of powerful imperial leaders, such as Charlemagne, the Great, who followed in Constantine's footsteps.

The core ideas in Greco-Roman philosophy and science emphasized logic, empirical observation, and the nature of political power and hierarchy.

Before Europe was taken over by Christianity, it was religiously fractured. While the German people believed in spirits and practiced animism, the Greeks developed a religion that included multiple gods and a complex narrative establishing relationships between them. The

Greek religion believed in gods and their intervention in regular people's lives. Greeks believed that gods could impregnate women (e.g., Hercules), determine the outcome of wars, and much more. Like the Jews, the Greeks believed in covenants. However, the Greek covenants were much simpler, and the stakes were much lower. The Greek idea of a covenant included common deals wherein the Greeks would make a particular sacrifice to a god and then that god would do something in exchange. For example, an architect could trade five pigs for a successfully built building.

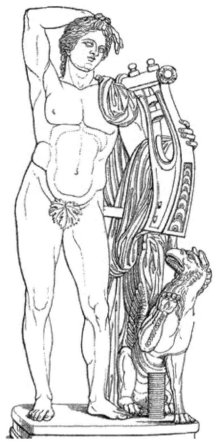

Greek mythology also includes titans who are like gods but less divine. The gods often discussed regarding the Greek religion are the Olympian gods, so named because they were thought to have lived in the Olympic Mountains. By the 5th century B.C.E., rationalism rose in Greece, which led to philosophers and historians beginning to think of their religion as a collection of myths. As a result, some began to criticize myth-as-history texts like the *Iliad* and the *Odyssey*.

Greek rationalism laid the foundations of Roman values and culture. The first philosophers were rather peculiar because they focused less on philosophy and more on mathematics, astronomy, biology, and primitive chemistry. While early Greek philosophers were scientists, Socrates is now considered the "father of Greek philosophy," for he was the first recorded philosopher.

The "big three" Greek philosophers were Socrates, Plato, and Aristotle. Socrates was an ordinary construction worker until someone told him that the oracle had said that he, Socrates, was the

Statue of the Greek god Apollo with lyre and griffin angels

smartest man alive. The foundation for Socratic philosophy is the question: "how much do I really know?" Socrates emphasized defining terms. He believed that people do not really know what beauty is, or what wisdom is, but can develop this knowledge through conversation. Socrates would ask a painter if he knew what beauty is, to which the painter would answer, "Yes, of course, I am a painter." However, when asked to define what beauty is, the painter could not come up with a definition that would not be challenged by Socrates.

Socrates argued that by a discussion with one person defending a point and the other challenging that point, people could arrive at a greater understanding of the point and what it means, thereby getting closer to the truth. By the end of Socrates' life, he was tried for not believing in Greek gods, in whom he did believe, and for introducing new gods, which he did not do. Socrates was still found guilty, arguably because the people of Athens got tired of his asking everyone questions, which made everyone uncomfortable and insecure about their knowledge. Socrates' punishment at the hands of the people of Athens was to drink a lethal dose of poison.

Socrates with his students

Socrates' legacy lived on because all of his teachings were written down by his friend and student, Plato. Plato was notable for being a superstitious philosopher who argued that the answers to humanity's problems and dilemmas are in the realm of the divine. He searched for answers in religion and superstition. Plato thought that before people are born, they see the original, pure versions of everything in the universe, and although they forget the pure versions of these things, the concepts are still in their heads. This means that everything there is to discover is already in people's minds.

Aristotle, Greek philosopher

Plato, Greek philosopher

Aristotle was a student of Plato's and is most famous for founding the study of logic. Aristotle wrote books on politics (e.g., *Politics*), justice (Nicomachean Ethics), and marine biology. (Note: Plato wrote *The Republic.* Aristotle wrote *Politics.*) He is most often referenced for his study of logic, including: what it means to be logical, what logical fallacies are, and how debates should transpire logically to determine the truth. An excellent book for greater insight into the field of Aristotelian logic is *Being Logical.* Aristotle's field of expertise is extensive, and he was considered the definitive authority on philosophical matters in medieval and Renaissance Europe.

The School of Athens by Raphael

Overall, Aristotle was more of a scientific philosopher, a direct opposite of Plato (that is why Plato points up to the sky, and Aristotle points down to the earth in Raphael's painting *The School of Athens).* Aristotle's rationalism laid the foundation for later Roman law, culture, and traditional values. Romans began to see sculptures and paintings as useless and focused instead on things they would consider useful, like building bridges, roads, irrigation systems, and aqueducts. Rationalism also greatly influenced the Roman government. The effects of Greek rationalism and philosophy cannot be overstated, for they are evident even today.

Artistic expressions, including literature and drama, architecture, and sculpture, show distinctive cultural developments. Literature and drama acquired distinctive forms that influenced artistic developments in neighboring regions and later periods.

The Greek theater was the foundation of all Western drama. Greek plays varied from comedy to tragedy, and the themes of those plays varied from everyday life situations to Greek myths. The *Iliad* and the *Odyssey* made such a grand contribution to Greek literature that these works of literature are still read today. Greek mythical literature, philosophical writing, and sculpture were so prodigious that the artists of the Renaissance looked to the work of the Greeks for inspiration.

Frontispiece of The Iliad

Distinctive architectural styles developed in many regions in this period.

Greek architecture, including the world-famous Parthenon, is still considered some of the greatest of the classical civilizations. Many temples like the Parthenon were built on high ground in Greek cities. Beneath them were forums, places for trade and dialogue, libraries, and other public places. The Greeks were famous for making things beautiful and proportionate, and this was also the case with their architecture. Greek buildings, especially temples, were built in proportion and used columns and patterns. Most of these buildings were made of marble.

The Roman architectural style was influenced by that of the Greeks since Rome's culture was a product of cultural diffusion from Greece; however, the Romans differed from the Greeks in their desire to make buildings and architecture useful. The Romans could appreciate great buildings, such as the pyramids, but they saw them as idle and useless while in Rome, everything had to have practical use. The Romans, in addition to building the structures that Greeks also built (such as libraries, amphitheaters, and places of worship), also focused on building baths, public fountains, aqueducts, coliseums, and roads. Roman architecture placed a great deal of emphasis on usefulness, which contributed to shaping and characterizing Roman culture.

Pont du Gard

Greek city-states and colonies

The Greeks were a great ancient civilization, but they lacked a centralized government. The Greek city-states were connected only by language and culture, which varied from city-state to city-state. Greece did not form a common identity until it became necessary when the Persians attacked them. The Greek city of Athens was the birthplace of modern democracy, science, and philosophy. The Greek city-states were not free or democratic. Even Athens was not as free a state as commonly thought - its population had a larger portion of slaves than free citizens. This changed because of reforms of the debt system, which decreed that one could no longer become a slave because of debt and that no Athenian citizen could be a slave of another Athenian citizen. Athens did not have a modern democracy either, as only the male population – who were not engaged in military service – could directly vote on the city-state's laws and policies.

Ancient Athens

Still, Athens was very democratic compared to the other Greek city-states, most of which were tyrannical and militaristic. Sparta and its allies practiced oligarchy or the power of multiple kings. Generally, one king would go to war, and the other one would rule the state at home. The Spartans had a militaristic culture and authoritarian government in which the army was the focus of regular peoples' lives. The Spartans sometimes practiced what is known today as eugenics, as they would kill babies who were born weak or with defects. The majority of Spartan men were trained for the military from the age of six and served until they were no longer able to.

Athens and Sparta were antagonistic towards one another for the majority of their history, but that changed when the Persians decided to conquer the Greeks. Sparta, Athens and other Greek city-states had to unite to protect what today is the Greek mainland. Darius I of Persia attacked Greece when they encouraged rebellions in the culturally and ethnically Greek territories in Asia Minor. Darius I was unsuccessful in this attack and was eventually defeated at the Battle of Marathon. Xerxes I led the second invasion of Greece but was defeated after several naval and land battles, which culminated in a humiliating military defeat at Salamis.

Sparta had been against waging war in Asia Minor; they saw it as difficult and unnecessary. Sparta emerged victoriously, but the victory took a large toll on both Athens and Sparta. The Athenians insisted on keeping their colonies, so Athens gained hegemony and later formed the Delian League. This led to the establishment of the Athenian Empire, which waged several victorious campaigns against the Persians. Sparta later destroyed Athens in the Second Peloponnesian War—which was motivated largely by the Spartan's dislike of Athenian political domination of the region—and the Spartan hegemony was re-established.

Corinthian helmet

While the war ended victoriously for Sparta and unsuccessfully for Athens, it did not end particularly well for either party. It was also damaging to Greece as a whole. Lasting for twenty-seven years, the war weakened Greece to the point that the Persians eventually were able to win back all the territory they had lost in the Wars of the Delian League. The Corinthian War weakened both Greece and Persia, thereby preparing both for the rise of Alexander of Macedon, also known as Alexander the Great.

The Hellenistic Alexandrian Empire

Alexander became a king in 336 B.C.E. after his father's assassination. He was a young king who gained notoriety in his empire when, as a teenager, he tamed a horse that no one else could break. The famous Greek philosopher Aristotle tutored the young Alexander. At the same time, Alexander was named the ruler of Macedon he was also awarded the Generalship, which brought with it the command of the Macedonian and the Greek armies. Alexander launched a series of campaigns on the Achaemenid Empire, which he conquered—a feat the Greeks had never been able to accomplish previously. By the age of thirty, Alexander had expanded his empire from Macedonia to Northwest India, stopping only due to the fatigue of his soldiers. Alexander died of fever in Babylon, which he had planned to make the base of operations for his eventual invasion of Arabia. There was subsequently much speculation about the cause of his death.

Alexander was never defeated in battle. He made no institutions to replace those he destroyed, and after his death, the empire was torn apart by civil wars between Alexander's generals, powerful families, and Alexander's friends who were all fighting over the empire. The people fighting for Alexander's territories became known as Diadochi, and the series of civil wars that divided the empire and shaped the post-Alexandrian Kingdoms were called the Diadochi Wars.

Drawing of Alexander the Great

The Diadochi Wars caused the spread of Greek culture and language throughout Alexander's empire because most of the Diadochi were Greek, which is why it is considered the beginning of the Hellenistic period. Hellenistic means "the ones who speak Greek," and it is characterized by the spread of Greek culture into the post-Alexandrian world. Greek culture spread and mixed with Egyptian, Persian, and Indian cultures. As a result, Greek theatre spread into India and mixed with Sanskrit drama, the Persian coins wrote the word "king" in Greek, and the Byzantine Empire rose.

The Roman Empire

Around the 7th century B.C.E., the Latins, Greek colonists of the Italian peninsula, founded a city upon seven hills. They called this city Rome and formed the Roman Kingdom, which was ruled by the ethnic group called the Etruscans and consisted mainly of Latins, who would later become the Romans. The Etruscan kingdom existed from the 7th century B.C.E. to the 5th century B.C.E., after which it was overthrown by the Latins to form the Roman Republic.

The Roman population was divided into two classes: patricians and plebeians. The patricians were the nobility, and the upper class and the plebeians were the laborers of the empire. In most ancient civilizations, workers were a majority but held little to no power; however, in Rome, this working majority did hold power because they lived in a democracy. The Roman Republic was created to please Roman plebeians, so they would not leave Rome and form another city of their own, which they had threatened to do.

The new republic was akin to the modern representative democracy that existed at that time. Representative democracy differed from Athenian democracy in that in Athens, people voted on policies directly, while in Rome, people voted on which patricians would represent the plebeians in the Senate. The Roman Republic differed from other states and became such an influential force in human history due to its open militarism, which is evidenced by its defeat of the Etruscan Kingdom, the unification of present-day Italy and expansion beyond its borders into Spain, the Balkans and North Africa (i.e., Carthage).

Rome continued to expand and fight its enemies, which spread civilization, Roman culture, and irrigation to less developed tribes and promoted Romanization throughout Europe. Less-developed people often voluntarily joined the Roman Republic because it brought infrastructures such as roads, canals, aqueducts, libraries, amphitheaters, irrigation, and public toilets, which greatly improved the living standards in these less developed regions. In return, these people had to become Roman citizens—essentially altering their identity—and as Roman citizens, they had to perform military service when drafted and pay the Roman government taxes.

Rome had existed as a republic for at least four hundred years when Gaius Julius Caesar rose to power. Caesar was from a famous and beloved Roman family. He united with Crassus, who was very wealthy due to his fire business, and Pompey, who was a powerful military general at the time. They established the First Triumvirate, in which they used their power to achieve each other's goals.

Julius Caesar later became a general of the army himself and was elected consul of Rome. He would subsequently go on to fight a campaign in Gaul (modern-day France) and assimilate it into the Roman Empire. As the governor of Gaul, Caesar developed a terrible reputation for corruption and irresponsible management of tax revenues. He eventually developed a rivalry with his former ally Pompey.

When Caesar arrived at the Rubicon River, which is the northern border of the Italian peninsula, he was ordered to disarm his legion. Doing so would mean he would go to prison for abusing his power as consul. But not giving up his legion would lead to a civil war in which he was the less powerful side. Caesar had to choose between the two. He chose the latter because his legionaries were experienced war-hardened men while the legions in Rome were fairly young and inexperienced.

Gaius Julius Caesar, Roman ruler

Caesar's reasoning proved sound, and he won the war. He took Rome and was elected consul and dictator of Rome for life; however, this was only a politically convenient decision by the Senators. In reality, the Senate did not like the fact that Caesar made all the decisions, so they organized a plot to kill him. Caesar had adopted a nephew of his named Octavian in his will, which led to a crisis over succession. The Senate killed Caesar, and after a civil war, which led to the Roman conquest of Egypt, Rome was taken over by Octavian, who adopted the name of Augustus and became Caesar Augustus, the first Emperor of Rome, in 29 B.C.E. After this coup, Rome, now an empire, continued to expand, reaching its peak in the 2nd century C.E.

In the 3rd century C.E., the empire was divided into two separate states: the Eastern Roman Empire and the Western Roman Empire. The East is often called the Byzantine Empire because the ancient name of its capital was Byzantium, but the Eastern Romans thought of themselves as Romans. The Eastern Roman Empire became the more powerful half because its trading center, Constantinople (Byzantium), was a link between Asia and Europe and the Black and Mediterranean Seas.

The Eastern Romans spoke predominantly Greek, and Emperor Constantine allowed Christianity to be practiced openly. They still followed Roman laws, its citizens were still guaranteed the same rights as Roman citizens, and even though Rome was in possession of the Eastern Empire only once and not for a very long time, the people of the Eastern Roman Empire still considered themselves Roman. They used Roman currency, and the eastern legionnaires were still the best army in the region.

While the Eastern Empire prospered, the West fell to Germanic Barbarians in 476 C.E. Under Emperor Justinian, the Eastern Roman Empire later tried to reconquer the Western Roman Empire, but its budget would not sustain that level of expansion. Rome never regained its previous size, but the East existed for almost a thousand years after the fall of the West.

Greek Democracy

Democracy was first implemented in the Greek city-state of Athens. In the beginning, Athens was ruled by archons, king-like rulers who were put in place by the constitution and not by divine power. Therefore, the ruler did not have absolute power over the government. The concept of absolute monarchy arrived in Europe after Alexander the Great invaded Persia. As a result, the Greek city-states had pluralistic oligarchic governments ruled by a noble family or a few noble families. Some were more attached to their constitution than others, but it was the founding of the principle of a government ruled by laws, not by people.

The Athenian government was not well managed. The families that ruled were selfish, debt slavery thrived, and food shortages occurred. To fix these crises, Athens implemented a system of electing a tyrant to have absolute control to fix the state. This happened in the early 6th century B.C.E. when Athens elected Solon. Solon laid the foundations for democracy by implementing a system

Solon, Athenian ruler

of allowing ordinary people to participate in the judicial system and by extending the circle of people who could become archons to wealthy people (not just people of noble descent). This laid the foundation for the idea that anybody can rule or assist in ruling the state.

However, tyranny and political instability eventually came to Athens. In 510 B.C.E., a nobleman named Cleisthenes launched a coup against the tyrannical government with the help of the Spartan army. Cleisthenes wanted to reform the government in such a way that the people would receive more representation. The people eventually turned against Cleisthenes, and he was sent into exile. The Spartan army created an even more tyrannical government in which a few noble families had absolute power, which enraged the citizens of Athens. A popular revolt made it possible for Cleisthenes to return to Athens and continue with his reforms, from which the first recorded democratic political system emerged. In this system, the General Assembly had primary control of the government.

The way direct democracy worked in Athens was via three main bodies of power: the ecclesia, the boule, and the jurors with the magistrates as the "Justice Department." Athenian democracy was based on a lottery in which eligible people (adult, male, full citizens of Athens) participated. Those who were picked met in the "ecclesia" (assembly) several times per year to discuss policies, lawsuits, and political matters. In the ecclesia, there were a total of six thousand people who discussed and voted on laws, foreign policy, military strategy, war, and issues that anyone in the ecclesia brought forward.

The "boule" was a group of 500 people, also chosen by a lottery, who sorted out which laws to discuss and essentially guided the assembly and created order during its meetings. A lottery also picked the jury, and this branch of the government had unlimited power in court and handled judicial matters such as lawsuits. The people who were eligible to be in the lottery represented a small amount of the population. Children, women, foreigners, slaves, and people currently engaged in the military were excluded. Out of 200,000 Athenian citizens, only 50,000 were eligible for government service; however, this system was far more democratic and free than any other in Greece at that time.

Other Greek city-states may have adopted some aspects of Athenian democracy, but most of them were ruled by a few noble families and were oligarchies. The most well-known example of such an oligarchic rule was Sparta. Sparta was ruled by two kings, one of which led an army to war while the other stayed at home and ruled on domestic matters. Many Greek governments of this age were organized in this way. It was only later that generals were de jure separated from politics. The two kings participated in the council of elders, the governing body similar to the Athenian boule but different in that the boule was chosen by lottery while the Gerousia (the council of elders) consisted of twenty-eight male Spartans who were elected by the apella (the Spartan version of the ecclesia) for life. The Gerousia gave a set of issues on which the apella voted.

The difference between the Athenian ecclesia and the Spartan apella was that the ecclesia had much more importance in governance, for it served the same function as a king, of which Sparta had two and Athens had none. The ecclesia was also far less limited in what it was voting on than the apella. The Spartan apella only voted on a small set of issues and policies that the council of elders brought to the apella. Since both of the Spartan kings were on the council (the Gerousia), the apella voted only on what the kings and the rest of the Gerousia could not agree on. The boule in Athens only helped set order in the ecclesia and would sort out anything less important or judicial.

This oligarchic control over policies and decisions in government was most prevalent in the Greek city-states who were not as democratic as Athens. Greek city-states thought the Athenian form of government was radical and laughable because a populous could not govern itself without knowledgeable people governing with or for them. However, Athens became a very successful state both economically and militarily, considering that it proved a challenge for the Spartans without becoming a militaristic society.

Roman Democracy

The Roman Republican system was the system that laid the foundation for almost all modern democracies. This form of democratic government arrived in 509 B.C.E. when the Roman plebeians overthrew their Etruscan overlords. The fundamental difference between the Roman Republic and direct democracy was that while in Athenian democracy, people voted on laws and policies directly, in the republic, people voted for representatives that would make decisions for them.

In Rome, the governing body consisted of the consuls, the Senate, and the Assembly. The Roman Republic was divided into two groups: the patricians and the plebeians. Consul was the highest position in government, and the person who occupied this position was in charge of the army, oversaw the work of the Senate, and was essentially the leader of the country, undertaking virtually all the roles that the President of the United States undertakes today. In Rome, there were two consuls. Sometimes they agreed to be in charge of different things. If they disagreed, they could veto one another, but the term for a consul was just one year, so it was in the consuls' interest to agree and come up with solutions quickly before their term ended. If that did not happen and the republic was in a crisis, one man was chosen to be the dictator of Rome and held supreme command until the crisis ended or he was replaced.

Coins of the Roman Republic

Below the consul was the Senate, a governing body that made laws and served as a treasury and the ministry of foreign affairs in Rome. It consisted of 300 patricians, from whom the plebeians in the Assembly elected the consul. Plebeians did not elect the Senate. Instead, senators were appointed by the consul for an indeterminate term, meaning they could serve for life. The Assembly voted and elected the consuls of Rome, so according to Roman law, the plebeians had the highest authority in choosing their leaders. The Assembly also protested policies the plebeians did not like, held debates with the consuls—such as those with Cicero— and elected Tribunes.

The tribune was the highest position in the Assembly and provided another layer of checks and balances. The position was filled by a plebeian who could veto legislation and intervene in the business of the Senate. In Athenian democracy, the commoners of Athens could individually propose legislation. In Rome, the people chose their representatives but were not wholly deprived of the power to propose legislation. The Tribune had the power to summon the Senate to discuss legal matters and propose the best laws and policies in his expertise that the plebeians offered for discussion in the Senate.

This system of government was one of the many major achievements of Rome. As the republic grew, it was hard for every part of the population to be involved in government. This system would have worked well when Rome was a city-state, but the more it grew, the more control it needed. Furthermore, Rome was far too vast for information to travel as quickly as it does today. In Rome, information was transported through messengers, which made it essential that the Roman Empire adopted a system of both central and regional bureaucracy.

Bureaucrats were appointed by the consul to rule and execute the consul's orders in the regions of the republic that the consul would not be able to manage by himself. The principles upon which the bureaucracy worked were Roman laws and duty to the government and the people of Rome. Many times, these officials were appointed from among the people living in the region, because the Romans understood that people would be more welcoming to their kind.

The social structures of empires displayed hierarchies that included cultivators, laborers, slaves, artisans, merchants, elites, or caste groups.

In Greece, politics was much more plebeian-oriented after Cleisthenes. However, only the wealthy could become archons (a group which did not have much power, though still possessed far greater influence over the Assembly than regular Athenians). In Sparta, only the nobles could become kings and members of the council of elders, and many other city-states gave more power to the noble and the rich than to the regular people.

Rome's decline was reflective of systemic problems in their government and military.

Rome was an empire of masterful legions that swept enemy armies out of their way and brought civilization to many people. Romans also saw themselves as masters of the whole world. Without Rome's influence, Europe would not be what it is today. Rome was once a great empire, and there are many reasons for its decline, including the weakening of the Roman military, a decrease in Rome's commerce, wars with Germanic tribes, and societal problems stemming from the concept of a free Roman citizen.

The Western Roman military was in decline for a long time. As the empire grew, it became more difficult to train soldiers, and the Roman generals hired Germanic mercenaries for use in war. As Machiavelli later wrote, "Mercenaries and auxiliaries are useless and dangerous. If you are counting on mercenaries to defend your state, you will never be stable or secure...Why? Because the only interest they have in you and their only reason for fighting is the meager salary you're paying them, and that's not reason enough to make them want to die for you."

The Roman practice of hiring mercenaries was not beneficial to Rome as the mercenaries were not loyal to Rome, but to their respective generals and salary, Rome provided. Not every soldier—not even every general—had been to Rome, so if a general was ambitious enough, he could try to take Rome because he was fighting for himself and his mercenary soldiers were fighting for him, not out of loyalty to the empire. Many over the years were that ambitious and declared themselves emperors of Rome.

Rome was drowning in corruption, for even though the state had turned into an empire, the Senate did nothing but act as a stamp that ratified treaties and could obtain access to the state treasury. Even the government served themselves and not Rome.

Trade declined over time as the concepts of free and slave became more of a dividing line between the people of Rome than the concepts of patricians and plebeians. As the population of slaves grew, the division between the patricians and the plebeians increased. This division paled in comparison to the division between slaves and free, mainly because slaves did the majority of the work.

The idea was spreading that it was not a free Roman citizen's obligation to perform hard slave labor. A Roman could be an engineer, a politician, a general, a soldier, an architect, a landowner, or an artisan, but did not have to undertake hard labor. Due to this view, the duties of herding animals and farming crops were given to slaves, while free Romans designed aqueducts and grand buildings. However, these buildings were built by slaves, and Rome grew to be dependent upon slavery for much of its industry and agriculture.

Another problem for the Roman Empire was that it was too vast to control efficiently. A collection of disloyal armies, the collapse of the Roman military, corruption in Rome and local governments, and the dependence of Rome on slave labor grew to be massive weights that Rome could not carry. In the 5th century C.E., Western Rome finally fell when Germanic tribes invaded it, and Rome was captured. The Eastern Roman Empire was reduced to a vassal city-state when Constantinople was sacked by an alliance of Christian crusaders in 1204 and ceased to exist entirely in 1453 when the Ottoman Turks overran it.

Greek and Persian decline allowed conditions for Alexander the Great's rise.

After the Athenian Empire came to an end when Sparta won the Peloponnesian War, Persia learned to play Athens and Sparta against each other, delaying hostilities between itself and the Greeks, but still engaging in the Greek wars either on the side of the Athenians or the Spartans. After the last war between Persia and Greece, the Corinthian War, Persia, and Greece were exhausted and weakened. During the conflicts of the post-Peloponnesian Wars period, Sparta was defeated by Thebes, and Greece was exhausted by war. Thus, it was much easier for Alexander of Macedon to conquer Greece several decades later, making him the leader of the Greek army and eventually giving him the power to destroy the Achaemenid Empire.

Roman conquests increased global trade.

Goods from the Silk Road that were traded across the Mediterranean Sea eventually became internal trade goods in Roman markets. The Romans conquered Egypt in 31 B.C.E., and trade with Egypt was much more accessible for the Romans after that. The same thing had happened with Carthage earlier in history, making it easier for Rome to trade with the Africans for salt and gold, making it easier to trade Silk Road goods across the Mediterranean Sea and making the Indian Ocean Trade route accessible. After the fall of Western Rome, Eastern Rome still controlled much of the world's trade, but it conflicted with the Germanic tribes.

Notes for active learning

Notes for active learning

Major historical events of the period:

7,000–6,000 B.C.E.:	Egyptian domestication of cats
3,000 B.C.E.:	Egyptians create hieroglyphs
2,560 B.C.E.:	Construction begins on the Great Pyramid of Giza
2,400 B.C.E.:	Egypt constructs its first road
1,500 B.C.E.:	*The Book of the Dead* is written
539 B.C.E.:	Phoenicia is conquered by the Persians
218 B.C.E.:	Hannibal of Carthage crosses the Alps into Italy during the Second Punic War
146 B.C.E.:	Carthaginian Empire falls after the Third Punic War
500s C.E.:	Land trade routes are established connecting West Africa with East and Sub-Saharan Africa

PERIOD 1: Prehistory and Civilizations to the year 500 C.E.

AFRICA

Egyptians provided examples for subsequent civilizations.

The Nile River Valley also emerged during this period, with Egyptian and Nubian settlements and societies forming in approximately 4000 B.C.E. As with the Mesopotamian cultures, agricultural surpluses allowed for the formation of states that could now exchange goods, services, ideas, and traditions. The Egyptian civilization slowly turned into a great empire and set an example for later civilizations, such as the Persian, Macedonian, Greek, and Roman Empires.

Nile River Valley's agricultural abundance provided the foundation for cultural exchanges.

In the Nile River Valley, agriculture was a prominent feature of the early settlements; the agricultural relationships eventually expanded into further trade, conflict, and warfare. For example, the Sudanic people populated Africa during this period. They shared agricultural knowledge with the Egyptians, allowing for the creation of vastly successful planting and harvesting schedules organized around the flooding patterns of the Nile. Such agricultural advancements were seen between 4000 and 3000 B.C.E. when agricultural surplus led to an expansion of the Egyptian population and raised the quality of life.

Agricultural communities had to work cooperatively to clear land and create the water control systems needed for crop production.

The introduction of irrigation systems exemplifies the urban cooperation experienced during this period. One such example of cooperation seen during this period comes again from Egypt, where climate change caused the Sudanic cultivators to embark farther down the Nile River, eventually coming upon the Egyptian and Nubian settlements with whom they shared watermelon and gourds. With these new crops, the Egyptian farmers were able to cultivate crops easily due to the summer flooding plains of the Nile. These examples of cooperation are crucial to understanding the traditions and social expectations of these civilizations and the later empires of Western Europe.

Egyptian lack of mineral resources influenced their development.

The geographical position of Egypt during this period is crucial to understanding its success as a core civilization. While Egypt itself lacked mineral, gold, and silver resources, it negotiated extensive trade agreements with neighbors, such as Nubia; when such agreements were unsuccessful, military action was the next step. However, Egyptians also tried diplomatic means to solve their expansion and competition problems, by initially assimilating the Hyksos invaders into their culture, though this later proved unsuccessful.

Egyptians developed hieroglyphs.

By about 3000 B.C.E., Egypt had created hieroglyphs as a means of recording religious rituals. These hieroglyphs were typically carved into wood or stone, though later they would be transcribed on papyrus. Ancient hieroglyphs were comprised of over 2000 different symbols and, for religious texts, would sometimes be written in a cursive form detailed in *The Papyrus of Ani*.

Section of the Papyrus of Ani manuscript showing Thoth's declaration to the Ennead

It is important to note that hieroglyphics were not a written language known to or used by the commoners—or even by most of the nobility. It was hieratic, only used by the small minority who were literate and had a need for written records. Hieroglyphics were special religious symbols, which were considered to be magical and were used exclusively by the priests in tombs or to magically protect exceptionally important buildings.

Social and gender hierarchies intensified as states expanded and cities multiplied.

Egyptian ruling families were one of the few in the ancient world to allow women an active role in government, though this was limited to the roles of pharaoh and co-regent; this was not the case in most other early civilizations. However, as with Queen Hatshepsut, others within the culture were less inclined to allow women to rule, especially when an acceptable male heir was available, as was usually the case. Women typically acquired higher status with motherhood, as childbearing was seen as crucial to the expansion of the empire.

Statue of Queen Hatshepsut

Egyptian rulers undertook territorial expansion.

Empire expansion was also seen in the Nile River Valley and the Aegean Sea during this period. The Egyptian ruling elite had spent years influencing and trading with its neighbors, so it came as no surprise when military forces under Tuthmosis I (1504–1492 B.C.E.) led conquests to expand Egyptian territories into the Euphrates River in the north and Nubia in the south. Such policies were continued by future rulers and became a staple of Egyptian foreign policy. However, this type of expansion eventually created adversaries interested in acquiring what the Egyptians had, causing the decline of the empire and leading into the Roman period.

Massive building projects characterized Egyptian civilization.

This period saw an undertaking of massive building projects, including palaces and temples. One such example comes from the Egyptian temple complex at Karnak, housing cult temples to Amun, Mut, and Khonsu, with construction begun in 2055 B.C.E. Other notable temple projects include the funerary complex of Queen Hatshepsut, built in approximately 1551 B.C.E. at Deir el-Bahari. Queen Hatshepsut's successor went to great lengths to dismantle the complex, removing images of the queen and often replacing them with images of his likeness. Many academics believed this was done because of Egyptian ruling elites, notably the priests, disapproved of a woman as pharaoh. In ancient Egypt, even wealthy and noble women found themselves subordinate to men.

The Great Hypostyle Hall at the Karnak Temple Complex

The pyramids produced by the Egyptians during the Old Kingdom, beginning with Djoser in the Third Dynasty (approximately 2650 B.C.E.), were monumental architectural projects that were crucial to the religious rituals of the culture. In addition to the three major pyramids, the Egyptians also constructed various step pyramids, or mastabas, throughout the Nile River Valley.

The great pyramids at Giza served an additional religious purpose but also showcased the power, wealth, and status of Egypt as an empire during this period. While Egyptians viewed the funerary pyramids as a means to the afterlife, outsiders seeing these monuments for the first time must have been awed by their sheer size and placement. They would have deterred adversaries from angering the Egyptian Empire. Even so, at the end of this period, Egypt experienced repeated invasions and military threats.

Eastern Mediterranean civilizations fostered the arts.

Examples of wall paintings can be seen extensively in Egyptian monuments and sites. This form of art was seen mainly in the tombs of the elite of the period and began in approximately 3000 B.C.E. In addition to wall paintings, Egyptians created reliefs that were sometimes painted, often depicting the pharaoh as a deity or other scenes of gods.

We can also look to Egypt for the earliest signs of weaving, beginning in the Neolithic period around 5000 B.C.E. and evolving into more elaborate and decorative practices. Initially, Egyptians crafted baskets, mats, and sandals, all of which supplied these early civilizations with a new standard of living. However, elaborate weaving did not stay in Egypt but spread to Mesoamerica and the Phoenician, Minoan, and Mycenaean colonies.

States developed legal codes, including the Code of Hammurabi, which reflected existing hierarchies and facilitated the rule of governments over people.

Egyptian law was thought to be derived from the god Ma'at, who embodied truth, order, and balance within ancient Egyptian culture. From this ideology, all Egyptians—except slaves—were considered equal under the laws of the land. However, the punishment was sometimes harsh and impacted entire family structures. If a person was sent into exile, their children and immediate families were also exiled, and military desertion or failure to meet labor demands might result in the imprisonment of an entire family. In later periods, judgments were sometimes given by religious oracles; examples of this are seen in the Twenty-First Dynasty (1069–945 B.C.E.) in the oracle of Amun.

Regional and transregional trade in the Eastern Mediterranean fostered the development of empires.

The Egyptians shared this idea of trade and communication with neighbors, especially the ones who held vast economic and natural resources, such as Nubia. As civilizations continued to progress, technological advances allowed for more trade, sharing of ideas, and a feeling of cosmopolitanism among those who lived in these cultural and religious centers. This was certainly the case in Egypt where basic goods such as pottery, tools, textiles, linen, stone vases, papyrus, gold vessels, ox hides, lentils, and dried fish were constantly being imported and traded.

Egyptians were especially concerned with their trading partners to the south, the Nubians, who were wealthy with vast gold and mineral deposits, stone, ivory, ebony, and various livestock. To secure these goods, the Egyptians created and maintained caravan routes, which led both north and south, allowing for the most abundant trading abilities possible. These trade agreements and the resources acquired in such dealings allowed the ruling elite of Egypt to secure vast power and influence. Eventually, their status and wealth resulted in invasion and war.

Egyptian *Book of the Dead* provided a glimpse towards afterlife beliefs.

The *Book of the Dead*, which originated in Egypt in approximately 1500 B.C.E., is another example of a religious work that provides great insight into the religious traditions and beliefs of its followers as well as its ruling and elite classes. The *Book of the Dead*, also known as *The Book of Coming or Going Forth By Day*, was a compilation of magic spells, charms, passwords, formulas, and enchantments meant to help the deceased through their trials and their journey through the underworld. Initially, such texts were carved directly onto the deceased's sarcophagus; the text later came to be written on papyrus and placed inside the sarcophagus.

Each copy of the *Book of the Dead* was individualized, making no two copies identical. Many contained illustrations depicting the trials the deceased would face before being admitted into the next world. The earliest versions of the *Book of the Dead* came from the Eighteenth dynasty (1580–1350 B.C.E.) and were compiled versions of earlier texts that would eventually comprise the *Book of the Dead* as it is known today.

Carthage

Carthage, which was located in Northern Africa, was the last remaining city-state of the Phoenician Empire and had a powerful navy and extensive trading networks. While the Carthaginians had colonies in Sicily, they controlled only half the island; the other half was controlled by an ethnically Greek kingdom allied to Rome. In the 2nd century B.C.E., seeking to establish full control over Sicily, Carthage attacked the Greek kingdom of Messina. Rome was Messina's ally, and hence became involved in the First Punic War, a devastating defeat for the Carthaginians who had to restore their destroyed trading routes and lost control of Sicily, which became a Roman Province.

After the First Punic War, Carthage gained territories in Spain while Rome was focused on uniting Italy and conquering the Greeks. In 218 B.C.E., a Carthaginian general known as

Hannibal became a major threat to the Romans. Hannibal was taught that the Romans were the primary enemies of Carthage. This was partly true, for the Roman Empire eventually set their eye on Carthage. Hannibal trained an army of African and Spanish tribal mercenaries to attack Rome. The most dangerous thing about Hannibal's advance was the location at which he decided to attack. While the Roman Senate couldn't figure out whether Hannibal would launch his attack through Sicily or cross the Mediterranean Sea into Italy or Greece, Hannibal chose a much more dangerous and daring path, crossing the Alps and attacking the Roman legions where they least expected it.

Hannibal crossing the Alps on an elephant

Rome's military mainly consisted of units called legions. The key to Roman success was their effective military organization structure, which was much more efficient than those of other contemporary powers. The Romans' primary weapon was their infantry, rather than the cavalry or war elephants that Carthaginians usually used as their main attacking force. Even though Hannibal lost some of his war elephants in the Alps when he ascended, the Roman legionaries did not know how to fight the Carthaginian elephants. They were afraid of the giant beasts who could easily crush the Roman cohorts as they were organized into tightly packed squares.

While Hannibal was a good tactician, he was not a good strategist. After he destroyed the Roman legions, he lacked the proper siege equipment to take Rome itself and also lacked sufficient reinforcements from Carthage. For fifteen years, the Romans kept Hannibal out of large and strategically important Italian cities. Carthaginians were running out of supplies, but when the Roman navy cut off the supply lines completely and besieged Carthage, Hannibal understood that he had failed in Italy, and his only option now was to defend Carthage and continue his campaign from there. Hannibal was eventually defeated at the battle of Zama, and Carthage lost the war.

The Third Punic War proved to be the end of Carthage. The Romans thought Carthage was going to attack them, so they attacked Carthage first. Even though there were no such plans in the Carthaginian government, nor did the Carthaginians have a giant army ready to attack Rome, the Romans besieged and destroyed the city of Carthage. They slaughtered most of the Carthaginians, turned the surviving 10 percent into slaves, and leveled the city to the ground.

Final assault on Carthage during the Third Punic War

Demand for salt and gold expanded African trade.

The trans-Saharan trade routes that extended from the coast of West Africa to North Africa and eventually the Mediterranean Sea were also important. Gold was important in medieval Europe, in the Islamic world, and throughout history. It was used for decoration, jewelry, articles in Christian churches, and gold coins that were used throughout classical and postclassical civilizations and empires. The demand for gold was enormous. It was a commodity found in abundance in Africa that Africans were willing to trade via the trans-Saharan trade routes. From sub-Saharan Africa, gold made its way through the Sahara to North Africa. The African civilizations that controlled the gold trade grew rich and prosperous. The wealthiest person in history was an African prince who attained high status due to the gold trade.

Golden icon set in enamel and pearl

While both the abundant salt and gold-trading empires emerged around the 8th century C.E., trading routes for future booms were established around the 4th or 5th century C.E. with the appearance of camels from Arabia in Africa. By the end of the 5th century, the nomadic people of West Africa had traveled across the Sahara to sell salt and other goods to East- and sub-Saharan Africa to receive gold in return. They used camels, which are very well suited for desert travel, because they can transport large weights without needing to feed or drink for days and have special air passages that prevent them from inhaling sand during a storm.

Contemporary salt caravan using camels to tranverse the Saharan Azalai route

Later in history, the gold trade spread. This made the sub-Saharan and trans-Saharan trading routes swell due to the vast quantity of goods traded and the size of caravans traveling along these trade routes. These routes did not involve as many diverse civilizations; they were all people of Africa. Even though some spoke Bantu and some spoke other languages, Africa had relative cultural similarities until the spread of Islam. Salt from the trans-Saharan (west to east) trade routes went to the Indian Ocean Trade networks, and the gold traded through the trans-Saharan (south from sub-Saharan Africa to North Africa) trade routes went to the North African merchants and the Mediterranean Sea trade lanes.

Notes for active learning

Notes for active learning

Southwest Asia

Major historical events of the period:

7,000–6,000 B.C.E.: Mesopotamian domestication of goats, pigs and sheep

6,000–5,000 B.C.E.: Mesopotamia invents irrigation systems

5,000 B.C.E.: Sumerian civilization emerges

4,300 B.C.E.: Horses are domesticated in Central Asia

3,500–3,000 B.C.E.: Cuneiform, developed by the Sumerian civilization, is widely used

2,000 B.C.E.: Hebrew monotheistic movement

1,750 B.C.E.: Code of Hammurabi is written

1,700 B.C.E.: *The Epic of Gilgamesh* is written

1,600 B.C.E.: Hittites Empire is established

1,000 B.C.E.: Phoenician alphabet

700–500 B.C.E.: Zoroastrianism forms

600–500 B.C.E.: Jewish exile to Babylon

550 B.C.E.: Achaemenid Empire is established

334 B.C.E.: Alexander the Great invades Asia Minor, decline of Achaemenid Empire

247 B.C.E.: Parthian Empire emerges

224 C.E.: Parthian Empire falls and Sassanid Empire emerges

c. 15 C.E.: Christianity is founded by Jesus of Nazareth

PERIOD 1: Prehistory and Civilizations to the year 500 C.E.

SOUTHWEST ASIA

Mesopotamian advancements in agricultural production, trade, and transportation

In approximately 5000–4000 B.C.E., the first plow was introduced in Mesopotamia. Some scholars argue that animals were used to pull the plow, though substantial evidence for this has yet to be discovered. During this period, the potter's wheel was invented. Furthermore, stone tools were quickly replaced by bronze and, later, iron tools. By 4000–3000 B.C.E., wheeled vehicles were a staple of Mesopotamian culture and precursors to the war wagons and chariots that were produced between 3000 and 2000 B.C.E. These technological innovations were the foundation of modern transportation and instrumental for the practice of warfare.

Mesopotamian achievements propelled civilizations.

Many influential and important civilizations emerged from Mesopotamia, between the Tigris and Euphrates River Valleys in the Middle East, beginning in approximately 3500 B.C.E. These include the Sumerian, Akkadian, Babylonian, and Assyrian civilizations; all left their mark on Mesopotamia during this period and inevitably influenced other regions such as the Nile River Valley in Egypt and the Indus River Valley in south-central Asia. Important achievements that stem from Mesopotamian civilizations include the discovery of the wheel and the plow, cuneiform (one of the first written languages), wheeled vehicles, and the use of bronze tools.

Cuneiform

Phoenician and Hittite geographic and resource factors influenced their trajectories.

Notable expansions of this period come from the Phoenicians, who also used surplus agriculture and trade agreements to launch an empire in the Mediterranean. In hopes of limiting competition within the region, the Phoenicians set up extensive colonies, over which they exercised both economic and military influence. These growing populations were difficult to maintain, and Phoenicians attempted to colonize more areas as a result of lacking resources in their regions.

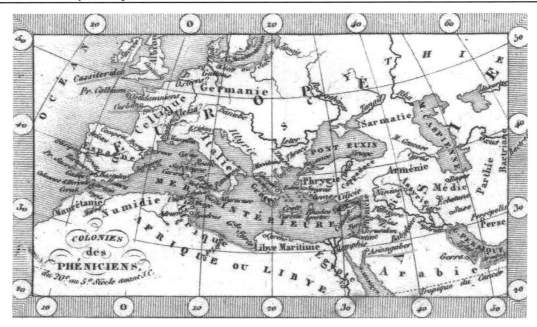

Phoenician colonies

In addition to the Egyptian and Phoenician successes, the Hittites also proved to be a formidable adversary for many civilizations of this period, including several in Mesopotamia. The Hittites occupied an elevated position within the global system at this time, as they were among the first peoples to domesticate horses and use chariots as a means of warfare. Additionally, the increasing use of iron in ceremonial, domestic, and military undertakings significantly altered the weaponry of the period, previously made from bronze. Such technological advances allowed the Hittites to invade and conquer Anatolia and go on to threaten the Egyptian Empire.

The technological advances of the Hittites also show the importance of geographic location and resources. As with other early civilizations, the Hittites would most likely have been less effective in their military campaigns had they not been able to master the use of chariots, iron weapons, and infantry, all direct results of the Paleolithic Revolution which began in approximately 10,000 B.C.E. Their access to these resources, combined with their innovation in learning to utilize them, is a major reason for their success. Horses, in particular, allowed the Hittites to travel farther and faster than anyone had previously believed possible—a military, economic, and social advantage.

Early regions of state expansion or empire-building were Mesopotamia and Babylonia.

As early civilizations began to establish themselves in the Nile River Valley and Mesopotamia, it became clear that the expansion and control of the territory was a priority of the ruling elite. These expansionist policies would continue into later periods, developed by later empires. In Mesopotamia, several states and regional powers emerged, including the Sumerian, Akkadian, and Babylonian cultures. These empires would mold the political and cultural norms of the region while also expanding their regional and transregional influence using trade and warfare.

Sumerian civilization, emerging around 5000 B.C.E., was responsible for creating cuneiform, the introduction of the plow, units of time and division of the day into measurable increments. The Sumerians had contact with Egyptians and Babylonians and likely influenced those cultures. Sumerian social life was dominated by the priesthood and devotion to the gods. Cities built temples at their centers as an indication of their importance. Artisans spent most of their time completing works for the temple or the warrior class charged with the protection of the temple. Notable cities of Sumerian culture included Eridu, Uruk, and Ur, all of which formed vast trading partnerships that characterized Sumerian foreign affairs.

Sargon of Akkad, Mesopotamian ruler

Sumerian civilization was quickly eclipsed by the Akkadian kings, who, during the Early Dynastic Period (2900–2334 B.C.E.), ruled the majority of Mesopotamia, including Sumer. Historians state that King Sargon the Great constructed the city of Akkad, united Mesopotamia, and created the first multinational empire. King Sargon and his scribes claimed that he conquered the four corners of the universe and that his empire spanned from the Persian Gulf, through the lower part of Asia Minor and into the Aegean Sea. To effectively rule an empire of this size, King Sargon created what Babylonian writers called the "citizens of Akkad," trusted governors and rulers of the Akkadian culture, placed in over sixty-five different cities throughout the Akkadian Empire. Outside invasion eventually brought about the demise of the Akkadian dominance in Mesopotamia and paved the way for the Babylonian Empire.

The Babylonian Empire emerged as one of the most famous empires of Mesopotamia and is famously known for King Hammurabi, who ruled from 1792 to 1750 B.C.E. This empire was based on diplomacy and occasionally warfare, and was vastly successful. By 1755 B.C.E., King Hammurabi had unified all of Mesopotamia under the Babylonian realm. Military offensives, eventually led to the unification of Mesopotamia, including the conquering of Uruk and Isin in approximately 1792 B.C.E. and the destruction of the city of Mari in 1761 B.C.E. However, like their predecessors, the success of the Babylonians would be short-lived. Following the death of Hammurabi and the weak rulers who succeeded him, Babylon was invaded by the Hittites in 1595 B.C.E., leading to the rise of the Assyrian Empire—which experienced a similar fate to those already mentioned.

These early empires would be crucial to maintaining the perception of power and influence within the region and inspired future empires to look towards Egypt, Mesopotamia, the Middle East, and China as the main source of influence regarding ruling classes and leadership. For example, the Macedonians, Persians, Greeks, and Romans hoped to duplicate the empirical actions of the Egyptian pharaohs and Macedonian kings.

Pastoralists were often the developers and disseminators of new weapons and modes of transportation that transformed warfare in agrarian civilizations.

As pastoral communities emerged following the decline of hunter-gathers, their expertise in weaponry was superior to their urban counterparts. Examples of their advanced skill can be seen in the use of chariots, horses, iron weapons, and the introduction of compound bows as an easily accessible weapon. Such technological developments would allow pastoral communities, such as the Hyksos, to effectively oppose the power of urban civic centers such as those of the Egyptians and Mesopotamians.

While the origin of the chariot is debated among academics, the first use of chariots is most widely credited to the Hittites in approximately 1700 B.C.E. Through the use of such weapons; the Hittites were able to conquer Anatolia and create an empire. Another notable example of the use of this technology was by the Hyksos, who, around 1720–1710 B.C.E., used chariots with great success as means of warfare against Egyptians in the northern regions of the Nile River Valley. As a result, the Egyptian pharaoh only ruled over Lower Egypt, while a Hyksos pharaoh ruled over Upper Egypt from the Nile River delta, for a century afterward. As a result of technology transference, the Egyptian military forces began using chariots themselves and eventually were able to expel the Hyksos using their innovation. Egyptian military forces were also comprised of infantry units who used spears, sickle swords, and daggers as tools of warfare.

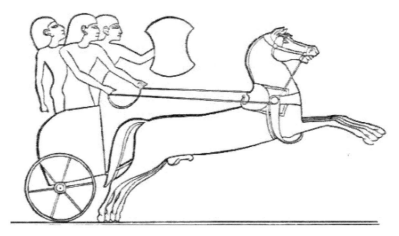

Hittite chariot

The Hittites maintained the first access to iron deposits. With the use of iron, they created lighter, more accurate weaponry and eventually phased out the bronze weapons of earlier periods. In addition to iron weapons, the military tactics used by the Hittites—like the Egyptians—encompassed infantry, chariots, lances, and thrusting weapons, in addition to the later compound bows. Such tactics made the Hittite forces an undeniable military power by about 1600 B.C.E.

The introduction of the compound bow marked the culmination of technological warfare advances during this period. The advanced bow now augmented warfare, which used domesticated horses, stable and successful war chariots and iron weaponry. The compound bow is attributed to the Akkadian Empire, ruled by King Sargon in approximately 2350 B.C.E. Many academics have argued that the development of the compound bow allowed the

Akkadian culture to emerge as an early power. This stronger, more accurate bow gave a great military advantage, as both infantry and chariot units could use the advanced weaponry; quivers could hold twenty to thirty arrows with wood or reed shafts tipped with bronze arrowheads.

The military technological advancements of the pastoral communities of this period would greatly influence subsequent periods. Such influence translated into other sectors, such as politics and trade, so that these tools could be said to have shaped world history. Similar technological advances would not be seen again for some years. It is important to note that without the domestication of horses in Central Asia around 4300 B.C.E., chariots and cavalry assaults would have been impossible. This domestication process was undertaken by the Indo-Europeans, who migrated to Central Asia in the Paleolithic period and eventually settled various river valley regions.

Ziggurats of Sumeria and Mesopotamia were constructed.

Sumerian and Mesopotamian cultures constructed "ziggurats," a precursor to the earliest experimental Egyptian pyramids. Ziggurats were step pyramids comprised of mud, which usually held a temple at the top. These structures emerged around 3500 B.C.E. and were the center of all Mesopotamian cities. Any formal religious ceremonies would be held at the temple atop the ziggurat, where food and drink—typically wine—would be left as offerings to the gods. Priests working in the temple would consume such offerings in the name of the gods. The emergence of the ziggurat as a civic center also speaks to the wealth and resources of the Mesopotamian cultures; before this, there had been few excess resources to store, and now they had resources requiring a ziggurat for storage.

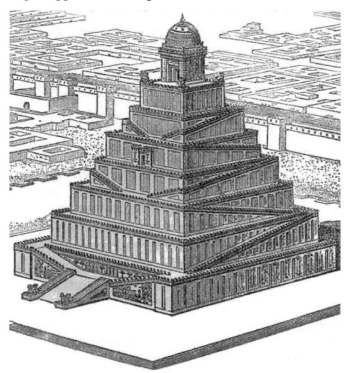

Ancient ziggurat: the Tower of Babel

Such monuments would later influence the Greek agora and the Roman Forum, keystones to Western civilization. The pyramids and temples also provide an understanding of the cultures that built them, as it is clear that Egyptians were concerned with their journey after death and believed that propitiating the gods would ensure a safe journey through the underworld. Like later Greek and Roman traditions, ancient Sumerians believed in deities that resided in the skies and used their temples as sources of influence and prestige on earth.

Eastern Mediterranean civilizations fostered the arts.

The art and sculpture that emerged from the New Kingdom in Egypt differed in function from most other early civilizations because much of it was created for the use of non-royals. Mesopotamians eventually evolved to produce works that could be used by both royals and non-royals. Like the sculptures of the Egyptians and Minoans, the early dynastic sculptures of Mesopotamia focused on deities and religious rituals. Archeological excavation at Nippur produced one of the largest caches of Mesopotamian sculpture to date and highlighted the ritualistic practices of the period.

States developed legal codes, including the Code of Hammurabi, which reflected existing hierarchies and facilitated the rule of governments over people.

The emergence of early civilizations and urban settlements prompted the creation of written laws and codes, most notably the Code of Hammurabi. Other civilizations in Egypt and China also enacted legal codes aimed at addressing the concerns of urban living and newly emerging civilizations.

The Code of Hammurabi was composed in approximately 1750 B.C.E. and consisted of 282 codes and laws, transcribed on various clay tablets and stone stelae (i.e., stone or wood slab). The legal code was produced during the reign of Hammurabi, a Babylonian king of Akkadian descent. The code uses cuneiform and is the earliest written law code found to date. Though much of the code addresses crime, such as assault, it also covers a range of law, including proper payment for services, the appropriate action taken for property disputes, maintenance of the social norms and standards regarding marriage, inheritance and family law. Historically, the code is known for its idea of "an eye for an eye," whereby compensation should be restricted to the value of the loss.

However, it is important to point out that not all social classes were viewed as equals under the Code of Hammurabi. If two men of the nobility were to harm one another, rather than receiving a reciprocal punishment, a fine might be imposed. A commoner accused of the same crime would be expected to pay in kind.

The Sumerians, during the Third Dynasty of Ur (2047–1750 B.C.E.), under King Ur-Nammu, created the Code of Ur-Nammu. This code predates the Hammurabi Law Code. However, the Code of Ur-Nammu is more of a moral guideline than a legal code. Unlike the Code of Hammurabi, which was based primarily on retribution and the idea of "getting even," the Code of Ur-Nammu uses monetary fines as punishment for inappropriate behavior and rarely used other forms of punishment.

Stela of Ur-Nammu, king of the Third Dynasty

These codes were based on the principle that the gods dictated laws and kings be meant to administer them. These variations in justice and religion point to a diverse world. There were many commonalities shared by these early civilizations in attempting to manage urban cities in the new elite classes of the period and the transition from nomadic gatherers to agrarian and pastoral communities.

These codes are important because they show what daily life was like within these cultures. By reading the assault codes in the Code of Hammurabi, historians know what types of crimes were occurring in Babylon during this period and the marital and family concerns of the culture. Additionally, the written record of legal codes set a precedent for future cultures that eventually resulted in the modern legal system. The universal understanding of the law codes of this period would not be the same without the Code of Hammurabi. As with military expansion, later empires would look to the legal codes of the Sumerians to create similar ideas.

Zoroastrian and Abrahamic religions become major religions contributing to the decline of polytheism.

Unlike the polytheistic religions of the time, Zoroastrianism was one of the earliest religions to promote partial monotheism. Zoroastrianism originated in contemporary Iran in the late 7th and early 6th centuries B.C.E. and was led by the prophet Zoroaster, also known as Zarathustra. The teachings of Zoroastrianism include a supreme god, Ahura Mazda, and six lesser deities who are part of the cosmic conflict between good and evil embodied in Ahura Mazda's constant battle with Angra Mainyu, an evil deity.

The teachings of Zoroastrianism were originally shared orally. However, during later periods, the magi or priests would transcribe these theologies into a collection of holy scriptures. The Zoroastrianism movement began to see a surge in popularity beginning in the 6th century B.C.E., garnering the support of the Persian ruling family. Historically, Zoroastrianism is known for its mantra of "good thoughts, good deeds, good words."

The first true form of modern monotheism was seen in the Hebrew monotheistic movement, which according to Judaic tradition, was founded in approximately 2000 B.C.E. by Abraham and the Israelites. Abraham and his followers initially lived in the great Mesopotamian city Ur but eventually migrated to Canaan and later into Egypt due to a protracted drought. After being enslaved in Egypt, the Israelites were eventually led back to Canaan by Moses, where they founded the kingdom of Israel. During this period, the Hebrew theology was a monotheistic oddity in a polytheistic world. Though they did not actively seek to convert non-Jewish populations, their culture greatly influenced many others and would become what we know today as Judaism.

Moses with the Ten Commandments

These religions were all important in the decline of polytheistic religions, which begins during this period, and the emergence of the dominant monotheistic religions (e.g., Christianity, Judaism, Islam) shaped the global system and resulted in prolonged warfare on a level never before experienced, such as during the Crusades.

Regional and transregional trade in the Eastern Mediterranean fostered the development of empires.

As communities developed and expanded in Egypt, Anatolia, and Mesopotamia, it became clear that regional and transregional trade was the course of the future and would propel these early civilizations into periods of the empire. These interactions not only served an economic purpose but had a cultural, religious, and political impact as well. By sharing technologies, religions, and languages, these early civilizations were engaging in an evolving global system.

Examples of regional and transregional trade during this period are highlighted by the actions of the Egyptians and Mesopotamians. However, the Phoenicians should also be mentioned as they conceived and maintained a seafaring empire with great influence and authority within the Mediterranean Sea. As the quality of life improved, the expansion of craftsmanship and artistry propelled the export and import of foreign goods via transregional trade.

The Phoenicians settled colonies throughout the Mediterranean—the most notable being Carthage—with other settlements on Cyprus in the 9th century B.C.E. and in Utica in North Africa in approximately the 10th century B.C.E. Some of these settlements were used as trading outposts from where they imported luxury goods and furniture; others exploited silver mines in North Africa and Spain, which financed the empire in the 8th century B.C.E. The Phoenicians also shared their extensive maritime skills, allowing other civilizations to travel longer distances and interact with a greater number of people.

In addition to these commodities, the importation of luxury goods was also common in Egypt during this period and included horses, cattle and other small livestock as well as mineral resources and deposits from Syria and Palestine, copper and ivory from Cyprus and Minoan and Mycenaean oil containers transported from the Aegean Sea.

Literature of Mesopotamia provided cultural insights.

The Epic of Gilgamesh was written in cuneiform in Sumer, Mesopotamia, around 1700 B.C.E. This epic literary work was one of the first of its kind and is widely considered to be the oldest written work of literature. This particular work is historically important as it gives an extensive insight into the Mesopotamian culture during this period.

The Epic of Gilgamesh

The epic tells the story of the great king of Uruk, Gilgamesh, who is part man and part god. He has remarkably attractive features and creates great architectural monuments and civic centers, but is viewed as a bad and harsh king. To remedy this problem, the gods create an equal in appearance, Enkidu, who teaches the king the beauty of the natural world. However, the pair scorned the gods, and Enkidu is put to death, which causes Gilgamesh great despair for the loss of his companion and his mortality. The epic ends with Gilgamesh accepting his mortality with the understanding that the human race continues and that he will be remembered for his architectural achievements, thus achieving a sort of immortality.

The association of monotheism with Judaism was further developed with the codification of the Hebrew Scriptures, which also reflected the influence of Mesopotamian cultural and legal traditions. The Assyrian, Babylonian and Roman Empires conquered various Jewish states at different points in time. These conquests contributed to the growth of Jewish diasporic communities around the Mediterranean and the Middle East

Judaism was built upon the beliefs of ancient nomadic Hebrew peoples that lived in Mesopotamia. As nomads, they traveled from the Tigris and Euphrates Rivers to the Mediterranean Sea. The Hebrew people were polytheistic, and they made sacrifices to their gods as a part of their tradition, which was in line with the practices of other peoples in Ancient Mesopotamia. This polytheism was eventually replaced by a belief in a single, all-powerful God who should be worshiped singularly. This idea of a single God would later become the concept that laid the foundation for dominant Western religions such as Christianity and Islam.

Another key concept present in the Greek, Roman and modern religions was the idea of a covenant. This meant that God could impact life positively or negatively depending on behavior and obedience to God's rules. One of the most famous covenants was made between God and Abraham. Abraham and his descendants would have to be circumcised and follow the way of life that was dictated to Abraham by God, and in return, they would be seen as a sacred nation (of Jews) that would walk under God's protection as His chosen people.

In this context, a key concept in the creation of monotheistic religion was the written codification of core beliefs and practices. The Jews wrote their experiences in the Torah, the Leningrad Codex, and different Hebrew scriptures. These

Abraham and the three angels

texts are partially what helped to keep the religion alive and the theology known to the people. The holy scriptures contain the Ten Commandments, which is the seminal treatise on the morality and ethical basis of both Christianity and Judaism. The codification of the Jewish tradition included the idea that God demanded social justice and moral righteousness and gave modern humans knowledge of God.

For most of their existence, the Jews were not accepted as the chosen nation, were disliked by others, and lacked the power of statehood and state protection. Throughout history, the emergence of a new empire near the Jewish homeland meant attempts at conquest by the emergent power. Their conquest by the Assyrian Empire led to the oppression of the Jews and the exile of a portion of the population of Israel to Mesopotamia. Likewise, the rise of the Babylonian Empire led to the famous Babylonian exile of the Jewish people (600 B.C.E.–500 B.C.E.) from Judah throughout the Babylonian Empire. The relocation of the Jewish population created Jewish communities throughout Mesopotamia. This led to further normalization of the idea of monotheism in Mesopotamia and thus a wider acceptance of Zoroastrianism and Christianity. The majority of accounts of these historical events are still accessible through the Hebrew Scriptures.

The main motivation for the Babylonian exodus was the weakening of the Jewish tradition and nation through the deportation of its political leaders. At the end of Babylonian dominance, during the takeover of the more tolerant Persians, the Jews were allowed to return to their homeland. This return from exile not only led to a return to Israel but also to the spread of Jews throughout Babylonia (present-day Iraq).

However, the Jewish people's troubles did not end there as the Persian Empire was taken over by Alexander the Great in 300 B.C.E. Alexander's kingdom was riled by Hellenism, which rejected the monotheism of the Jews. After this, the Romans arrived in the land of the Jews, absorbing the area into their Empire and calling it Judea. After the Romans put down a rebellion led by King Herod, a significant portion of the Jews were exiled into distant lands, thereby creating the Diaspora in Europe.

The Achaemenid Persian Empire

The Persian capital, Persis (Persepolis in Greek), was founded in the 600s B.C.E. Cyrus the Great formed a well-organized military and government, calling his state the Achaemenid Empire (or the First Persian Empire). The Achaemenids went on to defeat the Median Empire and the Babylonians, and later expanded from the borders of Iran and India to Egypt and what later became Constantinople and Istanbul. Xerxes and Darius later expanded this empire and strengthened its military power.

Darius the Great, Persian emperor

The Persian Empire would become successful in part because of its well-organized military—which neither the Babylonians nor the Medians had. Though the Persians had widely practiced a national religion called Zoroastrianism, they succeeded in the conquest of most of the Middle East partially because they did not enforce religious unity upon their subjects. The Persian Empire was a very religiously tolerant and liberal state. It did not enforce any regulations on the religious affiliation of Persians or conquered peoples, which allowed people who were formerly religiously oppressed to live freely. For example, the Jews were allowed to return to Israel from the Babylonian Exile.

The Persians utilized an organized bureaucracy with a central government, where the Emperor ruled over his bureaucratic subjects, which in turn, ruled over the people. He assigned satraps (governors) to different regions of his empire to serve as his proxy in places he could not directly rule. This meant the empire was ruled by local leaders, which improved the quality of attention and amount of time devoted to each region's development and problems. There was also a centralized component as local rulers had to report back to the emperor in the capital so the empire could work towards a single goal. This system allowed for some autonomy for the many regions of the empire, but it did not allow independence from the emperor or disorganization in general.

The Persian Empire also achieved success because it united many cultures and states under one single government. It utilized the trade networks of the conquered Phoenicians, the agricultural strength of Egypt and Mesopotamia, the governance and military structure of Persia, and Babylonian science (including astronomy and the Babylonian counting system) to create a well-functioning empire.

However, in their conquests, the Persians ran into problems. For example, Darius the Great started a long war with the Greeks and was defeated at the Battle of Marathon. Other Persian kings also tried and failed to conquer the Greeks. After many such attempts, the Achaemenid Empire was weakened, and Alexander the Great easily brought it into his realm.

The Parthian Persian Empire

India was not the only civilization that benefited from the fall of the Alexandrian Empire. The Parthian Empire rose after the fall of the Seleucid Empire, a Macedonian Hellenistic empire that spanned most of the Asian territory conquered by Alexander. The Parthians were a nomadic tribe that ended up conquering the Seleucids and establishing a state in Persia. They did not try to rid their empire of Hellenistic influences. The Parthian Empire was created in the 3rd century B.C.E. and fell almost 400 years later. It conquered much of the Achaemenid territory and beyond. It was arguably even more successful than its Achaemenid predecessor. While the Achaemenids could not conquer Greece, the Parthians proved to be a viable threat to the Roman Empire, challenging their hegemony in the West. The Parthian Empire controlled the Silk Road, and all the trade between the Roman and the Han Empires and the Parthian kings taxed all the goods coming through their territory. This made them wealthy because the trade between the Roman and Han Empires was extensive.

The empires above were all highly centralized. They united peoples and conquered states under a single government. The Parthian Empire, however, was different, for even though it was an empire, it did not have a centralized government. There was a capital, and it had a king, but it also had other economic and cultural centers outside of the capital. Those regional centers had a degree of autonomy beyond that of other contemporary empires. The regional centers had so much autonomy that even though the Romans conquered the Parthian capital three times, the empire itself survived.

This structure was not inconsequential as the decentralization eventually brought an end to the Parthian Empire. In the 1st century C.E., after an unsuccessful war with the Armenians, the Romans invaded Parthia and captured Mesopotamia and the Parthian capital. After a long series of civil wars between the vassal kings and autonomous regions of the empire, the Parthians were impoverished and destroyed morally as well as militarily. This conquest marked the end of the Parthian Empire and the beginning of the Sassanid Empire.

The Sassanid Persian Empire

The Sassanid Empire was the last Persian Empire before the rise of Islam and the Islamic conquest of the region. The empire has been noted for being much more centralized than its Parthian predecessor, emphasizing controlling the regions that were under its realm. It disposed of Hellenistic culture and Greek influences, placed more value on Persian culture and tradition, revived Zoroastrianism as the state religion, and remained tolerant of other religions (like the Achaemenids had been). The Sassanids experienced the rise of local landlords, which established a semi-feudal system of land ownership. Using its centralized government, the Sassanid Empire performed land and agricultural reforms throughout the region, while at the same time reforming the army so that it was more loyal to the centralized government rather than local lords. The empire then fought several wars with the Romans and, after steady offenses, won back much of the Achaemenid territory.

By that time, the Roman Empire was already divided into two. While the West was struggling to overcome the Germanic barbarian tribes, the East earned its reputation as the new Roman superpower by fighting empires—not tribes—which often included the Sassanid Empire. The Sassanid Empire existed for almost 400 years, but corruption in the government caused it to weaken. It could not sustain the invading Islamic armies of the 6th century, which marked the end of a non-Islamic Persian state.

The Mediterranean Region: Phoenicia and its colonies, Greek city-states and colonies and the Hellenistic and Roman Empires

Some of the civilizations that later caused trouble for the Romans were the Phoenician city-states, which were not an empire. There is little documentation of its people because they wrote on papyrus, which was easily destroyed due to its fragility. The Phoenician peoples developed and spread an alphabet, which was the foundation for the present Latin alphabet. The Phoenicians established ports throughout the Mediterranean Sea and grew incredibly rich from selling dyes and precious metals in the Mediterranean region. In Phoenician culture, maritime trading was very important, and their defense was also largely centered on naval military strength.

Ancient Phoenician coins

Although the Phoenician city-states shared the same culture and religion, they were not necessarily united because they could fight with one another and make alliances. Although there are not many records of their cultural traditions and religion, it is known that the Phoenicians influenced Greek and Roman culture and founded a city-state called Carthage, which later became a major empire. The Phoenicians were eventually defeated by the expanding Achaemenid (Persian) Empire of Cyrus the Great.

The Persian Empire's Bureaucracy

The Persian Empire rose to the east of Rome and was famous for its bureaucracy, which influenced practically all land-based, as opposed to maritime, empires. The Achaemenid Persian Empire introduced the concept of the absolute monarchic rule without any checks and balances, something the medieval European countries used extensively and founded one of the first government bureaucracies.

The Achaemenid Empire let the kings of conquered territories continue their rule, and they let conquered peoples maintain their own culture, for they respected the distinct homelands. The kings were only allowed to stay kings if they pledged allegiance to the Persian emperor and agreed to become the emperor's satraps.

Satraps were the government bureaucrats in Persia that ruled satrapies in the name of the Persian emperor. They had to pledge allegiance, contribute their wealth, and their army to the united Persian army, and they could not veto the Persian king's orders. However, they were allowed to preserve levels of autonomy that varied over time with the rise of the Parthian and Sassanid Empires, respectively. That is why the Persian king was called "The King of Kings."

Persian king and his charioteer

There was some mistrust between the king of Persia and the satraps, so the Persians had a system of Royal Inspectors, who were de facto spies of the Persian emperor. They reported on the current status of the region and whether the satrap was obeying the emperor's orders. This form of bureaucracy, combined with the religious toleration Persians promoted and Zoroastrianism's ban on slavery, provided the Persian Empire with a happy, loyal population that enjoyed the autonomy of their region while being part of a much larger empire.

Successive Persian empires declined after catastrophic military encounters with neighboring powers.

The Achaemenid, Parthian, and Sassanid Persian Empires fell in different ways, but for similar reasons. The Achaemenid Empire was a wealthy and free society with a powerful army, but once the Greeks defeated it in the Greco-Persian Wars, it started to decline. The Peloponnesian War stopped Athens' raids on the Persian Empire, damaging Athenian economies and sparking rebellions in Asia Minor. While Sparta and Athens had been fighting each other for thirty years, the Persian Empire once again enjoyed peace and growth, making the Greeks lose their advantage after the Persian invasions of Greece.

Crusaders attack Constantinople

The Parthian Empire was divided into satrapies, but not like the Achaemenid Empire. The Achaemenid Empire allowed a certain degree of autonomy, as the conquered kings were allowed to keep their kingdoms as long as they became subjects of the Persian Empire. In Parthia, captured kings were given such a degree of autonomy that there were several major administrative centers in the empire, and the capital was only the de jure capital. In reality, the Parthian Empire had many capitals. These were major political, logistic, and economic centers with high degrees of autonomy. While this autonomy may have saved the Parthian Empire from complete collapse after Roman advances, it did not work for long: The Romans eventually devastated the Parthians in a war, which led to local kings losing their loyalty to the larger empire. One such king would eventually overthrow the government and establish the Sassanid Empire.

The Sassanid Empire started strong with policies that were aimed at reducing the decentralization of Persia but, eventually, Persian bureaucrats became something like feudal landowners who were responsible for administering villages and collecting taxes from the farmers under their control. For four hundred years, the empire had been under constant pressure from the Romans, but it functioned well despite all the destruction Rome brought to Persia when the Parthians ruled it. Eventually, the Sassanid Empire grew exhausted by its wars with the Eastern Roman Empire. The corruption in the government grew, and the economy, armed forces, and ruler weakened. With the arrival of Islam and its conquerors, the Sassanid Empire could no longer withstand the pressure and gave in to the attacks of the Arab armies in 651 C.E.

Alongside the trade in goods, the exchange of people, technology, religious and cultural beliefs, food crops, domesticated animals, and disease pathogens developed across far-flung networks of communication and exchange. The spread of crops, including rice and cotton from South Asia to the Middle East, encouraged changes in farming and irrigation techniques.

In the 8th century C.E., the Islamic world experienced a sudden change in agriculture, which has been casually called the "Arab Agricultural Revolution." This was caused by trade. Arab traders had been the middlemen in the Asia-European trade for centuries, making money off of the trade of goods from Asia and bringing them to the Islamic world for consumption there as well. By the 8th century, Arabs decided to produce many of these goods themselves.

Art of the Indus River Valley civilization

New crops, such as cotton, were adopted from India along with the agricultural methods and tools related to them. The result of this was a better diet, increased food production, and increased wealth. Although the social mechanism was not capitalism in the modern sense, the Arab Agricultural Revolution is a good example of how free market activity has improved civilization and individual lives throughout history.

Notes for active learning

Notes for active learning

South & Southeast Asia

Major historical events of the period:

2,600 B.C.E.:   Harappa and Mohenjo-Daro use sewage and water systems

2,600–1,900 B.C.E.:   Indus River Valley civilization thrives

1,700 B.C.E.:   The *Rig-Veda* is written

1,500 B.C.E.:   Aryan nomads arrive in India

600 B.C.E.:   Buddhism emerges

326 B.C.E.:   Alexander the Great invades India

322–185 B.C.E.:   The Mauryan Empire, first centralized Indian state

320 C. E.:   Gupta Empire emerges

480 C.E.:   Nomads from the north invade the Gupta Empire

PERIOD 1: Prehistory and Civilizations to the year 500 C.E.

SOUTH AND SOUTHEAST ASIA

Agriculture developments in the Indus River Valley.

The early humans who settled in the Indus River Valley (present-day Pakistan and western India) were interested in urban development and agricultural advancements. This civilization thrived between 2600 and 1900 B.C.E.. It culminated in the Harappa communities, where an abundance of wood for a fire, clay for brickmaking, and richly fertilized soil made for an optimal river valley civilization.

A notable agricultural civilization of the period was the Aryan population. They were nomadic herders who evolved into an agricultural society upon settling in the Indus and Ganges River Valleys. This population would form the foundations of Vedic civilization following the success of the Harappa communities. The importance of the river valley civilizations cannot be overstated, for they were the foundations of later civilizations and empires.

Ceremonial Harappan vessel

Agriculture and pastoralism began to transform human societies.

The implementation of agrarian and pastoralist communities greatly impacted the development of human societies during this period, usually in a positive manner. As these civilizations expanded, the quality of life for average early humans, especially the new elite classes, drastically improved. One notable example is the Aryan population, which had initially been nomadic and became pastoral during their migration into the Indus and Ganges River Valleys. This particular group of pastoralists practiced what would become Hinduism, while also creating a self-sustaining empire that allowed the expansion of ideals and values within the newly settled region rather than by transregional means.

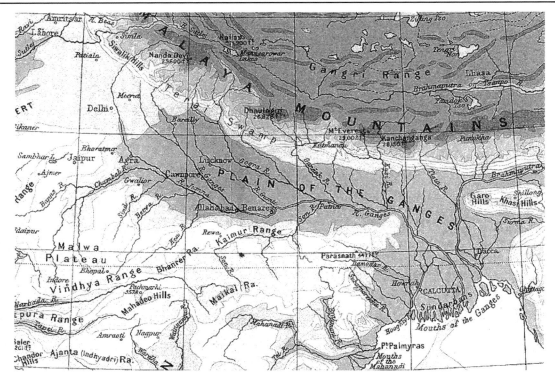

Map of the Ganges River Valley or "Plain"

Harappan and Mohenjo-Daro cultures thrived in Indus River Valley.

The Indus River Valley, in south-central Asia, was home to two influential civilizations: the Harappan and the Mohenjo-Daro cultures. The Mohenjo-Daro settlement, in present-day Pakistan, was constructed in approximately 2500 B.C.E.; its pinnacle was from 2500 to 1900 B.C.E. This settlement was most likely governed as a city-state using officials rather than kingship. The Harappa settlements in the region were instrumental in establishing the Indus River Valley as the center of Indian civilization. There was trading and a common sharing of knowledge and traditions between the Harappan settlements and those of Mesopotamia.

Aryans dominated the indigenous Indian population with the caste system.

The pastoral Aryan population living in the Caucasus areas eventually migrated into India, and some academics say they forcefully took control of various Indus Valley cities, eventually settling in the Ganges River Valley as agriculturalists. After settling the region, the Aryan rulers enacted a strict caste system imposed on the native population, one that allowed no social mobility. This system was based on the Brahma divine decree that there should be four groups: the Brahmin (priests, seers, and spiritual leaders), the Kshatriyas (i.e., the administrative class), the Vaisyas (i.e., the craftsmen and artisan class) and the Shudras (i.e., the laborer class, both skilled and unskilled). The Aryan culture and civilization are important to India and the global system because they became the foundations for Hinduism.

Emergent Vedic religion influenced modern Hinduism.

The Vedic religion came about as a result of the migration of the Aryan populations into India around 1500 B.C.E. The name is derived from the Vedas, composed in Sanskrit between 1500 and 1000 B.C.E. and made up of the *Rig-Veda, Sama-Veda, Yajur-Veda,* and *Atharva-Veda.* They are the oldest collections of Hindu scripture. This religious movement would greatly influence modern Hinduism and maintain a polytheistic base. Notable deities include Indra (the storm, sky and war god), Soma (a personification of the sacred soma plant), Agni (the fire god), and Varuna (associated with heaven, idealism, and ethics).

Ceremonial traditions and religious rituals were critical to the practice of the Vedic religion during this period; however, in the later periods, many began to reject these rituals and the role of the Brahmin class, or priests, within the religion. As the religion evolved, it would become the basis of Hinduism, which encompasses reincarnation, the law of Karma—also known as the moral law—and the caste system described above. Hinduism would become a crucial religion in India, the region, and the global system.

Trade led to cultural exchanges for the Indus River Valley.

Transregional and regional trade were evident in Mesopotamian culture via the Indus River Valley, which connected two blossoming cultures and therefore influenced the path that each would eventually follow. In the Indus River Valley, Harappan cities allowed for the trading of distant mining resources with rural agricultural communities. Again, this trade was not only an exchange of material goods but also an exchange of ideas, religions, languages, and traditions that would continue to influence various regions.

Specialized artisans worked in various regions and produced great ornaments, beadwork, metal tools, and pottery that were transported by animals, boats, and carts to various villages in the region. The same type of trade was seen between the Indus River Valley and various Mesopotamian cities such as Susa and Ur, where archeological evidence has been found to support these theories of trade. These Harappan cities also traded in present-day northern Afghanistan, acquiring the bright blue gemstones for which they would later become famous.

Religious Vedic texts emerged in South Asia.

Important texts from this period are seen in the form of religious works such as the *Rig-Veda*, which emerged from India in approximately 1700 B.C.E. along with the Vedic period. The *Rig-Veda* is one of the most important Vedas texts and contains the oldest and some of the holiest scriptures of contemporary Hinduism. The title, *Rig-Veda*, is translated as the "Knowledge of the Hymns of Praise," and was used for recitation in the early Vedic religion. This text is important because it shows the religious traditions of the period, which were seen in a different context than that of the epic poem.

The core beliefs outlined in the Sanskrit scriptures formed the basis of the Vedic religions—later known as Hinduism—which contributed to the development of the social and political roles of a caste system and in the importance of multiple manifestations of Brahma to promote teachings about reincarnation.

India was a vast land of people who rarely saw political unity but whose culture stayed strong despite political action. This land was dominated by Hinduism and the caste system, which has remained dominant in India for the majority of its existence. The caste system is even present in India today, undermining the actions taken by the British Raj, Gandhi, and the communists.

The Hindu religion, like many great contemporary religions, is based on an older religion, specifically the ancient Aryan Vedic religion. The Aryans were people who migrated from the Caucasus Mountains down to the Indus River Valley. The only way scholars know about them, and their religion is through the sacred texts they left behind, the earliest of which is known as the Vedas. The Vedas provide the foundational ideas for Hinduism, describe deities and hymns in praise of them, and act as a foundation for the social structure of the Hindu people by establishing a caste system.

A caste system is a form of social stratification that divides people into four groups: Brahmins, Kshatriyas, Vaishyas, and Shudras, with an extra group of people known as the "untouchables." The religious explanation for the caste system lies in the belief in a universal spirit, Purusha, which was divided into four parts that became the castes. At the top were the Brahmins, who were made from the mouth of Purusha and typically worked as priests and/or teachers. The Brahmins were the ones who spoke to the gods and taught members of the other castes their ways.

Next in the pyramid were the Kshatriyas, the warriors made of Purusha's arms. Purusha's thighs made Vaishyas, the merchants, and artisans, and from Purusha's feet came the Shudras, the laborers, and the farmers, who represented the majority of the society. These are the four essential divisions of people that have remained largely unchanged from India's founding to the present day. Additionally, the untouchables were a large part of society who were excluded from the system. This group typically consisted of people who did not accept the system, such as foreigners, criminals, and nomads.

The main incentive and the whole principle upon which the caste system stood is dharma, or a person's role or purpose as assigned by divine power. Dharma is particularly defined by caste, so the children of a Brahmin were also Brahmin and must fulfill their dharma by being the best Brahmin they could in their lifetime. People born into a particular caste had to stay within that caste and fulfill their purpose in life, as defined by the Dharma. This provided social order among the people. Moreover, while it limited personal freedoms, it was an essential part of Indian society, tradition, and the Hindu belief structure. However, why is it so important to fulfill dharma? The answer lies in the fundamentals of the Hindu religion.

According to this belief, the Jiva is the individual soul of a person, and the Ishvara is the supreme combination of each respective Jiva, so it follows that if the Jiva exists then, the Ishvara must also exist. The Brahman (not the caste) is the fundamental unit out of which everything, including Ishvara, is made. The individual soul follows the path of birth and rebirth, known as the cycle of reincarnation or the samsara. The Jiva is cursed with being stuck in samsara, and therefore the point of life is to escape that cycle and achieve moksha, or liberation.

Brahmin priest painting his forehead with the marks of his caste

The cycle of reincarnation is the concept that justifies the dharma and the caste system. Since the mechanism of life is one's soul being reincarnated every time one dies, the goal of life is to escape the cycle of reincarnation by fulfilling one's dharma to achieve moksha and be free and in harmony forever. Even those born as Shudras (farmers and laborers) have to be content with fulfilling their roles within their caste for their whole lives. By doing so, they are achieving a greater universal goal for their souls. According to the believers in the Hindu faith, this is justified because it results in the social order. This is how a religious, divine concept shaped the social structures and the everyday lives of millions of people in India for the vast majority of its history.

The core beliefs about desire, suffering, and the search for enlightenment preached by the historical Buddha and recorded by his followers into sutras and other scriptures were, in part, a reaction to the Vedic beliefs and rituals dominant in South Asia. Buddhism changed over time as it spread throughout Asia—first through the support of the Mauryan Emperor Ashoka, and then through the efforts of missionaries and merchants and the establishment of educational institutions to promote its core teachings.

Buddhism emerged around 600 B.C.E. This major religion began with Siddhartha Gautama, a prince of a kingdom in the North of India (present-day Nepal) who was kept under house arrest by his family due to a prophecy that foretold the fall of the kingdom if the prince left his house. Siddhartha was kept in sumptuous conditions all his life, but he suspected that there was more to life than just luxury, so despite his father's efforts to stop him, he went out to see his people.

On his way, Siddhartha encountered an older man and was fascinated by him. He did not know that people age. He encountered a sick man and a corpse and was similarly surprised to discover that people get sick and die. All of this resulted in a shock for young Siddhartha, so he resigned the crown and left his palace to become an ascetic and find meaning in himself and life overall. For about a month, he meditated under a tree and, in the end, achieved Nirvana, freedom of mind. He found the meaning of life, became the Buddha (or "the teacher"), and started teaching this meaning of life to the people.

According to Siddhartha, the key to the meaning of life is suffering, and to understand it, one must know the Four Noble Truths:

Face of the Buddha at Hong Hien

1. Life Means Suffering. Suffering in Buddhism is very vaguely defined, but essentially it includes physical pain, sickness, tiredness, and eventually death. It also includes mental illness, sadness, depression, and anger. Although there is also happiness, suffering is the default state for a human.

2. The Root of Suffering is Desire and the Ignorance Thereof. All humans have the desire, and this inevitably leads to suffering, as it is impossible to fulfill all desires. To Rid Oneself of Suffering is to Rid Oneself of Desire. Since all desire eventually leads to suffering, it follows that the path for getting rid of suffering is getting rid of desire.

3. To Rid Oneself of Desire is to Follow the Eightfold Path. The last three truths establish a logical path: life is suffering, and suffering is desire, so the absence of desire means the absence of suffering. It is human instinct to have desires, so the Buddha explains that following the Eightfold Path is the way to expel desire and, thereby, suffering.

The Eightfold Path is divided into three broad categories: wisdom, or how to use and interpret the knowledge of getting rid of desire and achieving Nirvana; concentration, or how to work specifically to get that knowledge; and ethical conduct, or how to live regular everyday life to obtain knowledge. Wisdom includes the first two Eightfold Path factors: right view and right intention. Ethical conduct includes the second three: right speech, right action, and right livelihood. Concentration contains the last three: right effort, right mindfulness, and right concentration. This is the basic lifestyle and mindset promoted by the Buddhist tradition to achieve peace and harmony within oneself and others to get rid of suffering.

Of course, this represents only the basic teachings of Buddhism, which did not stay the same throughout its history. Buddhism did not gain much popularity until the reign of a king known as Ashoka the Great, who ruled India in the Mauryan Empire around 260–230 B.C.E.

After defeating a neighboring kingdom in a battle, Ashoka was so astonished by the brutality of the fighting that he adopted Buddhism as his kingdom's religion. He converted to Buddhism himself and sought to spread the faith throughout India. From this period onwards, Ashoka's guidelines for governing and policies were peaceful and focused on the betterment of his peoples' lives.

At this time, Buddhism appealed to a lot of lower-class people because there was no caste system in Buddhism, and it was a nontheistic religion, which meant greater social mobility and opportunities for economic and spiritual development. The reactionary school of Hinduism began rioting and trying to revert the people to their old worship habits and away from the new Buddhist faith. Due to this concerted effort, Buddhism has almost entirely disappeared in India.

Buddhism has traveled all the way from India to Southeast Asia, China, and Japan. Throughout Buddhism's history, different cultures interpreted its teachings differently, and while accepting the basic principles, interpretations, and implementations differ. This led to the rise of Theravada Buddhism in Southeast Asia and Mahayana Buddhism in Nepal, China, and Japan. There are also a significant number of different sects of Buddhism. Even Mahayana Buddhism is not technically a school, but rather an umbrella encompassing many different schools from Tantra to Zen Buddhism.

All these differences arose essentially because of many countries and cultures adopting and implementing Buddhism by their cultural norms and traditions. Theravada Buddhism differs from original Buddhist teachings in that it calls for the worship of the Buddha as a god or as a divine figure. The spread of these variations was facilitated by trade throughout Asia via the Silk Road, the Indian Ocean Trade, and the efforts of Buddhist scholars, monks, and missionaries.

Buddhism deemphasized gender roles.

Women were allowed to participate in Buddhism on roughly the same scale as men. The Buddha also introduced the revolutionary concept of husbands respecting their wives. Additionally, women could become lamas (teachers) in Buddhism. Buddhism was more focused on the distinction between laypeople and monks than the distinction between genders. Buddhism did not emphasize gender roles, but it focused instead on human roles. It encouraged behavior, thinking, speech, and a monastic lifestyle similar to that of Christian monks, to rid people of materialistic needs and wants so they could focus on achieving Nirvana.

India chose Greek influences in India.

It is unknown exactly how Sanskrit drama developed—whether it was independent of or dependent on Greek influence; however, after Alexander the Great's conquest of the Greek city-states and Persia, he led his armies into the Indus River Valley, which spread Hellenistic culture not only throughout Persia, Greece, and Egypt but also to India.

India didn't change much and largely rejected this foreign influence. However, Indians did take some of the great inventions of the Greeks and use them to reflect their own culture. One famous example is the Indian Sanskrit theatre that developed in approximately the 1st century C.E. and reflected Indian culture and tradition. This theatre utilized the concept of stock characters such as the hero, heroine, villain, and clown, along with the addition of other roles that were added during the Gupta Dynasty's "Golden Age." Many of these plays influenced European writers, such as Goethe.

Similar to Greek architecture, Indian architecture is usually characterized by Hindu and Buddhist temples and places of worship. For the Hindus, temples were considered to be a link between the people on earth and their sacred deities, so they tried to make them magnificent. They were frequently made out of wood and rock. India was famous for rock-cut architecture, in which pictures of people, gods, messages, and entire buildings were carved out of the rock. Buddhists usually built smaller structures. They were called stupas and consisted of a circular base with a dome as a roof. Stupas became popular in Southeast Asia and were one of the symbols of Buddhism. Much later, the Hindus began to build bigger buildings such as the Angkor Wat in Cambodia.

Angkor Wat

The Maurya and Gupta Empires

To the west of the Han dynasty was India. India was a decentralized state for a long time, but in the wake of Alexander's conquest, it was able to gain the biggest empire it ever had due to the expansion of Magadha. When Macedonians tried to expand their influence into the Mauryan Empire, the Indians pushed them back and took over much of the territory beyond the Indus River, defeating post-Alexandrian satrapies.

The Mauryan Empire existed for around 400 years and is most famous for two things: unifying India and spreading Buddhism. The Mauryan Empire united all but the southern tip of what is now modern-day India into one Raj. Further, Ashoka, the Great defeated the competing Kingdom of Kalinga, adopted Buddhism and then sought to spread the faith throughout his empire, which eventually led to fifty years of peace. However, Hindu rebellions and weak leaders' eventually led to the overthrow of his empire.

In the 3rd century C.E., after 500 years of political instability and disunity, the Gupta Empire began, marking the beginning of the Golden Age in India. During that age, India developed the ten-numeral system still used today. Chess was created, philosophy and literature were expanded, and plays were written that would later influence European literature. During the Gupta Empire, trade and science flourished, and the heliocentric theory was developed. The Gupta Empire united the northern half of India and used a system of provinces and a centralized government bureaucracy. The Gupta Empire eventually declined because of invasions from the north. It existed for approximately 200 years, leaving an enormous legacy forever remembered as the Golden Age of a united India.

India's Bureaucracy

East of Persia lies India, which was decentralized for a very long period of history and contained many small kingdoms united in faith and culture, though not in government. The political decentralization of India changed upon the arrival of Alexander of Macedon. Alexander's forces, though they did not go far into India, brought political change by destabilizing India's various kingdoms, breaking the stalemate between these kingdoms and allowing for one to grow and the rest to fall. This happened with Chandragupta Maurya's kingdom, which later turned into the Mauryan Empire in India.

The Mauryan Empire was the first attempt at centralization of India. It was the largest Indian empire in history, even though it did not include the southern tip of India. The Mauryan dynasty fought many wars to unite India. To manage such a vast territory, they had to create a system of government that would not only be efficient but also prevent rebellions. To prevent rebellions, the Mauryan Empire kept an enormous armed force consisting of cavalry, infantry and war elephants, thanks to which it was able to fight and defeat various other kingdoms in India. The Mauryan Empire had a centralized bureaucracy that consisted of a council of advisors who also acted as government officials in different provinces. The Mauryan leaders also sent people from the royal family to govern these provinces, act as judges, make policies, administer laws and oversee construction alongside a vast number of collectors, treasurers, clerks, and other government officials.

Similar to the Achaemenid Empire, the Mauryan Empire had government inspectors and spies to fight corruption within the government. Moreover, while the dynasty fell because of weak rulers and the practice of nonviolence, this system of bureaucracy was also practiced in the next Indian empire, the Gupta Empire. Both the Mauryan and Gupta Empires were prosperous and influential throughout history due to big government control, sponsorship of agriculture and sciences, Hinduism's promotion of an ideal social order where everyone is assigned a job they must keep to help themselves in future life and efficient bureaucracies.

Overextension and poor leadership contributed to the declines of the Mauryan and Gupta empires.

The Mauryan Empire was the largest empire India has ever seen, which was not only an accomplishment for the Mauryans but also the cause of their demise. The Mauryan Empire was a successful state with an efficient bureaucracy. A strong empire needs a strong ruler, and Ashoka was the last strong emperor of the Mauryan dynasty. He defeated the kingdom of Kalinga in brutal battles, gaining more and more territory for the Mauryan Empire, but when he saw what he had done on the battlefield, he felt remorse for all the bloodshed he had caused. Ashoka broke down and started searching for a way to end this kind of bloodshed. He found it in Buddhism.

Ashoka started following the Buddhist way of nonviolence and made it one of the key requirements for the Mauryan government. Perhaps Ashoka's spirit did find peace in Buddhism, but many were enraged by the empire's blasphemy of the Hindu religion. The emperors that followed Ashoka could not hold this huge empire together; they were not strong enough to suppress rebellions, and parts of the empire started declaring independence. The path of nonviolence adopted by Ashoka ended up bringing even more violence to the empire in the form of politicians competing for the throne and wars fought over Mauryan territory. A successful coup was eventually made against the last Mauryan emperor, and the Mauryan Empire disintegrated.

The Gupta Empire fell in a similar way. The Gupta dynasty is considered the Golden Age of India, and while it saw a lot of progress and invention in many fields, it also saw India succumb to chaos. While the first three rulers of the Gupta Empire were strong, effective, and decisive (Chandragupta, Samudragupta and Chandragupta II), the leaders that followed were not as strong. In 480 C.E., the nomads from the North invaded the Gupta Empire, plundering whatever they could and leaving destruction and death in their wake as they were driven off.

Chandragupta II coin

The cost of fighting and reconstruction caused heavy taxation on the rich, which they did not like. The nobility would no longer stand high taxes on their property, so they led protests and rebellions, and some even declared independence from the Gupta Empire. This turned the current state of the Gupta Empire into chaos, and the nomads launched another attack upon Gupta, this time successfully. Chaos arose in India, and wars were fought by the newly-established kingdoms against their invaders, amongst themselves and against the Gupta Empire until it fell in 550 C.E.

Indian Ocean trade linked distant economies.

The Indian Ocean routes, which extended from East Africa to East Asia—including West Africa, Arabia, India, China, and the small commercial city-states of East Asia—are known today as the Indian Ocean Trade. Everything was traded along multiple sea routes, including grain, Arabian ivory, Indian textiles, Chinese china, books, and wood. The Indian Ocean was a very large and profitable market in which many trading ports such as Zanzibar, Canton, Mombasa, and Mogadishu flourished. The monsoon winds of the Indian Ocean enabled such lucrative and extensive trade. Monsoon winds were strong and very predictable winds that went east in one season and west in the other. The trading ships that sailed from India to China could go there and back relying on the predictable seasonal winds, and reliable winds would make possible an accurate and more reliable estimate of the safe arrival of goods.

The boom in Indian Ocean Trade occurred around the 7th century C.E. but had been in place long before that time, allowing Rome and India to establish trading relations around the 1st century C.E. This extensive and lucrative trading network shaped the governments and people involved, both directly and indirectly, by the creation of more jobs due to the need for people to participate in the transportation of goods and the making of goods; or, through the new demand for people to participate in turning the raw materials they received through trade into finished products. The monsoon winds allowed for many countries' dominant production of a specific good, such as India's long history with textiles, and established trading port city-states and communities.

Innovations in maritime technologies and advanced knowledge of the monsoon winds stimulated exchanges along maritime routes from East Africa to East Asia.

Many innovations that improved trade on maritime routes was made as well. The Indian Ocean had the very beneficial monsoon winds, but to utilize them, the Indian Ocean merchants had to build ships that could take advantage of them. The lateen sails originally made in Greece in the 2nd century B.C.E. were very popular in shipbuilding across the Indian Ocean. A ship called a dhow was developed that could use the wind very efficiently. The dhow ships were small trade ships with triangular sails that could catch the wind and greatly take advantage of it. Later, these sails would be improved to be used on bigger boats that could transport more goods and were equipped with more lateen sails.

Buddhism dispersed throughout Asia.

Stamp depicting a dhow

Hinduism was not a missionary religion. It had a very loyal following but was mostly relegated to India and some of its surroundings. Buddhism, not being practiced mainly in India, spread via the Silk Roads and Indian Ocean trade to Southeast Asia (e.g., Singapore, Indonesia, Laos, Cambodia, Vietnam, etc.). To the West, it spread less successfully but did reach Persia and the central parts of Asia. It had the greatest success in China and Japan and was dominant there for a long time. This spread took place through trade and contact with other cultures, which meant it was combining with other cultures and not only spreading as a religion but also changing as a religion.

Notes for active learning

East Asia

Major historical events of the period:

7,000–6,000 B.C.E.:   Copper smelting is practiced in China

6,000–5,000 B.C.E.:   Yellow River Valley domesticates chickens and cultivate rice

4,000–3,000 B.C.E.:   Yellow River Valley domesticates sheep, cattle and water buffalo

3,000–2,000 B.C.E.:   Yellow River Valley domesticates dogs, goats, pigs, oxen and horses

1,766–1,027 B.C.E.:   Large swaths of China are unified and ruled by the Shang Dynasty

551 B.C.E.:   Confucius is born

475–221 B.C.E.:   The Warring States period

221 B.C.E.:   Qin dynasty emerges as first unified Chinese empire

206 B.C.E.:   Han Dynasty emerges

108 B.C.E.:   Han Dynasty conquers parts of northern Korea

200s C.E.:   Mahayana Buddhism arrives in China, spreads to Korea and Japan

220 C.E.:   Han dynasty falls

PERIOD 1: Prehistory and Civilizations to the year 500 C.E.

EAST ASIA

Yellow River Valley inhabitants pursued animal domestication.

The Yellow River Valley had domesticated chickens from 6000 to 5000 B.C.E. They also cultivated rice, a staple of their diet. Between 4000 and 3000 B.C.E., the Yellow River Valley also had domesticated sheep, cattle and water buffalo; between 3000 and 2000 B.C.E., they domesticated dogs, goats, pigs, and oxen. Finally, by approximately 2000 B.C.E., horses became domesticated in the region.

Natural conditions of Huang He Valley agriculture shaped Chinese foreign policy.

The Yellow River, or Huang He Valley, emerged as an influential settlement around 4000 B.C.E. and was the foundation for all Chinese culture emerging during this period, most notably the Shang and Zhuo dynasties. Due to geographic constraints, such as mountainous regions, the Chinese farmers were primarily self-sufficient and relied upon the internal production of foods and goods, rather than relying completely on trade. The Silk Road connected China with the outside world and allowed for the transportation of goods and ideas, but apart from this trading avenue, the Chinese engaged in less trade than their counterparts in the Mediterranean or the Middle East.

Marco Polo caravan traveling to India on the Silk Road

Yellow River Valley's dynasties generated key technological innovations.

The Yellow River Valley, located in the northern Chinese plain region, was home to several powerful and influential Chinese dynasties, including the Shang Dynasty (1766–1027 B.C.E.) and the Zhuo Dynasty (1000–256 B.C.E.). The technological achievements of these cultures include extensive metallurgy and, with the development of new, more dependable tools, the creation of an effective standing army, and the technological advances of the Chinese Iron Age. Politically, the Shang dynasty was the first instance of Chinese unification and the levying of taxes on a domestic population.

Shang Dynasty propelled statecraft and technological advancements.

The Shang Dynasty of China (1766–1027 B.C.E.) is notable for its ability to unify and manage various regions of China, which before this period, had no central authority or ruling government. The Shang Dynasty's technological advancement via metallurgy—specifically bronze workings—allowed the creation of advanced weaponry and ceremonial tools, all of which were required to mount a territorial offensive that enabled the continued expansion of the dynasty. Many scholars have pointed to the frequent renaming of the capital during this period as evidence of the evolving expansion of the Shang dynasty.

Bronze tiger from the Shang Dynasty

The arts flourished in early East Asian history.

Sculpture and other arts played an important role in East Asian cultures. For example, it is recorded that over 15,000 Japanese Dogū were crafted from 14,000 B.C.E. to 400 B.C.E. Dogū are small clay figures shaped like humans, animals, and deities. Additionally, the Zhou Dynasty of China boasts beautiful examples of wine vases dating to 1000 B.C.E.

Dogū

Oracle bones were the first form of written records used in China.

Notable early written records from this period originate from the Shang Dynasty in China. The writing was found on oracle bones—bones carved with prayer and scripture, used in rituals for divination— dating to approximately 1200 B.C.E., but were likely used much earlier. While this discovery initially seemed to be only of a religious nature, it is important to the written record and language systems of the period because it proves that the Chinese culture maintained and shared a written language. This had previously been questioned by some academics as there was no archeological evidence to support that the Chinese had a written language at this time.

The prominent status of literature was evident in early Chinese culture.

Notable literary works from this period include the *Book of Songs*, also known as the *Book of Odes*. Written in China around 1000 B.C.E., the *Book of Songs* is composed of 305 poems and is the earliest known collection of Chinese poetry. It is extremely influential within Chinese culture—as Confucius embraced the reading of poetry—and maintains its cultural significance even today.

Another notable example of literature from this period also stemmed from Chinese culture in approximately 1200 B.C.E. and is seen in the use of oracle bones that were used to communicate with deities, known as divination. These bones were important because they show the written language of the Shang dynasty and give insight into the religious practices of the culture and the period. Divination was a popular concept among many civilizations and would greatly influence later cultures such as the Greeks and Romans who used oracles, divination and "casting the runes" as part of their religion.

Confucianism's core beliefs and writings originated in the writings and lessons of Confucius. They were elaborated by key disciples who sought to promote social harmony by outlining proper rituals and social relationships for all people in China, including the rulers.

Confucius did not view his teachings as religious, but rather as philosophical, which is why Confucianism was able to coexist with Buddhism in the beginning stages of Buddhism's introduction to China. The emergence of Confucianism stemmed from the hundred schools of thought – new and flourishing schools of thought that emerged in the late-Zhou Dynasty and during the Warring States period. Due to the chaos, confusion, and conflict that resulted from the end of the Zhou dynasty and the beginning of the Warring States, scholars and ministers tried to come up with clever and simple ways to fix the Chinese government and to make the society and its people live in peace and harmony once again.

Statue of Confucius

From these hundred schools of thought, three major schools became the most popular: Taoism, Confucianism, and Legalism. The most influential of these schools was Confucianism, for many future governments adopted its ideas, and it became the core of modern Chinese society. Confucius was a minor official in China during the Warring States period who had some ideas on how to improve Chinese society. No government would apply these concepts at the time, yet his ideas were later implemented in the Han dynasty and all of the following Chinese dynasties. Confucius did not write down his teachings, but his followers did.

Confucianism supports a series of social hierarchies, and Confucius believed that order could be achieved if a person knows his or her place in this hierarchy and acts accordingly. That way, grandparents respect their grandchildren and grandchildren respect their grandparents. There are a few relationships focused on Confucianism, the most important of which is the relationship between the son and the father. Confucius taught that the son has to respect his father, but his father must also respect his son for society to live in harmony. Confucianism emphasizes the construct of filial piety or the respect of one's elders. Altogether, Confucianism emphasizes ethical behavior. Included in the Confucian philosophy was the idea that the emperor also had to respect his people.

The code of conduct for emperors included the Confucian idea of following ethical behavior towards the emperor's subjects, and the Mandate of Heaven, the traditional Chinese religious explanation for why dynasties rise and fall. The Mandate of Heaven is the idea that emperors are granted legitimacy—the right to be emperors and rule—by some divine power known as heaven. Heaven judges the emperor's ability to rule his country by his ethical conduct here on earth. If an emperor does not act ethically, he might lose the Mandate of Heaven, and his dynasty would be overthrown. When Chinese Confucian scholars recorded Chinese history, they explained the fall of dynasties by the emperors' loss of the Mandate of Heaven.

In the major Taoist writings, the core belief of balance between humans and nature assumed that the Chinese political system would be altered indirectly. Taoism also influenced the development of Chinese culture.

The second most influential teaching of the hundred schools of thought was Taoism (Daoism). Taoism believes that everything in the universe, be it an ant, a rock, the sun, or anything at all, is an embodiment of nature. This natural spirit is called Tao (or Dao). Tao can't be understood through the physical senses because it is immaterial, but it can be experienced and sensed spiritually. The universe, according to Taoism, does not have multiple living things, but rather all living and nonliving things *are* life. Everything is a representative of the Tao that is present in everyone and everything.

The monks of Taoism believe that humans are different because they think. Humans think and reason, thereby altering the way of Tao and not letting it manifest itself. Moreover, the way that believers of Taoism believe one can let the Tao manifest itself in oneself is by following Wu Wei, or the practice of not doing anything. Wu Wei does not mean that one should lay down and be idle, but that one should not have a reason to do something and should let the Tao manifest itself by doing actions that one feels like doing. One's actions have to be instinctive and intuitive for that way, Taoists believe, Tao takes over, and the natural way of things flow. One old Taoist writing says that if a man sits by the river long enough, he will see the corpse of his enemy floating in it.

Taoism became a dominant ideology and religion during the Zhou dynasty, and it had an immense effect on Chinese culture. Taoism influenced traditional Chinese religion and partly became the new traditional religion of China. It also influenced traditional Chinese medicine practiced today, such as acupuncture; Chinese writing, such as poetry and books; and Chinese architecture, such as Taoist temples. Additionally, Taoism is evident because Confucianism has taken over the social systems in China, and the socialist government and culture are in place.

Taoist Trio

At the time of its spread to China, Taoism mixed with and added to Buddhism, and now many martial arts schools and temples practice Taoism and teach Wu Wei as a part of kung fu training. The Zhou dynasty even accepted this religion as their government religion, but it did not last long as China divided into smaller kingdoms, which started the Warring States period. Eventually, the Zhou dynasty and other Chinese states were overrun by the Qin dynasty that finally united China, and even gave it its name.

Confucianism emphasized filial piety.

Confucianism—which was a secular philosophy, not a religion—had a colossal effect on Chinese society. Confucianism affected gender roles and gender relationships in the same way it affected any social relationship. It promoted a hierarchy that determined who was more powerful in society. Everyone in the hierarchy was expected to be respectful and kind to those below them. Generally, gender relationships were improved by this system of mutual respect between the people on the low end and the people on the high end. For example, a son would respect his father and mother both when they were taking care of him and when they needed care.

Filial piety, respecting and taking care of one's elders, whether they be dead or alive, was greatly emphasized in Confucian philosophy. Confucius was recorded as saying, "In serving his parents, a filial son reveres them in daily life; he makes them happy while he nourishes them; he takes anxious care of them in sickness; he shows great sorrow over their death that was for him, and he sacrifices to them with solemnity." This also affected gender roles, for it implied that a female elder was just as important as a male elder. Confucian society wasn't divided by gender, but by social class, so the people of the same class were forced to treat each other equally.

Ancestor veneration persisted in many regions.

Ancestor veneration is a form of religious conduct that was present in most regions of the world, but especially in China. Although most people do not venerate their ancestors today, it is traditional in most cultures to treat the elderly with reverential respect. A common eastern belief is that the older one gets, the smarter one is, so ancestors were deeply respected and venerated. Besides trying to tell the future by reading oracle bones, the Chinese—as well as most other cultures—sought advice and help from their ancestors. The early Chinese believed that after their death, parents could help their children in this life. Therefore, even though animistic and shamanistic religions are not widely practiced today, they were widely practiced in the ancient nomadic and isolated populations and influenced some aspects of present society and culture implemented by most people across different cultures and religious beliefs.

The convergence of Greco-Roman culture and Buddhist beliefs affected the development of unique sculptural developments.

After Alexander the Great came into India, Hellenistic influences started to appear, especially in Buddhist culture. The Indo-Greek kingdom of Afghanistan and the Kushan Empire allowed collaboration between Greek and Buddhist cultures, which led to Greek sculpture appearing in the Buddhist tradition. For example, the Buddha was depicted in marble, which had never been done before.

Marble statue of the Buddha

This Greco-Buddhist synthesis and depiction of the Buddha have largely affected Mahayana Buddhism, prevalent in Central Asia, China, and Japan. This style of Buddhism saw the Buddha as a divine figure, so the depiction of him led to further developments of Buddhist art and Buddhist belief. Such developments were very important in Korean, Chinese, and Japanese cultures for a long time, for they were dominated by Mahayana Buddhists and often ruled by them, too. Statues of the Buddha exist all over the world. The tallest structure in Asia is, in fact, a sculpture of the Buddha, which was influenced by the Greek synthesis with Buddhist art from the 3rd century B.C.E. to the 7th century C.E. and the Islamic conquests.

The Qin and Han Empires

After the decline of the Zhou and the arrival of the hundred schools of thought into the political arena, smaller Chinese states grew in power and entered a period known as the Warring States period. The Zhou, who practiced Taoism, lost power to another state called Qin. Qin Shi Huang Ti, the leader of Qin, practiced Legalism and was characterized as being a dictatorial ruler. He attempted to control the Chinese population by burning all books except Legalist ones, executing people who criticized the state and overseeing massive building projects in which many people died. Still, Qin was said to be the first state to have united all the Chinese dynasties in one government during the Warring States period.

Also, in the Warring States period, smaller states built walls to protect themselves from the nomads up north while they were busy fighting elsewhere. To solidify his imperial rule of a unified China, Qin connected those walls to form the single Great Wall. The Great Wall of China—through solidifying a united China, has been called the great graveyard rather than the great wall because so many people died during its construction, with the bones of thousands of the deceased being used as mortar in the construction. The Qin dynasty was also famous for building roads and canals to connect the newly formed Chinese Empire. However, after all of the deadly construction, executions, government control, and heavy taxes, the peasants launched a series of uprisings against Qin Shi Huang's son. The Qin Empire was eventually successfully overthrown by the peasants, and a new Imperial order was established.

Liu Bang was the leader of the peasants who overthrew Qin, and he became the first emperor of the new Han dynasty. The Han dynasty adopted Confucianism as their official governing philosophy, stopped executing scholars and those who criticized the government and behaved benevolently towards the people. Liu Bang was a peasant himself, which gave him insight into how the peasants lived and what they needed. The Han dynasty existed for nearly 400 years—from the 2nd century B.C.E. to the 2nd century C.E.—and expanded the Silk Road trade.

Liu Bang, Han emperor

The Han Empire established trade relationships with the Romans, who were located on the Silk Road. It paid tribute to the Xiongnu nomads in Mongolia to prevent them from fighting the Han dynasty; however, despite this payment of tribute, the nomads attacked the Han anyways. As a result, the dynasty displayed its military strength by pursuing the nomads and conquering a portion of their land. Han China's influence and military involvement also spread to Korea, which they annexed closer to the 1st century BC.

Han rulers valued education. They subsidized historians and established universities. The bureaucrats of the Han Empire went through Confucian testing based on the education provided by the universities on government, society, economics, and Confucianism. Han China was a relatively successful state and existed for almost 400 years, during which time it dominated world trade on the Silk Road. The Han Empire owes its success in part to the pre-existing Qin dynasty's unification of an area that had been previously occupied by competing states.

Empires and states developed new techniques of imperial administration based, in part, on the success of earlier political forms.

The Han Empire employed government bureaucracy in which state-elected representatives addressed the problems faced by each region of the empire. The Han government had to obey the Confucian principles of a ruling that called for benevolence and mutual respect between the emperor and his subjects. As was characteristic of most states that had government bureaucracies, local rulers (like the local satraps in the Persian Empire) wanted to improve their regions because they lived there too.

The Chinese Empire's Bureaucracy

A highly efficient bureaucracy was created in China upon the emergence of the Qin dynasty in 221 B.C.E. The Qin dynasty united all the Chinese states in the Warring States period and subsequently proclaimed itself an empire with Qin Shi Huang as the first emperor of China. The Chinese Empire, like many others, had a vast territory to govern. To do so, Qin Shi Huang formed a system of government officials and secret and open police – similar to the Nazi Gestapo or Soviet NKVD – that attempted to control almost every aspect of human life under the dynasty's rule.

Qin Shi Huang,
Qin dynasty emperor

Not even the rich and noble families were spared from central oversight. To diminish their power, the emperor seized their land and sent them to live in places where it would be easier for him to control them. The regular people's lives were controlled, from their education level to their level of support for the government. Their jobs were also picked for them. The bureaucracy assigned people to work that the state deemed necessary—from state projects, such the building the Great Wall, to make commercial products, such as silk. The army and the police were under the sole control of the emperor.

Qin Shi Huang's state philosophy was Legalism, which taught that the state was to control the population in every way and that such control, combined with strict laws and enforcement, would create a society in which all people knew their place. The state could work efficiently without the social disorder. This philosophy not only allowed Qin to wield absolute, totalitarian power, but also justified his actions in the eyes of people who were obedient and loyal to him due to their belief in Legalism.

After the death of Qin Shi Huang, his son came to power. He was young and weak, so he couldn't maintain the same level of control as his father, ensuring China's first empire was short-lived. After seventeen years of Qin rule, the dynasty was overthrown by massive peasant rebellions in the 2nd century B.C.E. The will of the people crushed Qin armies, and a new empire, the Han, rose in China. It was headed by a peasant, Liu Bang (or Gaozu, his temple name).

The Han dynasty was quick to discredit any Legalist ideas and adopt something new and completely different from the totalitarian and dictatorial Legalist philosophy. Instead, the Han dynasty adopted Confucianism as its state philosophy. Confucianism is based on a social hierarchy, and mutual respect within the hierarchy is pivotal. Confucianism didn't create a need for government control over the people's lives; on the contrary, the emperor had to rule with benevolence and respect all the people as if they were his children, with respect given back to him from the people as though the emperor was the people's father.

This did not mean that the government had less power. The emperor still wielded absolute power and kept a powerful army to suppress any rebellions and instability. Therefore, the Han dynasty did not completely adopt Confucianism, but rather a mix of Confucian morality and Legalist authority. The Han dynasty created a system of government officials representing each region of the empire which they were in charge of. The government handpicked officials and not only from the wealthier segment of society, which meant that anyone could become a government official. This was probably the largest change the Han dynasty made to the Chinese bureaucracy.

Vessel with a design of a Chinese Confucian Scholar

The Han dynasty promoted education. To become an official in the government, one had to pass a very difficult Confucian examination. This ensured that only people who knew what they were doing could rule China. The Han Empire created the idea of a scholar-official, an official that would know Confucian principles and respect his subjects and the emperor. These scholars would not only act like people who performed government jobs but were also scholars of Confucianism and could make contributions to writing history.

While China did see dynasties rise and fall numerous times after the fall of the Han dynasty in the 2nd century C.E., the governmental structure remained practically the same. The bureaucracy—with regional capitals in all parts of the empire, government officials serving as local rulers under imperial rule, the Confucian examination system, and the concept of a scholar-official – did not change until the Revolution of 1911 and the arrival of Sun Yat-sen. This is truly an enormous legacy left by a dynasty that was founded initially by peasants.

Imperial governments projected military power over larger areas using a variety of techniques.

The Mongols had sophisticated supply and communication lines, with messengers who could move rapidly. Their strategy was to have stations at regular short intervals where fresh horses were kept ready. A messenger would race from one station to the next as fast as his horse could go, then change horses at the next station. Also, when a messenger needed to rest, other official messengers were ready to take over for him. This way, a messenger could continually travel at top speed for hundreds of miles. This rapid and reliable communication was one of the pivotal techniques used by the Mongols to outmaneuver their enemies and continually expand and effectively manage an empire that eventually stretched from the Pacific to the Mediterranean.

Peasant rebellions and political instability collapsed Qin, Xin, and Han dynasties.

The Qin Empire in China fell due to peasant uprisings that sprung up because of Qin's practice of Legalism and collectivist control over people's lives. After Qin Shi Huang died, the people of China saw the chance to liberate themselves from Qin rule and rebellions arose throughout the empire. After Liu Bang came to power leading his army and the peasants, the Han dynasty took power. While the Han dynasty prospered, marking a new age of development in China, political instability plagued the new empire. Wang Mang, the nephew of a Han Empress, launched a government coup in 9 C.E., proclaiming himself the emperor of the Xin dynasty. This rebellion ended in 23 C.E. The Han dynasty nearly lost power, but because Wang Mang was not successful at governing an empire, he was overthrown by peasant uprisings.

After the overthrow of the short-lived Xin dynasty—which controlled the capital, but not all of China—the Han dynasty was restored, and the history of Han is now divided into two parts: the Early Han and the Later Han (or West Han and East Han). The Early (western) Han was the more prosperous state, while Later (Eastern) Han, which existed for 200 years more, was overcome by trouble.

High taxes on the peasants and a state monopoly on the production of iron and tools worsened the quality of Chinese production. Han China used forced peasant labor to build fortifications and protect the Silk Road, creating the devastating Yellow Turban Rebellion in 184 C.E. Approximately one million Chinese people died during this twenty-year rebellion. The Han dynasty was victorious but was politically, militarily, and economically weakened. Corruption in the government, the decline of the Silk Road trade, and conflicts with the Xiongnu in the North made it possible for local warlords to rise to power. This gave way to the complete collapse of the central government, with the emperor losing all of his power and the empire succumbing to the period of The Three Kingdoms. The Han dynasty was no longer.

Three brothers during the Yellow Turban Rebellion

Religious and cultural traditions were transformed as they spread.

The Buddhism that dominated in Korea, Japan, China, and Central Asia was called Mahayana Buddhism and differed from original Buddhism, Theravada Buddhism, in many ways—the largest of which was seeing the Buddha as a god. The Buddha did not claim any divine power or authority. However, the majority of Buddhists today see him as such because the religion spread to different cultures through the Silk Road. Chinese culture added the concept of heavenly afterlife instead of Nirvana, and Buddhism changed more as it spread farther afield, branching off into two or three (historians debate how many) major groups and many smaller ones.

Notes for active learning

Notes for active learning

The Americas

Major historical events of the period:

4,000–3,000 B.C.E.:   Andes region first establishes permanent farming and fishing communities

3,000 B.C.E.:   Incan quipus writing system is developed

3,000–2,000 B.C.E.:   The Andes cultivates potatoes, beans and tomatoes, domesticates alpacas and lamas;

3,000–2,000 B.C.E.:   Mesoamerica cultivates corn, establishes permanent farming and fishing communities

1,200–400 B.C.E.:   Olmec civilization dominates Mesoamerica

900–200 B.C.E.:   Chavin civilization thrives in Andes region

700 B.C.E.:   Mayans develop pictographic written language

100–200 B.C.E.:   Teotihuacán is founded

PERIOD 1: Prehistory and Civilizations to the year 500 C.E.

THE AMERICAS

Agricultural advancements emerged in Mesoamerica and the Andes.

In Mesoamerica, agricultural advancements were slower than in other regions, with stone tools tracing back to about 6700 B.C.E. in what is present-day Mexico. With the cultivation of maize and other crops, permanent fishing and farming communities were established between 3000 and 2000 B.C.E. These communities excelled in varied areas, including pottery and Mayan astronomy.

Great examples of the vastness of these cultures can be seen in the Olmec civilization, which dominated the Mesoamerican landscape from approximately 1200 to 400 B.C.E. and is considered the predecessor of all subsequent Mesoamerican cultures, such as the Mayans and the Aztecs. Initially, the Olmec civilization occupied the area that is now the Mexican states of Tabasco and Veracruz, before greatly expanding. Some parts of Olmec culture, which were passed on to later Indian civilizations, included animism in their religion, religious stone architecture (e.g., enormous pyramids and sculptures of their gods), and ball sports that confined athletic contests with ritual human sacrifice. They also gave the world cacao.

Olmec colossal head

Technological innovations led to improvements in agricultural production, trade, and transportation.

Between 4000 and 3000 B.C.E., in the Andes region of present-day Peru, permanent fishing villages and agricultural centers produced exquisite pottery that was valued within the global system. Different crops or animals were domesticated in the various core regions, depending on available flora and fauna. In the Andes region, the cultivation of potatoes, beans, and tomatoes are all seen at approximately 3000 to 2000 B.C.E., while the domestication of alpacas and lamas was also being pursued during this same time.

The New World's Olmec and Chavin civilizations produced noteworthy achievements.

The Olmec civilization in Mesoamerica exemplifies many similarities between itself and other developing cultures during this period. During the early years of its history (approximately

6700 B.C.E.), the Olmec used stone tools and cultivated maize, a staple in the regional diet. They also centralized authority and religious rituals, as seen in their creation of statues, most notably colossal heads.

Sculpture was seen in a religious capacity, with monumental carvings and individual masks having been excavated at Olmec sites. One such example is the San Lorenzo Monument 3, which stands 173 cm (5 feet 8 inches) high and is given the nickname "Colossal Head." Seventeen of these heads have been found along the Gulf Coast.

The San Lorenzo Monument 3

In the Andes region of South America, the Chavin culture of Peru was the most developed pre-Columbian settlement, dating to about 900–200 B.C.E. This culture involved a sedentary agricultural existence and developed extensive basket weaving, pottery and stone carvings.

Region noted for Chavin agriculture and Mayan astronomy.

The Chavin civilization experienced a surge in agricultural production, causing an increase in the overall standard of living for the population. The Mayans' religious practices were combined with sophisticated scientific advances in astronomy. Observatories have been discovered and reconstructed in Mesoamerica.

Incans developed a quipus system.

The quipus, also spelled "khipus," was a record-keeping and communication system developed by the Inca civilization in approximately 3000 B.C.E. Like the other systems, this form of communication was meant to record quantitative and qualitative information and was used to communicate with neighboring villages and communities. The system is made up of different colored strings that depict a message using a variety of knot types. In this regard, it is unlike the previous languages mentioned because it is not written. Like other cultures, scribes were responsible for recording and sending messages, and the other classes were most likely unable to communicate using this method.

Depiction of a messenger carrying a quipus

New World civilizations enjoyed a diversity of architectural accomplishments.

Pre-Columbian Mesoamerican architecture is best known for magnificent pyramid-shaped temples, which were the heart of their cities and are the focal point of the study of Mesoamerican religions today. The Mayans were famous for building these temples, placing them in each of their numerous cities. Teotihuacán had temples for each of the most important gods, including the Temple of the Sun and the Temple of the Moon in the Avenue of the Dead. The people of Teotihuacán also built multistory buildings, which was an incredible achievement indicating that their civilization had a large population. More than just pyramids and pyramid-shaped structures were built; Native Americans constructed rectangular palaces out of the rock, decorated with sculptures composed of rock and marble, and sometimes even painted with red paint. The architectural styles of different Native American societies were variations on major themes, with pyramids and cities that became the symbol of their culture in the eyes of people today, revealing their distinctive cultural development.

Mesoamerica: Teotihuacán and Maya city-states

Although there is little known about the pre-Columbian Americas, there is evidence that some states in the Americas were as powerful as some empires in Afro-Eurasia were. One of these was the Toltec civilization of Teotihuacán. The Toltec did not leave many writings, but there is proof that their state was powerful and that the development of the city took place somewhere around 100 B.C.E. to 200 C.E. Teotihuacán was a large city and was able to sustain a population of 100,000 to 200,000 people, an enormous amount of people for that time compared to the rest of the Americas.

The Toltec built pyramids for their gods that were later considered one of the best examples of Native American culture. Teotihuacán was located in Central Mexico. There is much evidence that it had great influence and was a major economic and political center in Central America and came into contact with the Mayans and other Native American states and tribes. It may have been a multi-ethnic and multicultural city like Constantinople or other major economic and political centers. There is no documentation about the decline of Teotihuacán. However, the closest guess for the date of its decline is the 7th to the 8th century C.E. Teotihuacán was eventually taken over by the Aztec Empire, which came much later.

Pyramids in Teotihuacán

Another major civilization in the Americas was the Mayans, who most likely were united by culture but lived in city-states like the Greeks. The Mayans had a written language, so there is evidence of how they lived and traded. For example, the Mayans developed staple crops around 750 B.C.E., and by 700 B.C.E., they invented a pictographic written language, which means that the Mayans were far more advanced than other regional people who had not yet developed such a system.

The Mayans developed the calendar, of which they had two types: one calendar for agriculture and another for religion. The agricultural calendar told the Mayans when the rivers would flood and when to expect rainfall, while the religious calendar told them when to worship which gods and when to make sacrifices. These sacrifices varied from fruits to humans, and even though the Mayans made human sacrifices, they were not carried out to the same extent as the Aztec Empire.

The Mayans believed in many gods, had priests, and built grand pyramids to honor their gods. These pyramids became a symbol of Central American religions for later historians and people, and they are now a world heritage site. The Mayans were adept at constructing cities, and their culture was very powerful throughout Central America. Around the 3rd century

C.E., the Mayan civilization saw immense growth, built more cities, and saw their population rise to almost two million. Around 900 C.E., Mayan civilization eventually declined for unknown reasons. Not enough Mayan writing has survived to form an informed theory, yet it is hypothesized that a drought caused the decline. The Mayans left an impressive legacy even though they were not an empire and may not even have been a single united tribe.

Stucco Mayan glyphs

Andean South America: the Moche civilization

The Andes saw the rise of civilizations like the Moche, a fairly small civilization that later gave rise to one of the most important empires in South American history, the Incan Empire. The Moche and other relatively small civilizations of the Andes sustained themselves through fishing and terrace farming. The period from 600 B.C.E. to 600 C.E. saw the rise and fall of many great empires and civilizations. Additionally, there were many more states during that period that were small and not considered to have a large influence on world history. The most influential and vast empires came to be, not by fighting other great empires and conquering them, but rather by fighting the small nations, tribes, and city-states, thereby stabilizing the region of the world they conquered and uniting them under one culture, law and government.

Indigenous populations domesticated animals and adopted agricultural practices suited to their environments.

In the pre-Columbian Americas, there were no horses or camels. A popular animal used to facilitate trade in South America was the llama, which was the only beast of burden in the Andes. Certain populations, like some North American natives, used the farming method of slash-and-burn agriculture, in which they would set entire forests on fire to enrich the soil with nitrogen from the ashes.

Notes for active learning

Period 2

500 to 1500 C.E.

Expansion of communication, as well as cultural and commercial exchange networks, increased economic productive capacity

Although Afro-Eurasia and the Americas remained separate from one another, this period witnessed a deepening and widening of old and new networks of human interaction within and across regions. The results were unprecedented concentrations of wealth and the intensification of cross-cultural exchanges. Innovations in transportation, state policies, and mercantile practices contributed to the expansion and development of commercial networks, which in turn served as conduits for cultural, technological, and biological diffusion within and between various societies.

Pastoral or nomadic groups played a key role in creating and sustaining these networks. Expanding networks fostered greater interregional borrowing, while at the same time sustaining regional diversity. State formation in this era demonstrated remarkable continuity, innovation, and diversity in various regions. While some states attempted to preserve or revive imperial structures, less centralized states continued to develop.

The prophet Muhammad promoted Islam, which spread quickly through trade, warfare, and the cultural diffusion of this period. The expansion of Islam introduced a new concept of Caliphate to Afro-Eurasian statecraft. Pastoral peoples in Eurasia built powerful and distinctive empires that integrated people and institutions from both the pastoral and agrarian worlds. In the Americas, powerful states developed in both Mesoamerica and the Andean region.

Changes in trade networks resulted from and stimulated agriculture and industry. Increasing productive capacity had important implications for social and gender structures and environmental processes. Rising productivity supported population growth and urbanization, but also strained environmental resources and, at times, caused dramatic demographic swings. Shifts in production and the increased volume of trade stimulated new labor practices, including an adaptation of existing patterns of free and slave labor.

Global Comparative

Major historical events of the period:

540: First outbreak of the Bubonic Plague in Europe

700s: The Bubonic Plague devastates Japan

800–1300: Little Ice Age

900–1200: Collars used for draught animals to pull plows first arrive in Europe from China (invented in the 200s C.E.) via the Middle East and are increasingly used throughout the continent

1269–1293: Marco Polo leaves Venice and travels to and from China

1300–1400: The Black Death (the Bubonic Plague) spreads throughout Europe

1400: The Age of Exploration begins; the Old World diseases ravage the New World populations

1492: Christopher Columbus searches for a faster sea route to Asia

PERIOD 2: 500 to 1500 C.E.

GLOBAL COMPARATIVE

Improved transportation technologies and commercial practices led to an increased volume of trade, expanding the geographical range of existing and newly active trade networks.

Trade changed rapidly over this period in response to some important factors. All cultures begin as agricultural or pastoral, as people attempt to provide enough food for survival. As these food sources are secured, however, some leave these professions to pursue new ones. Thus as most societies move, there is a move toward the creation of artisans, who begin to produce new materials that they barter or trade for food. As society develops, new materials are created that need new markets. To get to new markets, people needed some new technological advances that made transportation to distant markets easier and more efficient.

During this period, several inventions made this increased trade possible, including innovations that improved transportation like the compass and the astrolabe. This change in trade, in turn, brought about a change in society as new financial institutions developed to facilitate the increase in trade and the creation of new money forms. This prosperity, in turn, led to both the rise and fall of some societies and empires over the course of the period.

Existing trade routes flourished and promoted the growth of powerful new trading cities.

As interregional trade began to expand, trade routes saw increasing amounts of traffic. Many merchants realized the potential for increased profits if they sold their wares outside of their immediate community. This meant that trade routes became dotted with major cities, as the traders needed both shelter and established markets for their wares. These cities became bustling centers of commerce and trade, giving way to a new era of interregional relationships.

This was an incredibly lucrative business. Merchants would set up businesses in port cities and run their operations through those offices. This led to fierce competition between these cities to attract more merchants. Taxes were collected on all goods sold in the city, so more merchants meant more revenue for the city-state and more power for the immediate region. Thus, as in Italy, where there was a similar social structure, fights sometimes broke out between the different city-states.

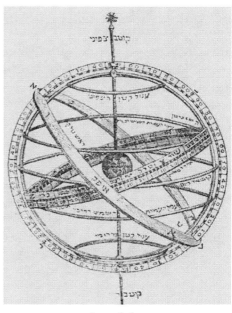

Astrolabe

Cultures, in turn, spread back along the trade lines, influencing several different regions. The city, because of the number of different cultures and belief systems that were sometimes in conflict with one another, had to be regulated by the merchants to avoid violence and upset. All groups shared general norms and practices meant to influence business and productivity positively. While this method could not be effective all of the time, it helped the city grow into a well-respected trading power.

The growth of interregional trade in luxury goods was encouraged by significant innovations in previously existing transportation and commercial technologies, including more sophisticated caravan organization; use of the compass, astrolabe and larger ship designs in sea travel; and new forms of credit and monetization.

Interregional trade occurred primarily because of innovations made in travel and finance. Simple systems, like those of most small medieval European towns, did not allow for expansive trade. Products from such towns were typically agricultural in nature, which meant that they had to be sold to an immediate market. As society developed and people began to devote more time to things outside of farming, artisans developed. In a barter-based society, an artisan would barter for the food needed by his family.

The development of money and trade greatly expanded this practice. People began creating items that went beyond basic needs. This is seen in most societies with things like ceremonial clothing and adornments. Wool and other coarse materials were the usual clothing sources. Therefore, materials like cotton and silk, which were soft and breathable, became commodities in high demand.

The wealthy used their clothes as a status symbol. Similarly, gems and metals in almost every culture worldwide are used to show wealth through jewelry or by adorning clothing or materials. Items that were considered exotic were the ultimate status symbol because such things were expensive and took time to procure. Spices from foreign lands, for instance, were in high demand. Foreign slaves and animals were also considered luxury items as they were curiosities that would draw the attention and jealousy of aristocratic peers.

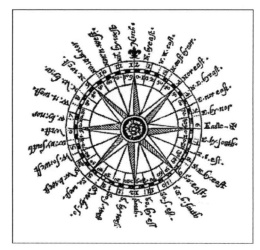

Compass

Procuring these items became possible due to new methods of transportation. The compass and astrolabe, for example, allowed for more accurate shipping routes. A *compass* uses magnetized metal to show the Earth's magnetic North. An *astrolabe* uses star positions to help with nighttime navigation. Using these methods, more accurate charts and maps could be created. This meant that shipping became more predictable, more of a science.

Land trade also changed with the development of camel saddles. While camels had been used as beasts of burden for years, their use was limited.

Camel riders knelt on cushions positioned behind the hump, but these were inefficient because they did not allow for the easy use of weapons, a necessity if caravans were going to be protected. The development of the saddle allowed for weapons to be used on camelback. This, in turn, led to an increase in camel breeding as the animals were much more practical than horses in the vast deserts of the Middle East. Using camels and the compass and astrolabe, these deserts became new trade routes for caravans willing to transport goods overland.

Another important innovation was a change in finance. Typically, if a person wanted to purchase an item, they had two choices: to barter or trade for the item with materials they had grown or created, or after coins were developed, a person could also purchase the product outright using the standardized currency. These options limited trade. They meant that a trader either always had to have a product to move so that he could barter with it, or it meant that he had to carry large quantities of money, which was dangerous to do. Some civilizations developed the solution to this problem at different times and with different levels of success.

Eventually, however, a banking system developed. Lenders would typically gather in places like temples where they would accept deposits of money or exchange money into different currencies. With so many different lenders offering to hold an individual's money, competition between these lenders was fierce. Many started to offer incentives to build their business. One such incentive was later named a *check*. In essence, a lender would accept a written letter as proof that a payment was due to the person holding it.

Now, a patron could write a note that a merchant could later cash at a bank instead of carrying money to a market. Similarly, lenders began allowing patrons to spend money before they had it. This is called lending credit. A lender might finance a merchant getting ready for a voyage with the understanding that the merchant will pay back his debt with interest once he has made the trip and sold his wares. These innovations allowed people to invest money and profit from it on a larger scale than ever before. It opened up an entirely new business, and people suddenly had much more access to resources than ever before.

Commercial growth was also facilitated by state practices, trading organizations, and state-sponsored commercial infrastructure.

As trade developed and changed, the political sphere had to change as well. Traders and merchants were creating a middle class, a bridge between the aristocracy and the common man. This new merchant class was very different from the lower class. They had political power because they controlled the flow of resources. The state-regulated trade, but it also forced the state to adapt. This is evident in the rapid changes occurring during the period to the social structure of most countries.

One such change is the development of currency. Evidence of coins can be seen as far back as the 6th century B.C.E. Coins were exchanged for goods, and their metallic content determined their value. In this way, a valued metal like gold would be worth more than a common metal like copper. The Romans were one of the first to standardize their coins, which were printed with the face and emblem of the Emperor of the time. These coins created one of the first exchange rates, with specific coins valued at different exchange rates with other coins.

This system had several inherent flaws, however. Counterfeit money was a problem as people could melt the coin down and use it as a covering for another base metal. It was also difficult to trade with coins, as their weight prohibited any large amount from being carried.

6th-century coins

As the banking industry exploded, however, the practice of using paper-based money began to spread. The system originated in China, where they used leather notes to avoid the inherent weight of trade using copper coins. The practice became popular, in turn, with lenders and banks. These institutions saw the potential in increased business if they started issuing receipts for deposits that would serve as a promissory note or check for payment. The practice eventually spread to Europe as well, with most cultures seeing the inherent advantage of lightweight money over heavy coins.

While trade was regulated in part by the state, it was also regulated by the traders themselves. Several organizations developed to create norms of business. In a single city, for instance, a guild might monopolize a trade. They would collect dues from members and regulate the quality and price of a product. In turn, a person wanting to join a profession regulated by the guild would have to seek permission, often serving under a master as an apprentice until they were eventually allowed to enter the profession as a qualified master themselves.

Multiple guilds often needed to interact to exchange or acquire supplies. A bookmaker would have to procure materials like vellum and leather from a tanner, for instance. Sometimes these interactions had to occur over long distances, which led to the development of trade organizations, or groups of guilds in distant places that had preferential agreements with one another.

The movement of peoples caused environmental and linguistic effects.

As people and societies develop, the need for resources and materials often drives them to move beyond their immediate surroundings, using trade or migration. When moving, they interact with some other cultures and people. This spread of knowledge and people causes important changes in the environment of a given area. It also plays an important role in language, as languages that develop in isolation tend to differ from those that develop near other languages. Thus the increased movement via the new bustling trade routes led to changes in the environment and the languages of the Eurasian and African peoples.

Long-distance trade routes bolstered by growing environmental knowledge and use of horses.

Long-distance trade became possible only with a society's adaptation to their environment. When a society forms, it develops technology to fit its specific needs. These needs are a reaction to their environment, as a way to work with it or against it. Many regions would be inhospitable without in-depth knowledge of the environment, allowing technological adaptations to be made. For instance, without practical knowledge of how to navigate through the shifting sands of the desert and where oases can be found for drinking water, one would quickly die in the desert.

Horses allowed the people of the Steppes to adapt to life in the same ways that camels helped people in the deserts. The Steppes were not fit, for the most part, for agriculture. This meant that food had to come from elsewhere. Therefore, the people of the Steppe became herders. The animals they herded provided them with food in the form of meat, milk, and clothing in the form of skins. To provide a flock with enough food, people like the Mongols and the Huns had to move around a lot. This was possible because of horses, which allowed them to move great distances to new pastures. Walking took too much time to feed a flock of any great size, so horses allowed for more range, as well as serving as a war machine when tribes came into conflict

Some migrations had a significant environmental impact.

Whenever people move from place to place, they take their culture with them. This can have immediate and lasting impacts on society. For instance, the spread of food can cause demand for products never before found in certain areas. Similarly, two societies in contact will trade for resources, which might lead to gems or metals being used in places where they do not occur naturally. Language, like culture, will spread as new people come in contact with it.

Some migrations and commercial contacts led to the diffusion of languages throughout a new region or the emergence of new languages.

Language spreads the same way technology or ideas do. As people interact, they need to have a common language to allow for accurate communication. While a trader might only pick up a few words from a specific area, someone who lived on the border between two societies would often learn enough of the language of their neighbors to communicate. Small tribes that lived in a specific area might all develop the same language, for instance.

Sometimes languages spread naturally due to environmental factors, like Swahili, but sometimes it occurred due to pressure from the ruling class to learn the status language. A good example of this might be Turkic, which spread as the status language of the Ottoman Empire after the fall of the Byzantines. When new people take over, they often require the lower class to learn the new language of their ruling class. Turkic is an example of this happening in a political arena, but it also happened in religious areas. The status language in the West was Latin because all church services were conducted in it. Similarly, with the prohibition of translating the Quran to avoid misrepresentation of the original text, Arabic spread as quickly as Islam. If people wanted to read their new holy text, they first had to learn the one language it could legally be written in.

Cross-cultural exchanges were fostered by the intensification of existing or the creation of new networks of trade and communication.

Culture is a difficult concept to quantify because it is more fluid than many other measures of people. Culture is a broad category that includes several sub-categories. Food is part of the culture, as is music and dance. Language is a very important part of the culture as well. Even within the same language, dialects can express vastly different identities and group ideologies. During this period, one of the largest impacts on culture was religion, because so many people tied their understanding of their world to the attitudes of their religious institutions. This is why people fought holy wars like the Crusades. Religion was one of the few unifying factors between peoples.

While culture is difficult to quantify, it is not difficult to spread. As trade resumed in many areas, like the Silk Road, and as new trade routes opened up trade with distant lands, culture traveled along these routes as well. As people interacted, they were forced to observe and understand the cultures of others. This can be read in the accounts of traders who express astonishment and culture shock when they encountered belief systems very different from their own.

In key places along important trade routes, merchants set up diasporic communities where they introduced their cultural traditions into the indigenous culture.

The term *diaspora* refers to a large migration of people from a similar background. Diasporic communities might be forced to leave their home due to invasion or disease. They might be forcibly removed, via the slave trade. They may represent a group that experienced a schism with the main sect or a dynastic change. In any circumstance, whenever a diasporic community was founded, they had a great impact on the area in which they settled, through cultural diffusion.

The writings of certain interregional travelers illustrate both the extent and the limitations of intercultural knowledge and understanding.

With transportation allowing for the movement of large population segments and the swift dispersal of ideas through a population, it is not surprising that explorers began seeking out foreign cultures to understand more of the world around them. Explorers' records of their explorations aid current historical research because they usually documented their travels. However, these writings typically display bias, as the limitations of cross-cultural understanding and conflicts between cultural beliefs often become apparent. Thus most accounts of explorers have to be scrutinized to understand how they saw the world versus how the world worked.

Increased cross-cultural interactions resulted in the diffusion of literary, artistic and cultural traditions.

As trade and culture spread, other areas experienced the impact of the spreading cultures. Buddhism settled into the same areas as Hinduism, as Buddhist missionaries often traveled with their countrymen to expand their religion's borders. In Burma, for instance, the capital city includes a Buddhist monastery where the monks educated children. Islam spread further than many other empires and influenced a huge number of people. With their religion came their language, as it is forbidden to translate the Quran. This, in turn, influenced the writing styles of many different peoples.

There was continued diffusion of crops and pathogens throughout the Eastern Hemisphere along the trade routes.

Trade led to the diffusion of both positive and negative items. On the one hand, more trade meant that food items diffused across cultural boundaries and helped to create a number of cuisines that are still enjoyed today. More importantly, it led to the diversification of the human diet, resulting in greater survival and health. On the other hand, as people moved, so did their diseases. As these diseases met new populations who had no immunity, they often devastated the local populations. This trade was the source of some concomitant benefits and harms that may not have been apparent at the time.

New foods and crops were adopted in populated areas.

One of the most environmentally impactful ways that trade influenced the world was through the spread of foods. Even though people were traveling greater distances, preservation techniques for food limited the amount that could be carried with the traders. This meant that merchants and traders had to forage for or purchase local food supplies as they traveled. Understandably, the merchants and traders found some new foods enjoyable and wanted to bring them back to the people of their region. Similarly, merchants who lived and worked away from their native homeland might import staples from their culture to allow for the consumption of their homeland's dishes even in a foreign country. This had an incredible impact on the environment and society.

Empires were also useful for spreading new items. Countries may not communicate effectively when separate, often due to past conflict. As an empire bridged these disparate peoples together, trade relations opened up, and new materials tended to diffuse quickly. This was particularly true of the Islamic world, which conquered territories never before under the same ideology. Therefore the diffusion of climate-friendly items like cotton, sugar and citrus plants is unsurprising from a historical perspective.

The spread of epidemic diseases, like the Black Death, followed the well-established paths of trade and military conquest.

One of the few negative impacts of increased trade was the increase in disease. As merchants and traders moved around the world, they often encountered diseases that they had no immunity to. A more modern example of this would be the impact that smallpox had on the Native Americans. Similarly, the Europeans were not prepared for the virulent diseases bred by the warmer tropical climates of their trading partners in the South and the Far East.

Plague Altarpiece

The most notable and well-known example of a disease spreading through trade is the Black Death, also known as the Bubonic Plague, caused by the Yersinia pestis bacteria. People of the time were unsure of how it spread, blaming it on bad air or the alignment of the stars. In actuality, the disease existed in China and the Far East, where people had built up immunity. As trade reopened along the Silk Road with the rise of the Mongol Empire, the disease made its most famous foray west. It is suspected that Justinian's Curse, which nearly crippled Constantinople and the Byzantine Empire centuries earlier, had been a strain of Bubonic Plague. However, the people of the time did not connect the epidemics.

The plague was a blood-borne disease, which typically meant that a person would have to come into direct contact with an infected individual to pick up the disease. The plague, however, adapted and was spread through fleas, which drink human and animal blood to survive. When a flea bit an infected individual and absorbed the infected blood, they also picked up his or her bacteria, which would rapidly reproduce. This rapid reproduction would block the flea's ability to drink more blood from another victim. The flea dealt with this by vomiting the infected blood back up to purge the bacterial blockage. This infected blood would enter the bloodstream at the flea bite, and the victim usually died within a week of developing symptoms.

Empires collapsed and were reconstituted; in some regions, new state forms emerged.

As previously discussed, this era was the focus of a significant period of change. As some empires collapsed because they were no longer able to change and endure, others rose to take their place predicated on changes in leadership and new styles of government. These reconstituted governments had to adapt to new ways of governing. They particularly embraced the new systems that were being introduced by the new religious orders. Those cities that were not capable of adaptation quickly died out or were abandoned, while cities that could adapt to the changing times flourished.

Following the collapse of empires, most reconstituted governments, including the Byzantine Empire, combined traditional sources of power and legitimacy with innovations better suited to the current circumstances.

Many of the new governments during this period were a blend of traditional and innovative ideas. Many traditional ideas were kept because they dealt with society's sources of power and legitimacy. For instance, most new governments continued the idea of patriarchy. *Patriarchy* is the idea that a male figure is at the head of the house both literally and metaphorically. Patriarchal societies require that men have positions of power in their homes and their governments. The Eastern Orthodox Church even named their leading representative's Patriarchs. This effectively barred women from roles in the church as the concept itself barred them from roles in government.

Similarly, the maintaining of a state religion was a common idea. However, while society would maintain a state-recognized religion, they had to have ways to deal with those who did not follow the same religious beliefs. Typically, a society would allow religious dissenters to practice their religion freely within their borders. It is a misconception that all people had to convert to one religion. Such strict rules would have interfered too much with trade relations. For instance, the Byzantines, as practicing Eastern Orthodox Catholics, allowed traders with other religious affiliations, like the Roman Catholics and Hindus, to trade inside of their cities while maintaining a firm belief in their church. The Islamic world dealt with religious dissenters as a taxable commodity. They allowed other religions to be worshiped freely, provided that they pay a special tax.

St. Maruthas, Bishop of Martyropolis in Mesopotamia, Eastern Orthodox Catholicism

These new governments were also loath to end the tradition of landowning elites. When the elite members of society-owned land, it was a two-fold benefit for the government. The government was only forced to regulate smaller portions of land that it owned directly, while the elite members of society were forced to pay for the upkeep of their territories. It also made the elite members of society less likely to interfere with the running of state-owned land, because they had their territory to contend with.

Several innovations were important during this era, however. Without some changes, these empires would die out as Rome and Alexandria had. Through innovation, they could continue to thrive. One of these innovations was the creation of new methods of taxation. In the ancient city of Rome, taxation was used for multiple reasons. Taxes could be levied to fund a war or to buy mercenaries.

Similarly, taxes could be levied on some different groups. They could be levied on animals of a particular kind of individuals living inside or outside of the empire. Taxes could even be levied on land that was owned by citizens. This type of taxation system was disliked by the people that it governed, which is one of the reasons that it was ineffective. People who disliked this taxation system might refuse to pay their taxes. This resulted in revolts that were expensive and time consuming to put down.

Instead, a new *system of taxation* was created. The Islamic countries instituted a single tax policy. They kept taxes on trades and customs but changed the way that taxes could be levied on their citizens. Taxes could only be issued on people and only adult males. This new Islamic system of taxes was much more effective than its predecessors. It was adopted all over the Empire and, after the fall of the Iberian Emirate, it was adopted into Western Europe.

Another adaptation that allowed these new governing systems to flourish where others had fallen was the creation of the *tributary system*. Tribute is money or goods paid by one party to another as a sign of respect. Typically, this was respect of their superior military or political position. Instead of attempting to control their territories through military force as the Romans had, new governments had to adapt to ways of maintaining control without losing their effectiveness as governing bodies. Tribute states would allow them to influence surrounding territories without having to become directly involved in their day to day ruling.

Tribute was also used in Western Europe where feudal serfs paid tribute to a protective lord. Similarly, vassals and peasants would often pay a tribute like a tax to make sure that they were given protection. Also, in Western Europe, citizens of the church were expected to pay a tithe based on their amount of income or production. This tithe was in support of the Roman Catholic Church and was a way to pay for the operation of church offices.

City-states emerged to sidestep the inefficiencies of centralized government.

City-states were a unique form of government that allowed for the control of larger territory. In Italy, the city-states were entrenched in Italian history. Most Italian city-states had their roots in pre-Roman civilization. Most had been founded even before the uniting of the Greeks and the creation of democracy. This meant that each of the city-states had histories with one another. This distinct culture and history meant that it was easier to allow the city-states to rule themselves than trying to bring them all under one centralized government. City-states also appeared in Africa at this time, in reaction to increased trade. Each of these port cities taxed the trade that came into them and, therefore, wanted to achieve the highest levels of trade for themselves to create the best chance at prosperity. This led to severe competition between the city-states to attract traders.

Some states synthesized local and borrowed traditions.

Many times, a new government might synthesize local cultural beliefs and integrate them into the governmental system as a way to ease the transition for newly conquered territories. Similarly, a territory that was exerting influence on another might be appeased if the territory adopted some of their cultural practices that they were attempting to exert control over. This might stop any further push for domination. A good example of the impact the local culture could have on a larger territory was the Persian influence on the Islamic world. While the Islamic world extended far outside the reach of the former Persian Empire, the Persians had served as one of the Islamic world's closest allies during their early years. This led to much cultural blending between the two powers.

Interregional contacts and conflicts between states and empires encouraged significant technological and cultural transfers.

French crossbowman

While most cultural diffusion took place over some years, using merchants and traders as its ambassadors, there were instances where the change occurred more rapidly. Typically, these rapid changes were the result of direct conflict between the two cultures. The way that a people wage war says a lot about their values system and society. Most civilizations wage war in unique ways. They use their unique weapons and surroundings to protect themselves as best they can.

In turn, when two cultures come into conflict, they must adapt and overcome the obstacles of the other culture's defenses. A good example of this would be the French crossbow as an answer to the deadly and accurate English longbow. While the French could not train longbowmen like the English, they could overcome this disadvantage by creating a weapon that could achieve a similar distance and striking power without years of training.

While these events were important, they came nowhere close to the impact of the Abbasid prisoners of war. During the fighting, the Arabs managed to capture several artisans, including Tou Houan, who knew how to make paper. This single instance changed the face of the Earth. While the Chinese had been making paper for years, this was the first time that the Western world had the same equipment. Within 500 years, paper making factories were spread from this eastern territory to Muslim-controlled Spain. From there, it spread quickly to the rest of Europe. Paper made possible a cultural advent for much of Europe. *Woodcut printing* allowed for the copying of pictures without artists recreating the images by hand. Books became less expensive without the cost associated with vellum sheets. This period was later known as the High Middle Ages and lasted until the Black Death came in the 1300s.

Innovations stimulated agricultural and industrial production in many regions.

Trade and population growth created a problem for many societies. They had to continue increasing the amount of food to provide for the increase in trade and to continue feeding the population. In some areas, the answer was simple, extend farmlands. However, in areas where farmland was limited due to population or environment, they had to adopt innovative and creative techniques to continue production. These innovations were often adopted by other cultures with similar problems as trade facilitated the increased spread of ideas.

Agricultural production increased significantly due to technological innovations.

Some of the most important innovations during this period were those that happened in agriculture. A society is only able to grow if it can produce enough food for its inhabitants. This means that innovation in agricultural practices would allow for faster growth in a society, for a society to become an urban center and for differentiation of trade and other products to become the focus of the society. To that end, several different innovations take place during the period that allowed the same end goal to be reached in very different ways.

An important innovation that happened at the beginning of the century was the development of the collar. While saddles had been developed to ride beasts of burden, the idea of using horses or camels to help with agricultural practices was predicated on a device that would allow them to comfortably pull forward against a structure that would not injure them. This was the basis for the development of the *beast collar harness*, which first allowed for a padded collar to be placed around the neck of a horse or camel. The horse or camel then had to walk forward slowly and could pull things behind it without injuring itself.

This opened up an entirely new world as far as agriculture was concerned because plows no longer had to be used by hand. Instead, a farmer could lead a horse forward and back down a field. This drastically increased production because the animal was stronger than a single farmer and could, therefore, do more work in the same amount of time. The earliest example of these collars appears in the 200s in China and eventually spread to Europe via the Middle East. They were introduced to Europe by the 900s, though they were not fully used there until the 1100s.

Another of these new agricultural innovations was called *terracing*. Terraces are human-made flat surfaces that are cut into the sides of hills, which allows for planting crops. This was used to increase the amount of arable land by utilizing previously ignored land on mountainsides where erosion, rocks, and slope previously caused problems. By building a terrace, a society could cut down on several of these problems because it became a set of flat landings, instead of an incline going up the mountain. Terraces were typically cut into a mountain in small inclines, almost like stairs. These stairs also changed the way that the land could be utilized by increasing water absorption and decreasing the amount of erosion done by wind and flowing water.

In response to increasing demand in Afro-Eurasia for foreign luxury goods, crops were transported from their indigenous homelands to equivalent climates in other regions.

One way to overcome the limitations of trade was to move the means of production elsewhere. As the desire for luxury items like tropical fruits, silk, and cotton increased, more stress was put on the original means of production in the home countries of these items. As far as food was concerned, the solution seemed easy. After all, many of the Eurasian countries had the same general climate because they are on the same lines of latitude. Therefore, foods that were in high demand, like bananas, could easily be uprooted and transplanted elsewhere, where a similar climate would allow them to continue flourishing.

The impact of this transportation of food was twofold. On the one hand, it was a way to diversify the products in a given area and to create new trade centers for specific luxury items. On the other hand, there was an ecological impact every time a new plant species was introduced into a particular environment. In many cases, the non-native species became an invasive species. An *invasive species* is a newly introduced species that takes over its new environment because of a lack of predators or natural counters. A good example of this is on the North American east coast, where the pine tree was introduced by Native Americans and became the dominant species because of its rate of growth. Invasive species can often upset an area's ecosystem, causing native plants and animals to die off.

Chinese, Persian, and Indian artisans and merchants expanded their production of textiles and porcelains for export.

While the Persians, Indians, and Chinese had been trading some luxury items like porcelain and silk for hundreds of years, this period saw the opening of Europe to these Asian influences. Several events encouraged trade to expand further into Western Europe. Pilgrimages to the holy cities of Jerusalem and Bethlehem became possible, which brought Christians into direct contact with many of the luxury items. The Crusades allowed more and more Europeans to witness the luxury items available to the rest of the world. This led to an increased demand in the market that the Chinese, Persian, and Indian artisans and merchants tried to fill. They typically tried to meet those needs by increasing the production of textiles and porcelain. China even sent silkworms to the Byzantine Empire, allowing for the Byzantines to begin production of silk as well, because the Chinese could no longer meet consumer demands.

The fate of cities varied greatly, with periods of significant decline, and with periods of increased urbanization buoyed by rising productivity and expanding trade networks.

With the large array of social, economic, and military changes occurring around the world, cultures, and civilizations during this period were quite unstable. Many cities fell into disrepair for some reasons: war, disease, natural disaster, or simply a city's inability to adapt to the times. Rome is considered to have lasted from roughly 500 B.C.E. to 500 C.E., eventually falling to the Huns. Athens fell into disrepair at this time, as did the city of Alexandria in Egypt. During this period, several cities fell because they were unable to compete for resources as effectively as emerging cultures like the Mongols and the Muslims. Although many cities were collapsing, technological advances made safer travel and better sanitation possible, which allowed for even greater populations and wealth in urban areas. The turbulence of this period is a result of the transition from somewhat isolated cities to a larger global network of trade and commerce.

Battle of Alexandria, Egypt

Multiple factors contributed to the decline of urban areas in this period.

There are four main reasons why cities fell into recessions and eventually disappeared. The first of these reasons is invasions. While some civilizations, like the Greek and the Roman, had been around for hundreds of years, other civilizations were only beginning to solidify their positions in the world. These new civilizations expanded their boundaries and created empires for themselves in the same way that the Greeks, the Romans, and the Egyptians had created empires hundreds of years before. With most areas under threat of invasion or suffering through the consequences of previous invasion attempts—successful or otherwise—maintaining civil order was difficult, and many cities collapsed.

The Islamic Nation, which was created by the Prophet Muhammad, expanded in the Middle East and created one of the largest unified territories during the age. The Mongols created one of the largest empires that were ever seen and changed the face of the Eurasian continent through conquest. The Vikings from the North began in Europe but soon extended their raiding into the Mediterranean. There, the Vikings caused several problems for established ports and their respective empires by quickly raiding port cities and ships. The Huns, like the Mongols, came out of the Eurasian Steppe, took over a significant portion of China and the surrounding territories, eventually expanding their raiding as far west as Rome. The Turks took control of the failing Byzantine Empire to create the Ottoman Empire, which lasted into the 20th century.

After invasions, the second most common problem which would cause a city to fall was a disease. Two major diseases became epidemics, killing large percentages of populations. The first disease was the Bubonic Plague, which was capable of killing a human, typically within two weeks of showing symptoms. There was no known cure, and societies had no way of containing the disease because they did not understand how the disease was spread. They blamed bad air and the alignment of the stars, when, in fact, the disease was spread from China to Europe and the Middle East by fleas that infested rats transported on trading vessels.

The Bubonic Plague is believed to be responsible for what the Byzantine Empire called the Plague of Justinian, which killed an estimated 25 million people in the 6th century. In the 14th century, it would be known as the Black Death and would kill somewhere between 75 and 200 million more people.

While the Plague was deadlier, the other major disease from this era, smallpox, did a significant amount of damage as well. In the early stages, it is spread typically by contact with infected fluids like spit or mucus or items that had come in contact with these infected fluids. Fabric, in particular, could preserve the disease until it could pass to another human host. Smallpox first appeared in Egypt.

In the earliest records, it is believed to have then traveled to Asia. At one point in the 700s, it transitioned to Japan, where it is said to have killed as much as one-third of the population of the island. It became entrenched in Europe primarily due to the Crusades, which allowed a large number of people to come into contact with the disease. By the 16th and 17th centuries, the disease had firmly entrenched inside European society. During the Age of Exploration, this disease would spread to all parts of the world, including the Americas, where it wiped out large numbers of Native Americans due to their lack of immunity.

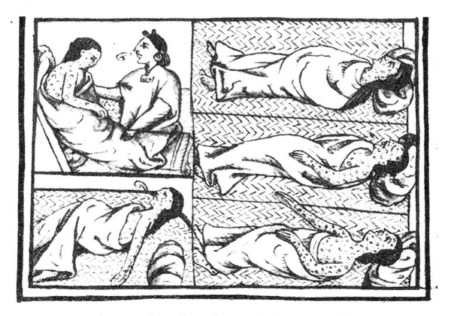

Infection of smallpox from a 16th-century folio

Another reason for the decline of urban areas during this period was a lack of agricultural productivity. Invasion and disease tended to result in smaller populations, which in

---

turn meant that there was a smaller population of farmers. Improvements to trade and travel had allowed urban centers to import food from more agriculturally inclined areas, but without a substantial farming population, there was not enough food to import. Likewise, in times of war, a city is often cut off from trade routes entirely. Therefore, in many situations, urban people were forced to either leave cities to find food or starve.

Harsh winters and global cooling led to a further decline in population. This was primarily because climate change had made the raising of staple livestock and production of some staple crops impossible. An example of this would be in England. Before the Little Ice Age, England was warm enough to sustain grapevines, which allowed people to make wine.

However, once the Little Ice Age struck, the English climate could not provide the necessary warmth and the grape crops were destroyed. Similarly, although citrus plants, cotton, and silk were able to grow in a variety of environments, many of the areas in which they had traditionally grown were no longer capable of cultivating them. The Little Ice Age disrupted trade and agriculture, leading to smaller populations.

Multiple factors contributed to urban revival: the end of invasions, the availability of safe and reliable transport, the rise of commerce and the warmer temperatures between 800 and 1300, increased agricultural productivity and subsequent rising population, greater availability of labor also contributed to urban growth.

Eventually, many factors would contribute to the regrowth of urban areas as centers of civilizations and life. The imperial and expansionist policies of many groups during this period lead to constant invasions and social instability, but as these cultures developed and solidified their global roles, stability returned to urban areas. These more sophisticated civilizations established urban areas as centers of trade, with the law, commerce, and innovative technologies.

For example, having built a powerful and large empire, the Abbasid Caliphate of the Islamic Nation needed a capital city and decided to build one along the Tigris River. Baghdad, the city they constructed, was soon a capital for not only the nation but also commerce and education. A different example would be the founding and success of Istanbul. When the Turks finally took the city of Constantinople, destroying the Byzantine Empire, they founded their own Ottoman Empire in its stead. Once the new empire was established, the area returned to peace and was allowed to recuperate as a center of commerce and trade.

The development of a global market and advances in trade between civilizations was another factor in the resurgence of urban areas during this time. The technology was making transportation and travel safer. Items like the compass and astrolabe allowed merchants to ship goods faster and more successfully. Saddles for camels allowed merchants in more arid areas to move more goods through desert routes.

The saddles gave traders a more defensible position on their camels, in case they were attacked by bandits, who were becoming more common as trade increased. Similarly, pirates and Vikings were an issue when traveling on water. However, once a civilization established themselves in an area, they often protected trade. An excellent example of this would be the peace that pervaded the Eurasian continent while the Mongols were in charge of their empire. The Mongols reestablished trade routes, like the Silk Road, which they policed in an effort to improve trade. They were incredibly successful, and the Silk Road saw an increase in activity, which the Mongols were able to tax, benefitting both the merchant class and the empire.

Norman pirates in the 9th century

Another positive impact on population and city growth was the period immediately before the Little Ice Age. Before the Little Ice Age, there was a rise in temperature; this warming period also contributed to an increase in trade by allowing traders to travel in areas where conditions were normally too harsh. The increased temperature and relatively peaceful times also lead to more farms being created, high crop yields, and surpluses of food. Food surpluses allow population expansion and the diversification of economies. With more people, food, and available jobs, urban centers were once again able to thrive and support large populations.

While cities, in general, continued to play the roles they had played in the past as governmental, religious, and commercial centers, many older cities declined at the same time that numerous new cities emerged to take on these established roles.

Global politics at this time were becoming increasingly complex as numerous civilizations grew and progressed simultaneously. While these societies advanced, others were struggling to maintain their previous status. As the empires of the period became larger, the world effectively became smaller. The cities founded by emerging and developed nations would rapidly shift, both in status as urban centers and between the nations that claimed them.

For example, Constantinople was the capital of the massive Roman Empire, which dissolved into two smaller empires in 395 C.E. These two empires, the Byzantine in the east and the Western Roman Empire in the west were both less formidable than the Roman Empire had been. Eventually, growing groups of Muslims and Persians began to take Byzantine land, and the Byzantine Empire asked for Western Rome's help in repelling the invaders. This led to the Crusades. However, by the Fourth Crusade, Western Rome turned on the Byzantines and sacked the Byzantine capital, Constantinople. The weakened Constantinople would be overrun by Turks and renamed Istanbul, the new capital of the Ottoman Empire.

Although the city of Constantinople existed as a capital in three separate empires, it held very different status in each, depending on the strength of the empire it was associated with at the time. Trade, technology, and military might have made global politics increasingly fluid and complex. Although cities, in general, maintained the same social roles, the specifics of which cities were prominent were highly contested as different civilizations; all pushed to have the most influence.

It is important to note that these rapid changes were not all happening at once. They also were not happening in the same place. As an empire flourished in the Middle East, it might be another one in China that was ending. These events were not predicated on being in the same place at the same time, though in a few very famous instances, it did happen in the same place. This meant that cities continued to play the same roles as they had in the past. They were governmental authorities that maintained peace, order, and stability. They were centers for religion and knowledge, typically through church offices. They were also centers of commerce, where people would gather to exchange goods, knowledge, ideas, and luxury items.

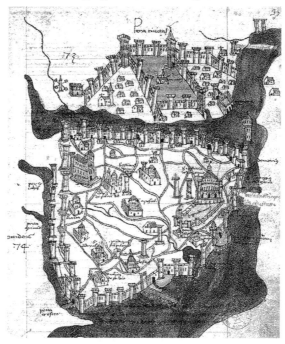

Map of Constantinople (1422)

However, as a city stumbled or started to decline, others quickly rose to take their place. This is seen in all parts of the world. For example, as the position of the Eastern Orthodox Church became tenuous due to pressure from the Roman Catholics and invading empires from Persia, Constantinople fell, and Istanbul replaced it. While this city is technically the same, it is important to think of them as two different organisms.

One was a city held by the Eastern Orthodox Church; the other is a Muslim Turkish city. This is meant to illustrate that sometimes the death of a city and the birth of a new city might happen in the same places. This was important for the people of the city because while the governments changed, the city itself did not. Many individuals who had been living in the city remained. To them very little had changed. They saw life continuing as it always had, even though, historically, a major shift had taken place.

Despite significant continuities in social structures and methods of production, there were also some important changes in labor management and the effect of religious conversion on gender relations and family life.

Over the period, there were some important changes to the social structure and methods of production. Advances in technology had allowed for larger populations and diversification of employment. New groups like artisans and merchants existed. Merchants were particularly important because they were a new *middle class*, existing in the socio-economic space between peasants and the leaders of civilization. The introduction of more fluid class stratification and increased efficiency in production lead to booming economies, and somewhat lessened the grip of the ruling class on social matters. Similarly, religion had a large impact on the era, particularly the changes in Christian power structures and the rise of the Muslim nation.

As in the previous period, there were many forms of labor organization: free peasant agriculture, nomadic pastoralism, craft production and guild organization, various forms of coerced and unfree labor, government-imposed labor taxes, military obligations.

This period was characterized by diversification of labor organization and management, resulting in a few new forms of labor and the continuation of others. One newly established group and form of labor were the lower class. These people are known as *peasants*. They would engage in *free peasant agriculture* or farming for the benefit of a town or city, often in exchange for being able to live in the town or city. This group represented the majority of the population. The word "peasant" comes from the French word for the countryside, which was used to name this group because that is where they were from. They were typically farmers on small farms. They also typically disliked the upper class for maintaining an amount of wealth that they could not hope ever to achieve. This led to resentment of those in power and, eventually, revolts against that power.

Another established labor group was the *nomadic pastoralists*. These were essentially herders and might be likened to present-day ranchers. Like peasants, they were of the lower class but did not have access to land that was arable, which meant that they could not engage in agriculture. Instead, they would have a flock of animals that they would follow around, typically moving them from one pasture to another as resources became diminished due to grazing. Their movements were also dependent upon the season: typically moving north in the summer when the lands in the North were green and then south again in the winter. This was, of course, reversed for those in the Southern Hemisphere.

Nomads were also warriors or had warriors as part of their social order in the event of a conflict with another tribe or group of people. Because they were so mobile, they often had to protect themselves from those who thought to take their animals. They were able to travel large distances over the course of a year, though not as much as traders or merchants might. Some animals could be considered for the pastoral lifestyle, not just cattle, sheep, and goats, but also horses and yaks. Camels were the animal of choice in the desert climates in the Middle East. Reindeer was one of the few animals that could survive the harsh winters of the Far North.

Another group of organized labor that changed this period was known as a *guild*. Guilds are a group of craftsmen who are all dedicated to a similar trade, so a guild would emerge when numerous people engaged in the same trade in the same area. Tanners had a guild, as did carpenters. Guilds were originally organized like a trade union or a secret society. They regulated both the means of production and the price that was charged for a good at the market. They also regulated the quality of goods by making sure that no one could enter the market in a particular craft unless he or she was part of the guild, and therefore subject to the guild for regulation.

Metal manufacturing guild

Guilds were typically made up of masters in the craft. A master would take on apprentices who would then work underneath that master until they became journeymen. A journeyman was above an apprentice level. They were someone trusted inside of the guild to be able to produce quality work. While an apprentice might assist a master or journeyman, it was unlikely that their work would ever see a market. A journeyman, however, was skilled enough to make and sell goods for public consumption.

Once they were made a journeyman, an artisan would begin working on what was known as their masterpiece. This is the piece that they would have to create and presents to the guild heads to get recognized as a master. Once they became a master, they could open their own shop, take their own apprentices, and go into business for themselves. Being a master was more lucrative than becoming a journeyman, but not all of those taken as apprentices were guaranteed to make it that far. Most people that entered a guild never became masters. Guilds were very widespread, and most major trade cities, like London, Paris, Venice, and Baghdad, would have some guilds—sometimes several hundred.

Not all labor was voluntary, however. A significant amount of coerced labor also characterized this period. There are two very important examples of coerced labor from this time. One comes from both Europe and Japan and is known as *serfdom*. Serfdom was part of the feudal systems of Europe and Japan during this time. Under the feudal system, the lower class or agricultural serfs were tied to the land they worked on.

This meant that although they were not slaves, they were not free to leave the land they worked or to pursue other jobs. *Serfs* were the lowest class in the feudal society and worked a specific plot of land owned by a lord. The lord's duty was to protect his serfs from other people who might wish to take their land or harass them in some manner. In return for this protection, the serfs paid taxes to the lord at every harvest, thus supplying the lord with food for his family and castle.

Taxes existed well before the invention of coins and paper money. In the original sense, taxes were a collection of part of someone's agricultural products for the year. For those living in ancient Babylon, each farmer might be forced to give ten bushels of wheat to the city every year as a form of tribute. Of course, the main reason for a lord to engage in feudalism was to tax serfs as a way to guarantee food through taxes. As paper money and coins became the way to do business, taxes began to change as well. Medieval taxes were paid to the ruling class: the king of an area or ruler in some way. Often taxes were paid on land or as customs.

Babylon

The idea of income tax and property tax came significantly later. At this period, there had to be an event occurring that would be the occasion for taxing someone. For instance, if a merchant was from Venice selling goods in the Byzantine Empire, every time he traded or sold an item, he owed a certain percentage of that trade to the Byzantines. This was known as a *customs tax*. Similarly, traders entering a city might pay a tax at the gate that would regulate their movement into and out of the city. This tax served two purposes. First, it kept most criminals and the poor out of the city. If a person was willing and able to pay the tax to enter the city, they were probably there for legitimate reasons. Second, the city provided a safe area for commerce and trade, so the tax functioned as payment for that service.

As in the previous period, social structures were shaped largely by class and caste hierarchies. Patriarchy persisted; however, in some areas, women exercised more power and influence, most notably among the Mongols and in West Africa, Japan, and Southeast Asia.

Despite changes that were happening in most of the world, this period was also characterized largely by the class and caste system hierarchies that had determined social order and positioning for hundreds of years. Some of the class systems and hierarchies were new and changed the way things had been done, but several older systems made resurgences during this period, and their antiquated ideas impacted the new social systems.

Feudalism was a new form of social structure with a king as the head of society. Underneath the king were his advisors; typically, this group included only members of the nobility. In Christian societies, in particular, members of the clergy who held a high rank might also be included. Underneath the nobility was an emerging merchant class, the beginning of the middle class.

The merchant class bridged the divide between the lower and upper classes in a way that made the upper class very uncomfortable. This was because all early merchants had been peasants at one point, and as they became wealthier, much of the nobility felt that their position in the social structure was being threatened. Social mobility jeopardized the power of the nobles because it potentially allowed for a more fluid and dynamic power structure; one where status and power were not permanent.

Underneath the merchant class was the peasants. These were free people who were able to move around as they so desired, though they typically stayed in cities or small towns. The serfs, who were below the peasants, were almost a slave class. Though they were not characterized as slaves at the time and are not considered that way now, serfs were tied to the land and unable to leave it.

This restriction on movement certainly classified their situation as a form of coerced labor. Serfs worked for a lord: a member of the nobility who owned land. Under that lord would be a hierarchy of less noble citizens. The lord would have lower nobles and knights fight for him if the need arose. He would essentially be the king of a small area, with the actual king serving as the overlord of the nation.

New forms of coerced labor appeared, including serfdom in Europe and Japan and the elaboration of the *mit'a* in the Inca Empire. Free peasants resisted attempts to raise dues and taxes by staging revolts. The demand for slaves for both military and domestic purposes increased, particularly in central Eurasia, parts of Africa and the eastern Mediterranean.

New forms of coerced labor characterize this period: serfdom, where individuals were tied to the land and expected to work it, though they were not characterized as slaves, and *mit'a* in the Incan Empire, which required entire towns to pay tribute to the Incans, typically through the forced labor community projects.

It is important to note that neither of these forms of coerced labor was slavery. They were not characterized that way at the time, and there were ways to escape these forms of labor.

A serf who could escape and live inside of a city for a year and a day was granted his freedom, meaning that he became a peasant instead of a serf. Typically, these institutions were seen as agreements, and while the labor was coerced, in that it was felt that it was owed to the higher power, it was not considered slavery.

The diffusion of religion often led to significant changes in gender relations and family structure.

The changes in religion also resulted in changes in gender roles and family structure. In particular, the role of women was changing. In many societies, women had typically been seen as the weaker sex. They had fewer rights and less responsibility than men. Among the ruling classes, women were typically viewed as chess pieces that could be married off for strategic advantage.

However, among the lower classes, women often worked alongside their husbands. Though they could not technically own businesses or enter guilds as masters, many of them still worked in the fields. As the merchant class began to emerge, the idea of women merchants came into being. With the peasant ideology that women needed to work alongside their husbands to help him prosper, it made sense to the lower classes that a merchant's wife would work in the same trade. As these ideas spread, with women taking a place in the new merchant class, each of the religions had to identify a central ideology for how they intended to view women.

Thus, each religion changed the way their people understood gender and family. Christianity, with its new convents, was breaking the cycle of marriage and birth by allowing women a way to escape their family roles and duties. A woman who no longer wanted to remain married to her husband, or who was seeking a way to escape a marriage to a husband she found distasteful, might escape to a convent for sanctuary. In Islam, the overshadowing of the religion by Persian traditions led to a breakdown of society. Women were suddenly offered fewer rights and less respect due to the dispersion of Persian traditions. Women became a segregated portion of the population, with less influence than in previous generations. The veiling and seclusion meant that women were limited to their family roles and barred from influencing the outside world.

Notes for active learning

Europe

Major historical events of the period:

540: First outbreak of the Bubonic Plague in Europe

711–788: The Umayyad Caliphate conquers most of the Iberian Peninsula

790–1066: The Viking Age

1096: First crusader invasion

1099: Jerusalem falls to crusaders

1200–1300: Firearms came to the Ottoman, Safavid and Mughal empires from China

1204: Crusaders invade Byzantium

1269–1293: Marco Polo leaves Venice and travels to and from China

1300–1400: Black Death (the Bubonic Plague) spreads throughout Europe

1358: The Hanseatic League is established

1400s.: The Renaissance begins in Italy

1453: Constantinople falls to the Turks

PERIOD 2: 500 to 1500 C.E.

EUROPE

Novgorod, Venitian, and Byzantine trade thrived.

In Russia, the trade capital was Novgorod. Novgorod was both an economic and cultural capital of the region, on a par with the powerful city of Kiev (the capital of modern Ukraine). Novgorod, at its peak in the 1300s, existed as an independent republic, stretching across Northern Russia to the Ural Mountains with a population of over 400,000. The city was ruled by a group of popularly elected politicians called a *veche*. This group was supposed to serve as a balance to the aristocracy but was dysfunctional and eventually lost power.

Novgorod served as one of the four major trade cities in the Hanseatic League. The other three were located along the trade route, moving from Novgorod to the West: Bergen in Norway, Bruges in Belgium, and London in England. The city specialized in specific items. German merchants brought animal furs and skins, wax, and honey. Cloth and metals came from the European mainland and were traded for corn from central Russia. In the East, trade with Central Asia flourished, and the city served as a meeting point for the East and West.

Venice served as the premier trading hub for Europe, mainly due to its position on the Adriatic Sea. It was a point of connection to Europe, but it was close enough that traders from the Middle East could make the trip with relative ease. The city flourished, especially in the 11th century. The Normans, a group of conquering Vikings from the North, arrived in the Adriatic Sea at the start of the century and quickly became a problem for the Byzantines by capturing important port cities.

The Byzantine Empire, in turn, reached out to the Venetians with a proposal whereby the Byzantine Empire would forgo all Venetian dues or customs in exchange for helping defend against the Normans. Essentially, this allowed Venetian merchants to trade for free in all Byzantine cities. Eager to take advantage of the deal, the Venetians readily agreed and worked with the Byzantines to protect their ports against Viking raids.

At the end of the century, the city's power increased again. The First Crusade began in 1096, with Christians fighting to regain their holy lands from the Muslims. Venice was perfectly placed to transport the troops and supplies needed for the Crusade. When Jerusalem was successfully reclaimed in 1099, it continued to facilitate travel from Europe as many Christians made pilgrimages to the holy city. As people from Europe traveled east in ever-increasing numbers, Venice was also contracted to begin providing the luxuries of the East to Europeans returning to the West. This economic prosperity gave rise to several competitors from rival Italian city-states like Pisa, but Venice would remain a strong competitor over the next several centuries.

Hanseatic League emerged as the dominant North Sea and Baltic Sea trade organization.

One of the most famous and longest-lasting trade organizations was the Hanseatic League. The Hansa started as an agreement between guilds in two different German cities: the salt mines in Hamburg and the herring fishermen in Lubeck. Both of these cities are ports that had a faster system of trading than going overland. Sea travel, however, had the added risk of attracting pirates or Vikings. Thus, the League, as it expanded, promised protection as well as prosperity. The League eventually encompassed a wide range of rivers and seaports connected by the North Sea, the Baltic Sea and the English Channel. These included Novgorod in Russia, Bergen in Norway, Brugge in France, and London in England. While the League no longer exists, its impact can still be seen. An excellent example of this is the German-based Airline Lufthansa or Air Hansa.

The expansion of empires facilitated Trans-Eurasian trade and communication as new peoples were drawn into their conquerors' economies and trade networks.

The development of empires changed the course of civilization. An *empire* is a collection of cities or countries under the control of a single ruler, typically a single person. Perhaps the best-known empire in the West was the Roman Empire, which conquered land as far north as England and as far west as the Persian Gulf. At its peak, it was estimated to control over 70 million people. It was by no means the only empire, however, and trans-Eurasian trade saw the rise of four incredibly powerful empires.

One of the most important trans-Eurasian empires was built from the proverbial ashes of the Roman Empire. The Roman Empire, at its peak, took an incredible amount of power to rule; it is not surprising that it broke apart into several smaller areas ruled by different people. Historians consider the east-west split of the Roman Empire as the start of a new empire. However, it is important to note that the people of the Byzantine Empire, or the eastern half of the Roman Empire, viewed themselves as Romans and continued to call their empire the Roman Empire. It was only later that historians renamed the empire after Byzantium, the city that Constantine I chose for his capital, moving it from Rome. This city would be renamed Constantinople in his honor. However, it did not separate from the western part of the empire until after Constantine I.

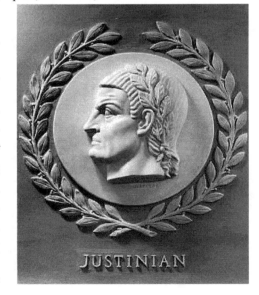

Justinian I, Byzantine emperor

In 395 C.E., Theodosius I split the empire between his two sons. The East managed to outlast the West, mostly because the eastern kingdom was willing to pay tribute to Attila the Hun, who moved on to the West and sacked the capital city of Rome. As the western half of the formerly united empire continued to destabilize under constant attacks from the Germanic Tribes, the eastern half flourished and achieved military and monetary success.

Perhaps the most famous Byzantine Emperor was Justinian I, who was responsible for the reclamation of much of the former Roman Empire. His military success funded some cultural feats in the empire, including the rewriting of the laws into a Code of Civil Laws, often called the Code of Justinian. These laws eventually became the basis of all civil law in Europe. He also commissioned the Hagia Sophia, a church that served as the focal point for the Eastern Orthodox Catholic Church. He was later named a saint for his contributions to Christianity. Justinian was also famous, in part, for his wife, Empress Theodora, who ruled the empire at his side. Unfortunately, the first known outbreak of the Bubonic Plague in the West (the so-called Justinian Plague) led to the first decline of the empire.

Despite the decline at the end of Justinian's rule, the Byzantine Empire persisted into the 15th century—not an easy feat by any means. Germanic Tribes from the North were a constant threat. Muslims in the West also gained control of much of the Empire. This led to the Byzantine Emperor reaching out to the Pope in Rome for aid. The Pope, in turn, started the first Crusade. While the early Crusades were helpful to the Byzantines because they allowed for pushback against the Muslims, later Crusades, like the Fourth Crusades, were failures and resulted in the ransacking of Constantinople, a Christian city, by the Crusaders themselves.

In 1204, Crusaders entered and looted the city, claiming that even though the Byzantines were Christians, they disrespected the Pope in Rome and were, therefore, the enemy of the Roman Catholic faith. While the Byzantines later reclaimed it, the empire never recovered the loss of their wealth and cultural items. Constantinople fell decisively in 1453 and was renamed Istanbul by the Turks. Splinters of the empire attempted to form throughout its decline, but with little success.

Inhospitable environmental conditions propelled Scandinavians overseas.

Transportation is one of the most common technological adaptations and can differ greatly depending on the environment and the people. The Vikings lived in the Far North near the Arctic Circle where most of the land was not suited to farming. Their environment was inhospitable due to the cold. This meant that land routes were dangerous because they meant exposure to the elements for extended periods. It also meant that animal life was scarce, and food had to be procured through alternative methods.

To circumnavigate these issues, the Vikings developed and perfected boats. They used the longship to travel from place to place. It allowed for fishing, which provided food. The Vikings realized that they were also able to use the boats to explore. This led to pillaging and raiding as far south as the Mediterranean. Many used the longboats to find more hospitable homes, like the Normans, who settled in what is present-day Normandy in France.

Vikings

Marco Polo traveled the Silk Road and returned with foreign accounts.

Marco Polo was another well-traveled man who told of his travels to inspire others. His *Book of the Marvels of the World* was said to have inspired some adventurers, including Christopher Columbus. His story began with his birth in Venice, Italy. His father and uncle left before he was born and did not return until he was in his late teens. They worked as merchants and traveled well into Asia, where Polo writes they met the Great Kublai Khan, who had never met Europeans and tasked them with a message for the Pope.

Marco Polo, Italian explorer

Years later, after several delays, Marco Polo, his uncle, and his father set off to finish his father's promise to the Great Khan and bring him letters from the Pope as well as the blessed oil and lamp he requested from Jerusalem. Upon their return to the court, they were very close with the Khan, who refused their requests to allow them to return home. From Marco Polo's text, it does not appear that they were captives, by any means. Many people suspect they may have served as political officers of some kind, as he often recounts trips to areas of the empire.

Eventually, they were allowed to leave with a wedding party headed to the Persian Khanate of Kublai Khan's nephew. From there, they traveled to Venice, which was at war. While in jail after capture, Polo recounted his journey to a fellow prisoner. Many people have claimed that Polo's account is false, claiming that it does not mention much of Chinese culture, such as foot binding. Others defend the text, however, noting the mentions of paper money and salt mining that are accurate for the period. They also point out that Polo was in Khan's court, where practices like foot-binding never became popular. It is also possible that Polo doctored his own story to avoid any cultural practices which would make the Europeans scoff at the Chinese, whom he greatly respected.

As the Eurasian peoples interacted, so did their literary, artistic, and cultural traditions. These were spread primarily as religion spread because so much of early culture was based on religious ideology, the uniting factor for most regions. As these religions interacted through trade and travel, people were exposed to art and literature that was new or different in some way.

A plague-ravaged Europe reacts to its trauma.

The Black Death's impact on Western Europe cannot be overstated. The death toll alone was in the millions. It is estimated that one-third of Europe's population was killed. In some places, like some parts of England, it was as high as two-thirds of the population. Because the disease was so widespread, it infiltrated all aspects of life. Religion and medicine were useless to stop the spread, causing some to forgo their faith and others to become near-fanatical, blaming outsiders like Jews for the wrath of God.

There are reports from the period of entire families of Jews being burned alive in their homes as punishment. Royalty retreated into their castles in hopes of remaining uninfected. This led to the destruction of most political systems for the duration of the plague. Farmers were needed more than ever to feed the people because as the population dwindled drastically, so did access to markets with fresh food. This led to a consolidation of people into cities and an end to the feudal system, as the serfs now controlled the means of production, and a middle class developed.

Dance of Death:
the Burgomaster and Death

Not even the fine arts could escape the Black Death's influence. A new fascination with death and life infected all aspects of creative thought. Artists created pictorial representations of Death as an entity. These images gave rise to the Grim Reaper iconography of the modern period. The creation of new genres like the *Danse Macabre* also changed the fine arts. The *Danse Macabre* or *Dance of Death* shows death as a "live" skeleton summoning the souls of those who must die.

It is most often seen as a motif in painting, but in literature, authors created several verbal *Danse Macabre* in the form of dialogues between Death and his victims. Songs and poems with plague prevention advice also became popular. The children's nursery rhyme "Ring around the Rosy" dates from this period and details advice on avoiding the plague, like stuffing your pockets with herbs or "posy" to ward off the bad air.

The Crusades shaped Christendom.

The Crusades serve as an example of a single instance of interaction, drastically changing the course of a specific culture. The Crusades started because a group of Turks took hold of a portion of the Holy Lands. The leaders of Constantinople saw the growth of these Turkish conquests and feared for the safety of their city. They called upon the Pope in Rome with the hope that he would be able to convince the western European monarchs to send aid.

This was important because Constantinople was Eastern Orthodox Catholic and not Roman Catholic, which meant that the Pope was not their religious leader. The Pope saw the advantage that answering this call might give him, hopeful that he could bring the Eastern Orthodox people under Roman Catholic rule if he provided aid. He called on the western Europeans to go on a holy pilgrimage to the city of Jerusalem, the place where Jesus Christ, the Christian's Son of God, was killed.

It is important to note that Christians did not have a concept of a holy war in the same way that Islam did. Christians, instead, were convinced to go on the Crusades because they were pilgrimages to holy sites with fighting on the way. While the First Crusade was a success at taking the city of Jerusalem and turning it into a Latin Christian center, the following Crusades were often considered failures because they did not achieve the end goal of establishing a Latin Catholic political power in the Middle East. Instead, the real impact of the Crusades was on religion and interactions between religions. The Christian faith was reinforced by the participation in these pilgrimages to the East, and it created a renewed interest in understanding the origins of the religion.

Crusader

Similarly, the conflicts between the Christian Crusaders and a range of different groups redefined what a *crusade* actually was. The definition changed from the original crusade, which was a holy pilgrimage to Jerusalem into a war that was fought on behalf of the Roman Catholic Church against any enemy of the church. During the Fourth Crusade, this even included other members of the Christian faith. Eastern Orthodox Catholics did not respect the Pope in Rome and were therefore considered enemies of the crusaders. This led to the sack of the city of Constantinople during the

Fourth Crusade, which, like the Battle of the Talas River, created a power vacuum in the Middle East, which was eventually filled by the Ottoman Turks as Constantinople never regained its full power after being sacked.

The Byzantine religion shifted.

The population was moving away from the Eastern Orthodox Christianity of the Byzantines and toward the Roman Catholic faith, which had established a system of patriarchy. The Catholic Church would eventually create convents where women, called nuns, could study the faith; but these women were still not allowed any power within the religious hierarchy.

Free peasants resisted attempts to raise dues and taxes by staging revolts.

This period was also characterized by rebellion. There were three important examples of peasants rising against the hierarchy. In the Byzantine Empire, there was a revolt in the 10th century started by a man named Basil the Copper Hand. Basil had impersonated a dead general to take power and had received punishment in the form of his hand being chopped off in Constantinople. He crafted, or more likely commissioned, a copper prosthetic hand. After this, he intended to raise a peasant militia to march on Constantinople to gain revenge against those that had punished him. This was quickly noticed by the leaders in the Byzantine Empire, who sent the Byzantine army to deal with him. He was quickly caught and burned at the stake in Constantinople, as an example to others who might try to emulate him.

In Europe, the peasant revolts in Flanders are perhaps among the best examples of rebellion. In 1320 C.E., there was an increase in taxes, which led to several small revolts. While none of these revolts were important in themselves, they evolved into a rebellion that lasted five years. When it became obvious that this was not going to be quelled easily, King Charles IV of France became involved, and a treaty was signed to bring the fighting to an end. The peasants did not honor the treaty because King Charles IV died and was succeeded by Philip VI. In the end, it was not until they were decisively defeated in battle that the peasants disbanded.

Edward III of England pays homage to Philip VI of France

Christianity offered women a limited role in the Church.

Christianity had a difficult time defining the role of women in that culture. Many women had been important in the creation and the spread of the religion but were not in positions of power. When the religion spread throughout the Roman Empire, in particular, it was typically spread from house to house, with meetings taking place around dinner tables.

In this informal setting, women had taken more prominent roles in decision making and planning. This was further supported by the iconography that developed around the Virgin Mary, Jesus' mother, and Mary Magdalene, whom he cleansed of devils. These women were partial founders of the religion and posed a real problem to the Church in Rome. Women could not be ignored, but the attitudes toward women also meant that they could never become teachers or leaders in the Church.

Artwork from Mont Sainte-Odile, a convent in France

A compromise was established with the creation of convents, places where women, called *nuns*, could worship and study their religion, like monks in their monasteries. Nuns were valued for their contributions to the religion but separated from the daily life of most people. *Convents*, as they began to appear, also gave women a way out of the cycle of marriage and childbirth and began to allow women access to the literacy and education they might have been otherwise barred from.

Notes for active learning

Notes for active learning

Major historical events of the period:

500: Bantu-speaking peoples reach modern-day South Africa

500s: Swahili spreads from coastal Kenya to the north coast of Mozambique

1100: The major trading center Timbuktu is founded in northwest Africa on the edge of the Sahara Desert

1325: Ibn Battuta embarks on first hajj journey to Mecca and the lands beyond

PERIOD 2: 500 to 1500 C.E.

AFRICA

Timbuktu and East African city-states provided crucial trade hubs.

In Northwest Africa, the major trade city was Timbuktu. Founded around 1100 C.E. by the Tuareg people, the city was supposedly named for an old woman who was tasked with overseeing the camp while her tribe roamed. The camp was uniquely located at the edge of the Sahara Desert, between the desert and the Niger River. This meant that it was positioned to receive trade from a variety of places and peoples, those who had adapted to trading along the river from city to city and those who had adapted to the harsh conditions in the Saharan Desert.

The city flourished over the next 300 years and became a cultural site as well as an economic site. Economically, it was the center of African gold and salt trades. Culturally, it soon became a major center for the Islamic faith. Three of the oldest African Mosques exist within the city, and they drew some devout scholars. By 1450 the city's population was about 100,000. It is estimated that as much as 25 percent of the population at that time were scholars. The city prospered for several years, but it was not the only African territory to do so.

Postcard of Djingereber Mosque in Timbuktu

The Swahili city-states on the Eastern coast of Africa were also considered vitally important trade centers. These city-states were on the Indian Ocean, which opened them to sea-based trade with a variety of regions. Sailors learned to harness the monsoon winds to take them from Africa to the East. There, they would pick up pottery from China or cloth and spices from India. Once they had a full cargo, they would utilize monsoon winds in the opposite direction. In Africa, they could travel to the port cities and trade the items for gold, ivory, or slaves.

The migration of Bantu-speaking peoples who facilitated the transmission of iron technologies and agricultural techniques in Sub-Saharan Africa.

When the Bantu speaking people from Northwestern Africa began to migrate to the South, it was probably in reaction to a need for grazing land. Archeological evidence shows that these people were pastoral and agricultural long before their surrounding neighbors, who were still hunters and gatherers. Assumedly, the Bantu migration had an immediate impact on the surrounding areas. As the Bantu pushed south over some decades, they would have interacted with local tribes. These tribes would have seen the technology used by the Bantu and recognized the potential applications in their own culture. They might even have been taught directly by the Bantu people. Thus, iron technology and farming methods would come to reflect the common knowledge shared by these groups.

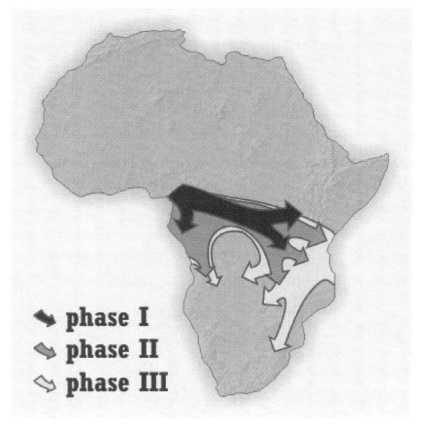

Bantu migration pattern

The Swahili language developed to facilitate trade.

For example, Swahili originated in Zanzibar, where the Bantu and Arabic languages collided. Both languages were important for trade in the region, and most traders would need to be fluent in both. This eventually led to the creation of a language that encompassed rules from both. Thus, Swahili could serve as a bridge, allowing for communication with Bantu and Arabic speakers without fluency in either language.

Muslim and Chinese diasporic communities exerted influence in South and Southeast Asia.

As a people, they were major players in the Indian Ocean trade markets, which led to contact with others, including Africans, who were often kidnapped and enslaved in India. Slavery in India was different from slavery in the Americas. Africans were not used on plantations, but rather as an exotic status symbol. They were often servants or bodyguards. Many Africans were already converted to the Islamic faith when they were taken, which meant that the Islamic faith was able to penetrate deeper into the Indian subcontinent than any other empire.

Ibn Battuta brought a global perspective back to Morocco.

Perhaps the most well-traveled explorer was Ibn Battuta, who is estimated to have traveled over 75,000 miles during his journeys. Born in Morocco to Islamic parents in 1304, his travels started as his traditional *hajj* to Mecca. Instead of taking the most direct route from Morocco, he chose to go through Egypt and Damascus, eventually traveling via Syria to Mecca. Once his *hajj* was complete, he decided to continue traveling instead of returning home. He chose the Mongol Ilkhanate for his next destination and continued to travel across much of Eurasia for the next twenty-five years. He claimed to have visited China, India, and several areas in Africa.

Ibn Battuta arrives in Egypt

Upon returning home and surviving several outbreaks of the Bubonic Plague, Battuta told his story to a scholar who wrote it down for posterity. The validity of the text is often questioned, as Ibn Battuta did not write down accounts of his travels as they occurred and spoke only from memory. This led to his biographer stealing several passages from other texts of the time. While the validity of these claims is questionable, they do paint a picture of how Battuta's people viewed the rest of the world. He admits several times to culture shock when witnessing other cultural practices, like the freedom of women in the Mongol Khanates and the too-revealing clothing styles of the sub-Saharan African Tribes.

Notes for active learning

Southwest Asia

Major historical events of the period:

570:    The Islamic prophet Muhammed is born in Mecca

632:    The Rashidun Caliphate emerges after the Prophet Muhammed's death

751:    The Battle of the Talas River results in an Abbasid Muslim victory over Tang Chinese forces

1096:   First crusader invasion

1099:   Jerusalem falls to crusaders

1258:   Baghdad is sacked by the Mongols

PERIOD 2: 500 to 1500 C.E.

SOUTHWEST ASIA

The central location of Baghdad linked East and West.

Baghdad, the current capital of Iraq, also took advantage of its positioning on several trade routes to prosper into a bustling economic center during the Middle Ages. Not only was the city on the Tigris River, but it was also close to the center of Mesopotamia, making it a good meeting place for caravans on the way to Khorasan in the East. At its peak in the 800s, the city boasted a population of between 300,000 and 500,000 people. This made it the second-largest city in the Middle East after Constantinople.

Baghdad was a major center of economic trade with a focus on leather, paper and cloth, and a center of academic knowledge and learning. After the fall of Rome, Baghdad and several other Middle Eastern and African cities became the premier centers of Western knowledge, preserving Greek and Roman culture. Scholars and academics from all over the region and beyond traveled to Baghdad's famous Bayt al-Hikma Academy to study. The city flourished until the 1200s when the Mongols raided it. While it still exists, it never regained its position in the modern world.

Caliphates solidified the Islamic world and expanded faith's reach.

In the Middle East, one of the most important empires of the period was created, the Islamic world led by the Islamic Caliphates. To understand the Islamic Caliphates, one must first understand the religion of Islam that gave rise to these empires. The religion of Islam started with a man named Mohammed from Mecca. Mohammed was a merchant in Mecca for some years. As a merchant, he was employed by Khadīja bint Khuwaylid, whom he later married. Khadija proposed marriage after she was given a vision of Mohammed as a prophet. She is considered the first person to convert to Islam. When he was 40 years old, Mohammed claimed that Gabriel visited him, an Angel mentioned in the Christian Bible.

Khadīja bint Khuwaylid,
wife of Mohammed

Several years later, at the urging of his wife and family, he began preaching the message that had been revealed to him. This caused him problems in polytheistic Mecca, and he was forced to flee to Medina with his followers. In Medina, he quickly united the disparate tribes under a single constitution. They marched with him on Mecca, and while it was a mainly bloodless takeover, it marked a turning point in the religion, as Mohammed got rid of the pagan idols in the *Kaaba* and claimed the spot for Allah, the one god. In this way, he united Arabia under one religion, creating the *Ummah*, or Islamic Nation, and setting the stage for the empires to come.

The Caliphates were the dynasties that arose in the wake of Mohammed's death. The first of these Caliphates was the Rashidun. The Rashidun formed immediately after the prophet's death, with Mohammed's father-in-law Abu Bakr taking control. This is important because his intervention kept the religion from falling apart. He tried to control dissenters, called the *Ridda*, and extended the Islamic world to the Red Sea.

The second Caliph was Umar ibn Al-Khattab who extended the empire significantly, conquering most of the Roman Empire and all of the Sassanid Persian Empire in his ten years as Caliphate. Umar was succeeded by another of Mohammed's companions, Uthman ibn `Affan, who continued to extend the empire but, more importantly, ordered the creation of the standardized text of the Quran, the Islamic Holy book. He also ordered the destruction of copies that differed from his to avoid schisms in the faith due to multiple interpretations. Rebels eventually assassinated him. The fourth and last Caliph of the Rashidun Caliphate was Ali ibn Abi Talib, the cousin and son-in-law of the prophet Mohammed. He, too, was assassinated during the first Muslim civil war, or *fitna*.

The second Caliphate was the Umayyad Caliphate. The Umayyad were the family of Uthman ibn Affan, the third Caliph of the Rashidun Caliphate. The first Caliph of the new dynasty was Muawiya ibn Abi Sufyan, cousin of Uthman and governor of Syria, which became a central base of Islamic power. The Umayyad differed from the Rashidun Caliphate in several ways. Where the Rashidun succession of Caliphs was based on the continuation of the religious message, the Umayyad was dynastic and was criticized by many later scholars for these dynastic leanings.

While many consider it to have been a little better than a dictatorship, the Caliphate was still a success in many regards. The relationship between the Muslims and the Christians living in the empire's territory was a strong one, as the Caliphs allowed minorities to practice their religion. This did not mean that there were no conflicts, however, for they were at near-constant war with the Byzantine Christians. As for conquest, the Caliphate was a huge success as well; it amassed the largest empire that the world had ever seen to that time and the fifth largest before the present time.

The third Caliphate laid claim to power through a closer familial connection with Mohammed than the Umayyad. The Abbasid descended from Abbas ibn al-Muttalib, who was Muhammad's youngest uncle. While the Abbasid Caliphate did not achieve the same amount of territorial power as its predecessor, and the Caliphate had an issue of factions breaking off pieces of their remaining territory, their rule signals a golden age in Islamic culture. From their seat in what is present-day Baghdad, they promoted knowledge above almost all else. People from around the world traveled to their House of Wisdom, turning Baghdad into one of the most important trade centers in the world.

Medicine and science evolved as the scholars created an early form of the scientific method. Mathematics was forever changed as the Arabic numeral system was developed. In literature, the lasting effects of *The Book of One Thousand and One Nights* can still be seen in movies like Disney's *Aladdin*. Sciences and fine arts like painting and architecture also saw the impact of dedicated study. The golden age came to an end with the arrival of the Mongols led by Hulagu Khan in 1258, which created a period of conflict and destroyed Baghdad. It did not, however, end the influence of the Islamic religion.

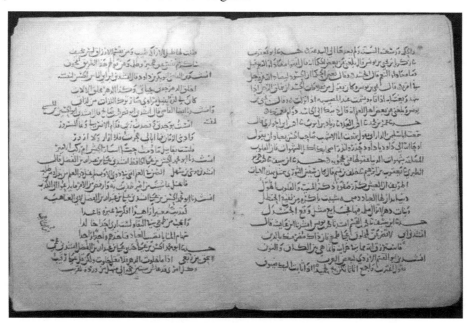

An original One Thousand and One Nights manuscript

Islam, based on the revelations of the prophet Muhammad, developed in the Arabian Peninsula. The beliefs and practices of Islam reflected interactions among Jews, Christians, and Zoroastrians with the local Arabian peoples. Muslim rule expanded to many parts of Afro-Eurasia due to military expansion, and Islam subsequently expanded through the activities of merchants and missionaries.

While many people view Islam as a religion separate from the Jewish and Christian influence in the same region, the Islamic faith is meant rather be a continuation of those religions. The Jewish faith is predicated on the belief that they are God's chosen people who will be saved by a messiah. Christians believe that the Jew known as Jesus of Nazareth was that Messiah.

Muslims, like Jews, believe that Jesus was a prophet. Jews think that the true Messiah has yet to come. Muslims believe that Mohammed was the last prophet and that their holy text, the Quran, was created to counter the textual "perversions" in the Torah and the Bible. Muslims believe these "perversions" were created when the Torah and the Bible were translated into other languages, which is why the Quran must always appear only in Arabic. All three religions are *monotheistic*, and all three worship one God and claim the same places as their holy lands.

Jesus Christ as the Christian God

There are five strict tenants of Islam which represent the influence of the other religions in the area. The first tenant is a profession of faith. In Judaism, this is done in a coming of age ceremony called the Bar Mitzvah, for boys, or the Bat Mitzvah, for girls. In Christianity, it is called a baptism or confirmation. Jews and Christians fast on their high holy days and during the period of Lent. Muslims fast for a month during Ramadan. All three religions call for the donation of money to the poor as well as a daily prayer. Even the pilgrimage to Mecca, which can seem strange to Westerners, is modeled on the pilgrimages taken to holy sites by Jews and Christians throughout history.

Like the Torah and the Bible, the Quran lays down lists of laws, called sharia law, for the people, many of which overlap. The Jews and Christians share the Ten Commandments, which also appear in the Quran, though in a different form. The Jews have dietary restrictions that are echoed by the Islamic faith, like being forbidden to eat pork products because they are "unclean." Islam, like Christianity, was intended as a conversion religion, while Judaism is more of ethnic religion.

Many people believe that conversion to Islam was mandatory as the Islamic world began to expand during the first Caliphate. This was not universally true. Like the Christian and Jewish faiths, Muslims believe that non-believers will not receive salvation, but they did not require new territories to convert. One reason that most new territories did convert was that the Islamic people's skill at fighting wars convinced many that their God must be the true God who had blessed them with their success. Others converted to Islam because it made sense to them financially: Muslims were subject to lower taxes and duties than non-Muslims in Islamic countries. In India, Islam was seen as a desirable alternative to the caste system. Therefore, while the Islamic faith spread successfully, it was for a multitude of reasons, of which forced conversion was only one.

Middle East trade networks relied on camels for transportation.

Those in the Middle East adapted to their environment by making the camel a central point of their culture. The *camel* is an important animal in a desert climate. It is a beast of burden, which means it can be used as transportation for materials and goods. Its ability to store water made it more valuable than the faster horses. Camels also served as a food source. Camels produce milk, which could be turned into several dairy products. Their meat is edible and was often dried into a form of jerky for preservation. Therefore, camel breeding opened the Middle Eastern deserts to new trade routes by providing transportation and resources.

Islamic world preserves and expands upon scientific and technological traditions of collapsing the Roman Empire.

During this time, a shift in mathematical and scientific understanding had to take place. Since the fall of Rome indicated a period of depression or recession in the West, most Roman and Greek texts were lost to the Germanic pillagers or were saved by communities in the Arab world. Thus, it was these Muslim scholars who continued the work of the Greeks and the Romans. Grecian mathematics was a complex system. The Greeks, though they had discovered irrational numbers, were not fond of the concept and tried to make a distinction between the magnitude of a number and the rationality of that number itself. Because of this inability to quantify irrational numbers as part of their mathematical thought, most Grecian mathematics was related to what present-day mathematicians call geometry.

Muḥammad ibn Mūsā al-Khwārizmī, co-inventor of algebra, on a postage stamp

The Greeks and Romans were focused on the mathematics of engineering. They were more concerned with how to build and complete new structures. When the Arab world took hold of these mathematical teachings, they jumped ahead to a new era of mathematical thought. Several Arab scholars created the field of mathematics known today as algebra. While the Greek mathematician Diophantus is known as the father of algebra, it was not until the Islamic Golden Age that his work was adapted into its present state through the efforts of Islamic scholars. With the quantification of irrational numbers, a multitude of possibilities opened up that did not exist in Diophantus' time, including the creation of the number zero, the concept of nothingness in mathematics.

As previously discussed, the Islamic influence during this time extended well into Europe and encompassed the entire Iberian Peninsula. This peninsula was renamed Al-Andalus by the Muslims. It was also known as Muslim Spain or Islamic Iberia. It was through this territory that the knowledge left by the Romans and Greeks was returned to Western Europe. In this territory, several discoveries were made in trigonometry, astronomy, surgery, and pharmacology. These discoveries drew scholars from around the Muslim world to the Peninsula and led to the territory becoming a major educational center.

With scholars flocking to study these new creations or ideas, the Iberian Peninsula was not closed to the West in the same way that much of the Islamic world was. It was significantly closer and less dangerous to travel to. Therefore, this territory was not only responsible for educating Muslim scholars but became a major educational center for the entirety of Europe and the lands around the Mediterranean Sea. In this way, it became a conduit through which culture and science could flow between the Islamic Middle East and the Christian Europeans. That does not mean, however, that this territory was peaceful. While it served as an educational center, this territory was at war with the Christian kingdoms to the north for most of its history.

Islamic states developed alternative forms of governance to manage burgeoning territory better.

Over the course of this time, many new forms of government emerged as a way to adapt to the new requirements of the ruling. These new governments witnessed the failures of their predecessors, like Rome and Alexandria, which had attempted to rule through military power. Instead, they adopted a new format to allow for the control of similar-sized areas without the same level of exertion. One of the major developers of these new systems was the Islamic world. The Islamic world was larger than could be easily controlled from one area.

Therefore, the government was separated into different areas. They were unique, however, because they all considered themselves to be a part of a larger Islamic world. A modern example of this would be how each state in the United States regulates itself while still holding to the laws, traditions, and ideology of the larger country of America. Therefore, the Islamic world was broken up into two distinct governments: the central government and the fringe Emirates.

The centralized power in the East was the Abbasid Caliphate. This Caliphate differed from the previous two Caliphates because, while the others attempted to maintain complete control of the Islamic world as a whole, the Abbasid quickly recognized that the entire Islamic world was too large for such control. They were quickly losing their territory on the fringes of their society and needed some way to combat this. Their solution to this problem was a system of vassal Emirates which controlled a small portion of the larger territory and were allied to the Caliphate. The Iberian Peninsula was an Umayyad Emirate, for example. One of the surviving Umayyad princes moved to the Iberian Peninsula and established himself as the Emir of Cordoba. While this Emir was at war with the Abbasid, who had deposed his family, many other Emirates were established, which made alliances with the Caliphate.

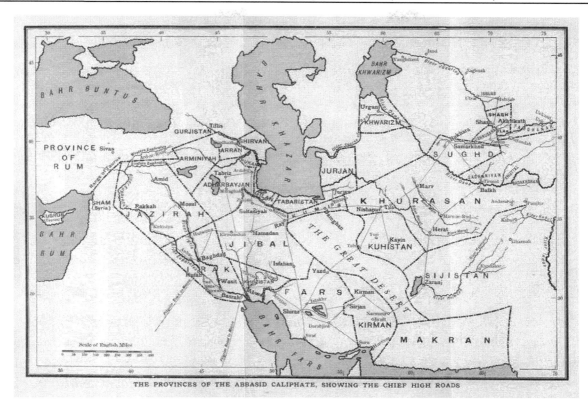

THE PROVINCES OF THE ABBASID CALIPHATE, SHOWING THE CHIEF HIGH ROADS

The provinces of the Abbasid Caliphate

Islamic-Persian exchanges shaped the emergent politics of the Middle East.

One benefit that the Persians had over the Islamic world was experience. The Persians had a fully developed government that was easy for the Islamic world to adopt. This led to the Caliphs adopting coinage, ministers, and set rules for bureaucratic institutions like collecting taxes. However, sometimes the Islamic beliefs were sacrificed for this close connection to the Persians. The Islamic Quran claims that all religions and their practitioners should be respected. The Persians disagreed, labeling foreigners as barbarians.

Therefore, the influence of the previous Persian Empire on the Islamic world was both a benefit to the state and a detriment. On the one hand, the Persian government assisted with the creation of a stable Islamic world with a functioning bureaucracy. On the other hand, some Islamic ideals conflicted with Persian beliefs, and the Persian beliefs often won out in the face of these conflicts. It is these Persian beliefs that started many of the misconceptions about the Islamic faith.

Chinese defeat by the Abbasids marked Central Asia's gradual shift into the Islamic world.

The conflict between the Abbasid Arabs and the Tang Dynasty of China is a good example of conflict sparking change. The Chinese, as one of the longest-reigning civilizations, controlled much of the area surrounding their homeland. While other empires, like the Romans, exerted their control through brute force, the Chinese preferred to use soft power. They would establish themselves as trading partners and negotiate treaties that would keep everything aligned with their wishes without military force.

In this way, they controlled much of central Asia, and they had some established alliances in the area. This did not mean that China was without enemies, however. The Chinese were in constant contact with several military opponents seeking land, influence, and resources. The people of Tibet wanted to control several western Chinese cities. The Turks were a constant threat from the West as their empire began to gain prominence. Similarly, the people of Laos and Thailand were threats to southern holdings.

It was while the Chinese focused on these threats to their rule that the Islamic Caliphate was created and gained power in the Middle East. The two powers came into direct conflict in 651 C.E. when the Umayyad Caliphate overthrew the Sassanid Persian capital of Merv and executed their King. China had a vested interest in the Sassanid Persians. They were a trading partner and a useful ally against the Turks. This made the Chinese understandably anxious to control this new player, and despite the Umayyad joining with the Turks for several campaigns, the Chinese won most early military encounters.

When the Abbasids overthrew the Umayyad Dynasty, the first steps taken by the new Caliphate were to consolidate the power of their sprawling empire. From their capital in Harran, Turkey, they turned their attention to the contested Ferghana Valley. In 750, the King of Ferghana had a border dispute with Chach, a neighboring kingdom. The Chinese sent their General, Kao Hsien-chih, to deal with the dispute.

The general offered the Chachan King safe passage from his central city as a show of mercy, but when the King took his offer, he was beheaded. The Chachan Prince escaped with his life and pled with the Abbasids to intervene. They sent the brilliant General Ziyad ibn Salih to meet Kao's forces. The two armies met at Talas for the–later named–Battle of the Talas River. Conflicting sources tell vastly different stories about the sizes of the opposing armies, but the understanding is that the Arab forces, with their allies, were the larger of the armies. Records say that the battle between the two armies lasted for five days. Several days into the fighting, the Tangs were surprised by a Turkish ambush from their rear flank, and the fate of the army was quickly sealed.

While the Abbasids considered pushing their advantage into China over the Hindu Kush Mountains, their supply lines would not allow them to continue west. This meant that many scholars of the time did not consider the battle to be of any real importance. It was only later scholars who recognized the impact that the battle had on Central Asia. With the Tang army permanently crippled, the Dynasty could no longer shore up its borders against the other military threats. The Dynasty had to withdraw from the west to take care of the more immediate threats like the Tibetans, who eventually captured the Chinese capital. The battle was important because this pullback by the Chinese left a power vacuum that was slowly filled by the Islamic world. Without the control of the Chinese, the people converted to Islam through the usual channels like trade.

Persian cultural gender beliefs shaped women's role in Islam.

During this period, Islam was forming and converting people in all areas of Eurasia. Islam did not have gendered ideologies at first and, in fact, even featured women in prominent positions—until it was heavily influenced by Persian culture. Persians had very strict gender roles that limited the power and status of women to be mostly passive members of society. This would be reflected in Islam as it continued to spread and convert followers. Overall, the new monotheistic religions of this period ushered in an era of even further gender disparity.

In Islam, the religion itself had teachings of gender equality. Like in Christianity, where several prominent figures were women, people pointed out that the Prophet Muhammad's wife was a highly valued member of society. She is considered to be the first convert to Islam, and she was a powerful figure in her own right, having employed the prophet as a merchant before he took up his role as a teacher.

However, these Islamic ideals had some conflict with cultural norms from the societies that they embraced. While gender equality teachings were inherent in the religion itself, the Persians, who had converted to Islam, began to influence Islam with their values. Persian culture required that women be secluded from men and that they should always be fully covered. This covering included the veiling of their faces.

Persian men also had *harems*, a collection of wives, and concubines all held by one man. These ideas spread from the Persian territories, using the same vehicles as the Islamic faith, and soon the ideas were too entrenched to remove. It is important to note that this was not due to the influence of the religion on converts but, instead, the influence that converts had on the religion.

Notes for active learning

South & Southeast Asia

Major historical events of the period:

550:        The Gupta Empire falls

600s: Boom in Indian Ocean trade

1511:   Malacca is conquered by the Portuguese

PERIOD 2: 500 to 1500 C.E.

SOUTH AND SOUTHEAST ASIA

Malacca controlled trade between the Indian Ocean and East Asia.

When ships left China, they might make for the trading hub at Malacca. Malacca is located on the Malay Peninsula, a landmass that separates the South China Sea and the Indian Ocean. In this position, it served as a major trading post for Chinese and Indian merchants. Traders who used the monsoons to travel back and forth between the two regions would often call Malacca home. Sometimes for several months, they had to wait for the monsoon winds. This resulted in the development of a bustling, cosmopolitan city.

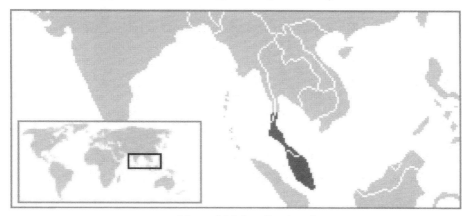

Map of Malay Peninsula

At its height, Malacca was the largest marketplace in the world for Indian, Chinese and Spice Island merchants. Recognizing the need to protect this trade and the merchants that were creating their economic prosperity, the Malays created a haven for the traders. Special districts existed for traders from the same areas, and warehouses were provided for the storage of their goods. A fleet of ships patrolled the waters surrounding the port to protect it and the merchant ships, especially from pirates. Malacca was such a powerful trade hub that its influence was even well recognized in the West. It was this fame that led to the city's eventual downfall. The Portuguese desperately wanted to control the port and invaded in the early 1500s. This led to the collapse of the port, however, as many traders simply moved elsewhere.

When traders used the monsoon winds to reach Africa, they were often traveling from major hubs located in Southeast Asia. In India, this hub was Calicut. Calicut was primarily a spice port. Most merchants were there to buy and sell the spices shipped from other Southeast Asian countries. The spice trade was not dominated by one particular group because different spices are native to different areas. This meant that several cultures intermingled in the city as representatives from different regions came with their particular set of spices, leading to a mix of Hindu, Buddhist, and Muslim cultures.

Indian caste system restricted social movement.

Feudalism existed in most of Europe and Japan during this period. In India, the caste system still existed. The *caste system* was predicated on the idea of reincarnation. Every time an individual died, they were either closer or further from Nirvana, based on how well they had filled their position in the caste during their previous life.

This meant that the *Brahmin* priests and academics at the top were the closest to achieving *nirvana*, or freedom from the cycle of reincarnation. The warrior class, underneath the *Brahmin*, included political leaders, who were less enlightened than the academics and priests but still held a respectable place. The merchant class was directly underneath the politicians and warriors. The peasants were under the merchants and were similar to the free peasants in Europe.

Sculpture of a person from the Brahmin class

One of the most notable classes in India was the creation of a caste called the Untouchables. These were individuals that had cast aside their religion or individuals that were separated from the society in some particular form or fashion. Often Untouchables would be those who were destitute. They were the homeless and those with the most menial jobs. They were called untouchable because they were unclean after being tasked with such jobs as cleaning latrines.

Muslim and Chinese diasporic communities exert influence in South and Southeast Asia.

An example of a diasporic community that had a huge impact on their new surroundings would be the diffusion of the Islamic faith into the Indian subcontinent. India was a difficult place for any outside community to penetrate. Several empires, including that of the Mongols, tried to bring them under their rule, but all failed. India had a very distinct culture with well-developed mythology and religion-based social system. This meant that they were less welcoming of change than an area where the society's ideals were less deeply entrenched.

Islam appealed to some people because it was a socially mobile religion, the antithesis of the current caste system. Therefore, most converts were of the lower classes, which made sense considering that they would gain the most from conversion, and they were the most likely to associate with the African slaves, which they would have to do to learn their religious beliefs well enough for conversion.

Another example of a diasporic community would be the Chinese who migrated and settled in Southeast Asia. No one is sure of the origin of this community, but many historians believe that these Chinese settlers were mainly fleeing dynastic change, particularly the fall of the Tang Dynasty. However, they were also known as merchants and may have come from traders who assimilated into a new society as part of a trading system with the indigenous people. These communities tended to appear in places where Chinese influence and beliefs were already held, for instance, the Buddhist faith. While many people intermarried with the local population, in some areas, there are still distinct "Chinatowns" that maintain Chinese cultural practices, even if the people themselves may have largely assimilated with the local culture.

People of the Tang Dynasty

Indian traders left lasting Hindu legacy in Southeast Asia.

Hinduism played a large role in shaping the culture of Southeast Asia. Records show that traders from India traveled to many of the major areas in Southeast Asia. Due to proximity, these Indian influences are often from the Western or Southern parts of India, those closest to the Southeast Islands. Proof of their influence is still seen today as Hindu communities have continued to flourish in Cambodia, Malaysia, Singapore, Thailand, and the Philippines. Some of the traditions have changed— the presence of Buddhism, in particular, influenced many—but they are still recognizable. Several holidays, like Diwali, the Hindu festival of lights, are still celebrated in these areas, and many cultural representations like traditional dances and sculptures of Hindu gods speak to the impact that Hinduism had on these areas.

Prambanan Shivaistic temple near Yogyakarta, Indonesia

Notes for active learning

Notes for active learning

East Asia

Major historical events of the period:

609: The Grand Canal completed by Chinese Sui Dynasty

700s: Paper is invented by the Chinese

800s: Gunpowder is invented in China

1012: Champa rice is imported from Vietnam

1162: Temujin (later renamed Genghis Khan) is born in Mongolia

1185: Feudalism begins in Japan

1200s: Gunpowder weapons begin to appear in China

1279: Mongols conquer China

1351–1368: The Red Turban Rebellion (White Lotus Revolution) overthrows the Yuan dynasty, ushering in the Ming dynasty

1405: Zheng He is sent by the Yongle Emperor of China to explore the Indian Ocean and East Africa

PERIOD 2: 500 to 1500 C.E.

EAST ASIA

Asian foods were brought west.

One of the most important foods was rice, a relatively quick growing grain that allows for the feeding of many people with comparatively little labor. Rice was grown in Asia for years, and the Chinese completed their Grand Canal as a way to move rice north faster. There is more than one strain of rice, and new varieties were introduced periodically to meet certain needs, like faster maturation or to combat disease. These grains were quickly adopted by the Persians, who turned rice into a staple of their food. This has happened several times throughout history. For instance, the Italians underwent a similar cultural shift with the discovery of the American tomato, which quickly became a staple part of their culture's cuisine.

Bananas are another food that made its way from eastern Asia to the West. Merchants from the Far East were particularly adept at setting up towns for trade in other territories. This meant that some citizens would remain in the town permanently, regulating its welfare, while others acted as traders between different regions. These small towns were almost like home bases developed to give traders a sense of home and community. Therefore they often included traditional plants and food that would provide traditional cuisine. Thus, bananas from the East were introduced to Africa by traders. Without a natural enemy, the plants would be able to spread quickly, until something adapted to keep them in check.

Hangzhou became China's major Silk Road trade city.

Gaozong, emperor of China

In China, the major trade city was Hangzhou. The city was a hub where many people gathered to buy silk and tea, but Hangzhou came to power when the Mongols attacked Kaifeng in the 12th century. Kaifeng had been the capital of the Song Dynasty in China but, after it was ransacked, Emperor Gaozong declared Hangzhou his new capital city. This meant that the Imperial court relocated to the city, as did the country's artists and scholars.

Its location on the Qiantang River meant that it had a direct connection to Beijing and the Pacific Ocean once the Great Canal was completed. Ships could leave Hangzhou and reach Japan and Korea. If they used the monsoon winds properly, they could reach India, Africa, or the Middle Eastern nations. Trade in the city expanded into tourism as Chinese officials came to visit merchants and enjoy the surrounding countryside. Several dynasties during the period named the city their capital because they were so impressed with the quality of living and culture found there.

Industrial production of iron and steel expanded in China.

Luxury items were not the only impact, however. China was far beyond other countries regarding their metallurgy capabilities. While the rest of the world was still working with copper, bronze, and some of the more malleable metals, the Chinese were creating iron tools and had developed steel. This technology would not exist in Europe until the Industrial Revolution. With these newer and stronger metals, the Chinese made unique advancements in production. This meant an increase in their production and transportation capabilities and also led to innovations in their agricultural systems and other technologies.

Chinese and Mongols united, capitalizing on the Silk Road trade.

The Chinese experienced several rises and falls in their power as a nation. During the Post-Classical Period, they achieved, in essence, a Golden Age. Silk was a commodity prized in the West, and China profited from increased sales in new markets, which in turn boosted production. The West also desired Chinese porcelain as a status symbol. Their participation in trade was only one aspect of the empire, however.

Perhaps the greatest accomplishment during this period was the reunification of China. Several ineffective dynasties had led to a disassociation between regions of the enormous territory. The Sui Dynasty changed that with the completion of the Grand Canal in 609 C.E. The Grand Canal was an amazing work of engineering. Over 1000 miles long, it linked the Yellow and Yangtze Rivers. The goal of the canal was to connect resources. Primarily, the rice grown in the South needed to be moved north to the more populated areas.

The next several dynasties continued the trend of Chinese culture and innovation. Paper, developed by the Chinese, spread to the west in the 8th century. Later in this period, the Chinese invented the idea of a moveable type, which would once again revolutionize the bookmaking process in their country as well as Europe. Gunpowder was invented accidentally during the 9th century, giving rise to weapons unlike anything in the West. It also led to the creation of fireworks, which became a part of many Chinese celebrations. The compass, while invented by the Chinese earlier, was first used for navigational purposes in the 12th century. Perhaps the greatest dynasty, the Ming, extended the Great Wall to its present size as a show of strength. Culturally, the empire reached an amazing peak with art, finance, science, and political influence.

The Mongols were different from every other empire, building people of the period. The Mongols, for most of their history, had been a quiet people living on the Eurasian Steppe. They were nomadic headers who used horses as their main form of transportation. This meant that they were on the move for most of the year. In turn, their homes, tent-like huts called *yurts*, had to move with them.

Mongols were rarely at war with outsiders, but there was often conflict between the different tribes, which meant that they had to have warriors who were skilled in weaponry. Mainly, they used a *bow* while riding on horseback. The bow was a re-curved composite bow, which means that it was smaller than other bows of the time; for it to be useful as a weapon, it had to be shot while riding a horse. In comparison, the English longbow was six feet tall. Similarly, the Mongols used a distinctive draw for their bow. While a typical Western archer would draw the string of a bow back using the forefinger and middle fingers of the dominant hand, the Mongols would draw the string with their thumb, the strongest joint in the hand. Despite its size, the bow was incredibly effective and could be accurately shot, some records say, from 500 meters away.

Representation of a Mongolian yurt

The Mongols eventually united under a strong leader called Temujin. Temujin was the son of a lower chieftain, who was later poisoned and was married young to a woman called Borte. Borte was captured by a rival tribe, which was not uncommon among the Mongol people. It is thought that the kidnapping of Temujin's wife may have even been retaliation for his father kidnapping his mother years earlier. Temujin, however, decided to get her back. He led his tribe against the rival tribe and won. This victory led to others, as Temujin sought to unite the different tribes under his leadership.

Genghis Khan,
Mongolian emperor

Eventually, he managed to bring each of the tribes under his control, primarily by using two unique methods. He would promote his leaders based on who was the most skilled instead of who came from the best family. This led to a competent and robust army. He also valued the citizens of the tribes that he conquered, making them part of his tribe instead of leaving them without representation. This earned him the hearts and minds of those he conquered. In 1206 he called for a kurultai, or general assembly, that ended with his election as leader of the Mongols. He took the name Genghis Khan.

The Mongol Empire under Genghis Khan was a complex machine. The Mongols had an incredibly effective military. Despite always traveling with a relatively small force, typically less than 130,000, they were greatly feared. Their horses made them faster than any other army. Similarly, their bows were more effective than the short-range weapons of other soldiers and more powerful than the bows of their enemies. They were also adaptive because their leaders were chosen based on merit and therefore were both creative and effective at overcoming obstacles like castles.

Genghis Khan's Mongols were so effective that he managed to extend his empire from his homeland to the Caspian Sea in the West. While he expanded the territory, his first wife, Borte, served as Empress and ruled the Mongol homeland on the Steppes. Their people so revered her that when Khan died in his sleep, only her descendants were considered for rulers of the four khanates: the Yuan Khanate, the Ilkhanate, the Chagatai Khanate, and the Golden Horde Khanate.

While often remembered for their violence, the Mongols also had several humane achievements. They reinvigorated trade along the Silk Road, even encouraging it because it was a taxable income. They made sure that traders were safe and even issued passports. They also developed a quick and efficient message system called the Yam. The Mongols moved so quickly on their horses that traditional messages might never reach them. Instead, a series of waystations existed for military messengers who could pass a message on much more quickly. This eventually developed into an effective system of communication for others as well, especially traders. Their system of meritocracy and religious tolerance were refreshing differences when compared to other empires.

Chinese scientific and technological advancements diffused westward.

It was the Chinese who invented both paper and the idea of movable type. The Far East had created these inventions significantly before they were shared with the rest of the world. The art of making paper was not shared until the Battle at Talas River which secured the knowledge for the West. The invention and spread of gunpowder and its utilization in weapons spread from the Far East to the West in a similar way. The Chinese developed gunpowder as early as the late 400s and quickly utilized gunpowder in fireworks.

By the 13th century, weapons utilizing gunpowder began to appear in China. In the Middle East, gunpowder traveled from China through India, possibly in reaction to the Mongol influence. There is evidence that the Chinese used these weapons against the Mongol Empire. The Mongols, in turn, adapted their weapons, including a "fire catapult," which was used during Ogdai Khan's invasion of Europe. The Islamic world also studied these weapons. The first evidence of the Islamic world utilizing firearms comes from the 13th and 14th centuries. However, the Islamic Ottoman, Safavid, and Mughal empires were called the "Gunpowder Empires" because they could use this invention from the Far East effectively.

Ögedei Khan

Mongols divided their empire to avoid unmanageable size.

The Mongol Khanates were a unique innovation in territory control and political leadership. Genghis Khan was successful where many other political leaders had failed. He conquered by leaving his faithful wife, Borte at home. In this way, his homeland was protected from invasion and dissent so that he was able to conquer the huge Mongol territory during his lifetime. He was also able to maintain that territory due to innovations in travel, primarily the use of horses. Genghis Khan recognized, however, that his territory would likely be too large for any of his sons to manage on their own.

Therefore, he approved of splitting the territory into sections which he called *khanates*. These khanates were all distinct but also similar. They all had different rulers, but by breaking down the territory into smaller sections, each ruler could make sure that he was more accurately dealing with the issues of his particular citizens. Thus the splitting of the Mongol Empire was effective where similar instances, like the splitting of the Roman Empire, had failed.

China used trade and tribute to exert power.

The Chinese were at any given point, fighting several different invaders. This meant that they did not have the time or resources to put down rebellions in their territories. Instead, they used trade regulation and the practice of tribute to exert their influence over Central Asia. This practice allowed them to exert control without having to exert force.

China profoundly influenced the religious, linguistic, and architectural development of Japan.

The Japanese had existed primarily as a closed society, but trade with the Chinese had opened them up to the same levels of cultural diffusion seen in the Middle East and Western Europe. Like the Chinese, the Japanese had an emperor who served as the head of their government. Chinese influence, however, led to the adoption of Confucian-based principles in the running of their government with Chinese titles and honorifics for politicians. While the Japanese were typically practitioners of the Shinto religion, Buddhism soon had a huge impact on their religious and artistic development. A significant portion of modern-day Japanese still practices traditional Buddhist values.

In architecture and agriculture, the Chinese encouraged the Japanese to use their city planning methods, which included long straight lines and dependence on regular rectangles to make navigation and communication easier. One of their largest impacts was on language. When the Chinese and Japanese began interacting, there was no written Japanese language. Therefore, the Japanese adopted and modified the Chinese script so that communication between the two languages was possible. This means that while the two languages are now unique in style, several words are similar due to the same base structure they had when the Japanese accepted the written script.

*Shinto painting of the Buddha
preaching the law*

Mongol dominance allowed commerce and cultural exchanges to thrive.

Like the defeat of the Chinese allowing for the Arab nations to spread Islam into Central Asia, the spread of the Mongol Empire changed the face of the modern world by creating peace that had not been seen since the *Pax Romana* of Rome. This Mongol peace allowed for trade to occur in a way it would not normally because most traders had to look to their defense and were often suspicious of others that they might meet on the road or in foreign cities.

However, the Mongols closely monitored trade in their region and protected those who traveled across their territory. This led to the saying that a girl could wear gold in her hair and travel safely anywhere in the Mongol empire. Because of the Mongols and the peace that they created across their entire empire, trade was able to diffuse in a faster way, and tradition and cultures were shared with an openness that would not have occurred naturally.

Papermaking in Ancient China

The importation of Champa rice into China enhanced their ability to feed the population.

Champa rice came from Vietnam in 1012 C.E. and was introduced to China during the reign of the Song Dynasty. The importance of this rice was seen immediately by Chinese farmers and politicians. An average rice crop took 180 days to fully mature. Champa rice had been bred to decrease that maturation time, cutting it to 90 days. This was an amazing innovation.

The Chinese tended to have rice fields in the southern part of their country, while most of their population lived in the northern part of the country. This is why their Great Canal was built: to move resources more quickly to the necessary parts of the nation. However, even this innovation was only so effective because crops still took a significant amount of time to grow. By introducing Champa rice, a larger amount of the population had a steady source of food. In time, this allowed for surpluses to develop, which took the stress off of rice farmers and those who controlled the means of production.

Chinese resistance to Mongol rule resulted in the overthrow and a new Ming dynasty.

In China, during the rule of the Yuan Khanate, a group of Chinese peasants rose up against the Mongol rulers. These peasants were known as the White Lotus Society, and the rebellion was called the White Lotus Rebellion. The White Lotus Society was a Buddhist sect. They were upset with the Mongol leadership, though their ire was sparked primarily because of natural disasters; particularly the Yellow River, which had been pretty consistently flooding.

These disasters caused unrest among the peasants who led to the rebellion itself. Surprisingly, the Mongols were unable to put down the rebellion, which lasted for 30 years. This was because the Mongols were constantly fighting among themselves and could not give their full attention to the rebellion. The White Lotus-Rebellion was considered a success because it did cause the end of that Khanate. In 1368, one of the leaders of the rebellion claimed that he had received a mandate from heaven that gave him the divine right to rule the Chinese people. He quickly declared himself emperor, starting the Ming dynasty.

Buddhism and Neo-Confucianism disagreed on women's roles.

Buddhism and neo-Confucianism came into conflict in a very similar way. Under Buddhism, all people were considered to have spiritual equality. This meant that men and women were equally important as far as their spirit or spirituality was concerned. A man was not valued more highly than his wife. Because of these beliefs, Buddhist tended to see gender equality as an important tenant of their religion.

However, neo-Confucianism taught that women were inferior or subordinate to men because of their belief that women generated disorder. Where men represented logic, stability, and order, women represented emotion, instability, and chaos. Thus under neo-Confucianism, a woman was worth less to society than her husband. Her only job was to give him male heirs to continue his family line. With these two religions being practiced in the same area, they sometimes came into conflict. In the end, the more aggressive neo-Confucianism prevailed, making women almost worthless in several eastern territories.

The influence of neo-Confucianism on the Buddhist regions led to practices like foot-binding, a painful form of disfigurement to make women's feet smaller and daintier. Women were now unable to rise to the same position that they had held previously. A famous neo-Confucianism proverb says that "a woman ruler is a hen crowing." This attitude was pervasive at the time. While the status of women in these cultures has improved, things are still unequal between the genders in much of the world.

Asian patriarchy competes with more gender-equal Asian models.

In many Asian cultures, the idea of *patriarchy*, or the persistent understanding that the father or eldest male is at the head of the family, was beginning to spread. This belief was in direct contrast with some of the ideals held by the Mongol people and those who were beginning to convert to Islam. In both of these cultures, women were given positions with significant influence.

Genghis Khan left his wife Borte as head of his empire in the Mongol territories while he went off to conquer more of the world. In Islamic areas, many people pointed out the position that the prophet's wife had held in his society, both as a businesswoman before he turned to teach, and at his side as an advisor when he took his rightful place as the prophet. In turn, Islam stressed social equality, as did Buddhism. This meant that in some areas, women were gifted with a sense of equality, while in other areas, this was very taboo. Women were particularly discriminated against in areas where neo-Confucianism was starting to take hold because it was based on the older patriarchal system.

Some migrations had a significant environmental impact.

Perhaps a more direct method belongs to the Polynesians. It is unknown exactly why the Polynesians moved from island to island in the Pacific, but they did so repeatedly. A possible reason is that an island only has resources to support a finite population. However, it is impossible to say for sure why they chose to move every few generations. Still, one notable tradition was that as they moved, they brought food and animals with them. This practice is understandable as they wanted to take food and animals that they were used to, but this practice had a huge impact on the new islands' ecosystems. The introduced plant or animal would have no natural predators on the new island. This meant they could easily become an invasive species, choking the life out of the native ecosystem and replacing it with theirs.

Painting of the Polynesian Islands

Notes for active learning

The Americas

Major historical events of the period:

600–700:	Teotihuacán goes into decline
900s:	Mayan civilization begins to decline
1050–1200:	Cahokia reaches the peak of its power
1100s:	Chinampas begin to be used for agriculture in Mesoamerica
1400s:	The Columbian Exchange begins

PERIOD 2: 500 to 1500 C.E.

THE AMERICAS

Tenochtitlán and Cahokia were major trading centers of pre-contact North America.

Tenochtitlán was a city inhabited by the Aztecs in what is present-day Mexico City. Like many trade cities, it developed in part due to a close supply of freshwater. In this instance, it was on an island in the center of Lake Texcoco. This provided security and allowed for amazing feats of engineering. The Aztecs used their knowledge of engineering to manufacturing canals, which used the lake to provide water for the hundreds of thousands of people who lived there. In the early days of the city, prosperity was bought through a tribute from surrounding conquered areas. In 1474, however, the social situation changed. Soldiers managed to capture a nearby trade city called Tlatelolco. By adding this city to their control, the people of Tenochtitlán were able to turn their city into a hub for trade and commerce.

Pre-contact Tenochtitlán

Conquistador Hernan Cortes was impressed with the amount of successful trade occurring in the city when he discovered it in the first half of the 1500s. He estimated in letters to the Spanish King that the marketplace averaged over 60,000 people every day and made particular note of the wide variety of metals the smiths worked with, including gold, silver, and copper. So much metal was available that it came to be used for farming implements as well as ornamentation.

While trade was well established, there was no formalized currency like that used in Europe and Asia. Instead, people bartered with items, though this did appear to be a formalized system. Gold was still used to purchase things of large value, but cotton or cacao beans might be used for lesser transactions. The establishment of trade allowed for the city to develop as they did overseas. There is evidence of schools for children, probably run by religious leaders. The Aztecs also had a distinct form of writing, though only a handful of examples exist today.

Further north, in the area near present-day St. Louis, on the Mississippi River, another important pre-colonial trade city existed. Cahokia is the present-day name for the city but dates back to the 17th century. Its original name is unknown. It was a large city with 10,000 to 20,000 inhabitants at its peak from 1050 to 1200. This meant that it was larger than comparable European cities at the time.

Centered near three rivers, the Mississippi, Missouri, and Illinois, Cahokia was a mound city that eventually included 120 mounds. These mounds were hand-built and played a central role in their culture, as the wealthy lived on top of them. The most impressive mound, called Monks Mound now, was some religious center with a temple-like structure on top. Farmland surrounded the city and the mounds, making use of the fertile land created by the shrinking of the Mississippi River to its post-glacier size.

Cahokia Monks Mound

The city seemed to have some craftsmen as well as farmers. Evidence suggests that they crafted knives and farming tools from flint. They do not appear to have traded these items extensively, yet there is evidence of trade from outsiders. Mica from the Carolinas has been discovered there, as has chert, a stone from Oklahoma. Shells from as far away as the Gulf of

Mexico have also been discovered in the city. This, along with a wall surrounding the city, implies a more passive understanding of the trade. The people there were wealthy and skilled in their own right, and while they would accept trade with outsiders, they did not actively seek it out like the Aztecs to the South.

New trade routes centering on Mesoamerica and the Andes developed.

While most people consider the importance of European and Asian trade routes primarily, important trade also occurred in the pre-colonial Americas. As in Europe and Asia, technology was developing in the Americas that allowed for an increase in trade and the creation of complex trade routes. These routes, in turn, gave rise to cities that flourished due to the expansive trade.

When discussing these trade routes and cities, it is important to keep in mind that archeologists are the primary source of this information. While written records from the Mesoamericans do still exist, they were more focused on documenting their religious and political matters. This exposes their cultural priorities but makes it difficult to analyze what trade and cities were actually like with any certainty beyond what is still visible in the ruins of these sites. The written record is more complete following the arrival of the European explorers. However, these explorers caused rapid changes to life in Mesoamerica, and therefore records do not always provide accurate accounts of life before European interference.

Trade in the Americas was similar to that of the Eurasians, as far as archeologists can tell, but a key difference was the geography of where these trade routes developed. Unlike in Eurasia, where most cities and trade routes developed along rivers, the Americas did not lend themselves to water-based trade. Most cities were inland and existed in lakes or reservoirs of water. Coastal towns were uncommon, and the traders in those that did exist tended to stay near the coast, instead of exploring the ocean.

An extensive system of roads would appear to indicate trade, but scholars question the numerous straight roads that dotted the Americas in pre-Columbian times. Straight roads might indicate a direct route between two trade cities.

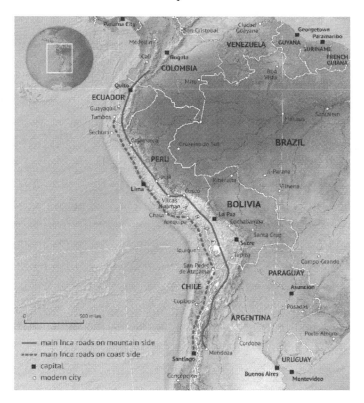

Incan road system

They might also mean that the road connected a city with a holy pilgrimage site. Still, some roads are positioned between known trading centers, which means that they were used for traveling merchants. Different cultures maintained their roads to different standards; Aztec roads show far less investment in infrastructure than the roads made by the Incan people. This might indicate that the Incan people used their roads as an extension of their influence.

The Roman Empire had a very similar system. Whenever they took control of an area, they would create sturdy roads that would allow for the easier movement of troops and supply lines. No such system of roads exists in the North Americas. While the people of the North must have had roads of some kind, it is likely that they were more temporary and had been covered up by vegetation. The North would have also facilitated more river-based trade. While South America boasts the expansive Amazon River, it was not as useful for trade as the Mississippi and Missouri Rivers in the North.

While it is difficult to say how specific tribes traded with one another, it is obvious that this trade did occur. Because these cultures did not develop money in the same way that their Eurasian counterparts did, most trade was made by barter. Thus, items from the numerous cultures on a trade route would inevitably become mingled and might show up far from their place of origin. Stones from South America have shown up in North American sites, indicating that there was intercontinental trade to some extent. The major North American trading centers likely existed without much direct contact with the South. Similarly, likely, the South Americans traded primarily with each other. The Aztec capital probably functioned as a hub to the north and as a connecting point between the northern and southern continents.

In the Americas, as in Afro-Eurasia, state systems expanded in scope and reach: Networks of city-states flourished in the Maya region, and at the end of this period, imperial systems were created by the Mexica ("Aztecs") and Inca.

While new governments were forming in the Eurasian continent, the Americas were going through a similar set of societal creations. Like the African and Italian city-states, the Mayan people also developed a system of interconnected cities ruled by one centralized government. Each of these cities had a large ceremonial center, which was the focus of the city, and a population estimated somewhere between 50,000 and 100,000 people. Each city-state was surrounded by an agricultural system based on sophisticated irrigation techniques that utilized reservoirs to water crops effectively. An extensive road network connected these city-states allowing for communication between them and also for them to trade with one another.

The Incan Empire had many cities also connected by centralized road systems, but these were separated into a federalist system, with four different quarters they called *suyu*. Originally, these four quarters were of the same size, surrounding a centralized district which functioned as the capital. However, as the Incan Empire grew, each of the *suyu* developed in their direction and became heterogeneous in size.

The Incans also had a unique imperial system in which the head of the government was tied very closely to the head of the Church. The leader of the Incan Empire was called *Sapa Inca*, or the sole ruler. It was believed that this ruler was the descendant of a sun god and therefore had

Atahualpa, the 14th and last Sapa Inca

a theocratic mandate from the heaven of divine right to rule. Because the emperor was essentially a demigod, it was believed that everything within the state, including labor, property, gold, silver, land, and people, all belonged to the *Sapa Inca*. This system is very similar to the Roman system of Popes, who are supposed to function as God's intermediary on Earth for the Catholic people.

Thus, while separated from contact with the developments occurring in the Eurasian continent, societies in the Americas were developing along similar routes. This has led many people to question the basis of human society and how much of a society's structure is unique or based on environmental factors and outside influence.

American agricultural innovations allowed growing populations.

In the Americas, unique methods were developed by native peoples to increase food production. One of these methods was called *chinampa*. *Chinampas* were gardens that were built into shallow lake beds. They utilized a wooden frame that would allow the garden to float at the top of the water. This meant that they did not have to irrigate the land. Instead, they built floating islands that would absorb water as needed by extending the plant roots into the lakebed. The system was incredibly useful because it made use of open, unused water space, and it was so widely used that two-thirds of all the food produced for Tenochtitlan was created using these *chinampas* fields.

Modern Waru Waru

In the Andes Mountains, people developed another unique irrigation system called *waru waru*. This system alternated between irrigation channels and plots of the Earth, where plants could be produced. This was similar to the modern practice of creating furrows for crops but also allowed for the collection of an increased amount of rainwater. By alternating earth with irrigation channels, the crops could be watered in a way that limited erosion from continuously opening and closing a flowing irrigation channel. It also increased rain collection by increasing the area where rain could be collected into the irrigation trenches. This differed from the normal method where water was collected in one area and then spread through the irrigation trenches.

Incans implemented an indigenous form of forced labor.

In the Americas, a form of coerced labor developed at the same time as feudalism in Europe and Japan: The Incans had a system known as *mit'a*. *Mit'a* is unpaid, mandatory labor done by those who were not citizens of the Incan society, but who were members of conquered territories. It was done as a tribute to the Incan people. The Incans only took *mit'a* from towns or tribes that had surrendered to them and swore fealty, meaning that a revolt would remove them from the reach and protection of the empire and thus end the need for the coerced labor. Typically *mit'a* was a large community project, like the creation of a statue or piece of art for the Incan city.

Period 3

1500 to 1900 C.E.

State consolidation and imperial expansion, fueled by global capitalism and industrialization, gave rise to new ideas of nationalism, revolution, and reform.

A key transformation of this period was marked by the interconnection of the Eastern and Western hemispheres. Empires expanded around the world, but they often had difficulties incorporating diverse subjects and administrating vast territories. Empires and states of varying sizes pursued strategies of centralization. African states shared some characteristics with larger Eurasian empires.

Migration patterns changed dramatically throughout this period and were closely connected to the development of transoceanic empires and a global capitalist economy. While some people benefited economically from migration, others were simply transported commodities. Forms of coerced and semi-coerced labor emerged in Europe, Africa, and the Americas, affecting ethnic and racial classifications and gender roles. The creation of European empires in the Americas quickly fostered a new Atlantic trade system that included the slave trade.

Although the world's production was still centered on agriculture, major changes occurred in agricultural labor and the systems of manufacturing. Demographic growth was restored by the 18th century and surged in many regions, especially with the introduction of American food crops throughout the Eastern Hemisphere. Industrialization fundamentally altered the production of goods around the world.

As states industrialized, they expanded their overseas colonies, establishing new transoceanic empires. The process was led mostly by Europe, which increased European influence around the world. The growth of new empires challenged the power of the existing land-based empires of Eurasia. New ideas about nationalism, race, gender, class, and culture emerged and were used to justify anti-imperial resistance. The 18th century marked the beginning of an intense period of revolution and rebellion against existing governments. These rebellions sometimes resulted in the formation of new states and stimulated the development of new ideologies.

Global Comparative

Major historical events of the period:

1450–1750:   The Age of Discovery (the Age of Exploration)

1494:   The Treaty of Tordesillas is signed

1500s: The Atlantic slave trade begins

1700s–1800s: The Age of Industrialization

1848:   Karl Marx and Friedrich Engels write *The Communist Manifesto*

PERIOD 3: 1500 to 1900 C.E.

GLOBAL COMPARATIVE

In the context of the new global circulation of goods, there was an intensification of all existing regional trade networks that brought prosperity and economic disruption to the merchants and governments in the trading regions of the Indian Ocean, the Mediterranean, the Sahara, and overland Eurasia.

The period from 1450 to 1750 has been given many labels, including the early modern period, the Age of Discovery and the Age of Exploration. All of these labels indicate the emergence of extensive travel, which eventually culminated in colonialism and global trade on a scale never before seen in history. Some of the trade routes which became influential were in Sub-Saharan Africa, connecting the Songhai and Mali Empires; the Eurasian trade routes which connected China to Europe using Siberia and Italy; the Silk Road; and the trade routes followed in the Indian Ocean and the Mediterranean Sea. Before this period, trade was dominated by the Silk Road and continental travel; however, by the period's end, global trade was being dominated by seafaring routes rather than transcontinental overland routes.

Trade was highlighted by the use of slavery by almost all the major powers of the period. One such example, not typically mentioned, was in the Sahara. While fewer slaves were transported to the Sahara than to the Americas, the numbers were still significant. Many of the slaves traded to the Middle East, and India were females; they were added to harems or used by wealthy families as concubines, with little to no status. Males were usually conscripted into various gunpowder armies.

Harem

The establishment of various trading posts created new zones of economic opportunity. These included posts on the Western coast of Africa, in the Caribbean, and various ports of Western and Eastern India. An early example of this expansion and trade growth in Portugal, which was the first empire to establish trading posts on and around the Cape of Good Hope. These new markets also created conditions for the growth of piracy, as a result of lucrative trading posts and maritime transports, which were attractive to both rival governments and criminals alike. The increase in trade also encouraged the spread of culture and religion, as with previous periods of prosperity and expansion. This increase in prosperity and technological development eventually led to the Renaissance, the Scientific Revolution, the Reformation, and the establishment of vast European empires in the 18th and 19th centuries.

The new connections between the Eastern and Western Hemispheres resulted in the Columbian Exchange.

The Columbian Exchange, like the Trans-Atlantic Slave Trade, linked the European continent with its colonies in the Americas. It was transformative in influencing the transport of goods, as well as the environmental landscapes of the Americas and Europe. The Columbian Exchange transported animals, plants—and also diseases—between Europe and the Americas. Animals brought from the Old World to the New World included horses, cattle, pigs, sheep, goats, and chickens. Turkeys, llamas, alpacas, and guinea pigs were transported from the New World to the Old. These animals also transformed the geographical landscape of the Americas, more notably than the Old World of Europe. Colonists were able to use horses and cattle as work animals and domesticated pigs, sheep, goats, and chickens as food sources, greatly increasing the diversity of foods available in the Americas at a time when supplies easily became scarce.

Plants moved from the Old World to the New World, included rice, wheat, barley, oats, coffee, sugarcane, bananas, melons, olives, dandelions, daisies, clover and—by accident— ragweed. The introduction of these plants into the Americas had an impact on plantation agriculture, slavery, and commerce. Sugarcane specifically transformed the economic and environmental landscapes of the Caribbean and the Americas during this period. It is also worth noting that various species of plants, such as ragweed, transmitted by the Columbian Exchange, proved to be an invasive species.

The plants transmitted from the New World to the Old World included corn (maize), potatoes (white and sweet varieties), beans (kidney, lima and snap beans), tobacco, peanuts, squash, peppers, tomatoes, pumpkin, pineapples, cacao, chicle, papayas, manioc (Tapioca), guavas and avocados. These plants were important for maintaining the colonies. For governments to continue investing in colonies, they wanted to see a return, and the cultivation of new crops for Europeans yielded that return. These new plants became staples of European diets. Notable examples are the introduction of potatoes, the cacao plant (used to make chocolate), and the chicle plant (used to create gum). Finally, the introduction of tobacco to the Europeans was transformative regarding the economic value and cultural influence, as smoking became a fad among the elite and displayed status.

This trade in new foods between Europe and the Americas also created a more diverse diet for Europeans, resulting in larger populations, increased health and longer life expectancies. Another long-term implication of the Columbian Exchange was further trade expansion between European empires and their colonies. Such progress, both economic and social, proved to be difficult to stop by the time of the American Revolution.

Portuguese trading animals in Japan, the Columbian Exchange

Old World adopted New World food imports.

As in the Americas, plants transmitted to Europe as a result of the Columbian exchange had transformative impacts. One example is potatoes. After the Spanish conquest of the Incan Empire by Pizarro, the returning Spaniards brought potatoes back to the European markets. As a result of the expansive trade systems in place, the new European staple was subsequently conveyed by European mariners to territories and ports throughout the world.

However, not everyone welcomed new crops, and in some regions, the potato was slow to be adopted by distrustful European farmers. After some success, the potato became an important food staple and field crop that played a major role in the 19th-century European population boom. Cassava, also known as manioc or tapioca, was also introduced into Africa by Portuguese traders, who had developed the crop in Brazil during the 16th century. Cassava became a staple of the region and led to further food security in Africa.

Populations in Afro-Eurasia benefited nutritionally from the increased diversity of American food crops.

As American crops were traded in European markets and, in turn, the Eastern markets, an expansion of food choices and quality led to population growth through diversification of the diet. In Asia, the diversification of diet caused by the introduction of maize and sweet potatoes resulted in population increase and longer life expectancy. Examples of this were seen in all regions where American crops were traded, including Africa and Europe. The cultivation of maize and cassava in foreign territories, such as Angola in Southwest Africa, was due to the Portuguese traders who initially brought the crop from Brazil. In Southeast Asia, the introduction of maize and cassava, which were naturally quite nutritious, allowed for population expansion and more stable quality of life.

In Europe, American staples diversified the diet of average Europeans. The potato, in particular, eventually became a better staple food for the poor, notably in Ireland, where 40% of the population came to rely solely on the potato crop. The results of these more diverse food choices were population growth, higher quality of living, and longer life expectancy. Better and more diverse diets led to larger, more robust populations, which in turn allowed for further exploration, expansion, and trade.

The increase in interactions between newly connected hemispheres and intensification of connections within hemispheres expanded the spread and reform of existing religions and created syncretic belief systems and practices.

The tremendous growth in population and quality of life allowed greater exploration in science, art, and religion. This led to huge social movements, particularly during the Reformation, the Scientific Revolution, and the Renaissance. These transformations fostered the spreading of dominant religious authority, whether that of the Catholic Church, Protestant Churches or Muslim mosques.

As a result of these great transitions, both in economic capacities and human interactions, many religions experienced a period of transformation or inception. Examples of such syncretic belief systems can be seen in Sikhism, the Cult of the Saints, and Vodun; they are all mixtures of two or more differing religious beliefs, integrated into one functioning religion. These new religions, most notably Protestantism, had a transformative influence in the early modern period and into contemporary times.

Traditional peasant agriculture increased and changed, plantations expanded, and demand for labor increased. These changes both fed and responded to growing global demand for raw materials and finished products.

As global markets grew—facilitated by new crops, the Atlantic Triangle, and the movement of goods—the demand for labor increased. In the Americas, following the decimation of the native populations during the era of exploration, this meant plantation slave labor, typically facilitated through the Atlantic Slave Trade. In the Russian Empire and parts of

Eastern Europe, this need for labor was filled by serfdom, which eventually became almost identical to slavery. This practice continued for close to 800 years and instilled an idea of working common property for the benefit of the community, called *krugovaya poruka*.

The Spanish implemented various labor systems in their Mesoamerican territories including an adaptation of the Mita system, formerly used by the Inca, as a means of providing labor for the Bolivian silver mines, as well as the Encomienda, used typically in agricultural practices where native populations were placed under Spanish authority and expected to produce labor and tribute according to Spanish needs. This type of forced labor was only seen during the 16th century. All of these labor forces were in response to the global trade emerging from the Atlantic Triangle and the Columbian Exchange. These raw materials were also transported east by giant companies, such as the Dutch East India Company, along with spices and luxury goods desired by the aristocracy, a new elite class emerging in European society.

Peasant labor intensified in many regions.

The use of forced labor was seen in empires looking to develop textile and silk production, most notably in the weaving industry in the Middle East, Iran, and Central Asia. All of these rivals were able to expand their trade extensively by the use of skilled and unskilled workers. Skilled craftsman in China produced great works, which included couched metal thread, cloth of gold, damask, velvet, and brocades. Examples of such works from the 16th and 17th centuries can be seen in texts detailing the travel of two French merchants, who were interested in the elaborate weaving process. They documented these works as important forms of tax revenue for the empires as well as examples of cultural prestige amongst rival weaving communities.

Slavery in Africa continued both the traditional incorporation of slaves into households and the export of slaves across the Mediterranean and the Indian Ocean.

The slave trade did not take place only in the American hemisphere, as millions of slaves were also transported to the east. Before 1650, almost all slaves were transported to Brazil or mainland Spanish colonies. However, by the mid-17th century, this was no longer the case; many forced laborers were sent to the Caribbean to work the sugarcane plantations of the Spanish, Portuguese, and later, the French. The slaves in these regions were predominantly young males, as the work was physically demanding. Many slaves in these regions lacked any family structure, unlike that seen on American plantations.

Caribbean and American plantations were unable to replenish the populations without replacements from slave trading in Africa. Slaves who did not travel into the Western Hemisphere went to the Middle East, India, and the Mediterranean region. In these regions, women were more prized than men, as many in India and the Middle East were introduced into harems and elite households, where they remained as concubines. While fewer slaves crossed into Europe and the Middle East than crossed the Atlantic, staggering amounts of forced labor were seen in this part of the world as well. Male slaves were conscripted into the gunpowder armies of the Mughals, the Ottomans, the Safavids, and Russia.

As new social and political elites changed, they also restructured new ethnic, racial and gender hierarchies.

Various cities continued to grow, and by the 1700s, Europe consisted of large metropolitan cities. These included Paris and London, which both had over 500,000 people; Amsterdam, which had approximately 200,000 people; and twenty other cities with populations of over 60,000. Life in major cities during the early modern period was drastically different from before. The early modern period also saw the rise of the middle classes, mainly as a result of the extensive trading and commerce achieved through the Atlantic System, mercantilism, and joint-stock companies. A dramatic rise in the gap between the poor and everyone else existed throughout the world.

In Christian nations, marriages were not arranged and took place later in life, allowing women more freedom, including education. Buddhism allowed women to hold a place of status within that religion, to a greater extent than in Christianity, Islam, or Hinduism. In some Muslim cultures, women typically had no social status; this was the case in the Safavid dynasty, for

example. The custom of Sati, which called for throwing one's self on the funeral pyre of a deceased husband as a form of mourning and reverence, was practiced in the Mughal Empire. Dowries were also reinstated, as well as the shunning of women who did not wear a veil.

The Ottoman Empire used harems as part of its political structure. In this capacity, royal wives and other women of status were able to gain some slight influence within the court on political matters. Class systems were implemented in Russia, which called for serfdom and contributions to the state according to one's class, through the "Table of Ranks" system. Under Peter the Great, Russia enacted compulsory state service. This led to the dissolution of the class system, as all were evaluated based on their skills and the performance of their duties.

Peter the Great of Russia

Both imperial conquests and widening global economic opportunities contributed to the formation of new political and economic elites.

As political and military successes were experienced across the globe, a new elite class emerged, which eventually molded the economic practices of the period. These included the Manchus of China, a new class of Creole elites found in the Americas, and an abundance of European gentry. The term "Creole" is derived from the Portuguese word for "native" and refers to someone with American and European heritage.

The European gentry was able to influence the great monarchies of the period by holding political offices in the newly expanding bureaucracies, as well as by becoming patrons of art, indicating status, prestige, and wealth. One notable example of this type of influence was the de Medici family of Florence, which rose to govern Florence and eventually control the Papacy. Global trade companies, such as the Dutch East India Company, also created a new wealthy merchant class, which continued to invest in the expansion of the empire, whether French, Dutch, Spanish, or English. New elite classes of this period show the diversity of the global system, which was greatly influenced by the Atlantic system and the global trade markets, which resulted due to the movement of goods, people, and ideas.

The power of existing political and economic elites fluctuated as they confronted new challenges to their ability to affect the policies of the increasingly powerful monarchs and leaders.

The established political powers of earlier periods were struggling with powerful monarchs who were embracing absolutism. Even those who embraced constitutionalism were not easy monarchs to influence. The nobility in Europe experienced this new sense of absolutism in Spain and France, where there was felt to be no real need for political advice from these elite groups. The emergence of rule by divine right had a dual effect on monarchs; it caused many monarchs to feel uninhibited in their authority and pitted them against equally powerful religious leaders, such as the pope and the most powerful bishops, to whom they often felt the need to answer to avoid ex-communication.

Zamindars in the Mughal Empire were aristocrats on the Indian subcontinent who wielded substantial power over the peasant population by owning large territories of land and collecting taxes. These types of class systems were similar to those seen in Russia and fostered resentment between the ruling and elite classes and peasant and working classes in the future. Such political tensions set the tone for future empire expansion and rule during this and later periods. As the populations continued to grow and become more diverse, the ruling classes continued to struggle to maintain their power, eventually leading to the French Revolution and the deposing of English monarchs.

Rulers used a variety of methods to legitimize and consolidate their power.

The empires of this period were more concerned than ever with the projection and maintenance of power. As a result, various methods were used to project power and maintain influence over often disparate populations and territories. Empires were able to acquire power through several means, the most common being the brute force of military expansions, typically seen in the Ottoman Empire, as well as the use of religion and the "divine right" to rule more "backward" lands and people. The introduction of absolute monarchies speaks to the ability of governments to instill power and influence within their respective regions. The most notable examples of absolutism come from Spain and France, whose leaders also ruled using divine right. The influence of the Catholic Church was vast and sweeping. Their success in making converts all over the world was proof of this.

The monopoly of trade by various governments and companies sponsored by monarchs also speaks to the control and authority of the monarchs. The English controlled the spice trade in the East Indies. For a long period, no other country could rival their control. The Spanish exercised the same type of control in the silver trade. To maintain power within an empire, monarchies also undertook great cultural and building campaigns to instill the idea of greatness, prestige, and power within their populations, as well as potential rivals.

Rulers used the arts to display political power and to legitimize their rule.

Across the globe, empires were eager to show their accomplishments to both their native populations as well as their European, Asian, and Russian rivals. They used art and architecture to flaunt their achievements. Examples of monumental architecture include the Taj Mahal, commissioned in 1632 by the Mughal Emperor, Shah Jahan, as a funerary complex for one of his favorite wives. The complex took over twenty years to complete and dominates the banks of the Yamuna River in Agra, India. The Red Fort was a fortified structure that was built by the Mughal Empire and served as the residential palace of the imperial family of Emperor Shah Jahan.

Another notable architectural monument of the period is the Suleymaniye Mosque, which was an Ottoman imperial mosque located on the second hill of Istanbul, Turkey. It is the second-largest mosque in the city and was constructed by the great Ottoman architect Mimar Sinan. Construction began in 1550, and the Mosque was finished in 1557, opening on August 16th of that year. Under Mehmet II, the Hagia Sophia, another monumental architectural treasure of the Middle East, was transformed into a mosque, eventually adding several minarets. This was another example of using monumental existing architecture to influence newly conquered peoples.

Titania from A Midsummer Night's Dream

Courtly literature was produced as a result of the vast patronage being seen throughout Europe. Examples of this include Queen Elizabeth's sponsorship of William Shakespeare. One example includes *A Midsummer Night's Dream*, where Shakespeare depicted Elizabeth and her Court in the most favorable manner, clearly showing his appreciation for her patronage of literary works and plays. The ruling elite used art as a means to remind their subjects of the power they wielded. The projection of power was important, regardless of the geographical region. The use of arts and culture to mark the success of an empire was again seen throughout history during other periods of transition and expansion.

Rulers continued to use religious ideas to legitimize their rule.

Empires and monarchs were able to use religious tools as a means of sustaining power and influence; this was true of various cultures throughout the world. European monarchs used the idea of divine right to rule, though this proved too overbearing for many Europeans. Religious ceremonies and rituals were used in Mesoamerica, where the use of human and animal sacrifice was an integral part of the religion. These cultures believed the gods were due to a blood debt, which coincided with religious calendars.

Recruitment and use of bureaucratic elites, as well as the development of military professionals, became more common among rulers who wanted to maintain centralized control over their populations and resources.

The use of janissaries was crucial to the Ottoman Empire. As a result, a never-tiring source of military men had to be developed, and this was done using "devshirme," which means "selection" in Turkish. The janissary system can best be defined as the system by which boys from Christian communities were taken by the Ottoman state to serve as special armed forces. These forces were instrumental in the expansion of the Ottoman Empire. The Chinese examination system was also important. It was used to select candidates for the state's vast bureaucracy. The Chinese examination system was influential throughout various Asian cultures, as well as the English East India Company, whose hiring/selection process it influenced. The use of salaried Samari in Japan was another example of military forces being used to create a stable and flourishing empire. The Japanese empire was less concerned with the expansion than its European counterparts.

Imperial expansion relied on the increased use of gunpowder, cannons, and armed trade to establish large empires in both hemispheres.

The early modern period saw the emergence of several land-based empires, including the Ottomans and the Safavids in Southwest Asia, the Mughals in India, the Ming and Qing in China, and the Russian Empire. All of these empires were able to emerge due to the use of large land armies, guns, and gunpowder. These empires also developed relatively independent of Western influence, counterbalancing the growth of European power and colonization. The Ottoman Empire (1453–1918) was established following the capture of Constantinople by Mehmed II (r. 1453–1481). Also known as Mehmed the Conqueror, he was a successful statesman and military leader who embraced the arts, literature, monumental architecture, and fine arts. Following the capture of the city, the Ottomans levied a heavy tax on European exports of goods from the East that traveled through their cities.

The Ming and Qing dynasties of China were also influential Gunpowder Empires that experienced expansion and influence via the Silk Road. Russia is also considered one of the Gunpowder Empires, rather than a European power. Peter the Great wanted Russia to have European status and be recognized at the French, Dutch, and British courts. He hoped to accomplish this through vast reforms such as the creation of a professional standing army, westernizing Russian culture, formalization of the social structure through the "Table of

Ranks" and promoting Russia's role as an emerging global power. The influence of the Gunpowder Empires was great; they were a counterbalance to European expansion and dominance of the world.

Competition over trade routes, state rivalries, and local resistance all provided significant challenges to state consolidation and expansion.

Many factors impeded the consolidation of new states and colonial empires. However, three are most important: competition over trade routes, state rivalries, and local resistance from indentured servants and colonized people. The Omani-European rivalry in the Indian Ocean and piracy are examples of competition over trade routes. The Thirty Years' War and the many Ottoman-Safavid conflicts are examples of how state rivalries played out. The Samurai revolts of feudal Japan, as well as numerous peasant uprisings and food riots, are examples of internal resistance.

Although rivalries over trade routes, border disputes, and internal rebellions seem to be separate phenomena, they did overlap. All major nations engaged in a game of attempting to undermine each other's pursuit of power. When this was not done overtly by war, it was done by encouraging or supporting internal rebellions in other countries' colonies and even in their heartlands; by funding disruptive piracy; and by forging alliances with non-European power brokers wherever and whenever possible.

Industrialization fundamentally changed how goods were produced.

The Age of Industrialization, which began in the middle of the 18th century and continued into the 19th century, was a period of rapid transition, innovation, and industrial-scale production of goods that had never been seen before. Before this period, the majority of cultures were agrarian. Many people lived in rural settings, with a select few living in urban dwellings. As a result, the majority of political influence not maintained by the monarchy was held by rural landowners and agrarian aristocrats, who supplied and fed the urban populations and ruling elites.

However, the Industrial Revolution changed this social structure by causing a massive migration from the countryside to the city; changing patterns of production, consumption, and use of goods. The monarchy began to align itself with urban populations, rather than the villagers and their masters. A new industrial and mercantile class emerged to produce the goods of the empires, which gave them a status previously unattainable. As a result, the monarchies were unknowingly embracing a new social order, which was based on economic production rather than hereditary status or class.

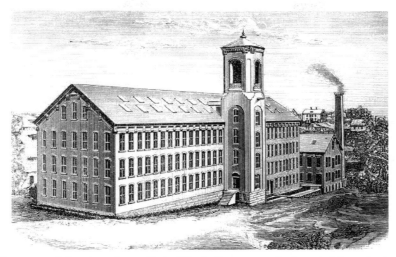

Factory of the American Hair Cloth Company, Industrial Revolution

During this period, manufacturing took off as a result of the introduction of massive machinery, which caused the production process to quickly transform by enabling faster production of finished goods. This particular transition had drastic impacts on the lives of Europeans and eventually had global ramifications. These innovative techniques caused a wider variety of goods to be available to a greater number of people than ever before, creating a higher standard of living across all social classes. Therefore, the Industrial Revolution not only influenced the production and manufacturing of goods and services but also transformed the social landscape of both Europe and the Americas. Although it is common to speak of an "Industrial Revolution," the process of industrialization was gradual and unfolded over the 18th and 19th centuries, eventually becoming a global phenomenon.

As the new methods of industrial production became more common in parts of Northwestern Europe, they spread to other parts of Europe, the United States, Russia, and Japan.

As the Industrial Revolution flourished on the European continent, it began to spread to other nations, including the United States, Russia, and Japan, who all adopted the new methods of production used by British industrialists.

Russia also industrialized its empire by creating thriving industrial centers. During the last years of the 19th century, Tsarist Russia struggled to meet the needs of a vast state that had up until then remained relatively entrenched in its traditions. Russia's stepping-stones to industrialization began in the late 19th century. The industrialization process was abruptly and temporarily interrupted by the communists when they came to power; however, it was revived in the Soviet Union with a fusion of Western production methods (the factory system and the assembly line) and involuntary servitude "for the state."

The "second industrial revolution" led to new methods in the production of steel, chemicals, electricity, and precision machinery during the second half of the 19th century.

The Second Industrial Revolution, also referred to as the Technological Revolution, was characterized by the mastery of steel production, the production of various chemicals, and the evolution of electricity. Most historians date this period between the years 1840 to 1870. During the Second Industrial Revolution, the most rapid development was seen in Germany and the United States, like Britain, Japan, and other European states had already experienced their initial wave of industrialization.

The industrial age modernization of steel manufacturing began with the introduction of Bessemer steel in America in the 1850s. This was the first mass-production application of ancient European smelting processes that used oxidation. Andrew Carnegie introduced the first modern method of steel manufacturing, the Siemens-Martin Open hearth furnace system, to America in 1865.

During the Second Industrial Revolution, railroads also emerged in North America (Britain was the first nation to have industrial rail, starting in 1825), transforming the United States, especially its Western territories. Further innovative designs in transportation throughout this period included steam-powered ships and boats. Another notable innovation that occurred during the Second Industrial Revolution was the electrification of factories, which began in America and allowed for even further efficiency of production lines and systems.

New patterns of global trade and production developed and further integrated the global economy as industrialists sought raw materials and new markets for the increasing amount and array of goods produced in their factories.

The nations that embraced the Industrial Revolution saw the emergence of new global trade patterns. However, this can also be said for nations that were less willing to employ new agricultural or industrial models, such as Latin America, sub-Saharan Africa, and parts of Southeast Asia. Global trade flourished, as it had in previous periods because governments and economies – both domestic and global – supported these new initiatives. Raw materials also became key goods as the Industrial Revolution sought to take raw goods (e.g., cotton, rubber, sugar, minerals and palm oil) and create finished products. Finished goods, like textiles, rum (produced from sugarcane), and other liquors, could more easily be traded on the global markets. As new goods were produced, empires looked for new markets in which to sell them; as a result, Imperialism was seen on an ever-expanding scale in Africa, India, China and much of Southeast Asia.

The need for raw materials for the factories and increased food supplies for the growing population in urban centers led to the growth of export economies around the world that specialized in mass-producing single natural resources. The profits from these raw materials were used to purchase finished goods.

The emergence of raw goods in the global market quickly became common, as more and more people – especially the majority who were low-income workers—were able to afford and access finished luxury goods. The emergence of urban metropolitan cities intensified the desire for consumer goods and can be seen as a direct result of the Industrial Revolution.

Cotton was extremely important during the Industrial Revolution in both Europe and the United States. At first, the introduction of the cotton gin allowed for the rapid production of cotton cloth. In the United States, this was seen most significantly in the South, where this cash crop was also tied to the increase of slavery in the United States. Sugar was another of the most prominent cash crops in the Caribbean and the United States. Meat was also a new staple during this period. The largest exporter of meat was Bolivia, a state which was able to create an

industrialized society as a result of the capital earned in this market. Additionally, rubber was grown in the Congo Free State by Belgian mercantile enterprises.

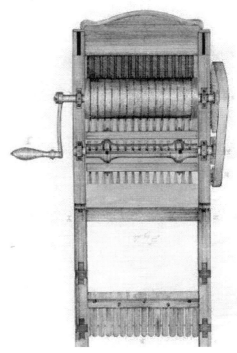

Eli Whitney's cotton gin

Metal and precious minerals were consumed at an even greater rate; as a result, various mining operations were created to meet the demands of the markets. Notable examples of such enterprises can be found in the Spanish copper mines of Mexico, as well as the British diamond and gold mines of South Africa.

All of these raw materials had an explicit influence on the Industrial Revolution but were also a direct result of such innovations. Without these supplies, the revolution could not have continued. However, the argument can also be made that without these goods, the global market would not have developed into one fueled by the desire for luxury goods and consumerism.

The rapid development of industrial production contributed to the decline of economically productive, agriculturally based economies.

Some states worked to shed their agricultural past, while others sought to continue traditional agricultural practices. An example of rapid industrialization can be seen in the development of the Indian textile sector during this period. British officials promoted the import of Indian cotton, which they were able to import at a below-market price, giving their textile markets substantial means for profit and increasing their capital. These textiles were produced at a lower price than similar products from abroad, making the demand for them extensive. Initially, Indian-produced textiles maintained the majority market share in India; however, within a short period, India's economy shifted to raw cotton exports. Once a dominant force in the textile trade (most notably in production), India now mainly exported cotton as a raw good as a result. This shift is an example of the influence the British Empire had over global trade.

The need for specialized and limited metals for industrial production, as well as the global demand for gold, silver, and diamonds as forms of wealth, led to the development of extensive mining centers.

In addition to various raw materials, the industrial age created a market for new precious metals and stones, including Mexican copper and South African gold, diamonds, and other precious stones. A new class of specialized laborers emerged, which included European and East Asian men sent to work in mines in places like Mexico and South Africa.

The copper mines of Mexico had originally been constructed and mined by the Spaniards. However, due to a decline in Spain's global status, various empires attempted to gain these valuable resources. Mining was extremely labor-intensive and mostly done by native workers who often rebelled against the conditions in which they were forced to work.

To facilitate investments at all levels of industrial production, financiers developed and expanded various financial institutions.

To finance the industrial giants created during industrialization, many governments and merchants strove to create a financial system up to the task of conducting transnational business, expanding global markets and dealing with a mounting surplus of capital. Some of the tools used for this were: expanded forms of insurance (which included life insurance), the selective implementation of the gold standard and the introduction of a stock market. These new economic enterprises found great success in the formation of banks, such as J.P. Morgan Securities, which came to dominate the banking sector. These modifications were important to the future of global markets as they established the economic system for modern leaders and lenders.

Financial instruments expanded.

Various tools were employed as governments and merchants aimed to address newly emerging economic realities. Notable examples include the emergence of the stock market, expansion of insurance companies, the implementation of the gold standard, and the introduction of limited liability corporations.

The Industrial Revolution saw a large increase in the stock market, where the new capitalist class was selling shares in their organizations as a means to raise funds for expansion. The stock market was organized to encourage investors to take risks to reap large rewards if the organization(s) in which they invested grew. The popularity of the stock market also surged because new wealth was engaging the market for the first time, which is another example of the economic and social transitions caused by capitalism.

The Industrial Revolution, which led to an increase in work-related accidents and deaths, also led to the implementation of insurance on a larger scale than previously seen. Insurance companies experienced a boom because anyone able to pay for the service could be awarded a contract of insurance. The policies seemed expensive to many in the working class but were also seen as necessary because insurance companies were able to better absorb unexpected debts than a family – even a wealthy one.

In hopes of stabilizing the market, the gold standard was also temporarily introduced. Citizens turned in their gold in return for state-issued currency, which could be used without penalty within the sovereign territory of the issuing state. However, if one wanted to transfer gold from England to France, each state would enact a penalty – in the form of fixed exchange rates – in hopes of discouraging such transactions. This was a development on the tariff system between countries which had been in existence since the 'mercantilist' era.

Limited Liability Corporations also allowed investors a more attractive investment option. With the passage of the Joint Stock Companies Act (1844) in the United Kingdom, this type of investment became even more widespread. Investors were able to enter into agreements with little to no risk, which encouraged additional investments and facilitated businesses' ability to more readily access the capital they needed to expand. Such practices became commonplace during the 19th and 20th centuries and are important for understanding the emergence of the global economy. All of these financial tools were important in creating the modern economic machine, and many of these institutions came to dominate today's markets.

The global nature of trade and production contributed to the proliferation of large-scale transnational businesses.

As local economic markets expanded globally, it became clear to various empires that there was a great need for them to conduct business transnationally, which would allow them to capitalize on the global markets. Two examples of transnational businesses created during this period were the Hong Kong and Shanghai Banking Corporation (HSBC) and the United Fruit Company.

HSBC, founded in 1865, was comprised of the Hong Kong and Shanghai Banking Corporations. The main offices of the institution were located in Hong Kong, which at the time was a British colony. Secondary locations were established in Shanghai and Japan to create a transnational banking institution. As previously mentioned, the British Empire founded Hong Kong as a means of keeping Chinese markets and ports open to European trade and merchants, and HSBC was a way of making this ambition a reality. HSBC allowed for stable monetary transactions in a period where uncertainty was rife. At the same time allowing foreign entities to invest in a market, they were unable to access. The creation of the HSBC allowed the British Empire to retain major influence in the global economy.

Hong Kong and Shanghai Banking Corporation

There were major developments in transportation and communication.

As the Industrial Revolution surged, there was a great improvement in transportation and communication technologies, which allowed the innovations above to continue to expand. One notable example of such improvement came from Robert Fulton, an American engineer and inventor responsible for creating the first commercially successful steamboat, the *Clermont*. This particular boat was able to transport passengers from New York City to Albany, a distance of over 300 miles, in only sixty-two hours. Due to his successes, Fulton was commissioned by Napoleon Bonaparte in 1800 to create the first practical submarine, the *Nautilus*.

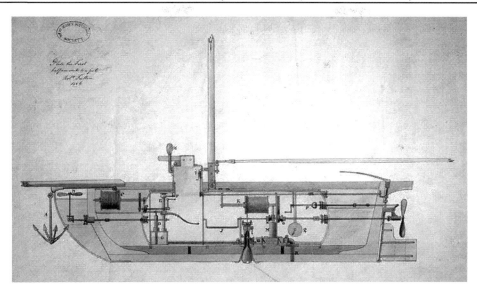

Fulton's design of the submarine

The first attempts at river navigation succeeded. After extended trial and error, a lock system was also designed to create the first modern canal. Canals were extremely influential in propelling empires and global trade forward because they allowed for the transportation of goods in the direction desired, rather than being constrained by the natural flow of the river.

The emergence of railroads in the United States and Tsarist Russia also indicates the innovation and the determination of their people to expand and grow. In the United States, the railroad was first seen in the 1830s and continued to expand until it covered the entirety of the Western territories. Between 1850 and 1890, American railways constituted close to one-third of global railways, highlighting an industry at the peak of its success.

By the 19th century, inventors had discovered how to harness electricity, leading to the creation of the electrical telegraph. The telegraph allowed information to flow at a quicker speed than ever before. It proved to be especially important during the French Revolution, as forces throughout the territories could access reliable information rapidly.

All of these technological advances were a direct result of the Age of Industry, but they also contributed to its continuation. Without the spread of more reliable and efficient modes of transportation, the migration that occurred during the period would have been impossible.

The development and spread of global capitalism led to a variety of responses.

As a result of the explosion of capitalism and other cultural transitions, different groups advanced various political and philosophical theories. Some of these included the emergence of Marxist theory, utopian socialism, and anarchy as a means of governing.

As with any period of transition, people and governments were struggling in an attempt to make sense of this new world. At this time, the world was dominated by an industrial giant; the emergence of capitalism on such a large scale was monumental and extremely influential. Today the majority of countries – even communist ones – use an adaptation of this economic system.

In industrialized states, many workers organized themselves to improve working conditions, limit hours, and gain higher wages. In contrast, others opposed the capitalist exploitation of workers by promoting alternative visions of society.

As the cities continued to expand, industrial workers continued to organize themselves according to their social classes, working classes, ethnicities, and political views. The predominant philosophy adopted by activists for economic reform was communism. Communism originated from the ideas of Karl Marx and Freidrich Engels, who promoted the ideals of socialism and communism to create a classless system, which theoretically functioned for the entire community at the expense of the entire community. Marxist theory argued that all social problems were a direct result of capitalism and could be eliminated if socialism was in place instead.

Marx and Engels detail their vision of a Marxist society in the *Communist Manifesto,* where they argue for a proletariat revolution (a workers' revolution) in hopes of throwing off the chains of capitalism. If successful, eventually the state would evolve to require no government, as the proletariat would rise to manage affairs themselves.

Utopian Socialist Theory also emerged as a response to the explosion of capitalism. This theory envisions a utopian civilization created using socialism that would provide for all members of its community. One example of utopian socialism was put into action by Robert Owen, a Welsh farmer who created a utopian center called New Lanark Mills, where he provided free education, improved working conditions, and increased wages. Owens' commune eventually failed, and its members left.

Anarchism, the complete removal of all governments as the only way to achieve true happiness and freedom, also emerged as a response to the political systems of this period. To maintain some form of organization, many people argued for locally elected councils. Others employed terrorism and fear as a means of ruling.

All of these philosophies influenced the political and social dialog of the period. Some were more influential than others; for example, Marxism culminated in the emergence of communism during the 20th century.

Marxism was given practical expression in many nations, starting with Russia after the successful Bolshevik Revolution of 1917. In reality, communism (Marxism) was a humanitarian catastrophe. Far from an egalitarian utopia with no government, communism led to brutal dictatorial regimes that murdered their citizens indiscriminately.

Lenin at Putilov factory in May 1917

Historians debate how many perished as a result of the famines and executions perpetrated by the Soviet government – such as the Ukrainian famine and the Tatar expulsion – but it has been established that the Soviet Union alone was directly responsible for the slaughter of at least twenty million people. While the plague was an unavoidable consequence of ignorance, that is not true of communism. The Soviet Union was only one of many communist nations, all of which have had a bloody history. Collectively, communist regimes have cost more lives than the two world wars combined.

In Qing China and the Ottoman Empire, some members of the government resisted economic change and attempted to maintain preindustrial forms of economic production.

While many states recognized the importance and power of the Industrial Revolution, others sought to avoid its influence altogether. These included Qing dynasty China and the Ottoman Empire. Neither of these two governments survived. The Qing dynasty of China experienced various periods of turbulence, including the Taiping Rebellion, where for the first time Chinese rulers were aware that reform was needed in hopes of continuing the Chinese empire. However, by the point of the Self-Strengthening Movement, the Qing dynasty had lost valuable influence, which was instead being replaced by foreign influence.

The Ottoman Empire also struggled to adapt to the industrial age and sought limited reforms only when all other means had failed. To prop up the Ottoman Empire, British forces stepped in to maintain their territories on several occasions—only because they feared a Russian Empire with expanded territories. However, such initiatives proved inconsequential as the Ottoman Empire earned the nickname "the sick man of Europe" until its collapse in the 20th century.

In a small number of states, governments promoted their state-sponsored visions of industrialization.

In states outside of the European Empire, there were various adaptations of industrialization occurring at different rates; for example, Japan under the Meiji government, Egypt under Muhammad Ali, and Tsarist Russia. The Meiji government of Japan was one of the only Asian governments to embrace industrialization, and this policy path led them to great success, both domestically and abroad. As the Industrial process took off, foreign influence in economic, political, and social customs grew in Japan. As a result of this industrial success, Japan gained autonomy in the world on a level it had never previously had. In the 1900s, Japan was able to wage wars against its neighbors, including China and Tsarist Russia. Japan also gained concessions from the dominant world powers in the post–World War I period, establishing it as the dominant regional power in the Pacific.

The Russian Empire also embraced the process of Industrialization by building railroads and giant factories. Some academics argue this process was a direct reaction to the military threat posed by Japan. Russia never achieved industrialization on the scale of the Western European nations, North America, and Japan. Later, Soviet Russia made a major effort to complete the industrialization that the Tsarists had started. However, because Russia did not have a capitalist economic system, with freedom for every citizen to contribute their ideas and with a reward incentive, the Soviet Union never caught up to the West, and the humanitarian cost of trying to do so was huge.

In response to criticisms of global industrial capitalism, some governments mitigated the negative effects of industrial capitalism by promoting various types of reforms.

The explosion of global capitalism shocked many people, as it was a system never before seen on such a scale. Despite the dramatic and rapid improvement in the lives of the poor under capitalism (e.g., vastly improved health and diet, housing, educational opportunities, and complete social and economic mobility), many only saw the negatives, such as discrepancies in wealth between workers and wealthy businessmen, pollution from factories and long workdays. Compared to the pre-capitalist economic systems that existed before the Industrial Revolution, wealth discrepancies, workday length, child labor conditions, and child mortality rates were much improved in industrialized areas. Most people were unaware of these improvements and reacted strongly to conditions they wished to change. Such reactions were permitted under the freedom of democratic societies but would have meant imprisonment or execution in many other regimes in history. In response to their citizens' unrest, many European governments attempted various reforms in hopes of maintaining peace and prosperity in their territories.

Germany introduced state pensions and public health care programs that were completely unheard of before this period. Chancellor Otto Von Bismarck, the unifier of the German state, introduced compensation for unemployment, medical insurance, and forms of social security after being greatly influenced by socialism.

Chancellor Otto Von Bismarck

Britain expanded suffrage, the right to run for government office, or vote. In 1832, the British Parliament voted to limit the number of qualifications necessary to vote. This eventually led to universal male suffrage and, later, total suffrage for all citizens. Additionally, various states worked to improve their public education systems. The expansion of freedoms and liberties—which are necessary preconditions to a capitalist system—was the starting point for movements, including universal suffrage for men and women and state-run welfare programs, which dominated America during the Great Depression and First World War.

How people organized themselves into societies also underwent significant transformations in industrialized states due to the fundamental restructuring of the global economy.

As urbanization boomed and people flooded across the Atlantic to seek a better life, it quickly became clear that a new form of social organization needed to be established. The emergence of a working middle class had never been seen before this period. Examples of such social change were seen in the ethnic enclaves throughout the Americas and West and South Africa, as well as the end of serfdom and slavery in Europe. All of these changes were a direct result of the Industrial Revolution, which increased the movement of people and goods and created a new global economic system that, in turn, allowed for the emergence of large economic powers in Britain, France, Germany, and the United States.

New social classes, including the middle class and the industrial working class, developed.

As a result of urbanization, the Industrial Revolution, and great migrations of the period, new social classes emerged – specifically the working and middle classes. These new forms of social status were a direct result of the widespread availability of improved modern job opportunities, such as factory work, and skilled manual labor jobs like mining, railroad building, and construction.

The increased wages of the middle class allowed them to have a higher standard of living and increased quality of life. Many middle and higher class people came to believe that lower-class people were guilty of designing their failures and futures by a lack of hard work and loyalty.

The emergence of such social classes was also monumental in shifting the political and cultural norms of the time; for the first time, aristocrats were not the only wealthy demographic in Europe. A merchant class had been established and would continue to mold the policies and practices of governments for many years. This particular transition also highlights the change from a government focused on a few elite citizens to one who had to seek the support of a wider variety of social groups.

Family dynamics, gender roles, and demographics changed in response to industrialization.

As the factories and cities grew, many more families were interested in relocating, and a rapid change in family structures occurred as a result. The social structure and demographics of both urban and rural dwellings were also transformed. As men left for higher-paying factory jobs, they quickly earned the title of "breadwinner," a concept that perpetuated in American culture until the 1960s and 1970s. Lower class women and children were seen as cheaper sources of employment and quickly integrated into the industrial machine. However, middle and upper-class white women were expected to maintain their homes and children and were largely excluded from political life.

Children working in a textile mill

As a result of these conditions, many elderly were seen as a burden in the urban setting and were typically discriminated against. Concerns regarding child labor also arose during this period, though that cause did not experience widespread popularity until the 20th century. The transition in gender roles cemented the roles of women and men and prevented women from being able to obtain many work and educational opportunities until the 20th century.

Rapid urbanization that accompanied global capitalism often led to unsanitary conditions, as well as to new forms of community.

Industrialization rapidly created opportunities for much higher wages than the poor could expect in pre-industrial economic systems, leading to the sudden and massive migration of rural and immigrant populations to the cities. Port cities were the first to experience explosive immigration and growth. After the port cities, factories developed in the cities of each nation's interior, where coal, iron, and other resources were harvested. Working-class people's wages and material standard of living improved in many ways. However, at the same time, the speed with which they migrated to the major cities, by the millions, meant that there were relative shortages of adequate housing, clean water, and waste removal. These shortages led to many public health issues.

The influx of the new populations overwhelmed European cities, which were all still basically medieval, designed to support only wealthy families and their servants. Access to necessities, such as clean water, was a major issue at first, even though lower-income families had greater access to quality food and solid shelter than they historically had. Two major health crises emerged in all of the major industrial cities – and were eventually mitigated by the same capitalist system which had created the overpopulation in the first place. One was pollution: the first factories, railroads, and mines used huge coal-burning steam engines and continued to do so for over a hundred years. The other issue was disease epidemics, triggered by unsanitary and crowded conditions.

London's history offers the best example of how overpopulation created epidemics and how the problem was resolved in a free market context. The lack of clean drinking water caused recurring cholera epidemics in London throughout the 19th century. London's citizens used the Thames River simultaneously as the main place to dispose of human waste and the main place from which to draw their drinking water. This practice had been established when London was created, almost two thousand years earlier. It had been tenable when the population was relatively low and, therefore, the waste which was thrown into the river dissipated reasonably well. However, with the industrial age population explosion and the additional sources of waste created by the consumer society, the Thames became seriously polluted.

Doctor John Snow used the scientific method to determine the link between cholera epidemics and polluted drinking water. He then successfully advocated for proper sewage and freshwater system for London, which led to the reduction and eventual elimination of cholera. This sewage system was an immense undertaking, which was possible only with the increase of wealth and technology which the capitalist system had brought.

There were many positive consequences of the growth of cities as well. New communities developed, including progressive thinking societies that fought for civil rights – their own, and those of the indigenous, colonial populations. The women's rights movement, anti-slavery movements, and temperance (anti-alcohol) movements are the most significant examples of political movements which had existed as nascent, powerless discussion groups prior to industrialization, but became major movements when millions of people came together in close proximity due to urbanization. The concept of unionization was also hatched in the industrial cities, where single employers employed hundreds or even thousands of workers at a single site, like a mine or a mill.

Industrializing powers established transoceanic empires.

As the great powers capitalized on the Industrial Revolution, they were able to strengthen their vast transoceanic empires in Oceania, Southeast Asia, Central Asia, and the Americas. This was a peak period, especially for the British and French colonial empires. Meanwhile, Spain and the Netherlands relinquished the final fragments of their once significant empires. Others—the United States, Japan, Germany, and Italy—entered the colonial empire-building game late, and some made false starts at empire-building, which did not succeed.

Empire expansion also highlights the effect of industrialization on global trade and trade patterns; for the first time, all corners of the globe were connected by the production of raw materials into finished goods. Without European industrial giants, the Industrial Revolution would not have spread to Asia and Africa. Without the colonial settlements created by these transoceanic empires, no colonial markets would have existed for European merchants to export their finished products.

States with existing colonies strengthened their control over those colonies.

As imperialism spread, it became even more important for empires to protect the colonies under their control from foreign capture and internal rebellion. Examples of this can be seen in the policies enacted by the British towards India, as well as the actions were taken by the Dutch in Indonesia. The British government actively ruled India from 1858 to 1947, following the transfer of authority from the British East India Company to the British Crown. This period is referred to as the British Raj and had a great influence on the development of the Indian subcontinent, as well as the British Empire as a whole. The Great Indian Uprising in 1857 greatly frightened the British operating in India; however, it was not catastrophic enough to derail the empire and can be seen as a turning point in British-Indian affairs. As a result of both external competition and internal struggle, the British Empire greatly tightened the reins it held over India.

In other parts of the world, industrialized states practiced economic imperialism.

As global powers looked to exert ever greater influence, European colonists sought new markets where they would face less competition from each other. As a result, the Opium Wars occurred in China, and both the British and the United States made a substantial investment in Latin America.

A similar strategy was also employed in Latin America by the United States and the British, who wanted to maintain their influence by controlling the ability of this region to industrialize. As a result, both the British and Americans attempted to limit industrialization in hopes of controlling the raw materials of the region to gain an economic upper hand in global markets.

Such initiatives continued to foster unhappy relationships between imperialists and the people they were taking advantage of. The resentful sentiment gave rise to nationalism, which emerged during the later part of this period.

Imperialism influenced state formation and contraction around the world.

As global powers worked to expand their influence, the emergence of imperialism was seen in the Americas, Europe and in the East, such as in the Russian Empire. All of these global powers belied the key to maintaining their successes and status through the use of imperial forces throughout their colonies. Examples of this type of ruling structure were seen all over the world, including in the French and British colonies of Southeast Asia, the American settlement in the Philippines, and the Dutch and French colonies in sub-Saharan Africa. Imperialism led many people to revolt against their imperialist masters. Revolts occurred in places like the Balkans, Philippines, Haiti, and Central Asia. These revolutions and rebellions were also caused by the cultural transitions and transformations stemming from the Enlightenment; however, the majority of grievances were a result of the treatment of native people by imperialists.

The United States and Russia emulated European transoceanic imperialism by expanding their land borders and conquering neighboring territories.

As the Russian and American governments looked to expand their influence, they sought to follow the European model of imperialism, believing it would produce beneficial results. American and Russian maritime forces led expeditions in hopes of creating new colonies and expanding their influence within the global system. Colonial territorial holdings were important because they were a means of asserting global power, but also of controlling the flow of raw goods in return for finished products.

As the Russian Empire looked to expand, it set its sights on Central Asia and made an aggressive campaign against British interests in India. Initially, the Russians were able to conquer various territories in Central Asia, including but not limited to the cities of Samarkand, Tashkent, and Bukhara. However, the Russian Empire was unable to gain a real foothold in India, which remained in the hands of the British.

America's expansion from its original thirteen colonies into its final continental scope followed an imperialistic course. One difference with the American imperialistic movement is that it did not have as much of a transoceanic scope as European colonization did. America did have some overseas territories in the Philippines, Hawaii, and Cuba that were subjugated by military force, but the bulk of American expansion occurred within the North American continent.

President James Monroe

The Monroe Doctrine specifically excluded American colonization outside of the American hemisphere. Expansionist (imperialistic) American presidents, such as Democrats Andrew Jackson, James Monroe and James K. Polk, and Republicans William McKinley and Theodore Roosevelt, focused on acquiring territory within the continent from the European powers and on removing native people so that European settlers could claim the land.

A few years later, a pivotal document known as the "Monroe Doctrine" was published by another Democrat, President James Monroe. This declared that the Americas were for colonization by the United States only and not by any other foreign power. This was used as the diplomatic pretext (or rationalization) for future expansionist presidents to use coercive measures to eject European powers—and then the native people—from more areas within the American continent.

In the 1840s, continuing the expansionist vision of the Democratic Party, President James K. Polk initiated a war of conquest against newly independent Mexico, which resulted in a treaty that ceded roughly half of the territory of Mexico to the United States. In that same war, Texas was wrested from Mexican influence. America also forcibly acquired the areas which soon became the states of California, Nevada, Arizona, Utah, and New Mexico.

Spain still retained remnants of the empire that it had established three hundred years earlier. In 1898, America and Spain fought a short war, which resulted in the United States acquiring the few overseas territories it would ever have: Cuba, the Philippines, Puerto Rico, and Guam. Under democratic president Grover Cleveland in the 1890s, Hawaii also became a

U.S. territory. The story was a distinctly imperialistic one: American sugarcane growers wanted control of Hawaii for their industry and the indigenous royal family; there was an obstacle. With the help of U.S. Marines, under orders from Cleveland, the royal family was ousted, and after the suppression of a series of rebellions, Hawaii was conquered.

New states developed on the edges of existing empires.

As European and American states expanded, they typically assimilated or removed the indigenous cultures they encountered. Several cultures, like the Cherokee Nation and the Zulu Kingdom, tried to find existence on the outskirts of the empires. Diseases following European conquest had almost completely decimated the Cherokee Nation. The Cherokee Nation lost between 5,000 and 15,000 of their people on the Trail of Tears between 1838 and 1839 when the U.S. military forced them to leave their lands and march from the Eastern Woodlands of the Mississippi River into Oklahoma. This treatment at the hands of President Andrew Jackson only strengthened the resolve of the Cherokee people to maintain their culture and traditions instead of assimilating into American society.

President Andrew Jackson

The development and spread of nationalism as an ideology fostered new communal identities.

As the new concept of nationalism spread across Europe and other regions, many new alliances were formed. Examples of nationalism were seen in Germany, the Philippines, and Liberia. The German nation was created during this period, having been unified in 1871 by Chancellor Otto Von Bismarck, who had developed a strong sense of German nationalism during his youth. Bismarck employed both diplomatic and military tactics in his quest to foster German nationalism.

New racial ideologies, especially Social Darwinism, facilitated and justified imperialism.

One popular school of thought was Social Darwinism. This and other racial ideologies supported by the pseudo-science of the period caused many in European and American governments to embrace imperialist and colonial policies, which in many instances placed white settlers ahead of other ethnicities and races. Social Darwinism made classifications not only between races but also between the wealthy and the poor.

Herbert Spencer

One of the first philosophers to promote the theory of Social Darwinism was Herbert Spencer, who applied these theories to social, political, and economic identity. Spencer made the argument that, according to the science available at the time, it was clear that the white European race was superior to others and therefore destined to rule other races. These ideas influenced eugenics and the philosophies of genocide promoted by the Nazis. Scientific racism was seen most notably in industrialized communities and made the argument that blacks and other minorities were less mentally developed, making them more fit for factory jobs and menial work.

The rise and diffusion of Enlightenment thought that questioned established traditions in all areas of life often preceded the revolutions and rebellions against existing governments.

As the Enlightenment transitioned into its later period, the social, political, and religious norms of earlier years were replaced by an era of science, rationality, and nationalism. The regional expressions of Enlightenment most heavily influenced this thought change seen across Europe, as each state or region experienced wavering periods of superiority.

Regardless of the location, the key figures of the Enlightenment (also referred to as the Age of Reason) were insistent on questioning the norms of their predecessors. In some cases, they even questioned the Roman Catholic Church.

In addition to the religious and cultural transitions of the period, there was a great transformation in government, both in practice and representation. This was seen in every part of Europe as well as in the Americas – most notably in the American and French Revolutions. However, progressive ideas of this period were also applied in less volatile instances.

One example, which embodies the ideas of the Enlightenment, comes from Jean-Jacques Rousseau in his last political, literary work, *Considerations of the Government of Poland,* which was published in 1782 and gave a detailed outline of a new constitution to be applied in Poland. This constitution shows the change occurring in political ideas and their application. Formerly, such brazen political deliberation would have been met with great force by monarchs; however, the political revolutions of the Enlightenment were shifting power away from monarchies and laying the foundations of modern Europe.

Jean-Jacques Rousseau

Increasing discontent with imperial rule propelled reformist and revolutionary movements.

As colonists and Europeans learned and expanded Enlightenment schools of thought, it became clear that the actions of the ruling governments were not typically in the interest of the people. As a result, rebellion—and in some instance revolution—broke out. Some of the most notable examples are the American and French Revolutions. Other examples include struggles for independence in Venezuela, the Haitian Rebellion and Revolution, and the Boxer Rebellion in China. This period was unlike any other regarding the political and cultural revolutions experienced around the world. When the American Revolution began, it was not known that its outcome would influence the ideas of the French Revolution, which toppled a monarchy that had been in place since the 9th century. Such events were inconceivable in the early modern period when monarchs were celebrated as extensions of God.

As revolutionaries aligned themselves with one another, it became more and more apparent to the French, British, and Spanish governments that imperial rule would be changed forever. It is almost inconceivable that in the American Revolutionary War, the American colonies defeated the British, who had the best-funded and trained military force to date. When American victory transpired, it inspired a sense of divine inspiration and focused on the colonies and other revolutionaries around the world. The nationalistic sentiment was sweeping through European and American cultures during this period.

The Haitian Revolution began as an uprising of slaves against French colonial rulers. Similarly, the Boxer Rebellion in China, which took place roughly a century after the revolutions in America, France, and Haiti, was a reaction to foreign influence in the country. It was not a slave uprising, but the Boxers had two primary things in common with their counterparts in those types of rebellions: they were ardent nationalists and anti-monarchists. Such revolutions and rebellions had widespread impacts and created the foundation of contemporary geopolitics. They questioned the authority of longtime rulers, such as the British and Spanish monarchs. Regardless of the outcomes of the American, French, and Haitian Revolutions, the new global powers included the British, French, German, Russian, and new American nation. The nationalism that developed during the colonial period also fostered animosity, rivalry, and war.

Foreigners are killed during the Boxer Rebellion

Religious ideas and millenarianism influenced some of the rebellions.

Religious ideas and prophecy are frequently reoccurring patterns in history, leading to rebellions of subjugated peoples. "Millenarianism" is a form of prophetic belief that has occurred in many subjugated societies throughout history, with similar characteristics in each unrelated case. The usual premise of a millenarian prophecy is that there is an oppressor who needs to be vanquished. Fundamental to each of these prophecies is a catastrophe. The catastrophe is within the power of the oppressed people to invoke, by performing some humbling sacrifice, and its function is to destroy the oppressor. These prophecies always predict a complete renewal of the world in the wake of the catastrophe, with the oppressed culture experiencing a revival. Some examples of rebellions that followed this model are: the Taiping Rebellion, the Ghost Dance, and the Xhosa Cattle-Killing Movement.

Responses to increasingly frequent rebellions led to reforms in imperial policies.

As a result of extensive rebellions and anti-imperial movements, some governments, such as the Ottomans and Chinese, enacted reforms to appease their populations. The Tanzimat Movement embraced by the Ottomans was a transformative movement that gave all subjects of the Ottoman Empire equal rights to life, liberty, and property, regardless of their religion. These reforms were a direct result of the uprisings and insurrections occurring in the Ottoman Empire, as well as an attempt at modernization. This was largely successful, yet the access that outside empires, such as France, Great Britain, and Russia, gained to the internal affairs of the Ottoman Empire led to fifty years of outside powers stoking the fires of minority discontent within the empire. This eventually led to the horrible mistreatment of minority ethnic groups, who were perceived to have been undermining the empire at the behest of an outside power. This mistreatment manifested in massacres, such as the 1878 repression of the Bulgarians after the imposition of the Treaty of Berlin, and the 1915 Armenian Genocide. The Self-Strengthening Movement in China was also an attempt at updating and reforming the empire in hopes of eliminating unrest and uprisings. The main goals of this movement were to update educational systems, diplomatic services, industrial factories, and the military. Many of the reforms were met with mixed enthusiasm from the government and Chinese people, and never really produced great changes within Chinese culture.

The global spread of European political and social thought and the increasing number of rebellions stimulated new transnational ideologies and solidarities.

As the Enlightenment period peaked, it was clear that new ideas, political theories, and movements were dominating both the European continent and the Americas. Improved methods of communication, the introduction of urban metropolitan centers of culture, and the openness towards change brought about by the Enlightenment and Industrial Revolution, allowed these new ways of thinking to spread quickly. This period embodied the transition from absolutism into new political models such as communism, democracy, and socialism. Before 1750, all empires in Europe, Asia, and the Islamic world were ruled exclusively by a monarch, who typically practiced absolutism. Two exceptions were England and the

Netherlands, who employed constitutional monarchies as a direct result of revolutions, rebellions, and upheavals that had previously occurred against the monarchies. Between 1750 and 1900, almost every absolutist monarchy had been overturned and replaced with a more liberal form of government that allowed for broader demographic representation.

This change in political and cultural behavior was especially important as it marked a change from loyalty to a bloodline or monarch, to loyalty to one's nation. This sentiment expanded and created strong sense of nationalism throughout Europe, as well as in the United States, where nationalist sentiment led to the beginning of the American Revolution. Another form of political change came in the form of rebellions or uprisings. While many monarchists in Europe and loyalists in the Americas saw the American colonies as rebels acting treasonously against the crown, others saw it as the birth of political theory and an application of Enlightenment philosophy. These ideas all originated from European minds like Locke, Voltaire, Rousseau, Montesquieu, and Hume and influenced monumental figures in American history, including Thomas Jefferson, John Adams, and Benjamin Franklin.

Migration, in many cases, was influenced by changes in demography in both industrialized and unindustrialized societies that presented challenges to existing patterns of living.

As many European states experienced the increased prosperity of the Industrial Revolution, migrants looked to these countries as potential lands of opportunity. The British and Dutch Empires had greatly expanded and continued to do so using imperialism. These empires were only able to expand as a result of the millions of migrant workers who labored to expand them. Migration also spread various cultures and traditions, which were not always welcomed. For example, ethnic enclaves created by Chinese immigrants struggled to adapt to their new setting outside of their familiar cultural context, and, as a result, many immigrants with a similar difficulty in adapting to their host culture were subjected to oppression and racism. All of these changes stemmed from the Industrial Revolution. This period had its challenges, but also brought about nationalism, urbanization, and a better quality of living for most social classes – especially the newly emerging working class.

Changes in food production and improved medical conditions contributed to a significant global rise in population.

Advances in agricultural production and practices during the Industrial Revolution often created food surpluses. This was a new concept for many Europeans and Southeast Asians, who were used to enduring food shortages, which still occurred but with far less frequency. The increase in food production during this time was astronomical and allowed many governments to worry less about feeding their population, allowing them to shift their focus to developing other sectors of the economy. One notable exception to this was in France, where food riots were an important part of the French Revolution. These surpluses caused an immediate population increase throughout Europe that proved to be important in later periods when mass labor was needed. In total, the European population increased from 100 million people in 1700 to 400 million people in 1900. This large and rapid increase is even more impressive given the drastic population decrease in Europe in earlier periods due to the Black Death and environmental shifts.

While the human race was prone to famines throughout history, disease pandemics wiped out even larger numbers of people than famine and wars. The great plagues were the most destructive, but they were not the only mass outbreaks of disease in history. Cholera and flu epidemics occurred almost every decade and killed millions (sometimes even tens of millions), such as the Spanish Influenza outbreak during the First World War that killed more people than the war itself. In the 19th century, public health research was done by individuals like Doctor John Snow, who determined the cause of repeating cholera epidemics in London and also proposed preventative measures.

Doctor Snow linked cholera to polluted drinking water and proposed sanitation measures, specifically proper sewage and freshwater system for London, as an antidote. The money he needed to finance the projects was made available by the surplus funds created by the Industrial Revolution and the unprecedented freedom of ordinary individuals to act without asking a king for permission. Snow's work not only prevented millions of future deaths in London but also rescued the entire world from continual death by disease. Enabled by the new freedom of the market, many other health researchers made other equally momentous contributions to the elimination of disease. The flu vaccine, which we take for granted today, was another discovery that put an end to perennial disease epidemics that used to kill millions of people.

John Snow, English physician

The population explosion of the 19th century was the result of unprecedented food surpluses and improvements in the public health arena, like better sanitation practices and medicines. The abundance of food and dramatic reduction of disease led to the population explosion not by increasing procreation, but by decreasing death rates, particularly those of children. Improvements such as food surpluses and public health measures were the result of the free market system of capitalism.

While many migrants permanently relocated, a significant number of temporary and seasonal migrants returned to their home societies.

Massive immigration for work was seen throughout the globe, with notable examples including Japanese laborers, Lebanese workers, and Italians who migrated to Latin America for seasonal work. Following the Meiji restoration in Japan, many laborers left to work on sugar plantations in Hawaii and guano mines in Peru. The plantation and mine owners typically welcomed these labor forces as they replaced a depleted slave workforce and were temporary inhabitants—they stayed only long enough to earn a decent wage and then return to Japan.

Another example of seasonal migration was seen in Argentina and Brazil, where Italian immigrants and laborers were crucial to coffee production in the region. Many of these Italian laborers replaced slave labor, as slavery had been abolished. The workers were paid directly by the Brazilian and Argentinean governments and returned to Italy following the coffee-growing season. Instead of being laborers, Lebanese merchants worked to establish trade networks for newly established American businesses.

The large-scale nature of migration, especially in the 19th century, produced a variety of consequences and reactions to the increasingly diverse societies on the part of migrants and the existing populations.

As migrants flocked to other regions, such as the United States, Oceania, and sub-Saharan Africa, many were met with difficult working conditions, racism, and other forms of oppression. As a result, many people attempted to adapt to the communities to which they were migrating while also maintaining their cultural traditions. These migrations and the creation of new ethnic communities led to a more diverse population in Africa; however, in the United States and Oceania, they were met with resistance from both imperialistic governments and others. Examples include the White Australia policies of the British Empire, as well as the Chinese Exclusion Act passed by the United States Congress.

Migrants often created ethnic enclaves in different parts of the world, which helped transplant their culture into new environments and facilitated the development of migrant support networks.

As massive influxes of immigrants continued to arrive in the Americas and other industrializing regions of the world, traditions and cultures were also transported abroad. Cultural enclaves were created as centers of support and culture for newly arrived immigrants, such as the Chinese and Indian populations.

Immigrant women

The Chinese who immigrated to the United States created secure areas, such as the Chinatowns in Brooklyn and San Francisco. These "cities within a city" allowed for newly arrived Chinese to seek advice, financial help, and banking services, as well as maintain their cultural traditions without infringement or jeering by others.

People who migrated from India to Africa created similar practices and traditions, and account for large portions of the African population today. Similar contemporary demographics in the Caribbean are a result of the descendants of indentured Indian immigrants who came to British Guiana between 1838 and the 1920s. Their descendants continued to play pivotal roles in government and culture throughout the 20th century and in contemporary times.

Notes for active learning

Europe

Major historical events of the period:

1500s:	Russian peasantry begins to be directly controlled by landowners
1517:	Martin Luther wrote "the Ninety-Five Theses," triggering the Reformation
1519:	Ferdinand Magellan leaves Spain and becomes first European to sail into the Pacific Ocean
1615:	Miguel de Cervantes completes writing *Don Quixote*
1618–1648:	The Thirty Years War
1702–1713:	Queen Anne's War
1730–1780:	High Enlightenment
1750:	Factory system introduced in England
1780–1815:	Late Enlightenment
1789–1799:	French Revolution
1833:	Slavery Abolition Act is passed in England
1861:	Russian Emperor Alexander II enacts the Emancipation Reform abolishing serfdom
1871:	Otto Von Bismarck unites Germany

PERIOD 3: 1500 to 1900 C.E.

EUROPE

European technological developments in cartography and navigation built on previous knowledge developed in the classical, Islamic, and Asian worlds and included the production of new tools, innovations in ship designs, and an improved understanding of global wind and current patterns—all of which made transoceanic travel and trade possible.

To facilitate advances in travel and trade, the English, French, Spanish, Portuguese, and Chinese Empires continued to develop various technologies and techniques that allowed them to travel farther, both faster and with more navigational certainty than was previously possible. This increased global trade and led to the creation of monopolies, such as the Dutch East India Company and the British East India Company.

The use of astronomical measurements was crucial to navigation during this and later periods. Technologies of the period included the astrolabe, which measures the angles of the sun and stars above the horizon, thereby making it possible to determine latitude. Other versions of astrolabes were found in the Islamic world and were introduced in approximately the mid-8th century. The astrolabe was extremely important for navigation before the invention of the sextant.

Universal astrolabes were also created during the 15th and 16th centuries. However, these were less popular than their smaller counterparts, as they were costly to build and complex to operate. Early manufacturing mainly took place in Augsburg and Nuremberg, Germany, as well as smaller operations in France. In addition to mastering navigational tools, explorers of this period began to understand and study the Trade Winds. The Trade Winds are known as the prevailing winds that blow southeast toward the Equator in the Northern Hemisphere and northeast toward the Equator in the Southern Hemisphere.

One example of this innovation is from Portugal, where navigation schools taught the concept of the Volta do Mar (Portuguese for "turn of the sea," or "return from the sea"), which used trade winds and oceanic currents to facilitate travel in a specific direction. Understanding oceanic current patterns were also important during the Age of Exploration and were extensively studied by many seafaring empires. The implementation of the sternpost-mounted rudder further improved the steering capacity of ships, allowing them to change course more quickly, thereby making them easier to navigate and manage. The first sternpost rudders were invented during the Han Dynasty in China. Evidence of their efficiency can be seen in the Chinese ships of the period, which were superior to most others.

Portuguese caravels are said to have originated in the 9th century as fishing vessels. However, they evolved to be the most navigable and speedy ships of the Age of Exploration. During the 15th and 16th centuries, these ships were distinct and possessed admirable qualities, such as quickness and agility. Many of these ships also used lateen sails, which were essential in creating vessels that were faster and better able to manage the winds. Greater efficiency in harnessing the winds also allowed for ships to travel faster over longer distances. Examples of the use of these ships are seen in the settling of West Africa by the Portuguese.

These vessels became prominent during the 15th and 16th centuries, due in part to the exploratory missions led by the Spanish and Portuguese Empires. Some have even claimed the Nina and the Pinta, which were part of Columbus's initial voyages to the Americas, were adaptations of caravels. The adoption of "skeleton-first" hull construction meant that ships could be strong and dependable during long sea voyages. This type of construction further strengthened the ability and desire for long-distance travel and exploration. The implementation of the dry compass was also important, and its use, coupled with astrolabes and cross-staffs, allowed sailors to travel more efficiently while making fewer mistakes and requiring fewer stops along the way. This was important as it reduced the high cost of operating such expeditions but also spoke to the technological status of the various empires.

As a result of extended and intensified travel, innovations in cartography were necessary to continue the exploration of the Americas and the East. During this period, maps became more readily available to a greater number of people, making travel easier and more accessible. Such accessibility proved instrumental in the European dominance of maritime travel and the maintenance of overseas colonies.

A notable example of advancing cartography was the work of Sebastian Cabot (1474–1557), who was born in Italy and known as an advanced mapmaker and explorer. Cabot worked as a cartographer for various monarchs of the period, including England's Kings Henry VII and Henry VIII, and Spain's King Ferdinand V. Some have argued that he may have even secretly explored on behalf of the Venetians. Cabot came from a family of explorers: his father was the explorer John Cabot. Cabot unsuccessfully searched for the Northwest Passage (a water route to travel across North America) in 1508, as well as unsuccessfully navigating a trip around the world between 1526 and 1529.

Sebastian Cabot, Italian mapmaker and explorer

The importance of these technological advances cannot be overstated, as they allowed for maritime travel, which dominated the period and led to the establishment of colonialism and world empires. These interactions had unbelievable consequences for the native populations of Africa, as well as the Americas. Additionally, they allowed the groundwork to be set for the empires of the 18th and 19th centuries, which would come to dominate global affairs in economics, politics, and military confrontations.

Remarkable new transoceanic maritime reconnaissance occurred in this period.

Transoceanic travel and reconnaissance had drastic impacts on both the European empires undertaking these expeditions and on the native populations of Africa and the New World. Starting with Portugal's exploration, the establishment of maritime trade and permanent settlements proved to be extremely lucrative during this and later periods. As Portugal began to explore Central America and Asia extensively, it quickly gained a prominent status within the trade markets. Access to luxury commodities and goods, which fetched high prices in European elite circles of the period, bolstered Portugal's reputation as an important and dominant economic entity.

One of the most notable Portuguese explorers was Bartolomeu Dias, who lived from 1457 to 1500 and explored the coast of Africa. Dias is well known for leading the first European expedition to sail around the Cape of Good Hope in 1488 successfully. Dias originally named the tip of Africa the "Cape of Storms," as its waters were perilous to navigate and had killed many sailors. This expedition was instrumental in opening extremely lucrative trading routes between Europe and Asia. Later expeditions included a trip near South America in 1500, where Dias became one of the first Europeans to see Brazil.

One of the first people to identify the Gulf Stream, which we now know is crucial to the global climate and oceanic systems, was Juan Ponce de Leon. Ponce de Leon was born in Spain in 1460 and led a European expedition hoping to find the mythical Fountain of Youth. However, he instead discovered the southeast coast of present-day Florida and went on to become the first governor of Puerto Rico.

Vasco da Gama, who lived from 1460 until 1524, was also a notable Portuguese explorer. Through his expeditions, he was able to find an ocean route connecting Portugal with the East. Sailing from Lisbon, Portugal around the Cape of Good Hope, on to India and back was a feat which was believed impossible at the time.

Ferdinand Magellan lived from 1480 until 1521. He is most famous for being the first person to circumnavigate the globe. In 1519, Magellan left Spain with a fleet of five ships, in hopes of discovering trading routes to the Spice Islands. However, during his three-year journey, he instead found the Strait of Magellan and is credited with being the first European to cross into the Pacific, reconnecting Asia with Europeans. His travels were instrumental in scientific discoveries and further advanced mapmaking through the implementation of his discoveries.

Portuguese motivations for maritime exploration and reconnaissance were similar to others during the period and included the desire to acquire vast wealth. The Asian continent produced goods that were in high demand by European elites. As a result, many Europeans sought to find a way to both acquire these luxury goods and manage their further trade for economic benefit. The desire to wield and hold power was extremely high, especially as global empires were emerging.

Notable Italian explorers of the period include Amerigo Vespucci (1454–1512), the first person to realize that the Americas were located on a continent separate from Asia - which was contrary to the commonly held notions of the time. As a result, the North and South

American continents are named after him. Giovanni da Verrazzano (1485–1528) was another Italian explorer who, in 1524, explored the northeast coast of North America from Cape Fear, North Carolina to Maine, while searching for a Northwest Passage to Asia.

The maritime exploration of this period established colonies and settlements, which would form the basis of maritime empires in later periods. These initial expeditions and exploration also allowed for the flow of goods across the globe, creating new social classes and expectations for those living in European Empires. The empires of this period were continuously expanding, growing, and envisioning a future dominated by their state.

Portuguese development of a school for navigation led to increased travel to and trade with West Africa and resulted in the construction of a global trading-post empire.

The Portuguese had a dramatic influence on the oceanic exploration and global trade of this period; they were among the first to engage in the slave trade, West African colonization, and the colonization of the Americas. Portuguese explorers were able to travel greater distances and engage in trade with various peoples who had luxury goods to offer. These two factors propelled the Portuguese state to the status of a maritime empire.

The Portuguese were extremely influential in the maritime success of the Age of Exploration, and much of this success was due to one man, Prince Henry the Navigator. Prince Henry (1394–1460) was a Portuguese prince, soldier, and patron of explorers. In approximately 1418, Prince Henry created the first school of navigation, with its astronomical observatory, in Sagres, Portugal. Those who attended this school learned the skills of cartography (map making) and trained in navigation and sailing, with the hope of eventually becoming skilled enough to sail the western coast of Africa. Using this school, Prince Henry sent various expeditions down the western coast of Africa, though he never made the journey himself. Some of the expeditions funded by Prince Henry's patronage included one to Cape Verde, in 1455; one to the Gambia River, in 1456; and one to the Cape of Palmas, in 1459.

Prince Henry the Navigator

Another notable expedition that took place as a result of Prince Henry's patronage was that of Gil Eannes, a Portuguese explorer who became the first person to sail beyond the Cape of Bojador and return successfully. Until this time, no European had successfully sailed beyond the

Cape of Bojador, which is located off of the Western Sahara Desert and subject to ferocious storms and powerful currents. With the support of Prince Henry, Gil Eannes was able to complete this expedition in 1434 successfully. This was monumental for further exploration and is an example of the influence and impact Prince Henry had on Portuguese exploration and global navigation.

Such schools were instrumental in creating new maps, expanding existing maps, and developing the field of cartography. These developments eventually led to the mapping of Western Africa and the spread of Christianity and commerce in the New World. As the Portuguese learned about West Africa and its waters, they began to construct a maritime empire using global trade and maritime advancements. Patrons of exploration like Prince Henry initially facilitated all of this. These advancements allowed Portuguese rulers to be the first to enjoy trading outposts in Western Africa and on the Cape of Good Hope (present-day Cape Town). Such economic success encouraged other Europeans to begin various expeditions into the Americas to look for additional trade routes connecting them with the East and the various goods of the region, which was so coveted among elites of the period.

In Oceania and Polynesia, established exchange and communication networks were not dramatically affected because of infrequent European reconnaissance in the Pacific Ocean.

Unlike the frequent attempts at colonization in the Americas, the regions of Polynesia and Oceania saw infrequent reconnaissance missions on the part of most of the European powers. One of the nations that did frequently explore this region was the Netherlands. This exploration was spearheaded by Dirk Hartog, a 17th-century Dutch sailor and explorer, who singlehandedly brought about the European impact on Australia. Hartog unintentionally came upon Australia after being separated from the rest of his expedition, following his landing at the Cape of Good Hope.

Willem de Vlamingh, Dutch explorer

Hartog initially named present-day Australia, "Dirk Hartog Island," and spent several days exploring its western coast. He was greatly disappointed and continued his voyage. Before leaving the island, Hartog placed a pewter plate detailing his landing and expedition. This was found by a later expedition to Australia, led by Willem de Vlamingh in 1696. Hartog's discovery also began the tradition of naming landings and leaving records of such events. Various explorers would continue this and left historians with archeological evidence of such expeditions, which had previously been questioned. Hartog's initial landing in Australia was also important as it mapped and detailed the terrain of land previously unknown.

The new global circulation of goods was facilitated by royal chartered European monopoly companies that took silver from the Spanish colonies in the Americas to purchase Asian goods for the Atlantic markets. However, regional markets continued to flourish in Afro-Eurasia by using established commercial practices and new transoceanic shipping services developed by European merchants.

As oceanic travel increased and maritime colonies were established, the movement of goods could not be stopped and would continue to propel global exploration and economies. As a result of such rapid economic expansion, new markets of trade within Asia, Africa, and the Americas developed and perpetuated the use of slave labor to meet the growing demands of the global market. In the early years of this system, Spain and Portugal dominated the global trade machine by holding trading posts on the western coast of Africa and maintaining vast merchant fleets. These two maritime empires were rivals and superior to maritime nations, such as the British, Dutch, Italian, and French.

The Manila Galleon facilitated Spanish trade between the Americas and the East for over 250 years. Such ships were large and well-armed; a necessity, as piracy was on the rise. Goods carried by the Manila Galleon included Asian luxury goods transported to Mexico, metal being traded with the Chinese during the Ming Dynasty and porcelain, and gold being taken from the Asian markets to the New World and back to Spanish and European markets. The dominance of Spanish economics and trade never transformed into total dominance of the European markets.

The Great Circuit, also known as the Atlantic Circuit and the Triangle-Trade, facilitated the Slave Trade, which the Portuguese, Dutch, French, and English each dominated at one point or another. The goal of such trade was to take luxury goods to areas where these goods were nonexistent or scarce, thereby creating demand and leading to profit. However, substantial risks and costs were also associated with the Great Circuit. It was not until the defeat of the Spanish Armada that English and Dutch maritime fleets experienced status or power.

As Spanish influence declined, both the British and Dutch Empires were able to flourish, which led to the vast empires of the 18th and 19th centuries. These two empires would drastically alter the trading system using the Dutch East India Company and the British East India Company. The European merchants' role in Asian trade was the transportation of goods from one Asian market to another. This varied during different ruling dynasties of China, but for the most part, European merchants were reliant upon East Asian culture and traditions when engaging in trade.

It is also important to note that governments facilitated the economic progress and expansion of trade in this period with various degrees of private enterprise. Monarchical governments granted exclusive charters to favored entrepreneurs, such as the Dutch East India Company and the British East India Company. In the 15th and 16th centuries, Spanish and Portuguese successes were funded by the state with the expectation of a great return for the monarchs. However, they were based on free enterprise, creating more competition among explorers than the British and the Dutch permit under their mercantilist systems.

The economic system of mercantilism was developed as a result of private companies gaining political and social power and was used by both the British and Dutch Empires in the Great Circuit and the Slave Trade. The trading institutions created were instrumental in forming the maritime empires found later in this period, but also the larger empires of the British in the following centuries. These same companies also impacted cultural norms and standards in India, as well as the political relationship between the British Empire and India, for decades to come. These early monopolies give us a glimpse into the origin of the economic models that followed, as well as the impacts such monopolies had on the global economy and markets.

The practice of Christianity continued to spread throughout the world and was increasingly diversified by the process of diffusion and the Reformation.

The origins of the Reformation can be seen in various capacities leading into this period. Average followers of the Catholic faith participated in ritual and ceremony. Many in leadership positions reaped the benefit of their status rather than remaining humble and pious. Additionally, the expansion of education and literacy by some Catholic sects allowed for many followers to ask theological questions that would have earlier been labeled as heretical. In addition to the theological and ceremonial decline of the Catholic Church, the emergence of the Scientific Revolution somewhat diminished the status of the Church, which continued to lose popularity with many followers. However, as a means of salvation, many continued to practice Catholic teachings.

This began to change with the emergence of Martin Luther, who spearheaded the Protestant Reformation and transition away from Catholicism. As a result of this dissatisfaction and growing decline in power, the Catholic Church attempted to make internal adjustments or an internal Reformation. However, these attempts were fleeting and produced no real results in the attempt to stem the tide of Martin Luther and Protestantism.

Martin Luther (1483–1546) was born in what is now Southeast Germany and became a friar, priest, theologian, and leading figure in the Protestant Reformation. Luther had not initially planned for a career in theology. However, he enrolled at the University of Erfurt in 1501, where he received a Master of Arts degree in grammar, logic, rhetoric, and metaphysics. At the beginning of his career, Luther aimed to become a lawyer, which greatly pleased his father and family.

However, by 1505, following a spiritual epiphany, Luther decided to become a monk. He did not find the theological satisfaction he was seeking and became ever more disillusioned with the Catholic Church. This sentiment was brought to a boil in response to a new series of indulgences called for by Pope Leo X. Indulgences were reductions in the amount of time one would have to spend in purgatory or serving penance sentences. The Church, and often imposters, claimed that by doing a good deed—generally giving the Church money—one's time in purgatory could be diminished, or entry into Heaven guaranteed.

On October 31, 1517, as a result of extended contemplation of and frustration with the wrong-headed teachings and practices of the Catholic Church, Martin Luther nailed what is called "the Ninety-Five Theses" to the door of his chapel in Wittenberg. Though he intended these points to be a source of theological discussion, the Ninety-Five Theses laid out a devastating critique of the Church's indulgences as corrupting people's faith. Luther also called upon the Archbishop of Mainz, Albert Albrecht, to end the practice of indulgences.

Martin Luther posts his Ninety-Five Theses

The Catholic Church worked tirelessly to discredit and ban the works of Luther. In October of 1518, following a meeting between Cardinal Thomas Cajetan and Martin Luther in Augsburg, the Church demanded that Luther recant his Ninety-Five Thesis. As a result of Luther's unwillingness to do so, the Church excommunicated him in January of 1521. In May of 1521, the Council of the Catholic Church published the Edict of Worms, banning all of Luther's texts and labeling him a convicted heretic.

This event also highlights the importance of the printing press, invented by Johannes Gutenberg in the mid-15th century. Printed copies of the Ninety-Five Theses spread throughout Germany in just two weeks, and throughout Europe in approximately two months. This was only possible due to advances in moveable type and the ability to replicate a text en masse.

Erasmus (1466–1536) was a prominent German humanist, Catholic priest, and theologian who interacted with Luther on theological topics in his later years. Following the publication of Luther's Ninety-Five Theses, Erasmus engaged in a ten-year battle with Luther, debating human nature, free will, and religion. Though Erasmus initially supported some Protestant ideas, he still outwardly supported the Catholic Church and condemned Luther's works and radical Protestantism in his work *De Libero Arbitrio*, in 1523.

Desiderius Erasmus,
German priest

John Calvin (1509–1564) was a French theologian, ecclesiastical statesman and founder of Calvinism, a branch of Protestantism. John Calvin was Martin Luther's successor as the preeminent Protestant theologian following a new wave of Protestantism. Calvin, like his predecessor, made a powerful impact on the fundamental doctrines of Protestantism and is widely credited as the most important figure in the second generation of the Protestant Reformation. The introduction of Calvinism in France eventually led to the French Huguenots and a new class of religious theology and elites, as well as rivalry amongst French Catholics and French Protestants.

As merchants' profits increased and governments collected more taxes, funding for the visual and performing arts, even for popular audiences, increased.

As a new middle class of merchants emerged throughout Europe, the ability to generate revenue using taxation also became a focus of European monarchies. This wealth and status eventually culminated in the emergence of patron classes and institutions that employed and supported various artists and commissioned many great cultural works, which include the masterpieces of the Renaissance.

The emergence of Renaissance art was transformational for Europe, as well as the rest of the world for centuries to come. These works were intended for the upper-class, elite, and ruling-class audience. However, many works were also for the average audience, who explored new concepts of religion or artistic expression during the Renaissance. The artists of the Renaissance period originated from various backgrounds and stations and were able to complete such accomplishments because of support from the patron class, most notably the de Medici family in Florence.

Typically, artists were given an apprenticeship or admittance to a guild where the artist could perfect his craft and eventually be commissioned by the Church, monarchies, or the elite classes to paint, sculpt or create various forms of art. Much of the art of this period was commissioned for religious purposes and ceremonial use; however, as elite families began commissioning personal projects, the newly emerging wealthy and middle classes sought art for their homes and personal enjoyment. These types of art focused on domestic life and everyday events, such as marriage, children, and the family. The influence of the artistic expression of the Renaissance cannot be overstated; it was the source of the vibrant European culture and tradition which emerged after the arid years of the Early Medieval Period. Such culture also expanded into literary works, social treatises, and works of political theory.

Innovations in visual and performing arts were seen all over the world.

The Renaissance—which translates as "rebirth"—was highlighted by various attempts to reintroduce the classical traditions of the Greek and Roman Empires. This included literary works, and a resurgence in Latin and artistic works, which at times challenged the Catholic Church. Philosophical influences of humanism can also be seen in the literature of this period. Humanism focused on the accomplishments and capabilities of man rather than God, and at times this upset Church leadership. This can be seen in humanist art, which focused on human physical and facial features. One notable humanist was Erasmus.

The Renaissance began in the 15th century in Italy. It quickly expanded to the rest of Europe and England using the Elizabethan court. Initially, the Renaissance was supported by the Catholic Church commissioning art. However, as the movement progressed, the patronage increasingly came from private entities or governments. Notable figures included Leonardo da Vinci (1452–1519) — considered one of the three great artists of the High Renaissance. Da Vinci was also considered the supreme Renaissance painter, as well as a scientist and innovator. Da Vinci is widely regarded as one of the greatest minds the world has ever produced. He developed extensive treatises and works regarding

Leonardo da Vinci, Renaissance artist

scientific discoveries. Important artistic works of his include the Mona Lisa (c. 1502) and The Last Supper (1498). Other notable works from Leonardo da Vinci include the Vitruvian Man (1485).

Michelangelo (1475–1564) was an Italian sculptor, painter, architect, poet, and engineer of the High Renaissance, also considered one of the three great artists of this period. His important works include David (1504); the Sistine Chapel ceiling (1541), which took seven years to complete; and The Pieta in St. Peter's Basilica (1499). Raphael (1483–1520) was another Italian painter and architect of the High Renaissance. Important works by Raphael include Saint George and the Dragon and the Sistine Madonna. Sandro Botticelli (1445–1510) was an Italian painter of the Early Renaissance. He belonged to the Florentine School under the patronage of Lorenzo de' Medici, again highlighting the importance of apprenticeship and patronage during this period. Important works by Botticelli include The Birth of Venus (1485) and The Mystical Nativity (1501).

Literacy expanded and was accompanied by the proliferation of famous authors, literary forms, and works of literature.

Like art, literature saw an explosion in prevalence due to the Renaissance. This can be attributed to the exchange of culture, ideas, and people during this Age of Exploration. Some of the most notable Renaissance-era writers included Shakespeare (1564–1616, also known as the Bard of Avon), an English poet and playwright, and England's National Poet. Some of his most notable works were published between 1589 and 1613. His early works included comedies and histories, while later works consisted of tragedies. Some of Shakespeare's most famous titles include *The Taming of the Shrew* (1592), *Romeo and Juliet* (1594), and *A Midsummer Night's Dream* (1595). Beginning in 1600, he began writing tragedies, such as *Hamlet* (1600), *Macbeth* (1605), and *The Tempest* (1611). In 1599, with the help of business partners, Shakespeare built his theater on the Thames River, called The Globe. Historical tradition states that Shakespeare died on his birthday, April 23, 1616. However, this is most likely inaccurate.

Miguel de Cervantes, author of Don Quixote

Other notable and popular authors of this period included Miguel de Cervantes, who was born the son of a deaf surgeon near Madrid in 1547. Cervantes became a soldier in 1570 and was severely wounded in the Battle of Lepanto. Captured by the Turks in 1575, Cervantes spent five years in prison. He was freed in 1580 and returned home. Cervantes did not achieve literary success until his later years. In 1605 he published the first part of *Don Quixote*, which became one of Spain's earliest masterpieces of popular literature. The novel tells the story of an elderly man who becomes so disillusioned by old stories of brave knights that he seeks out adventures. The main character soon gets lost in his fantasy world, begins believing he is a great knight, and convinces a poor peasant, Sancho Panza, to serve as his squire. Cervantes published the second part of the story in 1615, just before his death. After his death, Cervantes was praised as having written the first modern novel.

Tsarist Russia expanded into Siberia.

The emergence of serfdom in Russia and Eastern Europe allowed for the cultivation of agriculture, as well as frontier developments in Siberia. Beginning in the 16th century, the Russian peasantry was completely controlled by their landowners, with the class of serfdom becoming hereditary by the mid-17th century. Tsar Ivan IV ("Ivan the Terrible") implemented a system of conditional land tender as a means to encourage entrepreneurship and expansion beyond the European portion of Russia.

This system, known as *pomest'ie*, gave the Tsar the right to grant land to whomever he deemed fit, which meant that those nobles who were able to extract the most from their serfs were able to hold the territories under their control and potentially expand their landholdings. This created an incentive for nobles to expand into Siberia as a means to increase their wealth and the wealth of Russia as a whole. Modern Marxist historians speculate that without such forced labor, it would have been trying for Peter the Great to accomplish the "Europeanization" of Russia.

Rulers used tribute collection and tax farming to generate revenue for territorial expansion.

In Russia, taxation of farming and serfdom was common and was the beginning of heavy taxation of the peasant and working classes. In addition to taxing cultivated land, Peter the Great also implemented various other taxes in an attempt to finance his Great Northern War. He imposed taxes on everyday activities, such as bathing, fishing, beekeeping, having a beard, and paper goods. However, with every new tax, legal loopholes were found to avoid paying the tribute.

The solution was a sweeping new poll tax, which replaced a household tax on cultivated land. Each peasant was assessed a tax of 70 kopeks, to be paid in cash. This was significantly heavier than the taxes it replaced, and it enabled the Russian state to expand its treasury almost sixfold between 1680 and 1724. Peter also pursued protectionist trade policies, placing hefty tariffs on imports and trade to maintain a favorable environment for Russian-made goods. All of these measures allowed for territorial development and expansion in the Russian Empire, and eventually culminated in the Europeanization of Russia under Peter the Great and, later, under Catherine the Great.

Bolstered Russian military ushers in emerging world power.

The Russian Empire was different from those previously described, as it did not have a vast land army at the beginning of the early modern period. However, by the end of the period, it was able to undertake military campaigns such as the Northern War. Peter the Great made substantial progress in the westernization of the Russian Empire, and Russia came to be recognized as an emerging global power. His military reforms offered better pay and compulsory service in the army, as well as establishing naval forces.

European states established new maritime empires in the Americas: Portuguese, Spanish, Dutch, French, British.

As land-based empires expanded, so did the maritime empires made famous by this period of exploration. The Spanish and Portuguese maritime models were rather similar, as both countries' monarchs appointed viceroys or personal representatives to rule in the name of the king. The Spanish monarchs established the Council of the Indies, which was meant to pass laws and work in a supervisory capacity to the Spanish monarch. Lack of communication caused many viceroys to act independently. However, large bureaucratic institutions were established in metropolitan cities, such as Mexico City. During the 16th century, the Portuguese slowly faded as a power while Spain claimed and kept more and more land in the Western Hemisphere.

The English colonial model was different from those of Spain or Portugal. It avoided elaborate bureaucracies and allowed colonial settlements to develop their policies and practices. The English settled along the eastern seaboard of North America. Although the three great powers were destined to clash over land claims eventually, most such conflicts did not occur until the 18th century. This became known as "salutary neglect" and was the policy of the English monarchs until the mid-18th century. The French explored and settled the St. Lawrence River area through Canada, as well as the Mississippi River valley, south all the way to its mouth. Dutch colonies represented the second wave of colonialism, exemplified by the Dutch East India Trading Company's monopoly on global trade.

State-sponsored piracy, succession disputes, religious disagreements, and popular uprisings shake up European powers.

Piracy was sometimes a case of bold criminals attacking unarmed trading vessels in relatively unprotected areas, such as in the straits between Ireland and England in the 16th century. However, it was often state-sponsored "privateering," as was the case with Sir Francis Drake. Drake was commissioned by the Queen of England to harass Spanish trading vessels at a time when England could not compete with Spain militarily. Drake's attack on the Manila Galeon was an example of competition over trade routes, as well as a straightforward national rivalry. Royally funded piracy was also a big business in the Caribbean between about 1600 and 1830.

Francis Drake, British pirate

Queen Anne's War (1702–1713) and the Thirty Years' War (1618–1648) are good examples to compare because different types of crises triggered them. Queen Anne's War was fought over a succession crisis. The War of Spanish succession took place in Europe at the beginning of the 18th century. The catalyst was the confusion over succession after the monarch who presided over a large part of Europe passed away. The European conflict spilled over into the North American colonies of Spain, Britain, and France and was given the separate title of "Queen Anne's War." The result of this was a major change in territorial boundaries of Europe and some minor changes of territorial ownership in North America.

The Thirty Years' War was fought over the status and legitimacy of the Protestant faith. It had been slightly more than a century since the creation of Protestantism, enough time for it to have developed a large enough following to stand on its own in a war against European monarchs. Entire nations were dragged into the conflict because monarchs had different opinions about the legitimacy of this new religion.

Notable peasant revolts included the 1524–1525 German Peasants' War, as well as the 1606–1607 Bolotnikov Rebellion in Russia. In 1525, German peasants fought a series of simultaneous rebellions against local princes in the area that is now Germany and Austria. This is known today as the Revolution of 1525. The peasants wanted greater power for their town governments, as well as redress of some grievances against church leaders. These rebellions were generally not successful but had the long-term effect of making rebellions by the European poor more and more common.

The Bolotnikov Rebellion in Russia was a populist uprising organized by Ivan Bolotnikov at the beginning of the 17th century. Bolotnikov promised many of the same things communists promised three hundred years later, such as the total elimination of the wealthy and the class system in general. Bolotnikov's uprising failed but, like the German Peasants' War, set a precedent. Food riots in the Americas included the Boston Bread Riot, which took place in 1710–1713. This involved grain hoarding by the colonists, which was perceived as a public display of aggression directed at the wealthy.

Armed peasants of the German Peasants' War

A variety of factors led to the rise of industrial production: Europe's location on the Atlantic Ocean; the geographical distribution of coal, iron, and timber; European demographic changes; urbanization; improved agricultural productivity; legal protection of private property; an abundance of rivers and canals; access to foreign resources; and the accumulation of capital.

European industrial growth was facilitated by some conditions present at the time of the Industrial Revolution. These conditions included: the location of waterways and resources, improved means of agricultural production, massive waves of urbanization, and the protection of private property.

The geographic location of Europe, specifically its proximity to the Atlantic Ocean, allowed for the establishment of seafaring colonial empires, such as England and Spain. Large portions of the Americas, most of Africa and Oceania, were all part of European empires. The geographic distribution of raw resources, such as coal, iron, and timber, also influenced the Industrial Revolution. Europe controlled close to 40 percent of the world's population and resources. As a result, Europeans were able to wield significant influence over resources that were crucial to the explosive Industrial Revolution and rapid urbanization.

At the same time, improved agricultural capacities were seen throughout Europe. For example, in England, agricultural production rates of the 1770s were higher than the demand. Such increases in food supply had lasting impacts, most notably by increasing populations—a direct result of the improvement in agricultural efficiency.

The legal protection of private property was also crucial to the development of European capital. All of these economic factors were instrumental in initiating, continuing, and maintaining the Industrial Revolution and its effects.

The development of machines, including steam engines and the internal combustion engine, made it possible to exploit vast new resources of energy stored in fossil fuels, specifically coal and oil. The "fossil fuels" revolution greatly increased the energy available to human societies.

As raw resources became more readily available to a larger number of people, their increased use was seen in the advanced production of steam engines and internal combustion engines, which replaced water wheels as a means of energy. These new machines, fueled mainly by coal and oil, propelled the Industrial Revolution and shaped the landscape of modern Europe and the Americas. The use of these machines also increased the demand for energy.

The steam engines perfected during the Industrial Revolution were a result of the engines invented and produced by Boulton and Watt in 1769, which remained the standard steam engine models until 1775. One notable example of a modified Watt steam engine is the Newcomen engine. As early as 1823, Samuel Brown is attributed with creating the first internal combustion engine and applying it to industrial capacity. However, internal combustion engines became more prominent following the development of petroleum, which powered these engines beginning in the mid-1850s. The first internal combustion engine to be mass-produced was gas-fired and created by Jean Joseph Etienne Lenoir in 1860. These machines were especially important to the Industrial Revolution because they allowed for better transportation, production, and standards of living all across Europe and the United States.

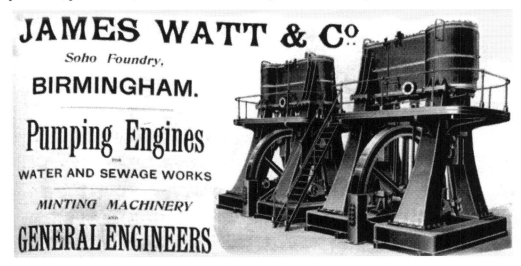

Advertisement for James Watt & Co. pumping engines

The development of the factory system concentrated labor in a single location and led to an increasing degree of specialization of labor.

As the Industrial Revolution boomed, the working classes in cities grew at an increasingly rapid pace, creating various skilled labor vocations. The factory system that had been introduced in England in 1750 and utilized a division of labor was quickly adopted abroad and used to propel various industries. This system formed the basis for specialized labor, where laborers worked on specified tasks.

Such a production system allowed for both skilled and unskilled workers to contribute to the overall output and production of the factory, which created greater successes in the factory production system. Another form of specialized labor from this period included the massive influx of immigrants, mainly to mining communities in the United States. This was an example of the impact of the Industrial Revolution on poorer people around the world and of the expansion of American settlers across the United States. Many of these laborers came as unskilled workers but were able to fill the demand for new types of labor.

The ideological inspiration for economic changes lies in the development of capitalism and classical liberalism associated with Adam Smith and John Stuart Mill.

As the economic change was seen throughout the European, American, and East Asian markets, the power and humanitarian success of capitalism and classical liberalism were becoming more evident. Previously existing only as theories, these ideologies began to be put into practice with the growth of capitalism.

Adam Smith,
Scottish philosopher and theorist

Adam Smith (1723–1790) was a Scottish moral philosopher and political and economic theorist, who was extremely influential in the Scottish Enlightenment. Two of Smith's best-known works are *The Theory of Moral Sentiments* (1759) and *An Inquiry into the Nature and Causes of the Wealth of Nations* (1776). Many academics have labeled Smith as the "father" of modern economics, as his models greatly influenced the economic policies of the period. Smith championed the idea of free-market economic theory and promoted the idea of capitalism with great success. However, it should be noted that Smith was extremely controversial as well. German economist Emile Durkheim later expanded on the vital concept of specialization, which Smith introduced in *The Division of Labor in Society*.

John Stuart Mill (1806–1873) was a British philosopher and political and economic theorist. Like many other political theorists of this period, Mill shared the idea that liberty required an individual to be free of state control or oppression. Mill became a great proponent of utilitarianism, which proposes that human beings do things to achieve a goal and that actions and objects have functions. Preference should be given to actions that achieve the most amount of good for the highest number of people. This idea was further expanded with the theory that utility can be quantified using units called "utils." The efforts of both Smith and Mill were instrumental in creating new economic theories for a new economic market and world. These theories were so influential and vital that they transcended this particular period of history and can still be found in today's economic discussions.

European states, as well as the Americans and the Japanese, established empires throughout Asia and the Pacific, while Spanish and Portuguese influence declined.

This period saw the decline of the Spanish and Portuguese empires of the early modern period, while the British, Dutch, French, and German empires expanded rapidly.

The British Empire was at the height of its historical glory. By leading the imperialist cause, the British came to dominate the Indian subcontinent (including portions of Burma, India, and Malaysia) and the global market for finished products. The British maintained colonies by both direct and indirect rule, which allowed them to influence vast amounts of resources and people.

The Dutch Empire continued to exercise hegemony in Southeast Asia, as it held the territories of the Dutch East Indies, a grouping of islands currently known as Indonesia. The Dutch government exercised an effective monopoly on the spice trade. It influenced the formation of modern-day Indonesia through the Dutch East India Company, as well as the Dutch government.

The German Empire also dabbled in colonial expansion in the Marshall Islands in the Pacific. By 1876 and 1878, the German government had annexed portions of the Marshall Islands, while also colonizing additional islands in the Pacific. Most importantly, Germany gained control of a significant portion of Northeastern China, known as Tangshan province, which was eventually ceded to the Japanese as part of the Treaty of Versailles. As a consequence of losing the First World War, Germany was also required by the victors to relinquish what remained of its colonial outposts.

Thinkers applied new ways of understanding the natural world to human relationships, encouraging observation and inference in all spheres of life.

Both the High Enlightenment (1730–1780) and Late Enlightenment (1780–1815) periods greatly influenced the people of Europe and the Americas. The Enlightenment was expressed differently in different regions. Thus, many scholars study the French Enlightenment, the American Enlightenment, or the British Enlightenment in their capacities. Some of the notable figures of the High and Late Enlightenment include Voltaire, Rousseau, Hume, Diderot, and Montesquieu, who wrote about government, human existence, and the interactions among men, and all greatly influenced the American and French Revolutions.

Voltaire (1694–1778) was born in France in 1694. He worked as a philosopher, writer, and historian and is recognized as one of the greatest writers of the French Enlightenment. Voltaire's personal history was turbulent as he experienced periods of exile from Paris. However, by his later years, he was welcomed warmly by Parisians and was considered to be a great writer and thinker. Some of Voltaire's most important and well-known works include the *Essay in the Customs and the Spirit of the Nations* (1756), *Candide* (1759), and *Dictionnaire Philosophique* (1764).

The literary works produced by Voltaire during the French Enlightenment were highly critical of the Roman Catholic Church and caused many people to view the human experience in a different capacity with the Church no longer enjoying the prominence it had in earlier periods. These writings created a very tumultuous relationship between the French government and Church, until the French Revolution when Voltaire was celebrated as a genius and philosophical mastermind.

Jean-Jacques Rousseau (1712–1778), another great figure to emerge during the High Enlightenment, was a philosophical figure as well as a songwriter, composer, and musical theorist. Rousseau was born in Geneva, Switzerland, and came to embody the Enlightenment movement both in his home canton and abroad. One of the greatest works compiled by Rousseau was the *Discourse on the Arts and Sciences,* which was released in 1750 and highlighted the struggle between nature and society. In it, Rousseau argued that civilization itself caused harm to humanity and would possibly lead to its destruction. Not all responses to Rousseau's work were positive, and in some places, his writings, specifically, the *Contrat* and *Emile* were burned. While many saw Rousseau as a great philosopher, one of his greatest critics was Voltaire. Some of Rousseau's friends included David Hume and Denis Diderot, both of whom were also monumental figures in the Enlightenment movement.

David Hume (1711–1776), a well-known philosopher and historian, was born in Edinburgh, Scotland. Hume became one of the most important of the British empiricists. John Locke and George Berkeley greatly influenced his works and ideas. Like many other philosophers of this period, Hume placed a great deal of value on the human experience, and he argued that all political and religious feeling and opinion is a direct result of everyday experience. During the 1750s, Hume became most renowned for historical works, such as the six-volume edition of the *History of England*, which consumed his life during the 1750s. Before *History of England,* Hume wrote several texts about religion and morality that were opposed and banned by the Roman Catholic Church.

Denis Diderot (1713–1784) was another French philosopher, artist, critic, and writer, who produced influential works during the High Enlightenment period. Diderot was educated by priests of the Jesuits order and earned a master's degree in the arts. His most well-known work is the *Encyclopedie* (1751–1752). This particular text had a great influence on Europeans, the French in particular, and by 1789 over 25,000 copies were in circulation across the globe. While Diderot produced a great literary reference in *Encyclopedie*, he was most influential in his role in the French Revolution and the promotion of democratic government across Europe and in the Americas. The philosophical, historical, and legal texts produced by these Enlightenment figures were extremely influential, especially in the revolutions in the United States and Europe. Their ideals stemmed from changing social and political systems and, in turn, contributed to further advancement in those areas.

Intellectuals critiqued the role that religion played in public life, insisting on the importance of reason as opposed to revelation.

The Enlightenment figures' religious commentary created tension with the Roman Catholic Church. While few philosophers spoke out directly against the Church, many of the undertones of the literary work from this period criticized the role of religion in daily life and the influence religious institutions held over governmental affairs. As a result, many works of this period encouraged readers to seek out rational council rather than council embroiled in religious iconography and ritual.

Montesquieu and the Catholic Church, in both Rome and France, had an antagonistic relationship. During his later years, Montesquieu was recognized as a forward thinker of the French Revolution. However, he was initially met with resistance, expulsion, and exile by the French monarchy as a result of his anti-Catholic rhetoric. For example, he criticized the vow of celibacy taken by those in the priesthood because he believed the Catholic Church was stopping European empires from reaching their full potential because they were causing depopulation. Montesquieu also described the Catholic Church as a highly oppressive institution and argued that, through its practice of strict laws and rituals, it was delaying the cultural rebirth created by the Enlightenment period.

Montesquieu, philosopher of the French Enlightenment

Voltaire also faced criticism from the Catholic Church during this period of intellectual progressivism. As a writer, Voltaire produced many satirical works about the dogma of the Roman Catholic Church, and as a result, many of his works were banned by the Church. Voltaire called upon the population to use reason and scientific thought rather than religious superstition when discussing things like the changing of the tides and weather patterns, the path to salvation or damnation, and the position of the Earth within the planetary system.

The importance of rationality, science, and inquiry during the Age of Reason and Enlightenment cannot be understated. The critical thinking of many key Enlightenment figures was also important because it inspired others to think more critically, which led to many innovations. The transition from primary concerns being about religion to being about politics developed throughout this period. For the first time, people were less concerned about the perception of God but instead focused on the new ideas and schools of thought emerging from the Enlightenment period. Texts of the time certainly had a religious aspect but were not focused solely on the Catholic Church anymore. Not since the early years of human civilization had the church had to share power.

Enlightenment thinkers developed new political ideas about the individual, natural rights and the social contract.

As the Enlightenment movement progressed, the role of human rights and the individual began to be viewed in a new light due to the ideas advanced in the philosophical works of the Enlightenment. Many of the works focused on the oppression and subjugation of the emerging working class. Such sentiment was felt across state boundaries and in the American colonies. However, Enlightenment ideas were centered on a new form of individualism, where for the first time, men were able to evaluate their lives by experience and natural-born rights rather than servitude and class structure.

John Locke (1632–1704), a political theorist and philosopher, is considered one of the most influential figures of the early Enlightenment. Locke's *Second Treatise on Government* was seminal to the American Revolution. In that work, Locke attacked the hereditary and divine justifications for absolute rule, which were the prevalent belief during his time. He proposed that human beings have rights that are derived from nature, as willed by God and that these rights are universal, and they also make us individuals. Locke argued that the claim by monarchs to have more political rights than others based on inheritance or a claim to a special relationship with God were false. Examples of the natural rights that Locke argued for were property rights and the right of a person not to have force used against him or her. These were the basis of the Declaration of Independence and the American Constitution.

John Locke, philosopher and theorist of the Enlightenment

Locke's other works, most notably the *Essay Concerning Human Understanding* (1689), focused on the human mind and its experiences, particularly its pursuit of knowledge. This concept fueled the minds and hearts of philosophers during the High and Late Enlightenment periods.

Charles des-Louis de Secondat, Baron de Montesquieu and de La Brede (more commonly known as Montesquieu), was born in France in January 1689. He is most well-known for his work as a philosopher and legal professional. Montesquieu's literary works also greatly influenced government during the Enlightenment and later periods following the American and French Revolutions. He is most known for his work *The Spirit of Laws,* which was published in 1748 and, for the first time, detailed the idea of legislative, executive, and judicial branches being the main parts of government and also separate from each other. *The Spirit of Laws* also criticized monarchies and was eventually banned by the Catholic Church.

These ideas greatly influenced the American Enlightenment and political figures. The newly formed American government adopted many ideas that had been set forth by Montesquieu and other Enlightenment thinkers. In 1755, Montesquieu died of natural causes. He was remembered and embraced by various politicians and ruling elites of this period, including various American Presidents, such as James Madison.

The works of Locke and Montesquieu were extremely important to the Enlightenment politically, economically, and culturally, and influenced the cultures and nations that emerged during this period. The expansion of economic theory and political revolution that was the focus of the period leading into the 20th century can be attributed to the works of John Locke, Montesquieu, and others from the Enlightenment period.

The ideas of Enlightenment thinkers influenced resistance to existing political authority, as reflected in revolutionary documents.

As the men of the Enlightenment period influenced their counterparts and other revolutionaries, many of them had been touched by the ideas proposed in various monumental texts. In France, this was the *Declaration of the Rights of Man and Citizen,* which would eventually be the platform used by French abolitionists. In the American colonies, this movement was most notably seen in the composition of *The Declaration of Independence*, which was important to both colonists and other nations, as it was a legal means of recognizing America's legitimacy in seeking independence from England. Another influential document that showed the perspectives of ordinary people of the period was the *Letter From Jamaica*, composed by Simon Bolivar about the independence movement in Venezuela.

The *Declaration of the Rights of Man and Citizen* is one of the most influential documents in French and world history. Composed in 1789 by General Marquis de Lafayette and passed by the National Constituent Assembly in August 1789, it was a direct result of General Lafayette's experiences in the American Revolutionary War. The *Declaration of the Rights of Man and Citizen* also shows the desire of the people of France to have their rights acknowledged by the government, not just as citizens of France, but as humans, with all the rights that entail. This can be seen as the first step in the direction of creating a notion of the idea of human rights. Such ideas were crucial to early abolitionist movements, as this document, like the American *Declaration of Independence,* makes no reference to race or ethnicity as a precondition for human rights.

The American *Declaration of Independence* is one of the most important documents in world history. Without it, the colonists would have failed to create the first modern state founded as a democracy. The document had 56 signatories and was passed by the Continental Congress on July 4, 1776. The *Declaration of Independence* is important in another regard as well. It was a legal contract stating the validity of the colonies as a group of organized states seeking independence from an occupier rather than a rebellious uprising like others seen during the age of colonialism. This was a crucial difference in the eyes of European states, especially France, which was the Americans' greatest ally against the British. It should be noted that many French who fought in the American Revolution did so to hinder the British Empire from harming French interests. However, others did so because they believed in the spirit of freedom.

These ideas influenced many people to challenge existing notions of social relations, which led to the expansion of rights as seen in expanded suffrage, the abolition of slavery and the end of serfdom, as their ideas were implemented.

Many of the Enlightenment philosophies and texts allowed for various groups to experience additional freedoms and rights. These included non-Caucasians, women and Russian serfs. The Abolitionist movement was the first of its kind. The early modern period saw an explosion of the transatlantic slave trade. However, by the 1800s, this system, which had propelled the world's economy in earlier periods, was being deconstructed by those who felt it was immoral. The texts that provided the basis for the American and French Revolutions expressed academic arguments against slavery through their proclamation of the notions of universal freedom and equality. The abolitionist movements in Europe seemed to produce more results than in the American colonies, where in some instances, the plantation model still proved to be the most profitable for agricultural production.

However, as the Industrial Revolution took precedence over agrarian economies, the decline of slavery began. The success of abolitionists in this period can be seen in the Slave Trade Act of 1807, which was passed by England's Parliament and outlawed slave-trading within the British Empire, specifically in the transatlantic slave trade, and called upon other European empires to do the same. America passed a law abolishing the importation of slaves only a year later. However, the actual market in slaves and the breeding of slaves on American soil remained legal for another half-century.

The Slavery Abolition Act of 1833, passed by England's Parliament, was also monumental as it proposed a process to "free" slaves using an apprenticeship-type program, similar to indentured servitude. The abolition of slavery was a huge achievement of this period, especially in light of the economic dominance the slave trade had supported in earlier periods. However, the abolition of slavery and the slave trade left people looking for economic opportunities, which were fleeting. As a result, many who had been emancipated continued to live a substandard existence in comparison to other Europeans and colonists in the Americas.

The expansion of the suffrage movement can also be attributed to the literary works and political movements produced during the Enlightenment period. This was most notably seen in the women's suffrage movement, where, for the first time, women asserted their equality and roles within society. While women made considerable strides in their quest for equality, it was a slow process, with many states and cultures reacting at their own pace. New Zealand achieved women's suffrage in 1893, but America and England did not do so until the end of World War I.

The end of serfdom in the Russian Empire was also an extremely monumental transition of this period, as for over 800 years, Russian agrarian culture depended on it. The Emancipation Reform of 1861, presented by Emperor Alexander II, guaranteed the abolition of serfdom throughout the Russian Empire, while the *Emancipation Manifesto* of 1861 called for the freedom of serfs living on private estates and domestic serfs who worked in households. As a result of these reforms, over 23 million people were set free from serfdom. They were able to gain the rights of full citizens living within the Russian Empire, including property and marriage rights. However, many serfs—particularly domestic serfs—struggled to acclimate to the new freedoms and lacked ways in which to earn money because they owned no land or property. As a result, many continued to work in the same fashion as before the end of serfdom in Russia.

Emperor Alexander II of Russia

The Enlightenment period influenced the public to pursue the ideas of equality and freedom, which led to some of the most important and lasting transitions toward civil liberties and human rights of this and later periods.

Beginning in the 18th century, peoples around the world developed a new sense of commonality based on language, religion, social customs, and territory. These newly imagined national communities linked this identity with the borders of the state, while governments used this idea to unite diverse populations.

As new social classes and forms of government emerged, so did common language, religion, and territory. As the idea of divine monarchies began to fade, people associated themselves less with a royal bloodline or monarch and more with the fellow people who shared their interests, struggles, and lands. While individuals were uniting based on common characteristics, governments frequently operated in the opposite direction. They wanted to unite people based on their ethnic and economic groups, which were composed of people who had different identities, such as minority groups who spoke different languages and practiced different religions. For example, the Austro-Hungarian Empire included ethnic Germans, Ukrainians, Hungarians, Serbians, and Croatians. These shared bonds and identity were the basis of nationalism – an idea and sentiment that had a significant influence on the European continent, as well as in the United States during the 20th century.

One of the first examples of a nationalist sentiment can be found in 18th century England where people began, for the first time, identifying primarily with the larger country of England rather than a province, town, village, or family unit. Many within the English community of this period embraced nationalism and employed banners, songs, mythology and symbolism as a way of identifying themselves with England. This movement also saw the adoption of a national flag as well as nationally-known songs like "Rule, Britannia."

People found unification through language as well. One example of this comes from the man who coined the term "nationalism," Johann Gottfried Herder. He argued that language was the one aspect of life that influenced national thought and culture. Those who shared a language also shared similar cultural traditions and a common means to express their interpretation of the world, which created a unified spirit in Germany.

The main reason governments found for supporting this movement was power, i.e., the ability to unite diverse demographics of people under one empire, which was the drive of colonialism. Governments that were able to wield the influence of vast peoples and lands were able to preserve their interests in the global markets and system, as the British did first using the East India Trade Company and later through imperialism.

Nationalism, on a global scale, proved costly for Europe and the United States as it eventually led to the events that ignited both World Wars and the Cold War during the 20th century. While empires were powerful, they did not have as much influence as absolute monarchs had had in the past. The usurpation of authority and the curtailment of individual rights and freedoms, frequent under despotism, were dwarfed by the oppression that occurred later under communism and fascism.

American colonial subjects led a series of rebellions, and French subjects rebelled against their monarchy.

The impact of the Enlightenment period culminated in the revolution in the American colonies, which was the first of its kind and, in turn, influenced revolutions in Haiti, Latin America, and France. The American Revolution took place from 1775 until 1783 and as a result of tense relations between the British Empire and its colonies in North America. One of the issues leading up to the outbreak of war was the lack of fair taxation and representation within the British Parliament. Americans were not happy about the British imposition of the Stamp Act of 1765, the Townshend Tariffs of 1767, and the Tea Act of 1773. The American Revolutionary War was triggered by the reaction of the British Crown to years of colonial unrest, including the Boston Massacre in 1770—where British military forces killed five colonists—and the passage of the Coercive Acts in response to the Boston Tea Party in 1773.

The American Revolution began with skirmishes at Lexington and Concord in April of 1775. The Battle of Bunker Hill took place on June 17, 1775, and ended in a British victory. Other notable battles of the American Revolution include the Battle of Trenton (December 1776), the Battle of Saratoga (September 1777), and the Battle of Yorktown (October 1781). In 1778, the French entered the war on behalf of the American patriots, escalating the conflict into an international war. Notable figures of the Revolutionary War include General George Washington, the commander of the Continental Army; William Howe, Commander and Chief of the British Army (1776-1778); Nathan Hale, an American spy caught and hung by the British in 1776; Benedict Arnold, an American officer who defected to the British; and General Charles Cornwallis, who surrendered the British forces to the Continental Army at the Battle of Yorktown in 1781.

Thirteen independent republics, each with its constitution, were created by the American Revolution. Today, the United States is generally thought of as a single nation with a preeminent federal government. However, the original arrangement made by the Patriots was that each of the thirteen colonies was an independent nation, or state, in an alliance of convenience that required a central organizing body, known as the Continental Congress.

This loose alliance of nations eventually evolved into a single nation. The first of several notable milestones in this journey was the creation of a single constitution in 1787. The next was the Civil War, which was fought over the question of whether the sovereignty of individual states or the preeminence of the federal government was superior. The victory of the Union decided the issue in favor of federalism.

The French Revolution was the product of several factors, including the Enlightenment period, the American Revolution, and the relationship between the French people, the monarchy, and the French aristocracy. Beginning in 1789 and continuing into the late 1790s, the French Revolution changed the political and cultural landscape of France forever, as well as influencing many other European affairs. Before the revolution, the French monarchy had spent lavishly and excessively, and as a result, was on the verge of bankruptcy. Furthermore, farm production in previous years had been disappointing, leading to vast food shortages and urban and rural unrest. Adding to this dismal situation was the existence of the first, second, and third estates, which greatly oppressed the lower classes. However, by this period, the third estate, which was made up of non-aristocratic members, was the largest class and could overrule the other two estates.

Napoleon Bonaparte, leader of the French Revolution

Notable events of the French Revolution include the Tennis Court Oath, where members of the assembly were able to achieve constitutional reform and the storming of the Bastille on July 14, 1789, where rebels infiltrated the medieval prison. On January 21, 1793, the Legislative Assembly condemned King Louis XVI to death by guillotine; nine months later Queen Marie Antoinette was also executed by guillotine.

By mid-1793, the French Revolution turned especially violent when Jacobin forces took over the government and enacted the Reign of Terror. In this ten-month period, close to 200,000 people were officially tried and executed by the acting French government. As a result of the Reign of Terror, the more liberal Girondins took control of the National Convention and instilled the five-member Directory, which was appointed by the Parliament. Napoleon Bonaparte (1769–1821) was a successful young general who supported the ideals of the Girondins. On November 9, 1799, he led a coup d'état, which eliminated the Directory. Upon his victory, Napoleon gave himself the title first consul of France, ushering in the Napoleonic era and the Napoleonic wars.

Slave resistance challenged existing authorities in the Americas.

While this period saw the beginning of the abolitionist movement, large numbers of slaves were still held by American plantation owners. As a result, the constant struggle for freedom was always being pursued by slaves. Slave resistance came in many forms in the

Western Hemisphere, as slavery existed in the United States, the Caribbean, and Brazil. Resistance came in two forms: passive and active. Passive forms of resistance included coded forms of communication, music and dance, secret meetings, and – most of all – religion. Active forms of resistance were manifested in rebellions, individual escape attempts, the formation of underground societies, and even legal challenges. Resistance posed serious challenges to the power of the dominant European groups. Authorities responded in many ways – politically, culturally, and with armed forces.

Several communities of escaped slaves formed throughout the American hemisphere. They are referred to as Maroon societies. Members of the Maroon communities shared a tight social bond and worked actively to preserve the freedom of escaped slaves. They existed in the Caribbean colonies, such as Jamaica and Haiti, several American states, such as Florida and Louisiana, and many places in South America.

Sometimes, slaves found the opportunity to plead their cases in courts of law. However, the legal system was always favoring slave owners. The pivotal trial of this kind in the U.S.A. was *Dred Scott v. Sandford*, 1857. Dred Scott was a slave who escaped to a free state and was pursued by his owner, Sandford. What is significant about this case is not so much the decision, but the major issue that it presented – citizenship. The Supreme Court justices at that time were generally in favor of slavery and used a loophole of citizenship to rule against Scott. They ruled that, as a non-citizen, he was ineligible to sue in a U.S. court of law. The issue of citizenship for freed slaves was settled later (in 1865).

The history of slave resistance is not as simple as one party altering the culture of another. Slaves and their overlords continually reacted to each other's moves, like a game of chess. The Underground Railroad was an attempt to resist the Fugitive Slave Act. The reaction of some whites in the south to Nat Turner's rebellion was an attempt to send a message to slaves that rebellion would carry a price that was not worth the risk. Both groups experienced significant cultural changes as a result of this conflict.

Discontent with monarchist and imperial rule encouraged the development of political ideologies, including liberalism, socialism, and communism.

As the political movements of the period transformed into revolutions, the political systems of the past were replaced with new and more modern ideologies such as communism, socialism, and liberalism. The spread of communism is typically attributed to the works and philosophies of Karl Marx (1818–1883) and Friedrich Engels (1820–1895). In later periods, this ideology came to be embodied by the Soviet Union, and there was ongoing tension between capitalist, democratic nations, and communist states. The goal of communism is to create a socioeconomic order void of social classes, with common ownership of the means of production by the people themselves to create a better social structure for all.

Friedrich Engels (left) and Karl Marx (right)

The spread of communism during the early 20th century is attributed to the Industrial Revolution and the rise of urban vocations, which created a new working class that felt it was being oppressed by the elites, members of government, and the state. The continued boom in urbanization increased the pool of people interested in communism and the transition from their current conditions to better ones. As a result of the spread in popularity, both Marx and Engels composed a text, *The Communist Manifesto* (1848), which greatly influenced later communists, such as Vladimir Lenin (1870–1924) and Joseph Stalin (1878–1953). *The Communist Manifesto* was the foundation for all future communist movements, including those seen in China, Southeast Asia, Europe, and South America.

Karl Marx was a radical journalist and political theorist who, in response to the political system of his time, sought to create a more utopian version of life. However, his ideals were seen by many governments of the period as extremely radical and subversive and resulted in his expulsion from Germany, France, and Belgium. Marx argued that socialism was a direct result of the flaws and impurities of the capitalist system, which would eventually lead to its destruction and replacement by the superior communist system. He deemed capitalism as a necessary step in the dialectical process of history towards the establishment of communism, with socialism as the intermediary step.

Marx lived his later years in London and began focusing his attention on economic theory. His benefactor and frequent co-author, Friedrich Engels, was a well-known German author, political theorist, and philosopher, who was equally influential in the communist movement. Along with Marx, he worked to unite the German working classes and sought to spread a counter-movement to capitalism, wherever possible. After Marx's death, Engels completed the second and third installments of *Das Kapital*, which used economic theory to promote communism over capitalism.

The spread of socialism is connected to communism and can be discussed in a similar context. Socialism is defined as a socioeconomic system focused on the co-operative management of the economic system and the production of goods. Like other political and social movements of the period, the rise in socialism is directly attributed to the Industrial Revolution and the privatization of property. Both Marx and Engels saw socialism as part of a materialistic phase of the transition to pure communism but discredited various socialist theories such as utopianism.

Removal of peasants' vegetables during Holodomor

In its practical application, communism resulted in the rise of brutal dictatorships, the slaughter of tens of millions of innocent individuals, and mass enslavement. One of many examples of the negative impact of communism is the Ukrainian "Holodomor" – a period of famine imposed by the Soviet government on Ukraine in the winter of 1932-33. During this time, the Soviet government stole Ukraine's entire food supply, which led to the starvation of at least seven million people, including over one million children. There are many more examples of mass slaughter and brutal political repression by communists.

Liberalism is defined as a political and social philosophy based solely on the ideas of equality and liberty. Some of the key ideas in liberalism include the rejection of absolute monarchies and the divine rights of royalty, as well as the removal of hereditary privilege and state-sanctioned religion. The rise of liberalism during the Enlightenment period has typically been attributed to John Locke, who argued that every man had the natural right to life, liberty, and the assumption and ownership of property. Locke claimed that no government should violate these natural rights, in direct opposition to the claim to divine rights made by the kings, queens, and absolute monarchs of the early modern period.

Such ideas were used by those participating in the American and French Revolutions as a means of dispelling tyrannical rulers who, according to the laws of liberalism, were violating the natural rights of men. Liberalism continued to grow and expand. During the 19th century, the movement took hold in the Americas and Europe. It also influenced later governments by creating liberal democrats, who transformed the policies of the United States in the early 20th century.

All of the political theories discussed above greatly influenced both the periods in which they emerged and subsequent periods of world history. During the Cold War in the 20th century, the spread of communism had drastic effects on the global economic system, as well as relationships between the East and West. Following the Great Depression during the early 20th century, the spread of liberal democracy greatly influenced domestic policies in America and set the tone for future government projects and expectations of the government by the American public. Without the contributions of Enlightenment thinkers, it is arguable that most of Europe would have continued to be ruled by monarchies with absolute power; however, as a direct result of the theories mentioned above, liberal democracies and other forms of government are active throughout the world today.

Demands for women's suffrage and emergent feminism challenged political and gender hierarchies.

As a result of the great transformations of the Enlightenment Age, women began to call for equal representation and suffrage. This was a long battle for many women across the globe. As women continued to organize themselves and work towards suffrage, several key figures emerged, including Olympe de Gouges, Mary Wollstonecraft, and Elizabeth Cady Stanton. Olympe de Gouges (1748–1793) was a notable French playwright and actively engaged in the women's rights movement during the French Revolution. She was executed by guillotine several years after the French Revolution.

Olympe de Gouges is most well known for her publication the *Declaration of the Rights of Women and of the Citizen*, in which she modeled her philosophies after the popular French Revolutionary text the *Declaration of the Rights of Man and Citizen*. De Gouges promoted the value of women's equality within the French government and culture. She spoke out against the suppression of women's sexuality and the expectation that women should be subservient to men on issues such as childbirth. Such ideas were not well received by the males in government following the French Revolution, and as a result, De Gouges was condemned to death.

Mary Wollstonecraft (1759–1797) was a famous English writer, social critic, and women's advocate. Wollstonecraft, inspired by the ideas of the Enlightenment, argued that it was essential that women be allowed to receive education on par with that of men, and that it was essential that traditional gender roles be challenged. Wollstonecraft had two children out of wedlock, which stalled the acceptance of some of her ideas. In later periods, she was described as "the mother of feminism." One of her greatest works was *A Vindication of the Rights of Woman*, which was released in 1792 and instantly became controversial. Wollstonecraft argued that the norms and standards of civilization had created a beast out of women, transforming them into tyrants of their households. She also argued for the expansion of women's education to the same capacity as men's education. For her period, Wollstonecraft was extremely revolutionary and, at times, was not well received. However, recently some academics and historians have argued that she was more widely accepted than previously thought.

Elizabeth Cady Stanton (1815–1902) was a monumental figure in the women's suffrage movement and inspired countless other activists and proponents of women's suffrage. Stanton argued for equal representation of women in various contexts, specifically education, as women were already often tasked with providing basic education to their children. Stanton is most famous for organizing the first women's rights convention in 1848 at Seneca Falls, New York. She is also well known for collaborating with Susan B. Anthony to form the Women's Loyal League in 1863 and later the National Woman's Suffrage Association. The efforts of Stanton and others in the women's movement were monumental in the passing of the Nineteenth Amendment, which finally gave all American citizens the right to vote.

Elizabeth Cady Stanton

The women discussed above are considered some of the first feminists who laid the foundation for future feminists in both America and Europe. These women were instrumental in popularizing the argument that while women were different from men, mainly in an emotional capacity, they were just as qualified to work outside the home and be equally represented in government. This newly emerging feminist movement was also a result of the Enlightenment and political revolutions in France and the Americas. For the first time in history, average men were able to emerge from the status of servitude. The desire for increased freedom from oppression was also felt by women who were suppressed by the social structures of the time.

Because of the nature of the new modes of transportation, both internal and external migrants increasingly relocated to cities. This pattern contributed to the significant global urbanization of the 19th century.

The emergence of new and more efficient modes of transportation, such as steam-powered ships, greatly influenced the migration patterns of this period. Steam-powered ships allowed many more immigrants to travel to the United States and for empires, such as the British and Dutch, to capitalize on overseas colonization. Within each country, advances in transportation stemming from the Industrial Revolution allowed for further expansion and development. For example, American railroads facilitated western expansion by making it easier to create a new wave of settlements, economies, and markets in the west. Eastern regions of the United States continued to develop at their own pace. They allowed for the migration of various people at different points, depending on the opportunities in each state. Western expansion led to a whole new culture and demographics in the United States.

East and west shake hands at the laying of the last rail of the Union Pacific Railroad

Migrants relocated for a variety of reasons.

As a result of the booming industrial and agricultural revolutions taking place in Europe and the Americas, many laborers—both skilled and unskilled—sought work in new markets and regions. This resulted in massive migration, which took place from the 1820s into the early years of the 20th century. Better economic opportunities enabled the poor to acquire and maintain a higher standard of living. In addition to the new working class, a thriving middle class emerged and was introduced to urban metropolises and industrial centers.

Many individuals chose freely to relocate, often in search of work.

In hopes of finding better forms of work and a higher standard of living, many migrants left their native lands for other regions, typically in Eastern Europe and East Asia. As people migrated, new groups of workers, as well as ethnic communities that supported their work initiatives, were established. Manual laborers emerged as a result of this great migration. Between 1820 and 1914, almost two and half million people migrated to work in factories, urban development and agricultural vocations on plantations. These laborers were typically welcomed as the end of slavery had created a vacuum of workers. In plantation settings, manual laborers were necessary to help maintain the economic viability of cash crops. Specialized professionals typically migrated to the U.S.A. from Eastern and Southern Europe and sought jobs in more specific fields, such as mining and railroad building. Migrants also sought better employment with fewer restrictions.

Many immigrants experienced animosity from native people with whom they were competing for work, which eventually led to very restrictive immigration policies during the late 19th and early 20th centuries. Migration was also extremely important in creating new social groups that dominated American and European societies in later periods. A monumental shift in the use of low wage labor supplied the workforce necessary to accomplish these industrial goals and ambitions.

The new global capitalist economy continued to rely on coerced and semi-coerced labor migration: slavery, Chinese and Indian indentured servitude, convict labor.

Various forms of labor and labor systems were introduced and transformed during the industrial age. Slavery continued into the early years of the industrial age in the United States, where slaves were used to grow and maintain cotton, sugar, and tobacco plantations. These particular crops were vital to the American economy in the pre-industrial age. As these cash crops continued to be in high demand, the need for slaves, and the profitability of slave labor continued as well. However, in Europe, slavery had already been eliminated and would be replaced with other forms of low-income labor. As industrial products displaced agricultural ones in value, slavery became unnecessary in the industrialized north. Convict labor, also known as penal labor, is an additional type of labor that was used extensively by the British and French empires to construct camps, farms, and colonies.

Indentured servitude was seen in the American colonies, typically as a form of payment for passage from the country of origin to America. It was also used in places like India and China. In the 1820s, the British Empire capitalized on this cheap form of labor and employed indentured servitude in many of its colonies in the Americas, and to a lesser extent, in Africa and the Indian subcontinent.

Slavery on an American sugar plantation

Due to the physical nature of the labor in demand, migrants tended to be male, leaving women to take on new roles in the home society that had been formerly occupied by men.

These migrations also shaped the gender and domestic roles of future Europeans and Americans. During the period of the Enlightenment, women and men began exploring different gender roles. Agrarian work required relatively low skill, which led women to adopt roles that formerly were considered to be exclusively for men. The factory jobs of the industrial age, by contrast, were labor-intensive, repetitive, and typically paid poorly;. However, for some immigrants during the industrial age, the low wages were a significant improvement from the subsistence level of existence they had experienced before industrialization. Many people had left agrarian jobs, where they made little money and found themselves in new jobs where workers did not control any aspect of the job - including the work hours and conditions.

Women were left to tend to matters of the household exclusively, though many men still regarded women incapable of effectively managing such affairs alone. Women argued that they were more than capable of such tasks and could perform them even better if they were afforded similar resources as men, namely an adequate education.

Receiving societies did not always embrace immigrants, as seen in the various degrees of ethnic and racial prejudice and the ways states attempted to regulate the increased flow of people across their borders.

As a result of immigration, social norms were tested, especially in Australia and the United States. Examples of racial and ethnic prejudice and tensions include the passage of the Chinese Exclusion Act in America and the White Australia Policy used by the British Empire. The Chinese Exclusion Act was passed in 1882 and placed a ban on the immigration of Chinese into the United States, as at the time, the Chinese were seen by many as a threat to the well-being of the United States. Many Americans seeking work in the United States were unwilling to compete with the massive influx of immigrant workers, specifically from China, and reacted with racism and bigotry. This legislation limited Chinese immigration to the United States for a total of forty years and caused a drastic decrease in the Chinese American population.

The White Australian Policy, passed in Australia by the British government, was also a response to a massive influx in immigration. During the mid-1800s, the influx of people of various ethnicities caused many white Australian settlers to take actions against both native populations and immigrants, most notably those from Asia.

Notes for active learning

Notes for active learning

Major historical events of the period:

1300s: *The Epic of Sundiata* is written

1652:   European colonization of South Africa begins

1805:   Muhammed Ali establishes an Egyptian Khedive in the Ottoman Empire

1847:   Liberia is founded in West Africa by emancipated U.S. slaves

1899:   The Boer War erupts in South Africa

PERIOD 3: 1500 to 1900 C.E.

AFRICA

Disease brought by ships arrived in South Africa.

The era of exploration and conquest also perpetuated the spread of viruses to parts of the world beyond the Americas. One example was the 1713 smallpox epidemic that took place on the Cape of Good Hope and decimated the South African Khoi San people, rendering them incapable of resisting the process of colonization and impacting the colonial status of Africa in later periods.

The Epic of Sundiata reflected the Malinke people.

The *Sundiata Keita* or *Epic of Sundiata* also referred to as the *Sundiata Epic*, is an epic poem of the Malinke people, which tells the story of the hero, Sundiata Keita, the founder of the Mali Empire, who died in 1255. The epic is an instance of oral history going back to the 14th century and is similar to those seen in Ancient Greece.

Europeans established new trading-post empires in Africa and Asia, which proved profitable for the rulers and merchants involved in new global trade networks. However, these empires also affected the power of the states in interior West and Central Africa.

Portuguese settlements on the west coast of Africa or the Gold Coast were the first of their kind and gave rise to the establishment of Portugal as a maritime empire. The Portuguese were attracted to the more fertile lands of Africa and sought to find a southern passage to India to trade with the East and Asia. This led the Portuguese to establish settlements along the west coast of Africa, such as the city of Elmina. Following fifty years of coastal exploration, the Portuguese made Elmina a permanent settlement, and it eventually developed into a fully functioning city, which was the embarkation point for future exploration and settlements on the western coast of Africa. The population of Elmina swelled, which indicates the number of merchants conducting trade on a global or regional scale at the time. By 1637, the Dutch had taken over the fort and improved its fortifications to prevent additional attacks.

The Atlantic system involved the movement of goods, wealth, and free and unfree laborers and the mixing of African, American, and European cultures and peoples.

As global trade expanded and empires increased their wealth and status, the emergence of the Atlantic System perpetuated slavery for decades during and following the early modern period. The Atlantic System is typically divided into two eras: the First and Second Atlantic Systems. The First Atlantic System began in the 16th century and was mainly comprised of Portuguese merchants transporting slave labor from Africa to Spanish and Portuguese colonies in the New World. This workforce was needed for labor-intensive mining and agricultural projects, replacing the native populations that had been decimated by disease and war.

The Second Atlantic System, in the 17th and 18th centuries, involved British, French, and Dutch merchants supplying African slaves to their countries' colonies. This period represented the greatest influx of slaves in American history. As with the Mesoamerican colonies, the North American colonies were also in need of a great workforce. Workers were needed to operate the plantations growing cash crops, which in turn facilitated the Atlantic System. An example of this is sugarcane. These cash crops later included rice, tobacco, and cotton.

The Triangular Trade included the transport of slaves from the Atlantic Systems but also included cash crops and manufactured goods shared between West Africa, the American colonies, and Europe. It was called the Triangular Trade because the flow of goods and human resources took the shape of a triangle. Typically, the colonies would send natural resources to Europe and West Africa. West Africa, in turn, provided slave labor to the colonies, and Europe exported finished goods to both.

Liverpool slave ship

The rise of the slave trade also saw a mixture of various cultures and people. Examples include religious adaptations of Vodun from West Africa, as well as the emergence of mulatto cultures in the Americas. Additionally, this mixing restructured social norms in the cultures that participated. In Africa, families were displaced and destroyed as rival kingdoms captured and sold each other into slavery. In the American colonies, the use of forced or slave labor continued until the end of the American Civil War. European nations also embraced slavery as it allowed them to prosper from the Triangular Trade and to establish great maritime colonies.

Many European states used both warfare and diplomacy to establish empires in Africa.

To attain their imperialistic goals, many European governments used military force in addition to diplomacy. The effects of these policies can still be seen in West Africa and the Congo today.

In hopes of maintaining a peaceful existence in West Africa, the British government used a program of indirect rule where native institutions were upheld, and British authorities made changes or gave advisement from a distance. However, this more hands-off approach seemed only to complicate things for both the native populations and the British authorities attempting to rule them. As a result, many other European empires decided against employing a similar ruling structure.

For example, the French chose to rule the colony of Algeria directly. The Algerian experiment was an entirely different iteration of colonization and seemed to be a bit more successful at maintaining a sense of authority in Algeria. However, the French experienced other problems associated with colonialism and imperialism, such as the exploitation of Africans, which resulted in tense relations.

French conquest of Algeria, Battle of Mazagran

In some parts of their empires, Europeans established settler colonies.

As Europeans sought the perfect recipe for global dominance, they employed various tactics, including the implementation of settler colonies in places like Africa, Australia, New Zealand, and French Algeria. Settler colonies were inhabited by entire family units who moved into a foreign region and were governed by an imperial power. Settler colonies were temporary and used to repopulate a colony that was depleted or struggling.

When a colonial power first began to explore a new land, its government sought to answer several questions. The government wanted to find out what was already in the territory that might be of benefit to them – who was living there and if they might be either a benefit or a threat to the colonists' ambition, what the geography of the land was like and if the potential colony would prove geo-strategically useful.

South Africa is a good case study of how colonial powers functioned throughout the world in the 18th and 19th centuries. The first European nation to establish a toehold on the southern tip of Africa was Portugal, whose monarchy wished to establish a safe harbor to have a strategic waystation for naval and trading ships. The Portuguese made the minimum necessary contact with the indigenous people there, and as they did not attempt to colonize, they were able to maintain their port—now modern Cape Town—in peace.

The first European power to truly colonize South Africa was the Netherlands. The Dutch established farms and pastures there to supply their vessels. Over time, these Dutch communities developed into a country in their own right, but on someone else's land. The Dutch settlements displaced the indigenous South African people, often leading to bloody conflict. For the Dutch, their South African colony was an economic resource. Dutch settlers were eventually partially displaced by the British, who arrived in South Africa in the 19th century. War eventually erupted in South Africa when major gold and diamond discoveries were made there.

The South African gold discovery provided a flashpoint for the Boer War.

In the South African region of Kimberley, the discovery of gold and precious stones resulted in a massive influx of British men. These migrations quickly created tensions between the native populations and those coming to mine their resources.

This dispute between European powers over the control of foreign resources, with the local population caught in the middle, culminated in the South African War of 1899–1902 (also known as the Boer War). This war was won by British forces and led to the creation of the Union of South Africa in 1910. It also led to the creation of the largest diamond and gold mines the world has ever seen. The manual labor in these mines was done primarily by the indigenous people of South Africa for wages, which were suppressed by law in the collectivist system called Apartheid.

The Battle of Majuba Hill in the First Boer War

Emancipated American slaves founded Liberia; repatriated settlers fought with indigenous Africans.

The Liberian nationalism movement also originated during the 1800s. The nation of Liberia was established in Africa as a place for free American blacks to live. President Monroe created a colony and legal framework—hence, the capital of the nation is called Monrovia. For the people who moved there, the dream was to live free of white racism on the continent populated by people with whom they shared a heritage. Ironically, the motivation of the white politicians who supported this project was to rid America of free blacks. The conflict came about as a result of tense relations between American settlers and Liberian natives, many of whom were willing to fight for an independent Liberian state, which became a reality in 1847.

South African Xhosa religiously protest colonization.

In South Africa, at the beginning of British domination, hundreds of thousands of head of cattle were killed by members of the Xhosa ethnic group in the belief that this would lead to their emancipation from European colonization. The story goes that two teenage girls reported meeting three of their ancestors, who had allegedly told them that if the Xhosa slaughtered all of their cattle, all of their ancestors would return from the dead and destroy the British settlers. The Xhosa chief accepted this story, and the Xhosa destroyed at least three hundred thousand head of their cattle. While this did not lead to the destruction of the British by ancestral spirits, it did lead to a famine that claimed the lives of about forty thousand Xhosa.

Egypt embraced early industrialization.

Muhammad Ali, who ruled Egypt, also embraced industrialization by creating a vast textile industry in Egypt. Though Ali was plagued by British intervention, he was ultimately able to stay loyal to his Ottoman roots.

Statue of Muhammad Ali of Egypt in Mansheya Square, Alexandria

Zulus were divided and conquered by the British.

The Zulu kingdom of Africa is an example of forced expulsion and imperialism. During the expansionist phase of the British colonization of South Africa in the late nineteenth century, the Zulu people were ordered to accept British authority. After refusing and being defeated in a subsequent war for territory, the Zulu were divided into thirteen political divisions—with the intention of keeping them at war with each other instead of united against the British. This policy succeeded, and the Zulu were soon relegated to a limited territory with no political rights and no citizenship. They remained a disenfranchised and stateless group—in this system and then under apartheid—until 1992.

Notes for active learning

Southwest Asia

Major historical events of the period:

1501: Safavid Empire reunifies Iran

1500s: Silver discovered in the Americas destabilizes Ottoman economy; Safavid Empire expands into northern India

1529: Ottomans begin and fail their Siege of Vienna

1500s–1600s: Ottoman and Safavid Empires engage in frequent conflicts over territory

1550: The Ottoman Suleymaniye Mosque in Istanbul is commissioned

1804–1835: Ottomans experience revolts in Serbian lands, bestow semi-independence

PERIOD 3: 1500 to 1900 C.E.

SOUTHWEST ASIA

As Islam spread to new settings in Afro-Eurasia, believers adapted it to local cultural practices. The split between the Sunni and Shi'a traditions of Islam intensified, and Sufi practices became more widespread.

The tensions of the schism of Islam are similar to those of the Christian Church in the sense that they grew and intensified over time, resulting in a political and concrete separation that forever altered the political and religious landscape of their respective regions, as well as the global picture. The 7th-century division of Islam took place over succession, following the death of Muhammad. No directive had been created for succession. As a result, the Islamic world divided into two communities over the true succession of the Muslim faith. One group believed the succession should remain within the bloodline of the family, placing the succession with Ali, Muhammad's closest male heir. This group eventually identified as Shi'ite Muslims.

Others believed the succession of the faith should lie with the most knowledgeable person, in this case, Abu Bakr, the father-in-law of Muhammad. This group eventually identified as Sunni Muslims. As a result, the Sunni Muslims recognized the legitimacy of several additional leaders, including Abu Bakr, Umar, and Uthman, the first three successors to Muhammad.

Abu Bakr,
Muhammad's father-in-law

Shi'ite Muslims only recognize the 4th successor, Ali Mohammad, who was Muhammad's son-in-law and cousin.

This division set the stage for tension and rivalry within the early modern period. By 1500, Sunni Ottomans and Shia Safavids were embroiled in a bitter conflict. Such resentment has been fostered and perpetuated throughout the world, regardless of region. In 1501, the Safavid Empire reunified Iran as an independent state and established Shi'ism as the official religion of the Empire. This became a monumental moment in Islamic history, establishing the geographical conflict of Sunni and Shi'ite Muslims for the following centuries, continuing to the present day. Today, the Safavid Empire would encompass Iran, Southern Iraq, and portions of Azerbaijan, all of which are still dominated by a Shi'ite majority. The Ottoman Empire was able to expand Sunni Islam into vast territories as it conquered its way across Eurasia. These expansions required mandatory conversion to Islam, but the practice of other religions was tolerated, as long as they did not offend Islamic law.

Sufism also emerged as a religious and political tool, which allowed for the expansion of Islam into Africa, India, and the Far East. Sufism, also known as Ta'sawwuf, is considered a form of Islamic Mysticism. Although Sufism is not an actual sect of Islam, both Sunni and Shi'a sects maintain components of Sufism, and many Sufis claim to be Muslims. Sufism is most well-known for active meditation of the Mevlevi Order, which focuses on abandoning personal ego and perception, instead of devoting oneself to Allah and spinning in a repetitive circular motion, emulating that of the stars. The division between Sunni and Shi'a cultures had drastic impacts on the period, especially seen in the rivalry of the Ottoman and Safavid Empires.

Safavid Empire became a bastion for Shia faith.

The Safavid Empire was able to build its foundations upon the growth of Islam and the use of Shia religious practices in a region that had been dominated by Sunni religious practices. By labeling Shi'ism as the formal and official religion of the Safavid Empire, the rulers gave tribute to their religion, but also called upon it as a source of strength.

Persians created new art genres.

Miniatures in Persia were also important artworks of this period and are found in both the Persian and Mughal empires. A new genre in Safavid art, which caused an explosion in demand for portraits, caused a new type of artwork known as miniatures to evolve. The ruler Akbar of the Safavid Dynasty was a great supporter of the arts and commissioned various portraiture works for himself and family members.

Ottoman Empire granted limited autonomy to minority groups.

The Ottoman Empire was multi-ethnic to its very core. At the height of the Ottoman Empire, there were significant numbers of Jews (in Palestine), Coptic Christians (in Egypt and the Levant), Orthodox Christians (in Armenia, the Balkans and parts of the Aegean) and various mystics, such as Sufis (in the Caucasus) that all lived within the territory of this vast empire. As with past successful empires, these varied ethnic groups were granted a certain degree of autonomy in the many *millets*, or regions, of the Empire. This is not to say that the non-Muslim subjects of the Ottoman Empire were treated equally to their Muslim counterparts, as they were forced to pay a tax, or *zakat*, due to their faith. However, they were respected in their regions and allowed to rise to high, influential positions in the regional bureaucratic apparatus.

Ottomans and Safavids become embroiled in conflict.

Additional expansion continued after the initial victories in Constantinople. Under Sulieman the Magnificent, the Ottoman Empire was able to maintain vast territories on three different continents. The military successes of the Empire were facilitated by the Janissary group, which formerly had been comprised of a Turkic Cavalry, which was quickly transformed into a warrior aristocracy. However, military power began to transition to the Europeans beginning in 1529 with the Siege of Vienna. It was cemented with the crushing blow at the Battle of Lepanto in 1571, where the Spanish and Venetian fleets defeated Ottoman forces.

The Ottomans were also unable to obstruct the Portuguese trade in the Indian Ocean. Such failures limited the revenue seen in tax collection, hindering the Empire's growth. The explosion of silver from the Americas in the 16th century further destabilized the Ottoman economy. The Ottomans were not interested in the Enlightenment or Scientific Revolution. As a result, they began to decline in the fields of warfare, technology, and trade. At its height, the Ottoman Empire was known for the effective administrative rule and tax relief, as well as sultans who operated as absolute monarchs and grand viziers who oversaw the running of the Empire. The Ottoman Empire was labeled "the sick man of Europe" as it declined in status and continued to lose its territorial integrity to European forces, which were more advanced as a result of the Renaissance, the Enlightenment, and the Scientific Revolution.

The Safavid Empire (1501–1722) was established by Ismail I (1487–1524, r. 1501) and ruled Persia from 1501–1736. Ismail led his followers to victory in the city of Tabriz, where he was originally proclaimed shah or emperor. Ismail also proclaimed Shi'ism the state religion. The establishment of the Safavid Empire was a threat to the rest of the Muslim world because the Shah's followers thought him to be the rightful head of the entire Muslim community. This brought the Safavids into conflict with the Sunni Ottoman sultans, who claimed the leadership of the Islamic community for themselves.

In 1514 Ismail was defeated by his Sunni rival, the Ottoman sultan Selim I. The Safavids were less militarily inclined and developed than their Ottoman counterparts, which led to the defeat, known as the Battle of Chaldiran. Isma'il became largely ineffective as a ruler following this defeat and only avoided complete Ottoman takeover as a result of the geographical location of the capital city of Tabriz in relation to Ottoman supply lines. As a result, Shi'ism remained relatively isolated in Safavid territories—present-day Iran and Southern Iraq.

Mehmed II, Ottoman sultan

One of the most significant Safavid accomplishments in the 16th century was Persia's eastward expansion into Northern India. Zahirud-din Muhammad Babur, a Persian ruler from the province of Ferghana, initiated the eastward expansion and became the first ruler of the Mughal court. The Safavid dynasty reached its peak under Abbas I, also referred to as Abbas the Great, who ruled from 1587 to 1629 and instituted slave regiments, similar to the Janissaries, to expand the Empire to its farthest reaches. Abbas also built up an army numbering close to 40,000. He moved the capital to Isfahan, expanded Safavid culture, and founded several colleges. Abbas was a patron of the arts, especially sculpture and architecture.

Ottoman Empire at its zenith, spanned three continents.

The Ottoman Empire was extremely extensive. At the peak of its territorial holdings, the Empire occupied three continents. The Ottomans were also interested in continuous expansion, as is evident from their invasion of the Balkans and Baghdad and their failed attempt to take the Austro-Hungarian city of Vienna. Large land-based armies also augmented the Ottoman forces, in this instance, greatly facilitated by the use of Janissary forces.

Ottoman janissaries grow and shaped empire.

Janissary

The Ottoman Empire employed the use of Janissary services, which entailed the selection of Christian boys recruited from conquered territories (e.g., the Balkans, Bulgaria) to enter into compulsory military service. These postings were typically long, dangerous and led to many casualties. However, janissaries were crucial to the rise of the Ottoman Empire as this warrior class greatly complimented their existing ranks, going on to conquer vast swaths of territory for the Ottoman Empire. Salaries and pensions propelled the janissaries to become part of the ruling class, though they increasingly came into rivalry with the existing Ottoman elite. This culminated in their entrenched power and corruption, increasingly preventing military reform. By 1826, the corps was abolished by Sultan Mahmud II.

Indian cotton production and Chinese silk production intensify.

Silk weaving centers were situated in metropolitan areas dotting the caravan route leading south to the major trading centers of Aleppo, Baghdad, Damascus, and later, in Ottoman dominions in the Aegean and Tunisia. Istanbul was famous for its embroideries and for brocaded silks produced in the imperial manufactory, while Bursa principally produced fabrics for trade. Shah Abbas I (1587–1629) implemented a series of reforms aimed at revolutionizing the textile industry. Abbas also made the production of silk into a royal monopoly and reorganized the imperial manufactories. The Silk Road traders dominated cotton textile distribution in India. In some instances, former trading alliances cemented a monopoly of the cotton textile trade by India. Examples of this are the Persian, Mughal, and Ottoman trading policies toward India and its cotton surplus.

Shah Abbas I of Iran

Religious-cultural divides sparked an Ottoman-Safavid conflict that lasted 150 years.

Religious and cultural rivalries facilitated the conflicts between the Ottoman and the Safavid dynasties. These were wars for territory and took place over roughly 150 years in the 16th and 17th centuries. These conflicts never resulted in the decisive defeat of either side, but they did weaken the Safavid Empire and contributed heavily to its later demise.

Anti-imperial resistance led to the contraction of the Ottoman Empire.

As the Ottoman Empire entered this period, it was clear that its nickname "the sick man of Europe" was more than accurate. The Ottoman Empire did not experience the abundant successes of other European empires. Instead, the Ottoman Empire experienced losses, including the independence of the Balkan states, the semi-independence of Egypt, and the emergence of French and Italian colonies throughout North Africa. One of the reasons for these losses was the Ottoman Empire's debt to the European treasuries.

In the Balkans, the Serbian struggle for independence was the first uprising against the Ottoman Empire. Between 1804 and 1835, various revolts ended in semi-independence for some regions of Serbia. British forces also influenced the struggle for independence in the Balkans. In Egypt, the emergence of Muhammad Ali, who adamantly believed in industrialization, was seen as a form of semi-independence as he was able to become an effective and respected ruler by 1820. Ali was able to rise to power due to the failed French attempts at invasion and a lack of effective influence exerted by the Ottoman Empire.

The British worked on behalf of the Ottoman Empire in Egypt to assert some influence in hopes of limiting the regional and sub-regional powers of the Russian Empire. French and Italian colonies also began to emerge in Northern Africa, displacing the former regional powers of the Ottoman Empire. As the power of the Ottoman Empire dwindled, many Europeans began to become concerned that the Russian Empire would become powerful enough to emerge as a European rival.

Notes for active learning

Notes for active learning

South & Southeast Asia

Major historical events of the period:

1500s: Portugal dominates Indian Ocean trade

1632:   The Taj Mahal is commissioned by the Mughal Emperor Shah Jahan

1800:   The Dutch nationalize the Dutch East Indies Company, giving the nation direct control over modern-day Indonesia

1857:   The Indian Revolt of 1857 (Sepoy Rebellion)

1858:   The British Raj (direct rule) in India begins

1898:   The conclusion of the Spanish-American War transfers the Philippines and Guam to the U.S.

PERIOD 3: 1500 to 1900 C.E.

SOUTH AND SOUTHEAST ASIA

Sikhism developed as a reaction to Hindu-Muslim struggles in India.

Sikhism is another syncretic religion, which was founded in 1499 by Guru Nanak. The religion's roots can be found in Hinduism and Islam, and its followers were found mainly in the Punjab Province of India, which is now divided between modern-day Pakistan and India. *Sikh* translates as "student," giving followers an indication of the superiority of the spiritual leader. The teachings of Guru Nanak (a guru is a master or a teacher), along with the work of nine other gurus who were part of his following, comprise the theological background of Sikhism. The Sikh faith is monotheistic and stresses good acts in place of ritualistic practices. The guiding principles of Sikhism include following Ik Onkar, the one God who prevails in all things. Sikhs also attempted social reform, demanding justice for all humans, in direct opposition to the caste system in place at the time.

Guru Nanak, founder of Sikhism

Some notable gender and family restructuring occurred, including the demographic changes in Africa that resulted from the slave trades.

In addition to the gender reforms already discussed, this period saw the rise of "powerful" elite women in Southeast Asian cultures. Other notable social changes taking place included the downsizing of the family unit. As many merchants descended upon Southeast Asia, they were shocked by the role of women in Asian markets. Women were able to sell goods at outdoor markets, facilitate money lending and currency changing services, and engage in long-distance trade—as was seen in the Atlantic system. As a result of these economic activities, some women were held in high regard in their society, although always secondary in relation to males.

Women in Southeast Asia were able to accumulate significant wealth and, for the most part, could use it as they wished. This was historically the norm in Asia and continued into the early modern period. This type of culture was perpetuated by historical inheritance customs, as well as the implementation of education for females. Overall, women's status in the Asian economic and political landscape was almost unheard of elsewhere. Even so, women were typically treated as secondary citizens and were controlled by their male kin.

Mughal Empire inherited Delhi Sultanate territory.

The Mughal Empire (1526–1858) was a continuation of the Delhi Sultanate seen under Mongol rulers, which is why they share a similar namesake. The lands maintained by the Mughal Empire include parts of present-day India, Pakistan, and Afghanistan. They were patrolled by a vast land army, which required heavy taxes to uphold and service. Military service was so valued in the Mughal Empire that many soldiers received land grants. This upset the elites in the government. The Mughal Empire engaged in limited trade and was able, using successful military campaigns and social reforms, to create a stable and peaceful empire.

Dancing Mughal Women

One notable ruler, Akbar, who assumed power in 1556, quickly established himself as a highly capable leader and a keen patron of the arts. He sought peace in his kingdom, instituting a policy of tolerance for all people regardless of religious affiliation. The Hindu population embraced him as a benevolent leader, and his capital at Agra drew scholars from all parts of India and the Muslim world. Akbar's court encouraged artistic excellence and innovation.

Artists began signing their work more often at this time. Akbar's death in 1605 transferred control of the extensive Mughal Empire to his son Jahangir, who ruled from 1605 to 1627, and, subsequently, Shah Jahan, who ruled from 1627 to 1658. Both of these rulers ruled during the peak of the Empire. Delhi, Agra, and Lahore were all major cultural centers.

Mughal Empire emphasized military prowess.

The Mughals were an extension of the Mongol Empire, which was vast and far-reaching in the Middle East. The Mughal Empire of the period was comprised of what is present-day India, Pakistan, and Afghanistan. Like other land-based Gunpowder Empires, the Mughals used vast armies to support and supply their settlements, also expelling foreign invaders.

The Mughal Empire in 1700

Subjects challenged the centralized imperial governments.

Challenges to authority and social norms were seen throughout the global system, not just in Europe and the Americas. One example is the Maratha power rivalry with the Mughal Sultanates. The Marathas were a group of militant Hindus, who engaged in guerilla warfare in hopes of maintaining a breakaway state in the southern portion of India. The Marathas were able to challenge the authority and power of the Mughal Sultanates over a period of almost thirty years by means of warfare. The Marathas' military successes contributed to the decline of Muslim dominance over India. However, these successes were short-lived, and the Peshwas, who created their lasting Empire in India, eventually overwhelmed the Marathas.

These rivalries also resulted in new powers emerging out of the political landscape. They directly resulted in the use of military means to gain and hold power, rather than political or religious means. Without the military advances of the Marathas, it would have been impossible to transition away from the Mughal Empire, which had formerly dominated the southern region of India.

Dutch imperial power coalesced after nationalizing Dutch East India Company.

In 1800, the Dutch East India Company nationalized the Dutch East Indies, which gave full control of the Indonesian territories to the Dutch government. Subsequently, with the axis of their colonies in South Africa, Indonesia, and the Caribbean, the Dutch experienced unbridled hegemony in the region, thereby becoming a tremendous transoceanic imperial power. During the 19th and early 20th century, the Dutch held a monopoly over the global spice trade, which allowed their Empire to reap the benefits of imperialism.

Boats leaving for East India from the City of Veer in Zeeland

British hold over India shook with the Indian Revolt of 1857.

As nationalism spread across the globe, rebellions and revolutions became more frequent and fiercer than before. One example is the Indian Revolt of 1857, where the tension between Indians and the British erupted into a full-scale rebellion. The revolt was initiated by Indian Muslims and Hindus, who were unwilling to complete the work of the British East India Company due to religious traditions and rebelled against the British forces, killing several officers. The revolt was met with staggering brutality by the British forces, who sought to instill fear and servitude amongst the Indian populations. The British also limited the extent to which Indians could own property and hold positions within the government.

British forces and their allies clash with mutineers

Portuguese-Ottoman hostilities erupted over trade competition.

In the late 15th and early 16th centuries, the Portuguese and Ottomans were the eminent powers in the Euro-Asian theater. The Ottoman Empire began its existence already in control of trade between Europe, Asia, and most of Africa. The Battle of Diu in 1509 was fought in the Arabian Sea between Portuguese and Ottoman supporters, highlighting the rivalry for the trade routes in the Indian Ocean.

The United States inherited Filipino unrest after wresting territory from Spain.

Filipino nationalism developed as a direct result of Spanish colonial rule, which lasted for close to three centuries, and culminated in the Philippine Revolution beginning in 1896. The Americans also imposed their form of colonial rule on the Philippine Islands after having promised the people of the Philippines their independence if they fought on the side of the United States in the Spanish American War. As a response, a U.S. naval detachment and marines were sent to the Philippines to quell Philippine resistance to newly imposed American colonial rule. The Philippines finally achieved independence in 1946.

The Battle of Manila Bay during the Spanish-American War

Notes for active learning

Copyright © 2021 Sterling Test Prep.

East Asia

Major historical events of the period:

1644:	The Manchus capture Beijing, overthrowing the Ming dynasty
1839–1842:	The First Opium War
1856–1860:	The Second Opium War
1861–1895:	China's Self-Strengthening Movement
1867:	Japanese isolation ends
1877:	The Satsuma Rebellion results in the disbanding of the samurai
1894–1895:	Japan emerges victorious in the First Sino-Japanese War, obtaining vast territory from the Qing Empire in Korea as well the island of Taiwan
1900:	Boxer Rebellion

PERIOD 3: 1500 to 1900 C.E.

EAST ASIA

China projected power in other regions via naval expeditions.

Chinese exploration in the same period was led by Zhu Di, also known as the Yongle Emperor, who used China's seafaring capability to display national power, assertiveness, and aggression. To accomplish this, he chose his most trusted general, Zheng He, to lead a series of expeditions to demonstrate China's vast power and influence. The Ming Dynasty also used these voyages for diplomatic means; sending gifts to their neighbors and showing off their immense wealth and access to highly desirable luxury goods. After completing seven different expeditions, Zheng He had navigated around Southeast Asia, India, the Persian Gulf, and even the east coast of Africa.

Official Chinese maritime activity expanded into the Indian Ocean region with the naval voyages led by Ming Admiral Zheng He, which enhanced Chinese prestige.

The Chinese maritime experience during the Ming Dynasty was dominated by the accomplishments of Zhu Di and Zheng He. In addition to exhibiting China's military status and power, the voyages and expeditions of Zheng He spread awareness of Chinese prestige and culture. In hopes of achieving respect, the politicians and emissaries of the Yongle Emperor presented various gifts during their journeys, including silk, porcelain, and gold. In return, Chinese diplomats received extravagant gifts from distant lands, including zebras and ostriches.

None of this would have been accomplished without Zheng He, also known as Cheng Ho. Zheng He was not born in Ming China but instead came from a Muslim family in the far southwest region of Asia. Zheng He had been integrated into Chinese culture following his capture by Ming military forces at a young age. Following this, he used various political connections and contacts to become a prominent general. The Yongle Emperor saw the value of Zheng He's Muslim background and recruited him to undertake diplomatic voyages, initially to India, later to Thailand and, eventually, to Eastern Africa. To please his Emperor and the Ming Dynasty, Zheng He addressed several issues of concern during his expeditions, including unsupportive neighbors (typically Sultans) and piracy within the region.

Following Zheng He's vast success and upon his death, the Ming Dynasty no longer had the ambition or desire to explore neighboring regions using oceanic travel. The Chinese people believed they had acquired vast and substantial wealth and that the need to find more from outside sources was unnecessary. Instead, they believed they should dedicate their means of creating further internal prosperity. As the Chinese did not see these expeditions as commercial in nature, it was easy to eschew the luxury goods of global markets. The purpose of

Ming exploration was expanding Chinese power among its rivals and peers; this had already been accomplished using vast battleships and treasure ships.

Zheng He's fleet

Additionally, the Yongle Emperor faced criticism from within China, due to his management of funds regarding the explorations. Several factions within the state opposed the Yongle Emperor's policies, and there was a constant struggle for power. New conservatives saw the monetary policies of the Yongle Emperor as wasteful and shunned all of his policies, which included sea expansion and exploration. Conservative rulers in China sought to limit European influence and closed the trade previously opened during Zheng He's expeditions. By 1525, an order from the government saw the destruction of all ocean-faring sea vessels, limiting Chinese interaction with Europeans for some time.

Chinese exploration under Zheng He and the Yongle Emperor was important because China was one of the dominant seafaring empires of the period, and Chinese culture experienced the negative consequences of the implementation of a global economic engine, rather than focusing only on the benefits, as the Europeans did.

European merchants involved in Asian trade were primarily transporting goods from one Asian country to another market in Asia or the Indian Ocean region.

The role of European merchants in Asia was to facilitate trade between states. The majority of trade was done by oceanic means of travel, rather than via continental overland routes. While the Silk Road continued to transport goods, people and ideas, it lost potency regarding global trade and markets following the emergence of the American markets. This shift was also a result of the decline in Chinese trade following the Yongle Emperor's death in 1424.

Yongle Emperor

In earlier periods, Christian missionaries and conditional trade agreements between Asians and Europeans were seen, though not frequently. In the 16th century, this practice was revived by Jesuit missionaries who entered China and shared both mathematical innovations—which impressed the Chinese—and the religious ideas of Christianity. At the same time, these missionaries returned to Europe with word of Chinese luxuries, creating demand for Chinese goods and the desire to establish a stable trade between Europe and Asia. The European elites saw Chinese luxuries as a symbol of status and wealth, which created a demand for Chinese teas, porcelain, silk, wallpaper, and other decorative items. As a result of this demand, the Chinese opened the southern port of Canton, while remaining skeptical of European influence and trade.

One exception to the norm regarding Asian trade was Portugal, who was able to dominate the Indian Ocean for a large portion of the 16th century. Ancient sea trade routes had been used by Southeast Asians, Indians, Arabs, and Persians; Portugal took them over with superior military technology and seafaring abilities. This resulted in Portuguese merchants having direct access to Eastern markets and goods, which they traded in European markets for a vast profit.

Asian empires of the period attempted to limit European merchant influence. This was seen in Tokugawa, Japan, where a conservative government sought to limit Europeanization. In the 1630s, the shogunate ordered the expulsion of Europeans, as well as the closing of Japan to outsiders and immigration. This government restricted trade to the outer islands of the region and effectively eliminated any chance of European merchants infiltrating the society. This reaction to European influence could be seen as a direct result of the Spanish conquest of the Philippines, which the Japanese saw as a possibility for themselves if they did not take action against Europeanization.

Buddhism spread within Asia.

The religion of Buddhism also experienced expansion and growth in this period. Buddhist beliefs center on the pursuit of Nirvana, which is a state of liberation and freedom. This can only be achieved when one eliminates worldly desires and obsession with self. Unlike its counterpart Hinduism, which emerged during the same period, Buddhism did not promote a social hierarchy and rejected the caste system so widespread in India during and leading into this period. Women were welcome in Buddhism as nuns, but in Hinduism and other religions, such as Islam and Catholicism, their role was extremely limited. As a result of its teachings and theology, many embraced the ideas of Buddhism, and the religion was able to expand beyond its territories. The primary reason Buddhism was able to expand was the Silk Road, which allowed for the flow of goods, people, and ideas throughout Eurasia. The main regions impacted by this movement of ideas and people were China, Siberia, Central Asia, India, the Middle East, and the Mediterranean Basin.

Woodblock printing emerged as characteristic Japanese art.

Woodblock printing was a form of art found in Japan during the early modern period. Unlike other art of the period, woodblock printing, which in Japanese is called Ukiyo-e, was accessible to ordinary people and became a source of decoration for many in the metropolitan culture of Edo, present-day Tokyo. Ukiyo-e, which translates to "pictures of the floating world," is commonly used to describe woodblock prints and paintings from the period (c.1670–1900). By the mid-17th century, woodblock prints were used to illustrate landscapes, tales from history, scenes from the Kabuki theatre, courtesans, geisha, and other aspects of everyday city life in Japan.

Japan and China produced a wide range of literary works.

Kabuki is one of the major art forms of Japan. Unlike the European Renaissance art, this classical dance drama is mostly known for stylization and the elaborate makeup worn by its performers. Kabuki is sometimes translated as "the art of singing and dancing." It greatly influenced Japanese culture. It is reflective of the geishas and the stylistic choices of the social elite.

One influential source of literature from China is *Journey to the West*, a 16th-century literary masterpiece of the Ming and Qing dynasties. This text is part of the Four Great Classical Novels in Chinese Literature, the others being: *The Water Margin, Romance of the Three Kingdoms,* and *The Dream of the Red Chamber. Journey to the West* is attributed to Wu Cheng'en and details the legendary pilgrimage of the Tang dynasty Buddhist monk Xuanzang, who traveled to the Western Regions (India) to obtain sacred texts (called sutras) and returned after much suffering and numerous trials. This text has influenced Chinese folk religion, Chinese mythology, and the Taoist and Buddhist philosophies. All of these literary works were influential in their regions. However, each of these examples also highlights the various sources of influence throughout the global system.

Qing Dynasty Manchu rulers discriminated against dominant Han ethnicity, adopted divide-and-conquer policies.

Another example of discrimination was the suppression of the Han Chinese after their capital fell to the Manchus from the Northeast of China. The Manchus were an ethnic group distinct from the Han Chinese and prided themselves as warriors in the Mongol tradition, as evidenced by the fact that their leader took the Mongol moniker of *Khan*. Upon the successful capture in 1644 of the Chinese capital, Beijing, the Manchus sought to firmly establish their rule by imposing regulations on everything from the manner of interaction to the styling of men's hair in the Manchu tradition.

Manchu assault of Ningyuan

In addition to their social suppression, a series of massacres were carried out across the country against citizens who pledged their allegiance to the former empire of the Ming dynasty. Interestingly, a large portion of the brutality was carried out by the former functionaries of the Ming dynasty, who had defected to the Manchu side. The dynasty the Manchu established, the Qing dynasty, was multi-ethnic at its core, as the Manchus themselves were a small minority within China. As a means to maintain their control, they played factions from larger ethnic groups against one another. This tactic was not unique to Qing dynasty rule and would eventually be used to great effect by the British and French in their overseas territorial holdings.

Manchus seized power in China.

The Manchus in China serve as an example of elites taking the place of former adversaries. They were able to overthrow the Ming dynasty in 1644. The Manchus were considered outsiders by the Chinese as they were a different ethnic group from the northern region of China. However, they saw themselves as the unifiers of China and ruled so effectively that they maintained power from 1644 until 1911.

Daimyos exercised significant local control in Japan.

In the Japanese Empire, daimyos (regional lords), who exercised great authority independent of the government before the early 17th century, emerged. These feudal leaders were eventually organized under one powerful family, the Tokugawa; however, not all feudal lords embraced this transition in power. Additionally, the Tokugawa were concerned with the infiltration of European theories and principles, which was aided by disgruntled daimyos. In the outer regions of the territory, the daimyos were quite difficult to govern. As a result of this tension, the Tokugawa shogunate closed Japan's borders in the 1630s.

Tokugawa Masako

Manchu Qing dynasty projected both internal and external dominance.

Emperor Kangxi of the Qing dynasty

The Manchu dynasty emerged as a direct result of the decline of the Ming dynasty, and eventually evolved into the Qing dynasty, which ruled China into the 20th century. As a result of Ming's weakness, the Manchus were able to take control of the empire and restore China to its former glory. The Qing dynasty was able to wield influence over the conquered Chinese people while at the same time maintaining a land-based gunpowder empire, which exercised considerable influence in the region and global affairs. Notable early rulers include Kangxi (1661–1722) and Qianlong (1736–1795), both cultured rulers who valued the arts and education but also saw the need for warriors and military expansion. The Qing dynasty became so successful that rulers sometimes canceled taxes because the treasury was full.

An elite Japanese group of Samurai disappeared.

The Samurai were local warrior-landlords in feudal Japan, who owed allegiance to the Emperor and yet were in constant tension with him. Throughout Japan's feudal history, there were numerous periods of protracted rebellions by the Samurai, some local and some that took place throughout most of Japan. The Satsuma Rebellion in 1877, against the Meiji Emperor, was the end for the Samurai; their order did not survive the modernization of Japan.

The expansion of U.S. and European influence over Tokugawa Japan led to the emergence of Meiji Japan.

The end of the Tokugawa era in Japan marked the beginning of the Meiji period, during which Japan emerged as a great power with the ability to influence both regional and global affairs. Great economical, social, and political reforms, modeled on the successes seen in the United States and Europe, occurred during this period, which overlapped with the Industrial Revolution. As the Japanese government began a period of rapid industrialization, the benefits were quickly evident and propelled the Japanese into an even more prominent position in the global market.

As a result of the rapid rise in power during the Meiji era, the Japanese were met with suspicion by their neighbors – including China and Russia, who were both notable adversaries. These tense relations culminated in several conflicts, including the Sino-Japanese War from 1894 to 1895 and the Japanese Russian Wars in 1904 and 1905.

Prince Yamashina Kikumaro on deck of a Japanese cruiser during the Russo-Japanese War

Japan lept ahead of other Asian nations in industrial development.

Japan was the first Asian country to become industrialized. As early as the 1860s, the Japanese government began studying Western technology to develop a more industrial nation. In the case of Japan, these new production methods spread as the result of deliberate government policy. An insightful new emperor came to the throne in 1867 and abruptly ended Japan's three-hundred-year policy of isolation from the West. Prince Matsuhito recognized that Japan could not survive as an independent nation in a rapidly modernizing world where colonial nations were the only ones industrializing. He ended isolationism and encouraged his people to learn everything the Western nations could teach them in regard to methods of production. Unlike China and India, its regional counterparts, Japan quickly emerged as an effective industrial state.

The Japanese royal family of 1904,
including Emperor Matsuhito

The rapid increases in productivity caused by industrial production encouraged industrialized states to seek out new consumer markets for their finished goods.

As the British and French Empires sought to expand their capital and economic influence, they quickly searched for new markets to which they could bring their finished products. British expansion into China eventually led to the Opium Wars.

The British had been secretly selling opium to Chinese merchants. Chinese officials quickly tried to stop this practice but were unsuccessful; the result was the Opium Wars. This was an attempt by the British to gain exclusive access to the Chinese markets, which it eventually achieved through Chinese concessions in the Treaty of Nanjing that was signed at the conclusion of the Opium Wars. The British Empire completed their monopoly on these markets with the founding of modern Hong Kong, which created a trading hub between China and the European continent.

As a result, the French and other Europeans sought to gain a hold on the Chinese markets in the same capacity as the British. This increased competition and eventually resulted in the opening of Chinese markets for some time.

Europeans and Japan militarily forced access to Asian trade markets.

Both the British and French were eager to corner the market on the opium trade in China, which led them to wage war against one another in hopes of gaining a monopoly on Chinese markets. Between 1839 and 1842, the First Opium War raged between the British and the Chinese as a result of under the table dealings between the two parties regarding the sale of Chinese opium. The British emerged victorious, establishing a monopoly on the Chinese trade and unprecedented access to the Chinese markets. The French, Dutch, Americans employed similar strategies, and later, the Japanese joined in hopes of making a great profit in previously untapped or underutilized markets.

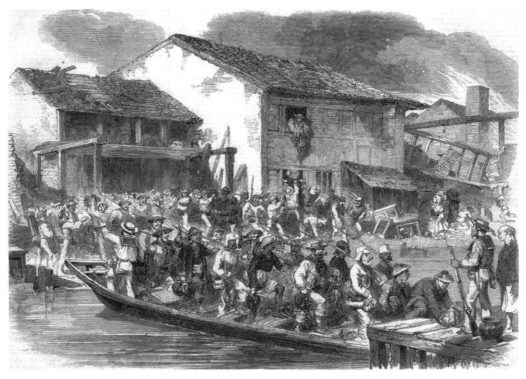

Return of soldiers during the Opium Wars

China sought industrialization through the Self-Strengthening Movement; The Boxer Rebellion contested European influence.

Qing China's Self-Strengthening Movement sought to combine the country's unique culture and tradition with the underlying principles of European Industrialization. This policy was embraced after China's numerous military defeats and ensuing concessions to Western European imperialist powers. The movement included the procurement of military equipment, the levying of taxes and the running of bureaucracies. It also included the construction of shipyards, railways, and weapons industries.

The Boxer Rebellion, which took place in 1900 in China as a result of rising nationalism, was a similar reaction to oppressive outside influence. The Boxers sought to limit the influence of colonists in China and to expel foreigners completely ultimately.

Chinese Taiping Rebellion rooted in a desire for gender equality and the dismantlement of public property.

An example of a rebellion from the industrial period is the Taiping Rebellion (from 1850 to 1864), which was the culmination of a religious and political movement headed by Hong Xiuquan. The movement sought to achieve equality for women and the end of public property. The rebellion was put down by the Chinese – with considerable help from their European counterparts – but was extremely costly in both casualties and money.

Scene from the Taiping Rebellion

Notes for active learning

Notes for active learning

The Americas

Major historical events of the period:

1505:   The first slave ship arrives in the Americas

1520:   Smallpox is first transmitted to the Americas

1521:   Cortes conquers the Aztec Empire

1531:   Veneration of Our Lady of Guadalupe and adherence to the Cult of Saints begins

1534:   Pizarro conquers the Incan Empire

1600s–1830:   Piracy thrives in the Caribbean

1765–1783:   American Revolution

1775–1783:   American Revolutionary War

1791–1804:   Haitian Revolution

PERIOD 3: 1500 to 1900 C.E.

THE AMERICAS

European nations explore and project power.

As many European states were competing for prestige and influence, the use of maritime expeditions was an extension of a state's power. Many monarchs viewed the conquest of unknown lands as increasing their status and authority against rivals and were eager to gain vast territories by various means. Finally, the Portuguese, like the Spaniards, used exploration as a means to impose religious conversion on thousands of Native Americans. Like in other European states, church and religion played an influential role in Portuguese culture, and most people believed it should be shared with the heathens encountered during explorations.

Francisco Pizarro, Spanish explorer

The Spaniards, like the Portuguese, were instrumental in the Age of Exploration. The reasons Spain undertook these exploratory expeditions were similar to those of Portugal and focused on three main concerns: accumulating wealth and resources, building political and military power, and spreading the Catholic faith to the heathen peoples of the Americas.

During his career as an explorer, Christopher Columbus undertook four expeditions. During his second expedition, he traveled with a fleet of ships and supplies, with the hope of establishing and sustaining a permanent colony in the Americas. Like other explorers of the period, Columbus was preoccupied with finding a navigable route from the Caribbean to Asia in hopes of gaining access to new markets and goods. His final expedition had the goal of locating the Strait of Malacca, in hopes of reaching the Indian Ocean.

Spanish explorers Francisco Pizarro and Hernán Cortes (also known as Hernando Cortes) set out on separate missions to South America. Cortes conquered the Aztec Empire in 1521, and Pizarro conquered the Incan Empire in 1534; both empires were taken by force with much bloodshed. Such settlements were instrumental in the influx of silver and gold to Spain, who continued to finance the Spanish expeditions and colonies in the Americas.

Notable French explorers of the period include Jacques Cartier (1491–1535), who led three expeditions to Canada while searching for the Northwest Passage. Other notable explorers from this period came from England and included Martin Frobisher (approximately 1535–1594), an English privateer (a pirate licensed by the British crown), navigator, explorer, and naval officer.

Frobisher was one of the first Europeans to explore Canada. He is also famous for taking part in Sir Francis Drake's expedition to the West Indies and for his military confrontations with the Spanish.

Spanish sponsorship of the first Columbian and subsequent voyages across the Atlantic and Pacific dramatically increased European interest in transoceanic travel and trade.

Like the Portuguese, the Spanish were instrumental in the founding of the Americas, the establishment of global trade markets and the expansion of their maritime empire. These ambitions began with Christopher Columbus and his expeditions, which took place in 1492, and were funded by King Ferdinand and Queen Isabella of Spain, who hoped Columbus would find a faster route to the Indies, bypassing the coast of Africa. Spain's desire to find this faster route demonstrates the influence and power held by Portugal as a result of being the first to find navigable waters around Africa and the Cape of Good Hope.

Ongoing tensions between the first two sea rivals led to the Treaty of Tordesillas, which was signed in 1494. The treaty effectively designated the eastern portion of the Atlantic Ocean to the Portuguese and gave the western portion to the Spaniards. This resulted in continued and intensified Spanish expeditions to the Caribbean, South America, and the southern regions of North America. Following these initial exploratory expeditions, the Spanish monarchs became interested in creating settlements and colonies. Construction of silver mines in the Americas eventually financed the Spanish Empire and allowed for continued investment and influence within Mesoamerica. It is reported that the silver mined from the Americas at one time constituted one-fifth of the total Spanish budget.

Bernal Diaz del Castillo, Spanish historian and soldier

The Spanish conquistadors of this period were able to conquer various territories in the Americas; most notably the Aztec and Incan empires in South America. However, due to their unwillingness to accept Christianity, these cultures were effectively decimated at the hands of the Spaniards. One notable example of this comes from Bernal Diaz del Castillo, also known as Bernal Diaz, a Spanish historian and soldier who chronicled the Spanish conquest of Mexico.

In 1514, Castillo accompanied Pedro Arias Davila (also known as Pedrarias Davila), a wealthy noble, on an expedition to Tierra Firme, in the Americas. By 1517, he had sailed to the Yucatan Peninsula of Mexico with Francisco de Córdoba's expedition. Castillo returned to Mexico with Juan de Grijalva in 1518 and again with Hernán Cortes in 1519. These various expeditions resulted in hundreds of battles, which showed the resolution of native Mesoamericans to repel the Spanish conquistadors. Castillo's final expedition saw the capture and surrender of Mexico City in 1521. For his military service, Castillo was awarded the office of governor of Santiago de los Caballeros, Guatemala.

Bernal Diaz del Castillo is also notable for publishing "Verdadera Historia de la Conquista de Nueva España" (True History of the Conquest of New Spain) in 1568, which gave graphic details about the Spanish conquering and colonizing machine, as well as the consequent decimation of native populations. Bernal Diaz del Castillo died in 1584.

To accumulate the wealth desired by Spanish monarchs, the voyages of Christopher Columbus and later explorers were undertaken to find the Northwest Passage, to reach Asia and its untold resources and goods. As Spanish explorers discovered wealth in the Americas, the ability to mine silver in Mesoamerica became transformative for the Spanish Empire. It is important to understand the draw of gold and resources; it was common for many Spaniards to be obsessed with the myth of El Dorado, also known as the City of Gold. As a result of intense European rivalries, the Spanish sought to assert their dominance over their European rivals, mainly demonstrated through the expansion of their maritime empire.

The Spanish believed this would be accomplished not only through global oceanic travel and trade but also through the establishment of colonies that mirrored the political and social models of Spain. The main push by Spaniards in America was for colonialism. As much as Spain wished to expand its power base and acquire new wealth, it was also immensely preoccupied with the conversion of Native American and Mesoamerican populations to Catholicism. This was a driving concern as many Catholics believed their religion superior and felt a moral obligation to share its wisdom and precepts with other peoples, primarily through missionaries. Some Mesoamerican people adapted their traditional religions to incorporate facets of Catholicism, while others like the Inca and Aztec cultures refused conversion and were met with hostility and death.

The implications of Spanish Columbian expeditions are monumental; many recognize Columbus as the first explorer to set foot in the Americas, though this is debated amongst scholars today. The colonies established were as important as the technological advancements that made them possible. Without the silver reserves from American mines, Spain would not have been able to maintain its status as a maritime empire and strengthen its position relative to the other European powers of the time. Additionally, other countries looked to Spain as an example to emulate in navigating and settling the Americas, eventually culminating in the American colonies of Britain, Spain, and France.

Northern Atlantic crossings for fishing and settlements continued and spurred European searches for multiple routes to Asia.

As a result of previous oceanic expeditions, other empires, such as the Dutch and the English, began showing an interest in establishing settlements in the Americas, while also hoping to find better oceanic trading routes with Asia. One notable example of this ambition was that of Henry Hudson. In 1608, the Muscovy Company of England and several English merchants from the East India Company hired Hudson to find a passage to Asia. He was unsuccessful and instead landed in Nova Scotia. From there, he continued south, discovering the Hudson River in New York. On his second expedition in 1610–1611, Hudson discovered the Hudson Bay and James Bay, before his crew mutinied and set him adrift in the cold arctic waters. Hudson's discoveries eventually led to extensive Dutch and English colonies in the area, capitalizing on abundant resources and vast habitable land.

Motives for Dutch and English exploration were less varied than those of the Spanish, as the Dutch and English were more concerned with finding a stable trade route between the Pacific and Asia. The Cape of Good Hope and its surrounding waters were unpredictable and dangerous. If some other route could achieve passage to Asia, there would be greater possibilities for expanded trade and increased economic benefits.

The Europeans felt pressure from the Ottoman Empire, especially in light of the capture of Constantinople in 1453 by the Ottomans. As a result of Ottoman control of traditional trade routes, many Europeans were forced to pay extremely high taxes on luxury goods, which were much desired among elites in all European cultures.

Henry Hudson, British explorer

The English traders and explorers were also concerned with reaching India in hopes of exploiting vast gold resources, as well as various spices and goods. Many saw the relationship between India and England as extremely lucrative and wanted to eliminate the "middleman" to make the most profit in the shortest period. Such ambitions led to a complicated relationship between India and England for decades to come, with Britain eventually establishing a monopoly on the export of Indian goods. This monopoly expanded as a result of emerging British maritime power in the 18th century.

Commercialization and the creation of a global economy were intimately connected to the new global circulation of silver from the Americas.

As Spanish and Portuguese settlements exported vast resources of silver and gold, a new market developed with the ability to buy, sell, and trade goods on a global scale by sea. Without the silver reserves found in Bolivia and Japan, it is unlikely that Spain could have maintained its status as a maritime empire. Without these resources, the Spaniards would have had to struggle to fund further expeditions, which made the development of Spanish colonies in Mesoamerica and other regions of North America possible.

Some historians have marked the silver trade as even more important than the spice trade of Eurasia, as it led to the development of the global market. Between 1450 and 1750, Spanish mines in Bolivia produced close to 85% of the world's silver. As a result, Spain dominated the trade of silver, which was mined from Mesoamerica to the Philippines, then traded for luxury goods in Europe. More specifically, the cities of Acapulco in Mexico and

Manila in the Philippines facilitated the great silver trade. This activity occurred in the Philippines, as it was a Spanish colony. The trade between these two regions was especially significant as the first period of substantial and continuous trade between the Europeans and Asia during the early modern period.

The output of Spanish silver mines was astonishing and reached close to 137 million pounds. It also provided the Spanish ruling and elite classes with access to lifestyles formerly unknown, full of grandeur and excess. These extravagant expectations continued as Spanish settlements yielded great results upon the backs of slave labor coming from Africa, the Caribbean, and the surviving members of native populations. By this point, native populations were almost completely decimated, following exposure to European diseases and slave labor instilled by the Spanish conquistadors. The average life expectancy of a slave forced to work in a mine was only six months. Much of the silver mined in Spanish settlements was also beneficial to the global economy, as the Spanish used these resources to pay off debts to fellow European empires, which in turn boosted the economies of those states.

Influenced by mercantilism, joint-stock companies were new methods used by European rulers to control their domestic and colonial economies and by European merchants to compete against one another in global trade.

As global markets expanded, exploiting the systems of the Great Circuit and Columbian Exchange, the acquisition of wealth was seemingly endless. One consequence of this was the implementation of mercantilism. Mercantilism is the economic theory that suggests that having a positive balance of trade will result in the accumulation of wealth. Mercantilist countries often imposed regulations that subsidized exports and domestic services while taxing the import of foreign goods from rival countries. This made citizens and companies less likely to look outside of their country for trade and kept their concentration of wealth local. Colonialism was a very important part of mercantilist practices because it allowed the import of raw resources from colonies for only the price of shipping. The European "mother countries" were able to create new markets for their goods at competitive prices by exploiting the resources of their newly established colonies and slave labor.

An important aspect of mercantilism in this period was the use of joint-stock companies, a necessary condition for the mercantilist system to flourish. A joint-stock company is defined as an organization that is formed to gather community resources of various merchants and skillsets, creating minimal risk for all those involved. By this means, the risk of colonization was drastically reduced and allowed for vast charters and expeditions to take place, which otherwise probably would not have.

Historically, joint-stock companies sold shares to investors in order to raise money for trading enterprises, such as the Virginia Company and the Swedish East India Company, effectively eliminating the risk and spreading it among a large pool of shareholders. If the company was successful in its endeavors, then original investors saw a return on their initial investment. Monarchies sought to encourage joint-stock companies by offering various monopolies. One example can be seen in the creation of the Muscovy Company of England and its monopoly on trade routes to Russia. Another was the spice trade monopoly maintained by the Dutch East India Company.

In 1600, Queen Elizabeth I of England granted a royal charter to the English East India Company, with a fifteen-year monopoly on all English trade in the East Indies. The goal of the charter was the development of extensive trade relationships with India, which had drastic consequences for India for several decades. The English monarchs were the first to use joint-stock companies in this manner, with the earliest recognized company being the Company of Merchant Adventurers to New Lands, which was chartered in 1553 and had 250 shareholders.

Imaginary seaport painted at the height of mercantilism

Other companies, such as the Virginia Company, sought royal charters to establish permanent colonies. Colonies like Jamestown were funded entirely by their mother government (in this case, England) because they were seen as investments. European empires viewed their colonies as a means to make a profit and not at all as independent entities. These joint-stock companies fueled the ambition of European colonialism and caused that pursuit to be undertaken for monetary reasons. However, some instances of colonization were due to social concerns.

Mercantilism also fostered tense relationships between the colonies and their European masters. As the Europeans exploited the resources of their colonies, colonists were expected to pay heavy taxes on goods imported from Europe. The colonists' resentment of such practices eventually led to the Boston Tea Party and became arguments in favor of the American Revolution. Mercantilism also cemented the seeds of slavery in America, as these companies employed forced labor to extract many of the resources.

European colonization of the Americas led to the spread of diseases (e.g., including smallpox, measles, and influenza) that were endemic in the Eastern Hemisphere among Amerindian populations and the unintentional transfer of vermin, including mosquitoes and rats.

As European explorers and conquerors made their way through the New World, a deadly killer aided them in their forced expulsion and religious conversions of the native populations: the transmission of various diseases. In the Americas, there had been less danger from diseases, as the populations were not in close contact or urban-type settings, reducing their vulnerability to contagion. Also, they did not domesticate as many species of animals as their European counterparts, reducing their exposure to diseases that thrive in the domesticated animal population. Smallpox, influenza, and measles can all be directly linked to Eurasian farming traditions. These diseases transformed over time, jumping from their host species and eventually becoming a threat to humans.

Diseases transmitted to the New World from the Old World included typhus, smallpox, measles, chickenpox, malaria, diphtheria, whooping cough, scarlet fever, yellow fever, influenza, and the bubonic plague. It is thought that Native Americans were largely disease-free before this period as they did not live in close quarters, did not typically keep domesticated animals, and interaction between populations was much less common than in Europe. This also meant that most Native Americans never developed the complex immune systems of the Europeans and were more susceptible to disease.

The introduction of such diseases had catastrophic ramifications for the native populations of the Americas. As a result of the deaths caused by these diseases, the European settlers were able to begin colonizing the Americas with little pushback. It is also thought that the Americas transmitted a form of syphilis back to the Old World. The transmission of disease into the Old World had little to no effect, except syphilis, as many of the European populations had developed immunities over long periods of exposure.

This side effect of the Columbian Exchange was far more deadly than the implementation of force and weaponry seen in the gunpowder empires of this period. Some academics have labeled the emptying of native inhabitants as a genocide, arguing that approximately 20 million Amerindians—80 to 90% of the native populations—were killed by disease upon European settlers' arrival in the Americas. An example of this can be seen in central Mexico, where the population in 1510 was 25 million people, but by 1605 the population was less than one million people. This was the work of smallpox and other disease epidemics in the region, which proved to be the most effective killer of the native populations of the Americas.

It is believed that smallpox was transmitted to the Americas in approximately 1520, on a Spanish ship that was sailing from Cuba and carrying infected slaves from Africa. The Incan Empire had already been devastated by smallpox, which killed its Emperor, Huayna Capac. This, in turn, unleashed a civil war by the time Pizarro arrived in the 1530s. Other diseases such as malaria and bubonic plague were transported and transmitted by animals, specifically mosquitoes and rats. However, the concept of communicability of disease was not yet discovered, and many people saw these diseases as the work of gods or other supernatural forces. It is also important to note that many European conquerors in the New World viewed these epidemics as God's punishment of those who refused to convert to Catholicism. Europeans were completely oblivious to their role in the transmission and spread of these diseases.

American foods became staple crops in various parts of Europe, Asia, and Africa. Cash crops were grown primarily on plantations with coerced labor and were exported mostly to Europe and the Middle East in this period.

The introduction of various crops in the Americas as a result of the Columbian Exchange had far-reaching implications outside of agriculture, including the perpetuation of slavery and the transformation of trade onto a global scale. The development of such crops also transformed the European continent and allowed Europeans to develop a more diverse and sustained diet. The impact of cash crops on the Americas seems much more far-reaching than any impact felt on the European continent. The slave trade escalated as a result of the transplanting of sugar cane to the Caribbean and the Americas. In 1505, the first slave ship arrived in the Americas, and this practice continued unabated for more than 300 years. It is reported that by the middle of the 19th century, approximately 10 million slaves had been forcibly transported to sugarcane plantations in the Caribbean and Brazil.

The cultivation of sugar cane specifically influenced the Atlantic system, as this was a product that could be transformed into a finished good in the Americas, often in the form of rum or molasses. The production of sugarcane accounted for nearly one-third of British profits from trade in this region. The British Empire recognized the profitability of this cash crop and continued to earn revenue from its taxation later in this period. As a result of such successes, those in charge of sugarcane plantations became enormously wealthy; some, from Jamaica to St. Kitts, was labeled sugar barons. Both Britain and France paid close attention to these territories as they were considered the lifeblood of the economy. Some historians have even argued that the British Empire was ill-prepared for the colonial revolution as a result of its preoccupation with its sugarcane territories

Tobacco cultivation was also extremely important in the Americas and served as a source of commerce for European trade. John Rolfe is credited with cultivating tobacco in both the Caribbean and American colonies. In May 1609, Rolfe, along with hundreds of new settlers, headed for Virginia. However, due to a storm, the group was stranded on Bermuda, finally arriving at the Chesapeake Bay in 1610. By 1617, tobacco exports from the American colonies to England totaled 20,000 pounds, and the following year shipments more than doubled. Approximately twelve years later, one and a half million pounds of tobacco had been exported. Some historians have argued that John Rolfe and tobacco represent the first great American enterprise.

The wedding of Pocahontas and John Rolfe

Afro-Eurasian fruit trees, grains, sugar, and domesticated animals were brought by Europeans to the Americas, while African slaves brought other foods.

Using the Columbian Exchange, various domesticated animals and plants were transported to the Americas and eventually East. There, various crops were able to thrive that had previously been unable to due to poor soil quality. Various crops were transported from the European continent, but the African continent also played an intricate role in the introduction of various crops and animals. Europeans introduced horses, pigs, and cattle to the Americas, as well as sugarcane; all of which were important to the agricultural and economic viability of the colonies.

Additionally, using the Triangular Trade, Africans introduced various new crops to the Americas, including rice, okra, Tania, black-eyed peas and kidney, and lima beans. Evidence of such cultivation comes from Sir Hans Sloane, a young physician living in the West Indies. As early as 1687, Sloane noted the cultivation of various beans, peas, okra, rice, and Tania on the island of Jamaica. These crops easily transitioned onto the American continent, where both African slaves and white settlers introduced them as staples of their diet.

Further evidence of such cultivation can be seen in the transport of black-eyed peas, reportedly first brought to the Americas by slaves, who carried them as food during the Middle Passage of the Trans-Atlantic Slave Trade. Historians have traced the pea's arrival in Jamaica to approximately 1675. It then spread through the West Indies, reaching Florida in 1700, North Carolina in 1738 and Virginia by 1775. However, it is also worth noting that a slave planter by the name of William Byrd mentioned the planting of black-eyed peas as early as 1738. Plants cultivated in Africa and Europe, then transported to the New World, were able to thrive there in various climates and cultures. The transfer of food from Africa to the New World also represents a transformation and integration of various cultures. As Africans brought their cultural customs and religion to America, they also introduced new foods and cultures using agricultural innovations and expansion.

Slaves stacked like cargo during the Middle Passage

European colonization and the introduction of European agriculture and settlement practices in the Americas often affected the physical environment through deforestation and soil depletion.

As cash crops and European colonies emerged, new methods of farming and agriculture were introduced in the Americas, similar to those used on traditional European farms. These similarities were derived from the establishment of colonies as extensions of an empire. The colonies produced goods unavailable in the other territories of an empire. Some of the problems that soon arose included soil depletion and deforestation, both of which were present in Europe. In Europe, deforestation came about as a result of the need for lumber to build ships, wagons and other modes of transport. Europeans also burned wood as a fuel source. Europe experienced wood shortages in the 1590s and, by the mid-17th century, saw full-scale deforestation. Such events led to large amounts of wood being exported to Europe from the Americas.

In the Americas, the result of deforestation was most notably seen in the Caribbean, where the Spaniards first brought cattle, which created a need for grazing land. They accomplished this by cutting down thousands of trees. Deforestation further accelerated upon the introduction of plantation farming. Trees were cut down to make room for vast plantations. Shipbuilding, popular in the northern colonies of the Americas, also facilitated deforestation. Soil depletion occurred because the majority of plantations in the Americas maintained a practice of planting one cash crop, which depleted the soil much faster than crop rotation methods.

Due to the expansive lands of the New World, new plantation farmers preferred using the single cash crop tactic. This practice was prevalent in the Caribbean, where sugarcane was extensively cultivated. Farmers cleared new lands, continuing to use the single crop method, eventually taking over other islands for this purpose. The lasting impacts of deforestation and soil depletion were seen in the lack of forests surrounding colonial settlements of the period.

Syncretic and new forms of religion developed.

The emergence of syncretic religions, which are adaptations of two or more separate religions into a single functioning religious system, can be seen throughout history. These were most prominent in the colonization of the Americas, where Catholic ritual merged with various native religions to form new and varying adaptations. These new religions show the influence of global trading and the movement of people and goods in the early modern period. Christianity combined with the West African religion, Vodun, to create hybrid religions in many colonies. These syncretic religions included Haitian Vodou, Puerto Rican Vodú, Cuban Vodú, Dominican Vudú, Brazilian Vodum, and Cajun Voodoo. The foundation of these faiths included the belief in an all-knowing and distant God, whom the Haitian sect called Bondye, as well as in lesser spirits, who maintained the day to day lives of practitioners. The American Vodun religions are based on ancestor worship, and practitioners believe that spirits are responsible for various aspects of life.

Though both Caribbean and African Christians actively suppressed these religions, nonetheless, they grew and evolved. After the introduction of Catholicism by Spanish and Portuguese priests, the religion evolved to include the worship of saints, as well as the use of altars and candles in ceremonial capacities. Slaves attempted to maintain their native religions while at the same time adapting to Christianity. There was a period of dual practice, where slaves attended mass and church as required, but continued to practice their native religions in private.

Virgin of Guadalupe

The Cult of Saints is another post-Columbian religion, with roots in Spanish Catholicism, found mostly in Spanish Latin America. Natives practicing their religions incorporated Catholic teachings into their beliefs, resulting in a syncretic religion where Catholic saints were the focal point.

The most notable of these saints is Our Lady of Guadalupe; on December 9, 1531, in Mexico City, Juan Diego, a peasant, saw a vision of a fifteen-year-old girl surrounded by light. She commanded him to construct a church in her honor. Juan Diego envisioned the girl as the Virgin Mary. The vision promised him a miracle if he completed the monument, and in return, she healed his uncle. This legend caused Our Lady of Guadalupe to become one of the most famous quasi-deities in the Cult of the Saints.

Codices provided insight into pre-contact indigenous groups.

Post-conquest codices in Mesoamerica were other forms of art commissioned by the ruling class and are defined as books written by pre-Columbian and colonial-era Aztecs. These codices provide some of the best primary sources for Aztec culture. Pre-Columbian codices differ from European codices, as they are largely pictorial and not intended to symbolize spoken or written narratives. The colonial-era codices contain not only Aztec pictograms but also Classical Nahuatl (in the Latin alphabet), Spanish and occasionally Latin; some are completely scripted with no pictorial content.

Notable examples include the Codex Borbonicus, which was composed by Aztec priests around the time of the Spanish invasion of Mexico. Like all pre-Columbian codices, it was originally composed of only pictures; however, Spanish notations were added later on. It is divided into three sections: intricate Tonalamatl (divinatory calendar), the Mesoamerican 52-year cycle, and a final section of rituals and ceremonies pertaining mainly to the 52-year cycle. The Florentine Codex is comprised of twelve books created under the supervision of Bernardino de Sahagun between approximately 1540 and 1585.

The growth of the plantation economy increased the demand for slaves in the Americas.

As agricultural advances took place in North America, the English colonies had varying bases for their economies, many of which were supported by slavery - especially in the South, where a vast opportunity for agricultural expansion presented itself. In the South, the soil and climate were better suited for large farms, which led to the development of a plantation system. One labor system initially used in North America was indentured servitude, in which an employer paid the passage of a person to the New World in return for several years of labor. The debt was paid in years of service, and upon completion, the indentured servant was freed. However, this initial system had limited success, especially in the Caribbean, where indentured servants often refused to go because of the harsh working conditions on the sugar plantations. The transatlantic slave trade emerged as a means of providing forced labor in industries and regions in which it was undesirable to work, or which had been depleted of their native populations due to disease and warfare.

As sugar plantations appeared, first in present-day Louisiana and later, in other southern colonies, the need for slave labor to support plantation farming increased. The planting and harvesting of sugar cane were very physically taxing work, and with the vast southern plantations, the insatiable need for additional forced labor continued. The introduction of tobacco and cotton later in the period only reinforced the need of the southern colonies, and the Americas in general, to be supplied with and supported mainly through the exploitation of slave labor.

As the free market made slavery a redundant source of labor, because of the growth of wealth with which to pay workers and an increasing need for skilled workers during the industrial age, slavery came to an end. This first occurred peacefully in British colonies and then at the end of the Civil War in the U.S. It should be noted that slavery was in decline in the United States prior to the Civil War; however, the southern plantation system's heavy reliance on slave labor slowed the rate of this decline.

Colonial economies in the Americas depended on a range of coerced labor.

In addition to the transatlantic slave trade, other forms of forced labor were seen. The use of chattel or property slavery was seen in Africa, predating the transatlantic slave trade. Such initial uses of slavery set the foundation for later slave trading. Indentured servitude was a similar practice where those interested in passage to the Americas, though unable to afford the journey, were provided the means to gain transport by lenders, who expected work in the New World as payment for these services. This was used to indebt people as a means of obtaining physical labor.

Both parties agreed upon the amount of time to be served; however, there is substantial evidence showing how difficult it was to get out of indentured servitude. Upon completion of said terms, the indentured servant was granted his freedom and was free to pursue his ambitions in the New World. The Spanish explorers were mainly concerned with finding mineral resources, such as silver and gold. They were among the first empires to employ the use of forced labor in the Americas as a means to extract the enormous silver and gold deposits of Mesoamerica. In hopes of extracting such reserves, the Spanish used an adapted version of the Incan work program mit'a in their Mesoamerican colonies.

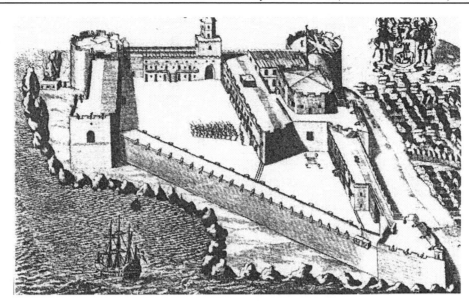

Cape Coast Castle used as a collection and shipping center of the Trans-Atlantic Slave Trade

In particular, the Spanish used this system to mine the silver veins of Bolivia, which came to finance the entire Spanish Empire. In practice, the mit'a required the work of one male for designated periods; however, as the native populations continued to die, the Spanish were forced to increase the work time required under the mit'a system, causing it to become ineffective eventually.

In addition to the mit'a, Spaniards also implemented the Encomienda system, which was a system used primarily for agricultural work. Natives in an area were placed under the authority of encomenderos, or Spanish bosses, who could extract labor and tribute according to the needs of the area and Spain. These various uses of forced labor represent the sentiment shared by Europeans regarding other ethnicities in terms of skill and labor, as these groups were seen as a means to complete the ambitious goal of colonialism and expansion, which preoccupied the elites and rulers of the Age of Exploration.

The massive demographic changes in the Americas resulted in new ethnic and racial classifications.

The social transitions of the period can also be seen in the emergence of various new classifications of ethnicity. The Mestizo can be defined as those having both European and Native American heritage. This group was seen as the middle of the racial hierarchy in Spanish and Portuguese colonies. The Mulatto classification can be identified as having both European and African heritage. The mulatto was considered to be of low status, due to their birth being the result of a relationship between a white slave plantation owner of European origin and a black slave of African origin. The Creole classification can be identified as having Spanish heritage but born on the American continent. However, this class also emerged as elite rulers of the American colonies. This was a result of their Spanish ancestry, which included wealthy and powerful white settlers—typically plantation owners and government officials. The English class structure was less minutely defined than the Spanish.

European woman visiting a Mestizo woman for tea

Creole identity emerged in Mississippi River Delta, elevated status.

Creoles experienced elevated status within the American colonies as their label identified them as French-speaking colonists, entailing upper-class white ancestry. Many legal documents from the period indicate that descendants of early European colonists in Louisiana began to refer to themselves as Creole in an attempt to establish their colonial roots. Many labeled themselves so to be distinguished from Europeans just arriving in New Orleans. Many Creoles were plantation owners and government officials during the Spanish and French colonial periods.

Spain adopted the caste system to govern New World territories.

Similar to the Ottoman style of governing through *millets*, the Spanish sought to govern the New World by establishing various governing districts. The districts were based on a caste system where the natives of the New World found themselves on the bottom. The Spaniards set up various "Republics of the Natives," where the native populations were treated quite poorly in an attempt to civilize them. This was largely a social experiment to see if one could remove the savage from an individual by exposing him to European morals and, above all, Christianity. Examples of this line of thinking were later seen in the French colonization of North Africa.

Simón Bolívar's articulated vision of decolonized Venezuela.

The Letter From Jamaica, written by Simón Bolívar (1783–1830), was also an important document because it highlighted an independence movement in another area of the globe, where Venezuela was revolting against the Spanish Empire. Bolívar was a respected military leader in South America, who fought tirelessly against the oppressive reign of Spain. After extensive battles for independence, Bolívar composed his vision of an independent Venezuela, which included a parliamentary government (modeled after England) as well as a life-long president. Bolívar embraced a form of divine kingship.

Simón Bolívar,
South American military leader

A forced labor island population sought Haitian independence.

The Haitian Revolution was also a direct result of the Enlightenment ideals of freedom from oppression and equality amongst humanity. In 1791, the island of St. Domingue, a colony of the French Empire, experienced a slave revolt that lasted for several years. As a result, France lost the colony to Toussaint Louverture, a former slave who led the Haitian guerilla forces against the French colonial forces. By 1795, Toussaint and his two top commanders, former slaves Dessalines and Henry Christophe, had reached a peace agreement with France due to its abolishment of slavery. In 1801, Toussaint went on to conquer the Spanish colonies on the island and led an additional slave revolt.

As a result of the use of force, Napoleon responded to Toussaint by sending French military forces to Haiti in January of 1802. These forces viciously engaged Toussaint and his forces, which led to a cease-fire agreement within a few months. The conflict escalated with the involvement of the British on behalf of Toussaint. The French were eventually defeated by Dessalines, who succeeded Toussaint following his death. In November 1803, General Dessalines was able to win the surrender of French forces, resulting in Haitian independence. By 1804, General Dessalines had become dictator of Haiti and proclaimed himself Emperor Jacques I. Ironically, Dessalines died putting down another revolt several years after leading Haiti to independence.

Toussaint Louverture, leader of a slave rebellion

Evidence of Latin American revolutions comes in the work and actions of military leader Simón Bolívar, who undertook the Venezuelan cause for independence from Spain. As a result of his successes and revolutions, Bolivar was able to acquire five nations, which constituted his empire and contributed to the decline of the Spanish Empire.

Indigenous tribes enact Ghost Dances in defiance of colonization.

The Ghost Dances of Native American folklore and practice were a means of restoring traditional practices and values. Native Americans hoped Ghost Dances would restore the buffalo and native tribes to their lands and expel the white settlers who had taken them over. The rituals were quickly banned because they were viewed as dangerous impediments to the assimilation of the native peoples to the Christian values of the American colonists.

Notes for active learning

Notes for active learning

Period 4

Post-1900 C.E.

Global conflicts and rapid technological advances fostered new conceptualizations of the global economy, society, and culture.

The 20th century witnessed a great deal of warfare. At the beginning of the century, a European-dominated global political order included the United States, Russia, and Japan. Over the century, peoples and states around the world challenged this order in ways that sought to redistribute power within the existing order and to restructure empires, while those peoples and states in power attempted to maintain the status quo. Other peoples and states sought to overturn the political order itself.

These challenges to, and the attempts to maintain, the political order manifested themselves in an unprecedented level of conflict with high human casualties. In the context of these conflicts, many regimes in both older and newer states struggled with maintaining political stability and were challenged by internal and external factors, including ethnic and religious conflicts, secessionist movements, territorial partitions, economic dependency, and the legacies of colonialism.

Rapid advances in science altered the understanding of the universe and the natural world, which led to the development of new technologies. These changes enabled unprecedented population growth, which altered how humans interacted with the environment and threatened delicate ecological balances at local, regional, and global levels. Scientific breakthroughs, new technologies, increasing levels of integration, changing relationships between humans and the environment, and the frequency of political conflict all contributed to global developments in which people crafted new understandings of society, culture, and historical interpretations.

The collapse of the global economy in the 1930s prompted changes in the role of the state in the domestic economy. New institutions of global governance emerged and continued to develop throughout the century. These new understandings often manifested themselves in and were reinforced by new forms of cultural expression.

Global Comparative

Major historical events of the period:

1900:	First successfully manned flight with Zeppelin airship
1903:	First airplane flight
1905:	Albert Einstein publishes *The Theory of Relativity*
1908:	Henry Ford develops the assembly line
1920:	Radio becomes first form of mass communication
1929:	The Great Depression
1930s–1960s:	The Green Revolution
1945:	The United Nations is created
1948:	U.N. adopts the Universal Declaration of Human Rights
1957:	Sputnik becomes first orbital satellite
1969:	First manned lunar surface mission
2001:	September 11 attacks

PERIOD 4: Post-1900 C.E.

GLOBAL COMPARATIVE

Researchers made rapid advances in science that spread throughout the world, assisted by the development of new technology.

During the 20th century, scientific knowledge advanced dramatically due to new and radical developments in the physical, life, and human sciences; all of which built upon the progress that was made in the 19th century. "Big Science" flourished, especially after the Second World War, as a consequence of the increase in science funding. Mathematics became increasingly specialized and abstract. New areas of physics, like special relativity, general relativity, and quantum mechanics, were developed during the first half of the century. The internal structure of atoms came to be clearly understood and was followed by the discovery of elementary particles. It was discovered that all known forces could be traced to only four fundamental interactions and that two forces, electromagnetism, and the weak nuclear force, could be merged into the electroweak interaction, which left only three different fundamental interactions. The discovery of nuclear reactions, in particular, nuclear fusion, finally revealed the source of solar energy. Radiocarbon dating was invented, which became a powerful technique for determining the age of prehistoric animals and plants, as well as historical objects.

NASA Pilot Neil Armstrong

A much better understanding of the evolution of the universe was achieved, its age was determined, and the Big Bang theory of its origin was proposed and generally accepted. The age of the solar system, including Earth, was determined, and it turned out to be much older than previously believed - more than 4 billion years, rather than the 20 million years previously suggested. The planets of the solar system and their moons were closely observed via numerous space probes. Pluto was discovered on the edge of the solar system in 1930, although in the early 21st century, it was reclassified as a plutoid instead of a planet. In 1969, Apollo 11 was launched towards the Moon, and Neil Armstrong became the first person from Earth to walk on another body that was in orbit around the Sun.

One of the prominent traits of the 20th century was the dramatic growth of technology. Organized research and the practice of science led to advancement in the fields of communication, engineering, travel, medicine, and war. The number and types of home appliances increased dramatically due to advancements in technology, availability of energy, and increases in wealth and leisure time. Such basic appliances as washing machines, clothes dryers, furnaces, exercise machines, refrigerators, freezers, electric stoves, and vacuum cleaners all became popular from the 1920s through the 1950s. Radios were popularized as a form of entertainment during the 1920s, which extended to television during the 1950s. Cable television spread rapidly during the 1980s. Personal computers began to enter the home during the 1970s–1980s as well.

The first airplane was flown in 1903. With the engineering of the faster jet engine in the 1940s, mass air travel became commercially viable. The assembly line made mass production of the automobile viable. By the end of the 20th century, billions of people had automobiles for personal transportation. The combination of the automobile, motorboats, and air travel allowed for unprecedented personal mobility.

Big science is a term used by scientists and historians of science to describe a series of changes in science which occurred in industrial nations during and after World War II, as scientific progress increasingly came to rely on large-scale projects usually funded by large businesses, private universities, private endowments and, to a lesser degree, by taxpayer-funded government initiatives. While science and technology have always been important to and driven by warfare, the increase in military funding of science following the Second World War occurred on a wholly unprecedented scale.

World War II has often been called the physicists' war, because of the role that scientists played in the development of new weapons and tools, notably the proximity fuse, radar, and atomic bomb. In the shadow of the first atomic weapons, the importance of a strong scientific research establishment was apparent to any country wishing to play a major role in international politics. After the success of the Manhattan Project, governments became the chief patrons of science, and the character of the scientific establishment underwent several key changes.

New modes of communication and transportation virtually eliminated the problem of geographic distance.

The military first used radio as a means of communication for Navy ships. In 1920, when it became the first form of mass communication, radio changed the way Americans received information and the way they were entertained. Radio programs, like the television programs of today, became a popular form of entertainment. Families sat around their radios listening to drama, mystery and detective serials, soap operas, news programs, and children's shows. Television was born in the late 1920s when the idea of "radio movies" was demonstrated before a large audience in New York City.

Radio station in Pittsburgh, PA in 1920

Television images continued to improve during the 1930s and early 1940s. By the end of the 1940s, broadcasting companies were presenting programs that brought families together to watch their favorite shows in front of television sets around the country. Since the 1940s, television technology has made great progress. Television programming developed rapidly, and television quickly became the fastest form of mass-communication. Color televisions, cable and satellite TV, video recorders, and remote controls are all features that have been added to enhance television viewing over the years.

Telephones had changed greatly since the late 1800s when they first became popular. Telephone lines connecting the east and west coasts of the United States were completed in 1915, making it possible to speak to someone across the country. Now cell phone use is booming. In the decade from 1990 to 2000, cell phone use increased by a factor of 20, while telephone lines started to carry fax and internet data. The computer is a 20th-century technological wonder that allowed everyone easy and convenient access to information and knowledge. As the computer was improved upon, various tasks could be performed, and more data and information could be stored.

Transportation also had a tremendous evolution beginning in 1900, when Ferdinand von Zeppelin launched the first successful airship, a dirigible that would take his name. In 1903, Orville and Wilbur Wright flew the first motor-driven airplane. In 1908, Henry Ford developed the assembly line method of automobile manufacturing with the introduction of the Ford Model T. In 1911, the first ocean-going, diesel engine-driven ship, *Selandia*, was launched. The first flight of the DC-3 – one of the most significant transport aircraft in the history of aviation - was in 1935. Twenty years later, the first nuclear-powered vessel, the submarine USS Nautilus, was launched.

In the second half of the 20th century, communication and transportation evolved rapidly. In 1957, *Sputnik 1*, the first man-made satellite, was launched into orbit; the first flight of the first commercially successful jet airliner, the Boeing 707, took place the following year. The first flight of the Boeing 747 – the first commercial wide-bodied airliner – and the first human-crewed Moon landing both occurred in 1969. In 1976, Concorde made the world's first commercial passenger-carrying supersonic flight, and in 1994 the Channel Tunnel opened. In 2004, the first commercial high-speed Maglev train started operating between Shanghai and its airport. In 2010, "Ultra PRT," the first modern commercial Personal Rapid Transit system, was installed.

USSR postage stamp depicting Sputnik 1

The Green Revolution produced food for the earth's growing population as it spread chemically and genetically enhanced forms of agriculture.

The term "Green Revolution" refers to a series of research, development, and technology transfer initiatives that occurred between the 1930s and the late 1960s and increased agricultural production worldwide. The impact of this was felt particularly in the developing world, beginning most markedly in the late 1960s. The initiatives involved the development of high-yielding varieties of cereal grains, expansion of irrigation infrastructure, modernization of management techniques, and the distribution of hybridized seeds, synthetic fertilizers, and pesticides to farmers.

The term Green Revolution was first used in 1968 by former United States Agency for International Development (USAID) director William Gaud. It spread technologies that already existed but had not been widely implemented outside industrialized nations. These technologies included modern irrigation projects, pesticides, synthetic nitrogen fertilizer, and improved crop varieties that had been developed using the conventional, science-based methods available at the time. The novel technological development of the Green Revolution was the production of wheat cultivars.

Cereal production more than doubled in developing nations between the years 1961 and 1985. Yields of rice, maize, and wheat increased steadily during that period. The production increases can be attributed roughly equally to irrigation, fertilizer, and seed development - at least in the case of Asian rice. While agricultural output increased as a result of the Green Revolution, the energy input to produce a crop has decreased at a greater rate, so that the ratio of crops produced to energy input has decreased over time. Green Revolution techniques also rely heavily on chemical fertilizers, pesticides, and herbicides and machines. In modern times, these chemicals and fuel are derived from crude oil, which makes agriculture increasingly reliant on crude oil extraction.

The world's population has grown by about four billion people since the beginning of the Green Revolution, and many believe that, without the Revolution, there would have been greater famine and malnutrition. Between 1950 and 1984, as the green revolution transformed agriculture around the globe, world grain production increased by over 250%. The production increases fostered by the Green Revolution are credited with having helped to avoid widespread famine, and for feeding billions of people. However, there are also claims that the Green Revolution has decreased food security for a large number of people.

Medical innovations increased the ability of humans to survive.

During the 20th century, large-scale wars were attended by medics and mobile hospital units, and advanced techniques for healing massive injuries and controlling infections, which thrived in battlefield conditions, were developed. Thousands of injured soldiers created a demand for improved prosthetic limbs and expanded techniques in reconstructive surgery, often referred to as plastic surgery. Those practices were combined to broaden cosmetic surgery and other forms of elective surgery.

Poster of Red Cross nurse

From 1917 to 1923, the American Red Cross moved into Europe with a battery of long-term child health projects. It built and operated hospitals and clinics and organized anti-tuberculosis and anti-typhus campaigns. Child health programs, such as clinics, playgrounds, fresh-air camps, and courses for women on infant hygiene, were a high priority. Hundreds of U.S. doctors, nurses and welfare professionals administered these programs, which aimed to reform the health of European youth and to reshape European public health and welfare along American lines.

In 1929, Alexander Fleming identified penicillin, the first chemical compound with antibiotic properties. Antibiotics revolutionized medicine in the 20th century and have, together with vaccination, led to the near eradication of diseases, such as tuberculosis, in the developed world. Their effectiveness and easy access led to overuse, especially in livestock raising, which prompted bacteria to develop resistance. All classes of antibiotics in use today were first discovered before the mid-1980s.

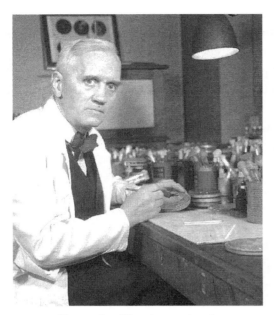

Alexander Fleming, scientist

The World Health Organization (WHO) was founded in 1948 as a United Nations agency to improve global health. In most of the world, life expectancy has improved since then, with the 2010 global figure standing at 67 years, with numbers well above 80 years in some countries. Eradication of infectious diseases is an international effort, and several new vaccines have been developed during the post- World War Two years to combat infections such as measles, mumps, several strains of influenza and human papillomavirus. Smallpox was finally eradicated in the 1970s, and Rinderpest was wiped out in 2011. The eradication of polio is underway. Tissue culture is important for the development of vaccines. Despite the early success of antiviral vaccines and antibacterial drugs, antiviral drugs were not introduced until the 1970s.

Cardiac surgery was revolutionized in the late 1940s when open-heart surgery was introduced. The transplant of organs, such as the heart, liver, and pancreas, was also introduced during the latter part of the 20th century. By the end of the 20th century, microtechnology had been used to create tiny robotic devices to assist microsurgery, using micro-video and fiber-optic cameras to view internal tissues using minimally invasive practices. The artificial heart was one of the greatest advancements in this field. Commonly known as a "pace-maker," it extended the lifespans of millions. The first successful experiment with an artificial heart was carried out by Vladimir Demikhov in the Soviet Union in 1937 when he implanted it in a dog. The first successful use on a human came in 1952 when a patient was sustained by one during open-heart surgery.

Jonas Salk developed the polio vaccine in 1955. Salk had previously created the vaccine for influenza. Before the vaccine, polio was a debilitating and potentially lethal disease that affected millions of children and adults worldwide. Polio has almost been eradicated but persists in some underdeveloped countries.

Energy technologies, including the use of oil and nuclear power, raised productivity, and increased the production of material goods.

Energy technology is an interdisciplinary engineering science that studies extraction, transportation, storage, and use of energy. Its research is targeted toward yielding high-efficiency energy while minimizing the side effects on humans and the environment. ("Interdisciplinary" means a combination of several fields of study. In this case, this includes such fields as geology, biology, and chemistry.) For people, energy is an overwhelming need and a scarce resource. The gathering and use of energy resources can be harmful to local ecosystems and may have global consequences.

Before the 18th century, wood was the main fuel for cooking food and heating homes during the winter. Coal began to be burned in Europe in Roman times, but only became a major secondary source of fuel in the 18th century, when industrialization brought coal-fueled steam-powered machinery. The scale of industry in the late industrial period could never have been fueled by wood alone, and to even attempt to do so would have caused catastrophic deforestation. By the late 19th century, a new fossil fuel became important: petroleum. Oil's potential as fuel was discovered in 1848 by Scottish entrepreneur James Young, who began to refine and sell it. After only a generation, this product was a major source of fuel. In the United States, the name that became widely associated with oil production was John D. Rockefeller. His company, Standard Oil, eventually dominated 90% of the oil market in the United States and a huge share of it in the rest of the world.

Nuclear technology involves nuclear power production from nuclear reactors, along with the processing of nuclear fuel and disposal of radioactive waste. It draws on applied nuclear physics, nuclear chemistry, and radiation science. Nuclear technology involves the reactions of atomic nuclei, and notable nuclear technologies include nuclear reactors, nuclear medicine, and nuclear weapons. Nuclear power generation has been controversial in many countries for several decades, but the electrical energy produced through nuclear fission is of worldwide importance. There are high hopes that fusion technologies will one day replace most fission reactors, but this is still an area of research in nuclear physics that has yet to yield any major new sources of energy. In biology and agriculture, radiation is used to induce mutations to produce new or improved species. Another use is in insect control with the sterile insect technique, where radiation is used to sterilize male insects, so they have no offspring, to reduce the insect population.

As the global population expanded at an unprecedented rate, humans fundamentally changed their relationship with the environment.

The concept of environmentalism refers to a broad philosophy, ideology, and social movement advocating the concern for environmental protection and improvement of the health of the environment. Environmentalism advocates the lawful preservation, restoration and/or improvement of the natural environment and may be thought of as a movement to control pollution or protect plant and animal diversity.

Environmentalism is an attempt to balance relations between humans and the various natural systems on which they depend, in such a way that all the components are accorded a proper degree of sustainability. The exact measures and outcomes of this balance are controversial, and there are many different ways that environmental concerns have been expressed in practice. Environmentalism is opposed by anti-environmentalism, which says that the Earth is less fragile than some environmentalists maintain and portrays environmentalism as overreacting to the human contribution to climate change or opposing human advancement.

Environmentalism deals today with new issues such as global warming, overpopulation, and genetic engineering. Many youths of today's society are more aware of the state of the planet because they grew up with Earth Day in place. School Eco Clubs are now working to create new ideas for the future through sustainable schools and other minor changes in student lives, such as recycling and sustainability practices.

Humans exploited and competed over the earth's finite resources more intensely than ever before in human history.

A non-renewable resource, also called a finite resource, is a resource that does not renew itself at a sufficient rate for sustainable economic extraction in meaningful human time-frames. An example is carbon-based, organically-derived fuel. The original organic material, with the aid of heat and pressure, becomes a fuel such as oil or gas. Earth minerals and metal ores, fossil fuels (coal, petroleum, natural gas), and groundwater in individual aquifers are all non-renewable resources. In contrast, resources such as timber (when harvested sustainably) and wind (used to power energy conversion systems) are considered renewable resources, largely because their localized replenishment can occur within timeframes meaningful to humans.

High Kölbling wind farm, St. Pölten, Austria

Renewable resources are replaced by natural processes and forces persistent in the natural environment. Soil, water, forests, plants, and animals are all renewable resources, as long as they are adequately monitored, protected, and conserved. There are intermittent and recurring renewables and recyclable materials, which are utilized during a cycle across a certain amount of time and can be harnessed for any number of cycles. The production of goods and services creates many types of waste during production and after the consumer has made use of it. The material is then either incinerated, buried in a landfill, or recycled for reuse. Recycling turns materials that would otherwise become waste back into valuable resources.

In the 20th and early 21st centuries, the use of natural resources grew like never before in history. Overfishing of the oceans is one example of industry practice or method threatening an ecosystem, endangering species, and possibly even determining whether or not a fishery is sustainable for use by humans. An unregulated industry practice or method can lead to complete resource depletion.

Renewable resources such as the movement of water, wind, and radiant energy from geothermal heat and solar energy are practically infinite and cannot be depleted, unlike their non-renewable counterparts, which are likely to run out if not used sparingly. Renewable energy and energy efficiency are no longer niche sectors that are promoted only by governments and environmentalists. Increasing levels of investment and the fact that more capital is from conventional financial actors both suggest that sustainable energy has become mainstream and will be the future of energy production as non-renewable resources decline.

This is reinforced by changing consumer choices due to climate change concerns, the accumulation of radioactive waste, high oil prices, peak oil (the notion that all easy access to oil has been exploited, and oil prices will always increase as a result) and increasing government support for renewable energy. These factors are commercializing renewable energy, enlarging the market, and increasing demand for the adoption of new products to replace obsolete technology and the conversion of existing infrastructure to a renewable standard.

Global warming was a major consequence of the release of greenhouse gases and other pollutants into the atmosphere.

Global warming and climate change are terms for the observed century-scale rise in the average temperature of the Earth's climate and its related effects. Multiple lines of scientific evidence show that the climate on Earth is warming. Although the increase of near-surface atmospheric temperature is the measure of global warming often reported in the popular press, most of the additional energy stored in the climate system since 1970 has gone into ocean warming. The increase in ocean temperature has melted a large portion of the world's ice, and this has, in turn, warmed the continents and atmosphere. Many of the observed changes since the 1950s are unprecedented.

Scientific understanding of global warming is increasing. The Intergovernmental Panel on Climate Change reported in 2014 that scientists were more than 95% certain that global warming is being caused mostly by increasing concentrations of greenhouse gases and other human (anthropogenic) activities. Future climate change and its associated impacts will differ from region to region around the globe. Anticipated effects include rising global temperature, rising sea levels, changing precipitation patterns, and the expansion of deserts in the subtropics. Warming is expected to be greatest in the Arctic regions, with the retreat of glaciers, permafrost, and sea ice continuing as a result.

Other likely changes include more frequent extreme weather events, including heatwaves, droughts, heavy rainfall, heavy snowfall, ocean acidification and species extinctions due to shifting temperatures. Effects significant to humans include the threat to food security from decreasing crop yields and the abandonment of populated areas due to flooding. The greenhouse effect is the process by which the absorption and emission of infrared radiation, by gases in a planet's atmosphere, warm its lower atmosphere and surface.

Over the last three decades of the 20th century, gross domestic product per capita and population growth were the main drivers of increases in greenhouse gas emissions. Carbon dioxide emissions are continuing to rise due to the burning of fossil fuels and land-use change. Emissions scenarios, estimates of changes in future emission levels of greenhouse gases, have been projected that depend upon uncertain economic, sociological, technological, and natural developments. In most scenarios, emissions have continued to rise over the centuries, while in a few, emissions have been reduced. Fossil fuel reserves are abundant and will not limit carbon emissions in the 21st century.

Pollution threatened the world's supply of water and clean air. Deforestation and desertification were continuing consequences of the human impact on the environment. Rates of extinction of other species accelerated sharply.

The concept of pollution refers to the introduction of contaminants that cause an adverse change in the natural environment. Pollution can take the form of chemical substances or energy, such as noise, heat, or light, and its components can be either foreign substances or naturally occurring contaminants. Deforestation is the removal of a forest or stands of trees where the land is after that converted to a non-forest use. Examples of deforestation include conversion of forestland to farms, ranches, or urban use. Tropical rainforests are where the most concentrated deforestation has occurred. Almost 30% of the world is covered by forests, excluding water mass.

Deforestation in Olympic National Timberland, Washington, due to drainage system

In temperate climates, natural regeneration of forest stands often will not occur in the absence of disturbance, whether natural or anthropogenic. The removal of trees without sufficient reforestation has resulted in damage to habitat, a loss in overall biodiversity, and an increase in aridity. Disregard of ascribed value, lax forest management, and deficient environmental laws are some of the factors that allow deforestation to occur on a large scale. In many countries, deforestation, both naturally occurring and human-induced, is an ongoing issue.

Deforestation causes extinction, changes to climatic conditions, desertification, and displacement of human populations. More than half of all plant and land animal species in the world live in tropical forests. Deforestation on a human scale results in a decline in biodiversity and, on a natural global scale, is known to cause the extinction of many species. The removal or destruction of areas of forest cover has resulted in a degraded environment with reduced biodiversity.

Disease, scientific innovations, and conflict led to demographic shifts.

The term "demographic transition" refers to the transition from high birth and death rates to low birth and death rates as a country develops from a pre-industrial to an industrialized economic system, a fact which is typically demonstrated through a demographic transition model. The theory is based on an interpretation of demographic history that was developed in 1929 by the American demographer Warren Thompson who observed changes, or transitions, in birth and death rates in industrialized societies over the previous 200 years. Most developed countries are in stage four or five of the model; the majority of developing countries have reached stage two or stage three. The major relative exceptions are some countries, mainly in sub-Saharan Africa and some Middle Eastern countries, which are poor or affected by government policy or civil strife, notably Pakistan, the Palestinian territories, Yemen and Afghanistan.

Although this model predicts ever-decreasing fertility rates, recent data show that beyond a certain level of development, fertility rates increase again. A correlation matching the demographic transition has been established; however, it is not certain whether industrialization and higher incomes lead to a lower population or if a lower population leads to industrialization and higher incomes. In countries that are now developed, this demographic transition began in the 18th century and continues today. In less developed countries, this demographic transition started later and is still at an earlier stage. This model became the basis for similar models, including the Migration Transition Model and the Epidemiological Transition Model, which predict the patterns of international and intra-national migration flow and the characteristics of a disease, respectively.

Diseases associated with poverty persisted, while other diseases emerged as new epidemics and threats to human survival. Also, changing lifestyles and increased longevity led to a higher incidence of certain diseases.

"Diseases of poverty" is a term sometimes used to collectively describe diseases, disabilities, and health conditions that are more prevalent among the poor than among wealthier people. In many cases, poverty is considered the leading risk factor or determinant of such diseases. In some cases, the diseases themselves are identified as barriers to economic development that would end poverty. Diseases of poverty are related to malnutrition. Together, diseases of poverty kill approximately 14 million people annually.

In the 20th century, diseases threatened to destabilize many regions of the world; new viruses, such as SARS and West Nile, continued to spread, malaria, and other diseases affecting large populations. Millions got infected with HIV, the virus which causes AIDS. At the global level, the three primary poverty-related diseases are AIDS, malaria, and tuberculosis. Developing countries account for 95% of the global AIDS prevalence and 98% of active tuberculosis infections. Furthermore, 90% of malaria deaths occur in sub-Saharan Africa. Together, these three diseases account for 10% of global mortality. Treatable childhood diseases also have disproportionately higher rates in developing countries, even though cures have been available for decades. These include measles, pertussis, and polio. Other diseases, such as pneumonia and diarrheal diseases, are also closely associated with poverty and are often included with AIDS, malaria, and tuberculosis in broader definitions and discussions of diseases of poverty.

Illnesses, such as influenza and cholera, came in reoccurring epidemics for centuries before solutions were found during the industrial age. Some, like cholera, was solved by adopting sanitation measures, especially in cities. Cholera is a deadly intestinal disease that is spread through contaminated food and water. In most pre-industrial societies, local rivers were simultaneously a source of drinking water and the place for human waste disposal. This enabled the easy spread of cholera and other infectious diseases. When Doctor John Snow determined that the Thames River was the source of reoccurring cholera epidemics in London, the issue was eliminated by the construction of proper sewer and plumbing systems and the provision of fresh water. In the undeveloped world, cholera epidemics persisted; particularly in rural Africa, where polluted water has been common, and there are no modern water sanitation facilities.

Ribbon hanging in White House in recognition of World AIDS Day

Reoccurring influenza epidemics were killing millions until a vaccine was developed. The 1918 influenza pandemic affected between one-fifth to one-third of the world's population and took the lives of an estimated fifty million people. Doctors Jonas Salk and Thomas Francis developed the first effective vaccine in 1938. It was an inexpensive way to save lives and easy to mass-produce. Since then, the number of lives claimed by influenza epidemics in developed nations has plummeted. For example, while the epidemic of 1918 killed 228,000 people in the United Kingdom, the epidemic of 1957 killed only 4,000, and the epidemic of 2009 killed 474 people in Britain.

Heart disease is one of the primary causes of death in the developed world and is attributed to both genetic and lifestyle factors. The excessive consumption of alcohol, sugar, trans-fats, and smoking are the primary lifestyle factors that fuel heart and lung illnesses. These all became common in the lifestyle of Europeans and Americans by the beginning of the 20th century, for many societal reasons. As people became wealthier and began to trade heavily with the rest of the world during the 18th and 19th centuries, their diet changed dramatically. In particular, the low-income majority attained a higher standard of living due to the higher-paying forms of employment in the industrial age. This higher purchasing power, combined with the increased efficiency to make foods available to more people, resulted in great health benefits in the form of better nutrition; however, unhealthy processed foods became available and among Western consumers.

Sugar was the most prominent and devastating dietary change. It was initially produced through the use of slave labor and became readily available to the working poor. It is also versatile and is used to make highly sugared foods and alcohol. The change from a diet that was primarily based on grain to a diet loaded with sugar, alcohol, cholesterol, and tobacco led to a generational increase in chronic heart diseases. High sugar diets also led to diabetes, which became more common and is continually affecting younger and younger people. The prevalence of neurological disorders, such as Alzheimer's disease, increased over the 20th century and is linked to unhealthy diets.

More effective forms of birth control gave women greater control over fertility and transformed sexual practices.

Birth control, also known as contraception and fertility control, are methods or devices used to prevent pregnancy, while the planning, provision, and use of birth control are called family planning. Birth control methods have been used since ancient times, but effective and safe methods only became available in the 20th century. Some cultures limit or discourage access to birth control because they consider it to be moral, religiously, or politically unpalatable. Some people regard sexual abstinence as birth control, but due to non-compliance, abstinence-only sex education may increase teen pregnancies when offered without contraceptive education.

Cover of Birth Control Review brochure, July 1919

Birth control use in developing countries has decreased the number of maternal deaths by 40% and could prevent 70% if the full demand for birth control is met. By lengthening the time between pregnancies, birth control can improve adult women's delivery outcomes and the survival of their children. In the developing world, women's earnings, assets, weight, and their children's schooling and health all improve with greater access to birth control.

Birth control increases economic growth because fewer dependent children are produced, and more women participate in the workforce. Teenage pregnancies, especially among younger teens, are at higher risk of adverse outcomes, including early birth, low birth weight, and infant mortality. In the United States, 82% of pregnancies in those between the ages of 15 and 19 are unplanned. Comprehensive sex education and access to birth control are effective in decreasing pregnancy rates in this age group.

After gaining political rights in the United States and much of Europe in the first part of the century, and with the advent of new birth control techniques, women became more independent throughout the century.

Improved military technology and new tactics led to increased levels of wartime casualties.

During the First World War, radically different military technology was used for the first time. The fundamental difference between World War One technology and the old-world equipment was that it was mass-killing technology, such as poisonous gas, machine guns, and explosives. Trench warfare resulted in an unprecedented rate of casualties.

Infantry used networks of man-made trenches, where soldiers would emerge from to race towards enemy trenches while being shelled and machine-gunned. This disastrous combination of outdated tactics and modern technology resulted in high numbers of casualties during every attack.

Soon after the invention of airplanes, military aviation became a significant component of warfare, though usually in a supplementary role. Two of the many types of military attack aircraft are bombers, which attack land-based targets, and fighters, which carry a much lower payload but are more versatile as they can attack targets at sea, on land or in the air. Military vehicles are categorized as land combat or vehicles. Military tactics answer the questions of how best to deploy and employ forces on a small scale. Some practices have not changed since the dawn of warfare: ambushes, seeking and turning flanks, maintaining reconnaissance, creating and using obstacles and defenses, etc.

Political changes were accompanied by major demographic and social consequences.

The right of nations to self-determination is a cardinal principle in modern international law, binding, as such, on the United Nations. It states that nations based on respect for the principle of equal rights and fair equality of opportunity have the right to freely choose their sovereignty and international political status with no external compulsion or interference. This can be traced back to the Atlantic Charter, signed on 14 August 1941, by President Franklin D. Roosevelt, of the United States of America and Winston Churchill, Prime Minister of the United Kingdom, who pledged The Eight Principal Points of the Charter. The principle does not state how the decision is to be made, or what the outcome should be, whether it be independence, federation, protection, some form of autonomy, or full assimilation. Neither does it state what the delimitation between nations should be—or what constitutes a nation. There are conflicting definitions and legal criteria for determining which groups may legitimately claim the right to self-determination.

On 14 December 1960, the United Nations General Assembly adopted United Nations General Assembly Resolution 1514 (XV) under titled "Declaration on the Granting of Independence to Colonial Countries and Peoples provided for the granting of independence to colonial countries and peoples in providing an inevitable legal linkage between self-determination and its goal of decolonization, and a postulated new international law-based right of freedom also in economic self-determination." Article 5 states: Immediate steps shall be taken in Trusts and Non-Self-Governing Territories, or all other territories which have not yet attained independence, to transfer all powers to the peoples of those territories, without any conditions or reservations, in accordance with their freely expressed will and desire, without any distinction as to race, creed or color, in order to enable them to enjoy complete independence and freedom.

Moreover, on 15 December 1960, the United Nations General Assembly adopted United Nations General Assembly Resolution 1541, which established the supremacy of self-determination over preparedness for self-government. To monitor the implementation of Resolution 1514, in 1961, the General Assembly created the Special Committee on Decolonization, referred to popularly as "the Special Committee," to ensure complete compliance with the principle of self-determination in General Assembly Resolution 1541. Resolution 1541 defined a free association with an independent State, integration into an independent State, or independence as the three legitimate options of full self-government compliance with the principle of self-determination.

The 20th century was plagued by unrest and conflict.

The number of people killed during this century by government actions was in the hundreds of millions. This included deaths caused by wars, genocide, politicide, and other mass murders. The deaths from acts of war during the two world wars alone have been estimated at between 50 and 80 million. It is estimated that approximately 70 million Europeans died from war, violence, and famine between 1914 and 1945.

The timing of the Great Depression varied across nations; however, in most countries, it started in 1929 and lasted until the late 1930s. It was the longest, deepest, and most widespread depression of the 20th century. The economic and political aftermath of World War I and the Great Depression in the 1930s led to the rise of fascism and Nazism in Europe and, subsequently, to World War II (1939–1945). This war also involved Asia and the Pacific, in the form of Japanese aggression against China and the United States. Civilians also suffered greatly in World War II, due to the aerial bombing of cities on both sides, and the German genocide of the Jews and others, which is known as the Holocaust. In August 1945, Hiroshima and Nagasaki were bombed by nuclear weapons.

During World War I, in the Russian Revolution of 1917, 300 years of Romanov reign were ended, and the Bolsheviks, under the leadership of Vladimir Lenin, established the world's first communist state, the Soviet Union. After the Soviet Union's involvement in World War II, communism became a major force in global politics, notably in Eastern Europe, China, Indochina, and Cuba, where communist parties gained near-absolute power. This led to the Cold War and proxy wars with the West, including wars in Korea and Vietnam.

Indian, American and South African activists pursued social justice, while the founding of Israel sparks region-wide unrest.

Gandhi's non-violence and civil disobedience influenced many political movements around the world, including the African American civil rights movement in the U.S.A. and freedom movements in South Africa and Burma. In 1948, the creation of Israel, a Jewish state in the Middle East, by the British Mandate of Palestine, fueled many regional conflicts. The vast oilfields also influenced these conflicts in many other countries of the mostly Arab region. The end of colonialism led to the independence of many African and Asian countries. During the Cold War, many of these aligned with the United States, the USSR, or China for defense.

The Cold War produced new military alliances, including NATO and the Warsaw Pact, and promoted proxy wars in Latin America, Africa, and Asia.

The Cold War was a state of political and military tension after World War II between powers in the Western Bloc and powers in the Eastern Bloc (established by the Warsaw Pact). The first phase of the Cold War began in the first two years after the end of the Second World War in 1945. The USSR consolidated its control over the states of the Eastern Bloc. At the same time, the United States began a strategy of global containment to challenge Soviet power, extending military and financial aid to the countries of Western Europe and creating the NATO alliance. The Berlin Blockade (1948–49) was the first major crisis of the Cold War, which was only overcome by the Berlin Airlift, where all the necessary supplies to sustain West Berlin were flown into Tempelhof Airport until the Soviets eventually relented. With the victory of the communist side in the Chinese Civil War and the outbreak of the Korean War, the conflict expanded.

The USSR and U.S.A. competed for influence in Latin America and decolonizing states of Africa, the Middle East, and Southeast Asia. Meanwhile, the Hungarian Revolution of 1956 was stopped by the Soviets, who used brutal military force. The expansion and escalation of the Cold War sparked more crises, such as the Suez Crisis of 1956, the Berlin Crisis of 1961 and the Cuban Missile Crisis of 1962. Following this last crisis, a new phase began that saw the Sino-Soviet split complicate relations within the communist sphere while U.S. allies, particularly France, demonstrated greater independence of action. The USSR crushed the 1968 Prague Spring liberalization program in Czechoslovakia, and the Vietnam War (1955–1975) ended with a defeat of the US-backed Republic of South Vietnam.

By the 1970s, both sides had become interested in accommodations to create a more stable and predictable international system, inaugurating a period of détente that saw Strategic Arms Limitation Talks and the U.S. opening relations with the People's Republic of China as a strategic counterweight to the Soviet Union. The United States and other Western nations increased diplomatic, military, and economic pressures on the Soviet Union to precipitate the collapse of communism. This policy was pursued by U.S. President Ronald Reagan and British Prime Minister Margaret Thatcher at a time when the communist state was already suffering from economic stagnation. Thatcher and Reagan realized that, with the capitalist system, they were able to bring to bear far more economic resources than the regimes operating under communism could. As a result, they began spending vast sums of money on building weapons, knowing that to maintain the principle of Mutually Assured Destruction (MAD), the Soviets would have to do the same. Even with the massive boon to the Soviet Treasury coffers due to the spike in the price of hydrocarbons in the early 1980s, the level of spending required to keep pace with the U.S. and UK was unsustainable.

In the mid-1980s, the new Soviet leader Mikhail Gorbachev introduced the liberalizing reforms of perestroika (1987) and glasnost (1985) and ended Soviet involvement in Afghanistan. Pressures for national independence grew stronger in Eastern Europe, especially in Poland, with the rise of the charismatic former Gdansk dockworker, Lech Walesa, and his Solidarity (Solodarnosh) Party. Gorbachev meanwhile refused to use Soviet troops to bolster the faltering Warsaw Pact regimes, as had occurred in the past. The result in 1989 was a wave of revolutions that peacefully (except the Romanian Revolution) overthrew all of the Communist regimes of Central and Eastern Europe. The Communist Party of the Soviet Union itself lost control and was banned following an abortive coup attempt in August of 1991. This, in turn, led to the formal dissolution of the USSR in December of 1991 and the collapse of Communist regimes in other countries, such as Mongolia, Cambodia, and South Yemen.

Although conflict dominated much of the 20th century, many individuals and groups – including states – opposed this trend. Some individuals and groups, however, intensified the conflicts.

An important thinker who contributed to the pacifist ideology was the Russian writer Leo Tolstoy. In one of his later works, The Kingdom of God is Within You, Tolstoy provides a detailed history, account, and defense of pacifism. Tolstoy's work inspired a movement named after him advocating pacifism in Russia and elsewhere. The book was a major early influence on Mahatma Gandhi, and the two engaged in regular correspondence while Gandhi was active in South Africa. Pacifism is opposition to war, militarism, and violence.

The word pacifism was coined by the French peace campaigner Émile Arnaud (1864–1921) and adopted by other peace activists at the tenth Universal Peace Congress in Glasgow in 1901. Mahatma Gandhi propounded the practice of steadfast nonviolent opposition, which he called "satyagraha," as instrumental in the Indian Independence Movement. Its effectiveness served as an inspiration to Martin Luther King Jr., James Lawson, James Bevel, Thich Nhat Hanh, and many others during the 1950s and 1960s American Civil Rights Movement. Pacifism was widely associated with the much-publicized image of the Tiananmen Square Protests of 1989 with the "Tank Man," where one protester stood in nonviolent opposition to a column of tanks.

Groups and individuals challenged wars and policy decisions.

Art is a common non-violent way to convey information and express sentiment about an event. Picasso's *Guernica* is an example of this: In 1937, in support of their statist allies in the Spanish civil war, the Nazis bombed the Spanish town, Guernica. Picasso was not an eyewitness – he had fled his native Spain in 1934 – but based his painting on other eyewitness accounts. His style Cubism, but the subject matter is indeed like that of Realism as it portrays the unmitigated reality of human suffering.

During the Cold War, many feared that a full-scale nuclear war would break out. This led to a continual campaign in the west for disarmament. During the early 1980s, in particular, mass-protest marches and public rallies were common. In communist nations, public protests were prohibited, and one faced severe criminal punishment if an attempt was made to protest as people did in the west publically. Political Action Committees in America are fundraising organizations for specific political causes, which endorse candidates who support the group's agenda. They raise funds to help their chosen politicians get elected. This was a strong component of the American anti-nuclear movement.

The anti-nuclear movement was not only about weapons. The protesters also believed that nuclear power plants were hazardous and wanted them to shut down. Several historic accidents at nuclear power plants have lent credibility to their fears, but these have, on the other hand, been extremely infrequent and benign compared to the alternative. There have only been three major crises at nuclear power plants since they came into use, one of which did not lead to contamination of the environment. In contrast, there have been scores of catastrophic oil spills, thousands of worker deaths in coal mine cave-ins and other fossil fuel disasters, and the combined total of environmental damage done by the damming of rivers and air pollution from fossil fuels dwarfs the damage done by the Chernobyl and Fukushima nuclear disasters.

Groups and individuals opposed and promoted alternatives to the existing economic, political, and social orders.

In popular understanding, the concepts of socialism and communism have often been viewed as the same. Marx saw socialism as the final stage of bourgeoisie capitalism, which would eventually lead to the onset of pure communism. However, it was Lenin who more strongly stressed the difference between "socialism" and "communism," stressing the importance of understanding socialism as the final stage in the dialectical process of overcoming capitalism and establishing communism. Marxism–Leninism supports universal social welfare. Improvements in public health and education, provision of child care, provision of state-directed social services, and provision of social benefits are deemed by Marxist–Leninists to help raise labor productivity and advance a society's development towards a communist society.

This is part of Marxist–Leninists' advocacy of promoting and reinforcing the operation of a planned socialist economy. It advocates universal education with a focus on developing the proletariat's knowledge, class consciousness, and understanding the historical development of communism. Marxist–Leninist and communist revolutions occurred in Asia throughout the twentieth century. The People's Republic of China under Mao Zedong developed its unique brand of Marxism–Leninism, known as Maoism.

The Non-Aligned movement was never established as a formal organization but became a reference to the participants of the Conference of Heads of State or Government of Non-Aligned Countries, first held in 1961. The term "non-alignment" was established in 1953 at the United Nations. Jawaharlal Nehru used the phrase in a 1954 speech in Colombo, Sri Lanka. In this speech, Nehru described the five pillars to be used as a guide for Sino-Indian relations, called Panchsheel (five restraints). These principles later served as the basis of the Non-Aligned Movement. The five principles were: mutual respect for each other's territorial integrity and sovereignty, mutual non-aggression, mutual non-interference in domestic affairs, equality and mutual benefit, and peaceful co-existence.

Militaries and militarized states often responded to the proliferation of conflicts in ways that further intensified conflict.

A military dictatorship is a form of government in which a member of the military holds authoritarian control. In a junta, power is shared by several military leaders. It may be different from civilian dictatorship in some aspects: their motivations for seizing power, the institutions through which they organize their rule, and how they leave power. Often viewing itself as saving the nation from corrupt or myopic civilian politicians or civil disorder, a military dictatorship justifies its position as "neutral" arbiters by their membership within the armed forces.

The military-industrial complex comprises the policy and monetary relationships which exist between legislators, national armed forces, and the arms industry that supports them. These relationships include political contributions, political approval for military spending, lobbying to support bureaucracies, and oversight of the industry. It is a type of iron triangle. The term is sometimes used more broadly to include the entire network of contracts and flows of money and resources among individuals, as well as corporations and institutions of the defense contractors, the Pentagon, Congress, and the executive branch.

Global conflicts had a profound influence on popular culture.

During the Cold War, the United States and the Soviet Union invested heavily in propaganda, especially motion pictures that were designed to influence the hearts and minds of people around the world. The Cold War remains a popular topic and is reflected extensively in entertainment media, such as the post-1991 Cold War-themed feature films, novels, and television shows. Soviet espionage in the United States during the Cold War was an outgrowth of World War II nuclear espionage and Cold War espionage was depicted in works such as the James Bond and Matt Helm books and movies. The James Bond video game franchise is a series of shooter games and games of other genres (including role-playing and adventure games) spun off from the James Bond film series and developed and published by a variety of companies. The games center on Ian Fleming's fictional British MI6 agent, James Bond. James Bond subtly represents the western government as the "good guys," as he works for the British government in its most elite counter-espionage department. Bond has all of the qualities of the archetypal male hero, his main fault being a womanizer.

The Dada art movement was an early 20th-century movement that began along with the establishment of the Cabaret Voltaire in Zurich in 1916. It was a counter-culture movement, consciously affiliated with international Marxism. Its American members sometimes referred to it as "anti-art." Dada-ism conveyed anti-war messages during the First World War and generally promoted anti-capitalist messages otherwise. Some of the anti-art involved gimmicks like presenting a photograph of a defaced toilet or a rendition of Mona Lisa in which she wears Salvador Dali's trademark beard and mustache. Sometimes a wild montage of newspaper photographs was made. Hugo Ball and Emmy Hennings were among the most prominent individuals behind the works of Dada.

At the beginning of the century in the United States and parts of Europe, governments played a minimal role in their national economies. With the onset of the Great Depression, governments began to take a more active role in economic life.

Economic historians usually attribute the start of the Great Depression to the sudden, devastating collapse of U.S. stock market prices on October 29, 1929, known as Black Tuesday. Even after the Wall Street Crash of 1929, optimism persisted for some time. The decline in the U.S. economy impacted most other countries first. The internal weaknesses or strengths of each country determined whether conditions got worse or better. Frantic attempts were made to shore up the economies of individual nations through the use of protectionist policies. By late 1930, a steady decline in the world economy had set in, but it did not reach rock bottom until 1933.

The New Deal was a series of domestic programs enacted in the United States, primarily between 1933 and 1938. They included laws passed by Congress, as well as presidential executive orders during the first term (1933–1937) of President Franklin D. Roosevelt. The programs were enacted in response to the Great Depression and focused on what historians refer to as the "Three R's": relief, recovery, and reform. This included relief for the unemployed and poor, recovery of the economy to normal levels, and reform of the financial system to prevent a repeat of the depression.

President Franklin Delano Roosevelt

Fascists advocated for a mixed economy, with the principal goal of achieving autarky through protectionist and interventionist economic policies. The terms neo-fascist and post-fascist are sometimes applied more formally to describe parties of the far right with ideologies similar to, or rooted in, 20th-century fascist movements. Fascist economics supported a state-controlled economy that accepted a mix of private and public ownership over the means of production. They also had great restrictions on freedom of competition, unlike capitalist systems. Economic planning was applied to both the public and private sectors, and the prosperity of private enterprise depended on its alignment with the economic goals of the state. Fascist economic ideology supported the profit motive but emphasized that industries needed to consider the national interest as superior to private profit.

While fascism accepted the importance of material wealth and power, it condemned materialism, which it identified as being present in both communism and capitalism, for lacking acknowledgment of the role of the spirit. In particular, fascists criticized capitalism, not because of its competitive nature or support of private property. However, due to its materialism, individualism alleged bourgeois decadence and alleged indifference to the nation. Fascism denounced Marxism for its advocacy of materialist internationalist class identity, which fascists regarded as an attack upon the emotional and spiritual bonds of the nation and a threat to the achievement of genuine national solidarity.

At the end of the twentieth century, many governments encouraged free-market economic policies and promoted economic liberalization.

Most first-world countries have pursued the path of economic liberalization in recent decades with the stated goal of maintaining or increasing their competitiveness in business environments. Liberalization policies include partial or full privatization of government institutions and assets, greater labor market flexibility, lower tax rates for businesses, less restriction on both domestic and foreign capital, and open markets. In developing countries, economic liberalization refers more to liberalization or further "opening up" of their respective economies to foreign capital and investments. Three of the fastest-growing developing economies today – Brazil, China, and India – have achieved rapid economic growth in the past several years or decades after they have "liberalized" their economies to foreign capital.

Many countries nowadays, particularly those in the third world, arguably have no choice but to "liberalize" their economies to remain competitive in attracting and retaining both domestic and foreign investments. Liberalization is also strongly encouraged by the Bretton Woods institutions (IMF, World Bank), as they attach liberalization "conditionality" to their loans. This "conditionality" is colloquially known as the "Washington Consensus," as the Bretton Woods institutions are based in Washington. For example, in 1991, India had no choice but to implement economic reforms. North Korea's economy is a "self-sufficient" economic system that is closed to foreign trade and investment; it is the complete opposite of a liberal economy. However, North Korea is not completely separate from the global economy, since it receives aid from other countries in exchange for peace and restrictions to their nuclear program. Other examples are oil-rich countries, such as Saudi Arabia and the United Arab Emirates, who see no need to further open up their economies to foreign capital and investments since their oil reserves already provide them with huge export earnings.

States, communities, and individuals became increasingly interdependent, a process facilitated by the growth of institutions of global governance.

Global governance is a movement toward the political integration of transnational actors aimed at negotiating responses to problems that affect more than one state or region. Institutions of global governance—the United Nations, the International Criminal Court, the World Bank, etc.—tend to have limited or demarcated power to enforce compliance. The modern question of world governance exists in the context of globalization and globalizing regimes of power. The term "global governance" may also be used to name the process of designating laws, rules, or regulations intended on a global scale.

The short historical period since the Industrial Revolution has seen a sudden and huge growth in global travel, both for business and leisure, as a result of the surplus income that ordinary people now have. This has brought a corresponding increase in security threats; it has facilitated the spread of disease, the travel of criminals, a huge new industry of human trafficking, and drug trafficking. The explosion of international business has also taken place even though the world is still comprised of independent nations with different economic laws. Another complication of the world's industrialization is the use of air and outer space, for which there have never been any divisions of territory.

The result of these factors is that governments have found the need to coordinate with each other more than ever before. There are conventions for cooperation in security and trade, which compel nations to act within certain norms and requirements. Agreements for trade are still a work in progress, which started at the level of small groups of neighboring nations and continues to develop towards very far-reaching global trade agreements. International standards have recently been created for the safety of air travel and the rights of passengers, as well as the use of outer space orbital paths for nations' satellites. However, the effectiveness of these agreements is only as good as the integrity of the world's leaders and governments.

New international organizations formed to maintain world peace and to facilitate international cooperation.

Armed conflicts have changed in form and intensity since the Berlin wall came down in 1989. The events of 9/11, the wars in Afghanistan and Iraq, and repeated terrorist attacks all show that conflicts can become lethal for the entire world, well beyond the belligerents directly involved. At the same time, civil wars continue to break out across the world, particularly in areas where civil and human rights are not respected, such as Central and Eastern Africa and the Middle East. These and other regions remain deeply entrenched in permanent crises and are hampered by authoritarian regimes, which reduce entire swathes of the population to wretched living conditions. Current wars and conflicts have a variety of causes: economic inequality, social conflict, religious sectarianism, colonial legacies, and disputes over territory and the control of the land.

The League of Nations was an intergovernmental organization founded on January 10, 1920, as a result of the Paris Peace Conference, which ended the First World War. It was the first international organization whose principal mission was to maintain world peace. Its primary goals, as stated in its covenant, included preventing wars through collective security and disarmament, and settling international disputes through negotiation and arbitration. Other issues raised in the Treaty of Versailles and related treaties included labor conditions, just treatment of native inhabitants, human and drug trafficking, arms trade, global health, prisoners of war, and the protection of minorities in Europe.

Removal of Berlin Wall in 1989

The League lasted for twenty-six years until it was replaced by the United Nations (UN) at the end of the Second World War. The UN is an intergovernmental organization that was established on October 24, 1945, to promote international co-operation and prevent another world war. Its objectives include: maintaining international peace and security, promoting human rights, fostering social and economic development, protecting the environment, and providing humanitarian aid in cases of famine, natural disaster, and armed conflict.

The International Criminal Court (ICC) is an intergovernmental organization and international tribunal located in The Hague in the Netherlands. The ICC has the jurisdiction to prosecute individuals for the international crimes of genocide, crimes against humanity, and war crimes. The ICC is intended to complement existing national judicial systems and may only exercise its jurisdiction when certain conditions are met, such as when national courts are unwilling or unable to prosecute criminals or when the United Nations Security Council or individual states refer investigations to the Court. The ICC began functioning on July 1, 2002, the date that the Rome Statute became effective. The Rome Statute is a multilateral treaty that serves as the ICC's foundational and governing document. States which become a party to the Rome Statute, for example, by ratifying it, become member states of the ICC. Currently, there are 123 states which are party to the Rome Statute and, therefore, are members of the ICC. The U.S. is not a member of this organization, though it has established a strong relationship with the Court.

New economic institutions sought to spread the principles and practices associated with free-market economies throughout the world.

The IMF was originally designed as a part of the Bretton Woods system exchange agreement in 1944. During the Great Depression, countries sharply raised barriers to trade in an attempt to improve their failing economies. This led to the devaluation of national currencies and a decline in world trade. The IMF formally came into existence on December 27, 1945, when the first twenty-nine countries ratified its Articles of Agreement. By the end of 1946, the IMF had grown to thirty-nine members. On March 1, 1947, the IMF began its financial operations, and on May 8th, France became the first country to borrow from it.

The IMF was one of the key organizations of the international economic system; its design allowed the system to balance the rebuilding of international capitalism with the maximization of national economic sovereignty and human welfare, also known as embedded liberalism. The IMF's influence in the global economy steadily increased as it accumulated more members. As the need for capital as a means to compete in the globalized economy has increased, the influence of the IMF has grown. After the fall of the Soviet Union, the IMF, along with the World Bank, became – and remains – the main source of large external investment. This is vitally important to developing countries, as often private financial institutions see investment in these economies as too risky.

Board of Governors, International Monetary Fund (IMF)

The World Bank was also created at the 1944 Bretton Woods Conference. The president of the World Bank is traditionally an American, while the president of the IMF is traditionally a non-American. The World Bank and the IMF are both based in Washington, D.C., and work closely with each other.

The General Agreement on Tariffs and Trade (GATT) was established after World War II in the wake of other new multilateral institutions dedicated to international economic cooperation—notably the World Bank and the IMF. A comparable international institution for trade, known as the International Trade Organization, was also successfully negotiated, but its treaty was not approved by the U.S. and a few other signatories and never went into effect. The ITO could have been a United Nations specialized agency addressing not only trade barriers but other issues indirectly related to trade, including employment, investment, restrictive business practices, and commodity agreements.

The GATT was the only multilateral instrument governing international trade from 1946 until the WTO was established on January 1, 1995. Despite attempts in the mid-1950s and 1960s to create some form of institutional mechanism for international trade, the GATT continued to operate for almost half a century as a semi-institutionalized multilateral treaty regime on a provisional basis.

Humanitarian organizations developed to respond to humanitarian crises throughout the world.

The United Nations Children's Fund (UNICEF) is a United Nations Program headquartered in New York City that provides long-term humanitarian and developmental assistance to children and mothers in developing countries. UNICEF was created by the United Nations General Assembly in 1946, to provide emergency food and healthcare to children in countries that had been devastated by World War II. In 1953, UNICEF became a permanent part of the United Nations System, and its name was shortened from the original United Nations International Children's Emergency Fund. However, it has continued to be known by the popular acronym based on its previous title.

UNICEF relies on contributions from governments and private donors. Overall management and administration of the organization take place at its headquarters in New York. UNICEF's Supply Division is based in Copenhagen. It serves as the primary point of distribution for such essential items as vaccines, antiretroviral medicines for children and mothers with HIV, nutritional supplements, emergency shelters, family reunification, and educational supplies.

The International Red Cross and Red Crescent Movement is an international humanitarian movement with approximately 97 million volunteers, members and staff worldwide, which was founded to protect human life and health, to ensure respect for all human beings and to prevent and alleviate human suffering. The movement consists of several distinct organizations that are legally independent of each other but are united by common basic principles, objectives, symbols, statutes, and governing organizations.

Amnesty International is a non-governmental organization focused on human rights, with over 7 million members and supporters around the world. The stated objective of the organization is to research and generate action to prevent and end abuses of human rights and to demand justice for those whose rights have been violated. Amnesty International was founded in London in 1961 and drew attention to human rights abuses and campaigns for compliance with international laws and standards. It works to mobilize public opinion to put pressure on governments that let abuse take place. In the field of international human rights organizations, Amnesty International has the longest history and broadest name recognition. It is believed by many to be the standard-bearer for the movement as a whole.

Médecins Sans Frontières, or Doctors without Borders, is an international humanitarian-aid non-governmental organization (NGO) and Nobel Peace Prize laureate, best known for its projects in war-torn regions and developing countries facing endemic diseases. Médecins Sans Frontières was created in 1971, in the aftermath of the Biafra secession, by a small group of French doctors and journalists who believed that all people have the right to medical care regardless of race, religion, creed or political affiliation and that the needs of these people outweigh the importance of national borders.

The World Health Organization (WHO) is a specialized agency of the United Nations that is concerned with international public health. It was established on April 7, 1948, and is headquartered in Geneva, Switzerland. The WHO is a member of the United Nations Development Group. Its predecessor, the Health Organization, was an agency of the League of Nations. Its current priorities include combatting communicable diseases, in particular, HIV/AIDS, Ebola, malaria and tuberculosis; the mitigation of the effects of non-communicable diseases; sexual and reproductive health, development, and aging; nutrition, food security, and healthy eating; occupational health; substance abuse; and the development of reporting, publications and networking.

World Health Organization flag

Regional trade agreements created regional trading blocs designed to promote the movement of capital and goods across national borders.

The North American Free Trade Agreement (NAFTA) is an agreement signed by Canada, Mexico, and the United States, creating a trilateral rules-based trade bloc in North America. The agreement went into effect on January 1, 1994. It superseded the Canada–United States Free Trade Agreement. NAFTA has two supplements: the North American Agreement on Environmental Cooperation (NAAEC) and the North American Agreement on Labor Cooperation (NAALC).

President George H.W. Bush, Canadian Prime Minister Brian Mulroney, and Mexican President Carlos Salinas participate in the North American Free Trade Agreement in San Antonio, Texas

Multinational corporations began to challenge state authority and autonomy.

A multinational corporation (MNC) is an organization that owns or controls the production of goods or services in one or more countries other than its home country. The actions of MNCs are strongly supported by economic liberalism and the free market system in globalized international society. According to the economic realist view, individuals act in rational ways to maximize their self-interest and, therefore, when individuals act rationally, markets are created and function best in a free market system where there is little government interference. As a result, international wealth is maximized by the free exchange of goods and services. For the first time in history, production, marketing, and investment are being organized on a global scale rather than in terms of isolated national economies.

A transnational corporation differs from a traditional MNC in that it does not identify itself with one nation. While traditional MNCs are national companies with foreign subsidiaries, transnational corporations spread out their operations in many countries to sustain high levels of local responsiveness. An example of a transnational corporation is Nestlé, which employs senior executives from many countries and tries to make decisions from a global perspective rather than from one centralized headquarters.

Sony building in Tokyo, Japan

Another example is Royal Dutch Shell, whose headquarters are in The Hague, Netherlands, but whose registered office and main executive body are headquartered in London. Sony Corporation (commonly referred to as Sony), is a Japanese multinational conglomerate corporation headquartered in Tokyo. Its diversified business is primarily focused on consumer and professional electronics with divisions, including gaming, entertainment, and financial services. The company is one of the leading manufacturers of electronic products for consumers and professional markets. A very famous transnational organization and brand is Coca-Cola, which can be found in even the most remote of villages around the world.

Movements throughout the world protested the inequality of environmental and economic consequences of global integration.

In 1969 at a UNESCO Conference in San Francisco, peace activist John McConnell proposed the creation of a day to honor the Earth and the concept of peace, first to be celebrated on March 21, 1970 (the first day of spring in the Northern Hemisphere). A month later, a separate Earth Day was founded by the United States Senator Gaylord Nelson as an environmental teach-in first held on April 22, 1970.

John McConnell with the Earth Day flag he designed

While the April 22nd Earth Day was focused on the United States, an organization launched by Denis Hayes, who was the original national coordinator of Earth Day in 1970, made Earth Day international in 1990, with organized events taking place in 141 nations. Today, numerous communities celebrate Earth Week, an entire week of activities focused on environmental issues.

Greenpeace is a non-governmental environmental organization with offices in over forty countries and with an international coordinating body in Amsterdam, the Netherlands. Greenpeace states that its goal is to ensure the ability of the Earth to nurture life in all its diversity and focuses its campaigning on worldwide issues such as climate change, pollution, deforestation, overfishing, commercial whaling, genetic engineering, and anti-nuclear issues. It uses direct action, lobbying, and research to achieve its goals. As an example, a common strategy used by Green Peace is to obstruct the operations of new off-shore oil extraction facilities. The global organization does not accept funding from governments, corporations, or political parties, relying instead on its 2.9 million individual supporters and foundation grants.

Greenpeace evolved from a group of Canadian and American protesters into a less conservative group of environmentalists who were more reflective of the counterculture and hippie youth movements of the 1960s and 1970s. The social and cultural background from which Greenpeace emerged heralded a period of de-conditioning away from old world antecedents towards new codes of social, environmental, and political behavior.

The Green Belt Movement (GBM) is an indigenous grassroots non-governmental organization based in Nairobi, Kenya that takes a holistic approach to development by focusing on environmental conservation, community development, and capacity building. Professor Wangari Maathai established the organization in 1977, under the auspices of the National Council of Women of Kenya. The Green Belt Movement organizes women in rural Kenya to plant trees, combat deforestation, restore their main source of fuel for cooking, generate income, and stop soil erosion. Since Maathai started the movement in 1977, over 51 million trees have been planted. Communities in Kenya have been motivated and organized to both prevent further environmental destruction and restore that which has been damaged.

Climate change and global warming are examples of the impact pollution have on the climate. Climate change over the past century has been attributed to various factors, which have resulted in global warming. One argument is that of global warming, and that it may be due (at least partially) to human-caused emission of greenhouse gases, particularly carbon dioxide produced by the burning of fossil fuels. This prompted many nations to negotiate and sign the Kyoto treaty, which set mandatory limits on carbon dioxide emissions. Whether or not global warming is happening at an abnormal pace and whether human industry is to blame, are currently being debated.

Global warming refers to the increase in the average temperature of the Earth's near-surface air and oceans since the mid-20th century and its projected continuation. Some effects on both the natural environment and human life are, at least in part, already being attributed to global warming. A 2001 report by the IPCC suggested that glacier retreat; ice shelf disruption, such as that of the Larsen Ice Shelf; rising sea levels; changes in rainfall patterns; and increased intensity and frequency of extreme weather events are attributable in part to global warming. Other expected effects include water scarcity in some regions and increased precipitation in others, changes in mountain snowpack, and adverse health effects from warmer temperatures.

People conceptualized society and culture in new ways; some challenged old assumptions about race, class, gender, and religion, often using new technologies to spread reconfigured traditions.

The term "society" is currently used to cover both a number of political and scientific connotations as well as a variety of associations. The development of the Western world has brought with it the emerging concepts of Western culture, politics, and ideas, often referred to simply as "Western society."

One of the European Union's areas of interest is the information society. Although the term "information society" has been under discussion since the 1930s, in the modern world it is almost always applied to the manner in which information technologies have impacted society and culture. It, therefore, covers the effects of computers and telecommunications on the home, the workplace, schools, government, and various communities and organizations, as well as the emergence of new social forms in cyberspace. Here, policies are directed towards promoting an open and competitive digital economy and research into information and communication technologies and their application to improve social inclusion, public services, and quality of life.

The International Telecommunications Union's World Summit on the Information Society in Geneva and Tunis (2003 and 2005) has led to some policy and application areas where the action is required. These include: promotion of ICTs for development, information and communication infrastructure, access to information and knowledge, capacity building, building confidence and security in the use of ICTs, enabling environment, etc. As the access to electronic information resources increased at the beginning of the 21st century, special attention was extended from the information society to the knowledge society.

The notion of human rights gained traction throughout the world.

Human rights are moral principles or norms that describe certain standards for treating humans and are regularly protected as legal rights in national and international law. They are commonly understood as inalienable fundamental rights which are inherent in all human beings regardless of their nation, location, language, religion, ethnic origin, or any other status. They are applicable everywhere and at all times in the sense of being universal, and they are egalitarian in the sense of being the same for everyone. They impose an obligation on people to respect the human rights of others. The doctrine of human rights has been highly influential within international law and in global and regional institutions.

Many of the basic ideas that animated the human rights movement developed in the aftermath of the Second World War and the atrocities of the Holocaust and culminating in the adoption of the Universal Declaration of Human Rights by the United Nations General Assembly in Paris in 1948. Ancient people did not have the same modern-day conception of universal human rights. The original human rights discourse was the debate over the concept of natural rights, which appeared as part of the medieval natural law tradition that became prominent during the Enlightenment. It included such philosophers as John Locke, Francis Hutcheson, and Jean-Jacques Burlamaqui, and featured prominently in the political discourse of the American Revolution and the French Revolution. From this foundation, the modern human rights arguments emerged over the latter half of the 20th century, possibly as a reaction to slavery, torture, genocide, and war crimes, as a realization of inherent human vulnerability and a precondition for the possibility of a just society.

Eleanor Roosevelt holds the Universal Declaration of Human Rights

Women's rights are the gender-specific human rights and entitlements claimed by women and girls worldwide. In some places, these rights are institutionalized or supported by law, local custom, and behavior, whereas in other areas, they may be ignored or suppressed. Women's rights include, though are not limited to, the right: to bodily integrity and autonomy, to vote, to hold public office, to work, to birth control, to have an abortion, to be free from rape, to fair wages or equal pay, to own property, to education, to serve in the military or be conscripted, to enter into legal contracts, and marital and parental rights.

The term "White Australia Policy" comprises various historical policies that intentionally favored immigrants to Australia from other English-speaking countries, and, to a lesser extent, from certain European countries, over aboriginal people. The term, although widely used, is a misnomer, as many white ethnic groups (especially those from Eastern and Southern Europe) received unfavorable treatment under the policy. This was an attempt by Australians to help shape their own identity after the federation. The policy was enacted in 1901, soon after the Federation of Australia, and was progressively dismantled between 1949 and 1973.

Increased interactions among diverse peoples sometimes led to the formation of new cultural identities and exclusionary reactions.

Various modern cultural studies and social theories have investigated cultural identity. Cultural identities are influenced by several different factors, such as: religion, ancestry, skin color, language, class, education, profession, skill, family, and politics.

Négritude is a literary and ideological philosophy, developed by francophone African intellectuals, writers and politicians, in France during the 1930s. The term was meant to be provocative. It takes its roots from the Latin "niger," which was used exclusively in a racist context within France.

Xenophobia is the fear of that which is perceived to be foreign or strange. Xenophobia can manifest itself in many ways involving the relations and perceptions of an ingroup towards an outgroup, including a fear of losing identity, suspicion of its activities, aggression, and desire to secure a presumed cultural purity. Another form of racism is an uncritical representation of another culture in which an unreal quality is ascribed to a culture.

Racism consists of beliefs and practices that seek to justify, or cause, the unequal distribution of privileges or rights among different racial groups. Modern variants are often based on social perceptions of biological differences between people. These can take the form of social actions, practices or beliefs, or political systems that consider different races to be ranked as inherently superior or inferior to each other based on presumed shared inheritable traits, abilities, or qualities. It may also hold that members of different races should be treated differently.

Among the questions of how to define racism are whether to include forms of discrimination that are unintentional, such as making assumptions about preferences or abilities of others based on racial stereotypes; whether to include symbolic or institutionalized forms of discrimination, such as the circulation of ethnic stereotypes through the media; and whether to include the socio-political dynamics of social stratification that sometimes have a racial component.

In sociology and psychology, some definitions of racism include only consciously malignant forms of discrimination. Some definitions of racism also include discriminatory behaviors and beliefs based on cultural, national, ethnic, caste, or religious stereotypes. While race and ethnicity are considered to be separate phenomena in contemporary social science, the two terms have a long history of equivalence in widespread usage and older social science literature. Racism and racial discrimination are often used to describe discrimination on an ethnic or cultural basis, independent of whether these differences are described as racial.

Believers developed new forms of spirituality and chose to emphasize particular aspects of practice within existing faiths.

"The New Age" is a term applied to a range of spiritual or religious beliefs and practices that developed in Western nations during the 1970s. Precise scholarly definitions of the movement differ in their emphasis, largely as a result of its highly eclectic structure. Although analytically the movement is often considered to be religious, those who were involved in it typically prefer the designation of "spiritual" and rarely use the term "New Age" themselves. The New Age movement drew heavily upon some older traditions, in particular, the occultist current of the eighteenth century.

A meeting of the New World Alliance, America's first national "New Age" political organization

Several mid-20th-century influences, such as the UFO cults of the 1950s, the Counterculture of the 1960s, and the Human Potential Movement, also exerted a strong influence on the early development of the New Age movement. Although the exact origins of the movement remain contested, it is agreed that it developed in the 1970s, at which time it was centered largely in the United Kingdom. It expanded and grew in the 1980s and 1990s, in particular within the United States.

Popular and consumer culture became global.

In the aftermath of World War I, the world started experiencing a second major period of globalization (the first period had begun in the 18th century and had been interrupted by the outbreak of the war). The United States gained a dominant world position in the wake of World War I, and therefore this process of globalization was largely Americanization. Other prevalent emerging issues of the post-World War I era were dictatorships, terrorism, and the spread of nuclear weapons. Also, there were many smaller-scale wars and violent conflicts taking place around the world, often caused or exacerbated by resource scarcity or ethnic conflicts.

Popular culture is the entirety of ideas, perspectives, attitudes, images, and other phenomena that are within the mainstream of a given culture. Heavily influenced by mass media, this collection of ideas permeates the everyday lives of its society. The most common pop culture categories are: entertainment (movies, music, TV), sports, news (as in people/places in the news), politics, fashion or clothes, technology, and slang.

Popular culture is often viewed as being trivial and "dumbed down" to find consensual acceptance throughout the population. As a result, it comes under heavy criticism from various non-mainstream sources (most notably religious groups and countercultural groups), who deem it superficial, consumerist, sensationalist or corrupt. The term "popular culture" was coined in the 19th century, though some argue that it was created earlier. Traditionally, popular culture was associated with poor education and the lower classes, as opposed to the official culture and higher education of the upper classes. The distinction from "official culture" became more pronounced towards the end of the 19th century.

From the end of World War II, following major cultural and social changes brought by mass media innovations, the meaning of popular culture began to overlap with those of mass culture, media culture, image culture, consumer culture, and culture for mass consumption. Popular culture changes constantly and occurs uniquely in place and time. It forms currents and eddies and represents a complex of mutually interdependent perspectives and values that influence society and its institutions in various ways.

Sports were more widely practiced and reflected national and social aspirations.

Some historians assert that team sports, as we know them today, are primarily an invention of Western culture. The traditional team sports are seen as springing from Europe, primarily the British Empire. This discounts some of the ancient Asian games of cooperation (e.g., polo, numerous martial arts forms and various, now assimilated, football varieties), as well as American sports (e.g., lacrosse). European colonialism certainly helped spread particular games around the world. The Olympic Games also ensured standardization when rules for similar games around the world were merged. Regardless of game origins, the Industrial Revolution and mass production brought increased leisure-time, which allowed individuals the freedom to engage in playing or observing spectator sports, as well as less elitism in, and greater accessibility of, sports of many kinds. With the advent of mass media and global communication, professionalism became prevalent in sports, and this furthered popularity of sports in general.

Several English schools, colleges, and universities, such as Winchester and Eton, introduced variants of football and other sports for their pupils. These were described at the time as "innocent and lawful," certainly in comparison with the rougher rural games. With the onset of the Industrial Revolution and urbanization, rural games were introduced to the new urban centers and came under the influence of the middle and upper classes. The rules and regulations for specific games devised at English institutions began to be applied to the broader game, with governing bodies in England being set up for some sports by the end of the 19th century.

The rising influence of the upper class also produced an emphasis on the amateur and the spirit of "fair play." The Industrial Revolution also brought with it increasing mobility and created the opportunity for universities in Britain and elsewhere to compete against one another in sporting events. This sparked increasing attempts to unify and reconcile various games in England, leading to the establishment of the Football Association in London, the first governing body in football (soccer).

England National Football Team

Changes in communication and transportation technology enabled the widespread diffusion of music and film.

The 20th century saw a revolution in music as the radio gained popularity worldwide, and new media were developed to record and distribute music. Music performances became increasingly visual with the broadcast and recording of music videos and concerts. Music of all kinds also became increasingly portable. Headphones allowed people sitting next to each other to listen to entirely different music or share the same music.

Twentieth-century music brought new freedom and wide experimentation with new musical styles and forms that challenged the conventions of the music of earlier periods. The invention of musical amplification and electronic instruments, especially the synthesizer, in the mid-20th century revolutionized popular music and accelerated the development of new forms of music, like reggae.

The history of film began in the 1890s when motion picture cameras were invented, and film production companies started to be established. Because of the limits of technology, films of the 1890s were under a minute long, and until 1927, motion pictures were produced without sound. The first decade of motion picture saw film moving from a novelty to an established large-scale entertainment industry. The films became several minutes long and consisted of several shots. The first rotating camera for taking panning shots was built in 1897.

Most forms of popular music express the realities of being poor, conflict, injustice, and life in the world for the ordinary person, just like the realist painters did. "Reggae" – a word derived from the lexicon of poverty "ragged" – is a genre of music that emerged in post-colonial Jamaica in the 1960s. Its litany includes songs about racism, slavery, the effects of poverty, and songs about romantic love. Reggae became popular around the world, particularly with Bob Marley and Jimmy Cliff, peaking in the 70s and 80s.

Spin-off musical movements developed in other regions. Young white musicians from the impoverished neighborhoods of Britain collaborated with Caribbean immigrants to create fusion music genres, like Sca and Punk. These also carried counter-culture political messages and songs about poverty. Punk carried the rebellion to the extreme with staged antisocial behavior and wild clothing and hairstyles. When a member of the band Clash was asked during an interview in Toronto in 1979 what he thought of the damage the fans had done to the auditorium, his response was to count the demolished seats and comment: "Only twenty, that's all – there's only twenty real rock fans in this whole city!"

The first film studios were built in 1897. Special effects were introduced into film continuously, and sequenced action (moving from one sequence into another) began to be used. In 1900, continuity of action across successive shots was achieved, and the first close-up shot was introduced. Most films of this period were what came to be called "chase films." Overall, from about 1910 on, American films had the largest share of the market in Australia and all European countries except France.

1920 film poster

Notes for active learning

Europe

Major historical events of the period:

1914–1918: World War I

1917: The Russian Revolution

1932–1933: USSR creates the devastating "Holodomor" famine in Ukraine

1933: Nazis rise to power in Germany

1936: Francisco Franco becomes fascist Spanish head of state after the Spanish Civil War

1939–1945: World War II

1989: Berlin Wall falls

1991: Dissolution of the Soviet Union

1999: The European Union is established

PERIOD 4: Post-1900 C.E.

EUROPE

New scientific paradigms transformed human understanding of the world.

The scientific revolution established science as a source of the growth of knowledge. During the 19th century, the practice of science became professional and institutionalized in ways that continued throughout the 20th century. As the role of scientific knowledge grew, it was incorporated into many aspects of the functioning of nation-states. The history of science is marked by a chain of advances in technology and knowledge that have always complemented each other. Technological innovations brought about discoveries and were bred by other discoveries, which inspired new possibilities and approaches to longstanding science issues. The beginning of the 20th century brought the start of a revolution in physics. The long-held theories of Newton were shown not to be correct in all circumstances. Beginning in 1900, Max Planck, Albert Einstein, Niels Bohr, and others developed quantum theories to explain various anomalous experimental results by introducing discrete energy levels.

The year 1879 is commonly seen as the beginning of psychology as an independent field of study. In that year, Wilhelm Wundt founded the first laboratory dedicated exclusively to psychological research (in Leipzig). Sigmund Freud's influence was enormous in the foundation of scientific psychology. However, the 20th century saw a rejection of Freud's theories as being too unscientific and a reaction against Edward Titchener's atomistic theory of the mind. Titchener brought Wund's structural-functionalist approach to psychology to America and attempted to create a praxis between applied psychology and theoretical psychology (which is the norm today). As such, he criticized Freud as being unscientific in his approach and was considered by Freud to be his main adversary.

This led to the formulation of behaviorism by John B. Watson, which was popularized by B.F. Skinner. Behaviorism proposed limiting the psychological study to overt behavior since that could be reliably measured. Scientific knowledge of the mind was considered too metaphysical, hence impossible to achieve. The final decades of the 20th century saw the rise of a new interdisciplinary approach to studying human psychology, known collectively as cognitive science.

Cognitive science considered the mind as a subject for investigation, using the tools of psychology, linguistics, computer science, philosophy, and neurobiology. New methods of visualizing the activity of the brain, such as PET scans and CAT scans, began to exert their influence as well, leading some researchers to investigate the mind by investigating the brain, rather than cognition. These new forms of investigation assumed a wide understanding of the human mind as possible, and that such an understanding might be applied to other research domains, such as artificial intelligence.

Albert Einstein, physicist

Albert Einstein published the *Theory of Relativity* in 1905. The series of relativity theories, which includes the general and then special relativity, explains the relationships between mass and energy, time and space, and gravity. Finlay-Freundlich wanted to prove Einstein's theory by demonstrating how the immense gravity of the Sun can bend light from distant stars. To measure this, he needed a solar eclipse to reduce the light coming from the Sun. The only opportunity for this in 1914 was in Russia, but his presence there coincided with the outbreak of the First World War. Being a German, Finlay-Freundlich was arrested and detained when the war broke out, and all of his photographic equipment was confiscated.

...ely separate field of physics developed between 1900 and 1905, mainly by the research of Max Planck and Albert Einstein. While it explains the interactions of sub-atomic particles, according to most physicists, its principles do not agree with the physics of larger objects. Hence, scientists have been searching for a unifying theory, a so-called "theory of everything," with the string theory emerging as a potential unifier.

During the first half of the 20th century, cosmologists began to seriously investigate the most fundamental question of all: "What created everything that exists?" Several competing theories were developed to explain the origin of the universe. In the 1920s, a Catholic priest who was also a scientist, named Georges Lemaitre, tried to reconcile the biblical explanation for creation with existing empirical knowledge. In the process, he developed the explanation of the creation of the Universe called the "Big Bang Theory," and it is the accepted theory today. Lemaitre used the evidence that the Universe is expanding, which had been confirmed by Edwin Hubble, and regressed the expansion to what he called a "primeval atom." The term "Big Bang" was a term of derision given to Lemaitre's theory by one of its greatest detractors, British cosmologist Fred Hoyle. Hoyle, along with Einstein, believed that the Universe existed in a "steady state" and that this was not incompatible with its expansion. He rejected the idea that the universe could have been created out of nothing and thought this was illogical.

The aerial bombing by the UK and the U.S. of Dresden, the capital of the German state of Saxony, took place in four raids between February 13 and 15, 1945. 722 heavy bombers of the British Royal Air Force and 527 of the United States Army Air Forces dropped more than 3,900 tons of high-explosive bombs and incendiary devices on the city. Approximately 25,000 people were killed. Germany surrendered three months later. German propaganda following the bombing and post-war discussions on whether it was justified led to the bombing becoming one of the moral *causes célèbres* (popular causes) of the war. The United States dropped atomic bombs on the Japanese cities of Hiroshima and Nagasaki in August 1945, during the final stage of the Second World War. The two bombings, which killed at least 129,000 people, remain the only use of nuclear weapons in the history of warfare.

During the Cold War, the world's two great superpowers at the time, the Soviet Union and the United States of America spent large proportions of their GDPs on developing military technologies. The drive to place objects in orbit stimulated space research and started the Space Race. By the end of the 1960s, both countries regularly deployed satellites. Both the United States and the Soviet Union began to develop anti-satellite weapons to blind or destroy each other's satellites. Laser weapons, kamikaze-style satellites and orbital nuclear explosions were researched with varying levels of success. Spy satellites were, and continue to be, used to monitor the dismantling of military assets by arms control treaties signed between the two superpowers.

The superpowers developed ballistic missiles to enable their nuclear weapons to have a global reach, without the need to maintain nuclear weapons at or near each other's borders. A significant portion of military technology relates to transportation, allowing troops and weaponry to be moved from their origins to the front. As rocket science developed, the range of missiles increased, and intercontinental ballistic missiles were created, which could strike virtually any target on Earth in a timeframe measured in minutes rather than hours or days. To cover large distances, ballistic missiles are usually launched into sub-orbital spaceflight.

Europe dominated the global political order at the beginning of the twentieth century. However, both land-based and transoceanic empires gave way to new forms of trans-regional political organization by the century's end.

The 20th century opened with Europe at an apex of wealth and power, with much of the world under its direct colonial control or its indirect domination. As the century unfolded, the global system dominated by rival powers was subjected to severe strains and ultimately yielded to a more fluid structure of independent nations, organized on Western models.

United Nations charter logo

Wars of unparalleled scope and devastation catalyzed this transformation. World War I destroyed many of Europe's empires and monarchies and and weakened both Britain and France. In its aftermath, powerful ideologies arose. Ongoing national rivalries, exacerbated by the economic turmoil of the Great Depression, helped precipitate World War II. The militaristic dictatorships of Europe and Japan pursued an ultimately doomed course of imperialist expansionism. Their defeat opened the way for the advance of communism into Central Europe, Yugoslavia, Bulgaria, Romania, Albania, China, North Vietnam, and North Korea. After World War II ended in 1945, the United Nations was founded in the hope of allaying conflicts among nations and preventing future wars.

The war had left two nations, the United States and the Soviet Union, with the principal power to guide international affairs. Each was suspicious of the other and feared a global spread of the other's political-economic model. This led to the Cold War, a forty-five-year stand-off between the United States, the Soviet Union, and their respective allies. The Cold War lasted until the 1990s when the Soviet Union's communist system began to collapse because it was unable to compete economically with the United States and Western Europe. The Soviet

Union's Central European satellites reasserted their national sovereignty, and in 1991, the Soviet Union disintegrated.

In the early postwar decades, the African and Asian colonies of the Belgian, British, Dutch, French, and other West European empires won their formal independence. These nations faced challenges in the form of neocolonialism, poverty, illiteracy, and endemic tropical diseases. Many Western and Central European nations gradually formed a political and economic community, the European Union, which expanded eastward to include former Soviet satellites and former republics of the USSR.

Colonial pressures helped pushed the world to war.

In Europe, Germany and Great Britain became rivals. Germany attempted to join the colonization game late in history and did establish colonies in Africa, China, and the South Pacific, which abutted British colonial territories in those areas. Germany and France – which was Britain's ally – had a mutual mistrust originating from the Franco-Prussian war, which had established Germany as a nation. One of the German government's earliest goals was to create a navy that could rival the British navy. They almost succeeded in it by the time World War I began.

Rising nationalism and increasing national awareness were among the many causes of World War I, the first of two wars to involve many major world powers, including Germany, France, Italy, Japan, Russia/USSR, the United States, and the British Empire. Civil wars occurred in many nations.

The United Kingdom drew reinforcements from Oceania.

The Australian and New Zealand Army Corps (ANZAC) was a First World War army corps of the Mediterranean Expeditionary Force. It was formed in Egypt in 1915 and saw its primary action in the Battle of Gallipoli, where the Entente powers sought to capture the strategic Dardanelles waterway. The corps disbanded in 1916, following the Allied evacuation of the Gallipoli peninsula and the formation of I Anzac Corps and II Anzac Corps. Following the evacuation of Gallipoli in November of 1915, the Australian and New Zealand units reassembled in Egypt. During World War II, the Australian I Corps HQ moved to Greece. As the corps also controlled the New Zealand 2nd Division, it was officially renamed ANZAC Corps. The Battle of Greece was over in weeks, and the corps HQ left Greece, with the name ANZAC Corps no longer being used.

An economically and militarily exhausted Tsarist Russia was toppled by a revolution.

The Russian Empire existed from 1721 until it was overthrown by the short-lived liberal February Revolution in 1917. At the beginning of the 19th century, the Russian Empire extended from the Arctic Ocean in the north to the Black Sea in the south and from the Baltic Sea in the west to the Pacific Ocean, and (until 1867) into Alaska in North America, in the east. Russia was an absolute monarchy until the Revolution of 1905 when it became a constitutional monarchy. The Empire collapsed during the February Revolution of 1917, largely the result of discontent at home with the war effort abroad.

Demonstration of Putilov workers during the February Revolution

Internal and external factors contributed to the collapse of the tsarist regime in 1917. World War I was a necessary external precondition because it created the internal conditions for the rebellion. Industrial workers and rural peasants suffered intolerable conditions that were triggered by the war. Peasants who were conscripted into the Imperial Russian Army lost their land to landlords who expropriated it while they were serving at the front. Food prices rose greatly, and food shortages had developed by 1917, due to a large number of agricultural workers having been conscripted to fight in the war.

Industrial workers were becoming cognizant of their importance for the first time, as they recognized that the government was dependent on their labor for the production of weapons and ammunition. However, regular citizens were hit the hardest by the food shortage, and they began to realize that the wages they received were not sufficient to weather the storm like the First World War. This made it easy for communists to agitate among the factory workers in major cities and to create guerrilla groups out of peasants and workers. The food shortages led to riots in Petrograd (the capital of Russia at the time) that were organized and promoted by communists. Tsar Nicolas was a relatively young leader and did not react adequately or anticipate the seriousness of the communist threat.

Emerging ideologies of anti-imperialism contributed to the dissolution of empires and the restructuring of states.

The notion of anti-imperialism was used in the context of nationalist movements, who wanted to secede from an empire or a multi-ethnic sovereign state. The term gained wide currency after the Second World War and at the onset of the Cold War as political movements in colonies of European powers promoted national sovereignty. Some anti-imperialist groups, such as in Guevarism, opposed the United States and supported the power of the Soviet Union. In Maoist doctrine, this was criticized as social-imperialism. In the Arab and Muslim world, the term is often used in the context of Anti-Zionist nationalist and religious movements.

In Das Kapital, published in the mid-19th century, Karl Marx suggested that imperialism was part of the prehistory of the capitalist mode of production. Lenin defined imperialism as the highest stage of capitalism, the economic stage in which monopoly-finance capital becomes the dominant application of capital. As such, financial and economic circumstances compelled national governments and private business corporations to worldwide competition for control of natural resources and human labor using colonialism. The Leninist views of imperialism and related theories such as dependency theory address the economic dominance and exploitation of a country, rather than the military and the political dominance of a people, their country and its natural resources. Hence, the primary purpose of imperialism is economic exploitation, rather than mere control of either a country or of a region.

In the 20th century, the USSR represented themselves as the foremost enemy of imperialism, and thus politically and materially supported Third World revolutionary organizations who fought for national independence; as such, the USSR sent military advisors to Ethiopia, Angola, Egypt, and Afghanistan. Nonetheless, the USSR behaved as an imperialist power when it asserted sphere-of-influence dominance upon Afghanistan and dominated the countries of Eastern Europe, the Baltic states and the Caucasus, as accorded in the Yalta Agreement (February 1945) during the Second World War (1939–1945).

Transnational movements sought to unite people across national boundaries.

Communism is a social, political, and economic ideology and a movement whose ultimate goal is the establishment of communist society, which is a socioeconomic order structured upon the common ownership of the means of production and the absence of social classes, money, and the state. Lenin brought Marxism into the 20th century, with his original theoretical contributions such as his analysis of imperialism, principles of party organization, and the implementation of socialism through revolution and reform after that. As the official ideology of the Soviet Union, Marxism-Leninism was adopted by Communist parties worldwide with variation in the local application. The economy under such a government is primarily coordinated through a state economic plan with varying degrees of market distribution.

Since the fall of the Soviet Union and Eastern Bloc countries, many communist parties of the world today continue to use Marxism-Leninism as their method of understanding the conditions of their respective countries. While this ideology seems innocuous in theory, its practical application has led to despotism, poverty, and murder. Since the Bolshevik Revolution, communist governments have murdered millions of their citizens—although a completely accurate figure is impossible to determine.

Spanish fascism rose, avoided World War II, and abated.

*Francisco Franco Bahamonde,
Spanish general*

Francisco Franco Bahamonde was a Spanish general and the head of state in Spain from 1936 until he died in 1975. Coming from a military family background, he became the youngest general in Spain and one of the youngest generals in Europe in the 1920s. Franco led a series of politically-motivated violent acts, mostly against political and ideological enemies, including but not limited to concentration camps, forced labor, and executions, which resulted in an estimated 200,000 to 400,000 deaths. Franco's Spain maintained an official policy of neutrality during World War II, except the Blue Division. However, he actively allowed the Nazi Luftwaffe to practice their techniques in the Spanish Civil War, which is part of the reason why many Luftwaffe pilots had already gained invaluable combat experience by the time World War II began.

By the 1950s, the nature of Franco's regime changed from an extreme form of dictatorship to a semi-pluralist authoritarian system. During the Cold War, Franco appeared as one of the world's foremost anti-communist figures; consequently, his regime was assisted by the United States, was asked to join the United Nations, and came under NATO's protection. By the 1960s, Spain saw progressive economic development and timid democratic improvements.

Vast numbers of refugees fled Nazi Germany.

According to the Geneva Convention on Refugees, a refugee is a person who lives outside his or her country of citizenship because he or she has well-founded grounds to fear persecution because of his or her race, religion, nationality, membership of a particular social group or political opinion, and is unable to obtain sanctuary from his or her home country or, owing to such fear, is unwilling to avail himself or herself of the protection of that country. Between the Nazi rise to power in 1933 and Nazi Germany's surrender in 1945, more than 340,000 Jews emigrated from Germany and Austria. Tragically, nearly 100,000 of them found refuge in countries subsequently conquered by Germany. German authorities deported and killed the vast majority of them.

Military conflicts occurred on an unprecedented global scale.

In Western Europe, since the late 18th century, more than 150 conflicts and about 600 battles have taken place. During the 20th century, the war resulted in a dramatic intensification of the pace of social change and was a crucial catalyst for the emergence of the Left as a force to be reckoned with. Recent rapid increases in the technologies of war, and therefore in its destructiveness, have caused widespread public concern and have, in all probability, prevented the outbreak of a nuclear World War III. At the end of each of the last two World Wars, concerted and popular efforts were made to come to a greater understanding of the underlying dynamics of war and to reduce or even eliminate it altogether hopefully. The first example of this was the League of Nations, proposed by U.S. President Woodrow Wilson. Unfortunately, the world was not yet ready for such an international organization, as the Armistice of 1918 did not fully resolve the underlying tensions that caused the First World War.

Shortly after World War II, as a token of support for this concept, most nations joined the United Nations. During this same post-war period, to further delegitimize war as an acceptable and logical extension of foreign policy, most national governments also renamed their Ministries or Departments of War to Ministries or Departments of Defense. The Human Security Report of 2005 documented a significant decline in the number and severity of armed conflicts that had taken place since the end of the Cold War in the early 1990s. However, the evidence examined in the 2008 edition of the Center for International Development and Conflict Management's Peace and Conflict study indicated that the overall decline in conflicts had stalled.

Cold War between superpowers fueled the arms race.

The Cold War caused an arms race and increasing competition between the two most powerful countries to emerge after World War Two, the Soviet Union and the United States. This competition included the development and improvement of nuclear weapons and the Space Race.

As the United Kingdom relinquished India and Hong Kong, overseas subjects migrated.

India, Britain's most valuable and populous colony, achieved independence as part of a larger decolonization movement in which the British Empire granted independence to most of its territories. For many, the political transfer of Hong Kong to China in 1997 marked the end of the British Empire. People migrated massively towards the imperial metropoles, mainly for economic reasons.

The dissolution of the Soviet Union effectively ended the Cold War.

The dissolution of the Soviet Union was formally enacted on December 26, 1991, as a result of the declaration of the Supreme Soviet of the Soviet Union, acknowledging the independence of the former Soviet republics and creating the Commonwealth of Independent States (CIS);. However, five of the signatories officially ratified the agreement at a later date and the three Baltic States (Latvia, Lithuania, and Estonia) never became members of the CIS. On the previous day, Soviet President Mikhail Gorbachev resigned, declared his office void, and handed over his powers as the leader of the Soviet Union to the Russian President, Boris Yeltsin. That evening, the Soviet flag was lowered from the Kremlin for the last time and replaced with the pre-revolutionary Russian flag.

Russian President Boris Yeltsin (left) with
U.S. President Bill Clinton (right)

Previously, from August to December, all the individual republics, including Russia itself, had seceded from the Union. The week before the Union's formal dissolution, eleven republics—all except the Baltic states and Georgia—signed the Alma-Ata Protocol formally establishing the CIS and declaring that the Soviet Union had ceased to exist. The dissolution of the USSR also signaled the end of the Cold War. The Revolutions of 1989 and the end of the Soviet Union led to the end of the decades-long hostility between the North Atlantic Treaty Organization (NATO) and the Warsaw Pact, the defining feature of the Cold War.

More movements used violence against civilians to achieve political aims.

The Irish Republican Army (IRA) is any of several armed movements in Northern Ireland in the 20th and 21st centuries dedicated to Irish republicanism: the belief that all of Ireland should be an independent republic. The original Irish Republican Army was formed in 1917 from Irish Volunteers who refused to enlist in the British Army during World War I. Most Irish people dispute the claims of more recently created organizations that insist they are the only legitimate descendants of the original IRA, often referred to as the "Old IRA."

The first split came after the Anglo-Irish Treaty in 1921, with supporters of the Treaty forming the nucleus of the National Army of the newly created Irish Free State, while the anti-treaty forces continued to use the name Irish Republican Army. After the end of the Irish Civil War, the IRA was around in one form or another for forty years, until it split into the Official IRA and the Provisional IRA in 1969.

ETA is an armed Basque nationalist and separatist organization in Northern Spain and Southwestern France. It was founded in 1959 and has since evolved from a group promoting traditional Basque culture to a paramilitary group intending to gain independence for the Greater Basque Country. ETA is the main group within the Basque National Liberation Movement and is the most important participant in the Basque conflict. The group is proscribed as a terrorist group by Spain, the United Kingdom, France, the United States, and the European Union. There are more than 400 members of ETA imprisoned in Spain, France, and other countries. On September 5, 2010, ETA declared a new ceasefire that is still in effect, and on October 20, 2011, ETA announced a definitive cessation of its armed activity. In 2012, it was reported that the group was ready to negotiate an end to its operations and disband completely.

States responded in a variety of ways to the economic challenges of the twentieth century.

The 20th century's initial climate of optimism was soon violently dismembered in the trenches of the Western Front. During World War I, production in Britain, Germany, and France was almost entirely refocused to support the war effort. In 1917, Russia descended into a revolution led by Vladimir Lenin, who promoted Marxist theory and sought to collectivize the means of production as a way to establish a state-based on equality rather than competition. After World War, I, Europe, and the Soviet Union lay in ruins, and the British Empire was in decline, which left the United States as the preeminent global economic power.

Before World War II, American economists had played a minor role. During this time, institutional economists had been largely critical of the "American Way" of life, especially the conspicuous consumption that characterized the Roaring Twenties before the Wall Street Crash of 1929. The globalization era began with the end of World War II and the rise of the U.S. as the world's leading economic power, along with the United Nations. To prevent another global depression, the victorious U.S. forgave Germany its war debts and used its surpluses to help rebuild Europe and encourage the reindustrialization of Germany and Japan. In the 1960s, it changed its role in recycling global surpluses.

John Kenneth Galbraith, Canadian and American politician and economist

After World War II, Canadian-born John Kenneth Galbraith (1908–2006) became one of the standard-bearers for pro-active government and liberal-democrat politics. In The Affluent Society (1958), Galbraith argued that voters reaching a certain material wealth begin to vote against the common good. He also argued that the "conventional wisdom" of the conservative consensus was not enough to solve the problems of social inequality. In an age of big business, he argued, it was unrealistic to think of markets of the classical kind. They set prices and used advertising to create artificial demand for their products, which distorted people's real preferences.

Consumer preferences came to reflect those of corporations, and the economy as a whole was geared to irrational goals. In Economics and the Public Purpose (1973), Galbraith advocated "new socialism" as the solution: nationalizing military production and public services, such as health care, and introducing disciplined salary and price controls to reduce inequality.

Introductory university economics courses began to present economic theory as a unified whole in what is referred to as the neoclassical synthesis. "Positive economics" became the term created to describe certain trends and laws of economics that could be objectively observed and described in a value-free way, separate from normative economic evaluation and judgments.

The Soviet Union proposed five-year economic plans, wielded artificial food shortages to suppress populations.

The Soviet Union's first five-year plan, implemented between 1928 and 1932, was a list of economic goals, created by General Secretary Joseph Stalin, based on his policy of "Socialism in One Country." In 1929, Stalin edited the plan to include the creation of "kolkhoz," collective farming systems that stretched over thousands of acres of land and had hundreds of peasants working on them. The creation of collective farms essentially destroyed the kulaks (middle management in the rural gentry) as a class. Also, it brought about the slaughter of millions of farm animals that peasants preferred to kill as opposed to give up to the gigantic farms.

The disruption of agriculture was deliberately used by the Soviet regime to create famine in Ukraine, Russia, Kazakhstan, and areas of the Northern Caucasus to ensure loyalty in those regions. Ukraine had its own culture, separate from Russia, and many Ukrainians, especially in the western part of the country, did not want to be a part of the Soviet Union. In the winter of 1932-33, the Soviet Union deliberately created a devastating famine in Ukraine by confiscating all of the output of Ukrainian farms. The event is called "Holodomor" in Ukrainian, meaning, roughly, "to exterminate using hunger." This was undertaken to terrorize Ukrainians into submitting to Soviet rule. It is impossible to know exactly how many Ukrainians perished in the Holodomor, but most estimates put the number between 2.4 and 7.5 million people. The Soviet government sold the confiscated Ukrainian grain to wealthy Western nations in order to boost its cash reserves.

The introduction of collective farms allowed peasants to use tractors for farming the land, unlike before when most had been too poor to own a tractor. Government-owned machine and tractor stations were set up throughout the USSR, and peasants were allowed to use these public tractors to farm the land, which increased the food output per peasant. Peasants were allowed to sell any surplus food from the land.

The fear of invasion from the West left the Soviets feeling the need to rapidly industrialize to be able to compete with its Western allies if need be. At the same time, as the war scare of 1927, dissatisfaction among the peasantry, due to the famine of the early 1920s and their growing mistreatment, was emerging in the Soviet Union. Also during this time, the secret police, the GPU, had begun rounding up political dissenters in the Soviet Union. All these tensions had the potential to destroy the young Soviet Union and forced Joseph Stalin to introduce rapid industrialization of heavy industry so that the Soviet Union could address these threats if needed.

Thatcher's leadership changed the UK economy.

Liberalization led to dramatic improvements in Great Britain after Margaret Thatcher and her Conservative Party took office in 1979. The assumption in all developed nations today is that governments derive their economic policies from "Keynesian economics," a field of economics created by British economist John Maynard Keynes. However, British Prime Minister Margaret Thatcher believed in a different, and often denigrated, approach to economics: "Austrian Economics," which was theorized by Ludwig Von Mises. As a result, when Margaret Thatcher's Conservative Party assumed office in Britain in 1979, it pursued liberalization policies, which confused most people because the policies were often contrary to what was expected. However, the liberalization Thatcher pursued did lead to the restoration of the British economy.

In 1979, Britain—the former pre-eminent global power—was justifiably referred to as "the sick man of Europe." In Lady Thatcher's own words during a retrospective interview, "Great Britain was a nation in decline but, what was even worse, they were *resigned* to it." Inflation and unemployment were extremely high, violence was rampant, and strikes were crippling the entire economy. The government was operating at a massive deficit, which meant that it could not afford to make any improvements to social services. There was a huge exodus of Britain's most talented people. The nadir was the infamous "Winter of Discontent" of 1978-79, when strikes, violence, and social collapse epitomized the decline of the once-proud nation. One example from the Winter of Discontent illustrates just how low Britain had sunk by then: bodies remained unburied

Margaret Thatcher,
British Prime Minister (1979–1990)

for two weeks as public gravediggers joined the pervasive strikes and plans were made to dispose of the backlog of dead bodies at sea.

Thatcher's government immediately set out to reduce taxation and cut government spending (except in popular areas like health and defense). The top tax rate in 1979 was 83%, which was immediately reduced to 60%, despite the government's deficits, and further reduced later - as were the tax rates on the lowest income earners. Thatcher confronted labor unions, whose bosses she believed were abusive, bringing in a law which made it very difficult to create a closed shop union in Britain. At the same time, much of the coal mining industry in Wales and much of the manufacturing base in the north of England closed down. Unemployment spiked in many of the towns of South Wales (Swansea, Cardiff) and Northern England (Newcastle, Sunderland, Carlisle). Many of those towns have still not fully recovered.

Thatcher's government also initiated a massive campaign of privatization, reversing the nationalization of major industries her Labor Party predecessors had engaged in. For example, British Gas – the primary gas company – was sold off. This resulted in a short-term boon, as the controls on prices were still, largely, in place. However, over the longer term, gas prices for consumers rose and is a problem that persists to the current day.

Following Thatcher's liberal economic ideology, the right to carry passengers from point to point on the British Rail Network was privatized. However, the most expensive part of running rail services, infrastructure and maintenance, was left in the hands of the taxpayer-owned Network Rail. Further, the rail companies all competed for the highest-yield routes between major urban centers, leaving Network Rail to guarantee break-even subsidization of routes between cities where the profit margin was not as high. This resulted in profits for the private rail companies and losses for taxpayers as they were still responsible for maintaining the rail infrastructure.

When Thatcher resigned in 1990, Britain was competitive on a global scale once again. It had the second most powerful military in the world, the government was spending twice as much on health care and education (per capita, in real dollars) as it was in 1979, inflation was low. The real incomes of millions of the poorest British people were double what they had been in 1979. Taxation was far lower, the government was not running severe deficits, and there were very few strikes. However, most of these benefits were limited to the Southeast of England (the Thames-river Basin), the area around London. The British Economy, in many ways, is still experiencing a boom due to Thatcher's policies; however, the disparity in income between the Thames River Basin and the rest of the country has continued to grow. Therefore, there are still many questions surrounding the success or failure of the policies of economic liberalization Thatcher set in motion.

European Union is created to enhance cohesiveness.

The European Union (EU) is a politico-economic confederation of 28 member states that are located primarily in Europe. The EU operates through a system of supranational institutions and intergovernmental negotiated decisions by the member states. The institutions are: the European Parliament, the European Council, the Council of the European Union (which is informally known as the Council of Ministers), the European Commission, the Court of Justice of the European Union, the European Central Bank and the Court of Auditors. The European Parliament is elected every five years by EU citizens.

The EU has developed a single market through a standardized system of laws that apply to all member states. Within the Schengen Area, passport controls have been abolished. EU policies aim to ensure the free movement of people, goods, services, and capital; enact legislation in justice and home affairs; and maintain common policies on trade, agriculture, fisheries, and regional development. The monetary union was established in 1999 and came into full effect in 2002. It is currently composed of 19 member states that use the euro as their legal tender.

Notes for active learning

Major historical events of the period:

1952:   Egyptian Revolution of 1952

1954–1962:   The Algerian War of Independence

1960s–1970s: Accelerated rate of decolonization

1961–1974:   The Angolan War of Independence

1970s: Idi Amin of Uganda expels South Asians

1975–2002:   The Angolan Civil War

1967–1970:   The Biafran War (The Nigerian Civil War)

1994:   Rwandan Genocide

PERIOD 4: Post-1900 C.E.

AFRICA

Gold Coast subjects of the British crown agitated for independence.

The Gold Coast was a British colony on the Gulf of Guinea in West Africa that became the independent nation of Ghana in 1957. The first Europeans to arrive were the Portuguese, in 1471, who named the area "The Gold Coast" because of its large gold resources. The slave trade was the principal exchange in this colony for many years. By 1901, all of the Gold Coast was a British colony, with its kingdoms and tribes considered a single unit. The British exported a variety of natural resources such as gold, metal ores, diamonds, ivory, pepper, timber, grain, and cocoa.

The British colonists built railways and the complex transport infrastructure, which formed the basis for the transport infrastructure in modern-day Ghana. By 1945, the native population was demanding more autonomy in the wake of the end of the Second World War and the beginning of the decolonization process around the world. By 1956, British Togoland, the Ashanti protectorate, and the Fante protectorate had merged with the Gold Coast to create one colony, which became known as the Gold Coast. In 1957, the colony gained independence under the name of Ghana.

France and Portugal unsuccessfully attempted to prevent the independence of African colonies.

The Algerian War of Independence was a war between France and Algeria from 1954 to 1962, which led to Algeria gaining its independence from France. An important decolonization war, it was a complex conflict characterized by guerrilla warfare, terrorism, the use of torture by both sides and counter-terrorism operations. The conflict was also a civil war between loyalist Algerians, who supported a French Algeria and their insurrectionist Algerian nationalist counterparts. Started by members of the National Liberation Front (FLN) in 1954, the conflict shook the foundations of the weak and unstable French Fourth Republic and led to its replacement by the Fifth Republic, which had a stronger president, in the form of Charles de Gaulle. Although the military campaigns greatly weakened the FLN militarily, with most prominent FLN leaders killed or arrested, and terror attacks effectively stopped, the brutality of the methods employed failed to win hearts and minds in Algeria, alienated support in Metropolitan France and discredited French prestige abroad. After major demonstrations in favor of independence from the end of 1960 and the United Nations resolution recognizing the right to independence, De Gaulle decided to open a series of negotiations with the FLN. The planned withdrawal led to a state crisis, to various assassination attempts on de Gaulle, and some attempts at military coups. Upon Algeria's independence in 1962, 900,000 European-Algerians (Pieds-noirs) fled to France, in fear of the FLN's revenge. The French government was unprepared for the influx of refugees, which caused turmoil in France.

The Angolan War of Independence (1961–1974) began as an uprising against forced cotton cultivation. It became a multi-faction struggle for control of Portugal's overseas province of Angola between three nationalist movements and a separatist movement. The war ended when a leftist military coup overthrew Portugal's Estado Novo regime in Lisbon in April of 1974. The new regime immediately stopped all military action in the African colonies, declaring its intention to grant them independence without delay. In Angola, after the Portuguese had stopped the war, an armed conflict broke out among the nationalist movements. The war formally came to an end in January of 1975 when the Portuguese government, the National Union for the Total Independence of Angola, the Popular Movement for the Liberation of Angola and the National Liberation Front of Angola signed the Alvor Agreement.

Algeria's struggles for independence resulted in the large transfer of colonial subjects to France.

In Algeria, upon independence in 1962, 900,000 European-Algerians fled to France. Pied-Noir refers to people of French and other European (usually Spanish, Italian, Portuguese or Maltese) ancestry who were born or lived in French North Africa, namely French Algeria, the French protectorate in Morocco or the French protectorate of Tunisia.

More specifically, the term Pieds-Noirs is used for those European-descendent citizens who returned to mainland France as soon as Algeria gained independence, or in the months following. After Algeria became independent in 1962, about 800,000 Pieds-Noirs of French nationality were evacuated to mainland France while about 200,000 chose to remain in Algeria. Those who moved to France suffered ostracism from the Left for their perceived exploitation of native Muslims and were blamed by them for the war.

Images and reports of civilian suffering during the Biafran War shook the world.

The Nigerian Civil War, also known as the Biafran War, which occurred from 1967 to 1970, was a war fought to counter the secession of Biafra from Nigeria. Biafra represented the nationalist aspirations of the Igbo people, whose leadership felt they could no longer coexist with the Northern-dominated federal government. The conflict resulted from the political, economic, ethnic, cultural, and religious tensions that preceded Britain's formal decolonization of Nigeria from 1960–1963. Immediate causes of the war in 1966 included a military coup, a counter-coup, and persecution of Igbo living in Northern Nigeria. Control over oil production in the Niger Delta also played a vital strategic role.

Within a year, the Federal Military Government surrounded Biafra, capturing coastal oil facilities and the city of Port Harcourt. The blockade imposed during the ensuing stalemate led to severe famine and was used deliberately as a strategy of war. Over the two and half years of the war, about two million civilians died from starvation and disease. This famine entered the world's awareness of mid-1968 when images of malnourished and starving children suddenly saturated the mass media in Western countries. The plight of the starving Biafrans became a cause célèbre in foreign countries, enabling a significant rise in the funding and prominence of international non-governmental organizations.

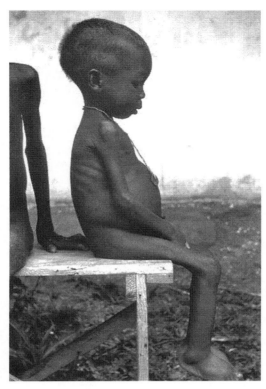

Starving girl during the Nigerian–Biafran War

Pan-Africanism surfaced as a unifying ideology for an oppressed people.

Pan-Africanism is an ideology and movement that encourages the solidarity of Africans worldwide. Based on the belief that unity is vital to economic, social, and political progress, it aims to unify people of African descent. The ideology asserts that the fate of all African peoples and countries are intertwined. As a philosophy, Pan-Africanism represents the aggregation of the historical, cultural, spiritual, artistic, scientific, and philosophical legacies of Africans from past times to the present. Pan-Africanism, as an ethical system, can trace its origins to ancient times, and it promotes values that are the product of African civilization and struggles against slavery, racism, colonialism, and neo-colonialism. In the United States, the term is closely associated with Afrocentrism, an ideology of African-American identity politics that emerged during the civil rights movement of the 1960s to 1970s.

African decolonization often led to violent social unrest and colonial population exodus.

Decolonization during the 1960s and 1970s often resulted in the mass exodus of European-descended settlers out of Africa—especially from North Africa, the Congo, Mozambique, and Angola. By the mid-1970s, Portugal lost its African territories, and nearly one million persons of Portuguese descent left those territories as destitute refugees. The Angolan Civil War (1975–2002), one of the largest and deadliest Cold War conflicts, erupted shortly after and spread out across the newly independent country. At least one million people were killed, four million were displaced internally, and another half-million fled as refugees.

In the 1970s, Uganda and other East African nations implemented racist policies that targeted the Asian population in the region. Idi Amin's anti-Asian policies in Uganda were among the most virulent, eventually resulting in the expulsion and ethnic cleansing of Uganda's Asian minority. Uganda's 80,000 Asians were mostly Indians born in the country. India had refused to accept them, and most of them were settled in the United Kingdom, Canada, and the United States.

In the aftermath of the 1994 Rwandan Genocide, over two million people fled into neighboring countries, particularly Zaire. The refugee camps were soon controlled by the former government and Hutu militants, who used them as bases to launch attacks against the new government in Rwanda. Little action was taken to resolve the situation, and the crisis did not end until Rwanda-supported rebels forced the refugees back across the border at the beginning of the First Congo War.

European countries bring water to Rwandan refugees

British helped lead criticism of Apartheid in South Africa through activism.

The Anti-Apartheid Movement (AAM), was a British organization that was at the center of the international movement opposing South Africa's system of apartheid and supporting South Africa's non-whites. The protests of 1968 comprised a worldwide escalation of social conflicts, predominantly characterized by popular rebellions against military and bureaucratic elites, who responded with an escalation of political repression.

AIDS/HIV and Ebola-ravaged Africa.

AIDS is a disease of the human immune system caused by the human immunodeficiency virus (HIV). HIV was causing an epidemic in southern Africa with primary modes of HIV transmission in sub-Saharan Africa being: unprotected sex, mother-to-child transmission (vertical transmission), and transfusions of HIV-infected blood. Many of the countries in sub-Saharan Africa are ravaged by poverty, and many people live on less than one

U.S. dollar per day. The poverty in these countries gives rise to many other factors that explain the high prevalence of AIDS.

The poorest people in most African countries suffer from malnutrition, lack of access to clean water, and have improper sanitation. Because of a lack of clean water, many people are plagued by intestinal parasites that significantly increase their chances of contracting HIV due to an already compromised immune system. Malaria, a disease still rampant in Africa, also increases the risk of contracting HIV. Many of the factors seen in Africa are also present in Latin America and the Caribbean and contribute to the high rates of infections seen in those regions. In the United States, poverty is a contributing factor to HIV infections. There is also a large racial disparity, with African Americans having a significantly higher rate of HIV infection than white Americans.

Ebola (a form of hemorrhagic fever) is arguably the most aggressive contagious disease on the earth. It severely and rapidly damages the internal organs of humans and can kill within days. Ebola is spread by contact with even minute amounts of an infected person's body fluids. The first recorded case of Ebola was in 1976. The most recent pandemic of Ebola developed in Africa in 2014 and killed over 11,000 people. It is believed that the first victims became infected by consuming contaminated meat from bats.

Egyptian President Nasser took strong measures to build the nation's economic power and influence but suffered the loss of prestige due to failed military ventures.

Gamal Abdel Nasser Hussein was the second President of Egypt, serving from 1956 until his death. A leader of the Egyptian Revolution of 1952 against the monarchy, he introduced neutralist foreign policies during the Cold War and co-founded the international Non-Aligned Movement. His nationalization of the Suez Canal Company and the brief union he presided over with Syria was acclaimed throughout the Arab world. However, his intervention in the North Yemen Civil War was mostly unsuccessful, and his prestige took a blow with Egypt's defeat in the Six-Day War. Nasser made Egypt fully independent of British influence, and the country became a significant power in the developing world under his leadership.

One of Nasser's primary domestic efforts was to establish social justice, which he deemed a prerequisite to liberal democracy. During his presidency, ordinary citizens enjoyed unprecedented access to housing, education, jobs, health services, and nutrition, as well as other forms of social welfare, while feudalistic influence waned. As a means to achieve these ends, he adopted a policy of Non-Alignment, though he remained strongly committed to the principles of socialism and state-planning of the economy. His economic policy became a textbook example of what is known as "Import Substitution Industrialization," where the resources of one's own country are utilized more effectively, thus reducing the need to rely on imports from other countries to sustain oneself.

*Gamal Abdel Nasser Hussein
(center), president of Egypt*

By the end of his presidency, employment and working conditions improved considerably. However, poverty was still high in Egypt, and resources allocated for social welfare had been diverted to the war effort. The national economy grew significantly through agrarian reform; major modernization projects, such as the Helwan steelworks and the Aswan Dam; and nationalization schemes, such as that of the Suez Canal. However, the marked economic growth of the early 1960s took a downturn for the remainder of the decade, only recovering in 1970. Egypt experienced a "golden age" of culture during Nasser's presidency and became a model among the African states.

African socialism combated neoliberal trends.

African socialism has been and continues to be a major ideology around the continent. Fabian socialist ideals inspired Julius Nyerere, and he was a firm believer in rural Africans and their traditions and ujamaa, a system of collectivization that according to Nyerere, was present before European imperialism. In South Africa, the African National Congress (ANC) abandoned its partial socialist allegiances after taking power and followed a standard neoliberal route. From 2005 through 2007, South Africa was wracked by thousands of protests in poor communities. One of these gave rise to a mass movement of people living in the impoverished townships that, despite major police suppression, continues to work for popular people's planning and against the creation of a market economy in land and housing.

Julius Nyerere, African politician

Notes for active learning

Notes for active learning

Southwest Asia

Major historical events of the period:

1915:   The Ottoman Empire expels Christians from its territory

1915–1917:   Armenian Genocide

1947:   Beginning of a long term refugee crisis in the Middle East

1948:   Modern Israel is created

1950s–1960s: Pan-Arabism ideology emerges and takes root

1977:   Israel and Egypt reach peace agreement

PERIOD 4: Post-1900 C.E.

SOUTHWEST ASIA

A weakened Ottoman Empire, increasingly subject to self-autonomous movements among its ethnic minorities, tried to establish security by creating alliances with Western powers.

During the period of decline and modernization of the Ottoman Empire (1828–1908), the empire faced challenges in defending itself against foreign invasion and occupation. The empire ceased to enter conflicts on its own and began to forge alliances with European countries such as France, the Netherlands, Britain, and (later) Germany. However, these alliances normally came at a cost, as the Western European powers always sought to exact a price on the 'sick man of Europe' for the assistance they provided. Often this was in the form of trade concessions, which the Ottoman Empire was in no position to refuse or negotiate too strongly against.

The rise of nationalism affected territories within the Empire, which external powers were more than willing to exploit to their ends. Within the territory of the Ottoman Empire, there were many ethnic minorities - an easy point of interference on the part of outside actors. The most consistent example of this was on the part of the Russian's, who waged war against the Ottoman Empire on various occasions in defense of their Slavic Orthodox brothers in Serbia and Bulgaria.

Additionally, there were increased moves on the part of non-Anatolian Islamic peoples, who found themselves under Ottoman Turkish control, to establish a degree of autonomy within the Empire. The most notable of these cases was in Egypt, where Muhammed Ali, with the tacit support of the British Empire, established a Khedive (semi-autonomous region) in 1805 within the Ottoman Empire. To a lesser extent, similar movements took place in the Levant. All of these moves by the great powers of the day laid the foundation for the eventual mandates given to the victorious powers at the end of World War I.

The attempted Tanzimat reforms to modernize the Empire were not enough to help the Ottoman Empire catch up to the level of development present in Western Europe. It was an important restructuring and modernization period, which caused most aspects of Ottoman society to improve; however, the implementation of the reforms called for greater foreign assistance for financing and constructing the modernization program. As a result, the Ottoman Empire was further weakened by its reliance on external assistance. These factors, when combined with the onset of World War I in 1914, made the continued existence of the Ottoman Empire impossible.

Jewish Zionism (re)claimed Middle East territory.

Zionism, as an organized movement, was founded by Theodor Herzl in 1897. The Hovevei Zion, or the Lovers of Zion, were responsible for the creation of 20 new Jewish settlements in Palestine between 1870 and 1897. After the Holocaust, the movement focused on the creation of a Jewish state, attaining its goal in 1948 with the creation of Israel. The Zionist movement continues to exist, working to support Israel, assist persecuted Jews, and encourage Jewish emigration to Israel. The success of Zionism has meant that the percentage of the world's Jewish population who live in Israel has grown steadily over the years. Today 40% of the world's Jews live in Israel. There is no other example in history of a nation being reestablished after such a long period of existence as a diaspora.

The struggle between Arabs and Jews in Palestine culminated in the 1947 United Nations plan to partition Palestine. This plan attempted to create an Arab state and a Jewish state in the narrow space between the Jordan River and the Mediterranean. While the Jewish leaders accepted it, the Arab leaders rejected this plan, as it called for them to lose territory their ancestors had lived in for thousands of years. In the 1948 Arab–Israeli War, which immediately followed, the armies of Egypt, Syria, Transjordan, Lebanon, Iraq, and Saudi Arabia intervened and were defeated by Israel.

Theodor Herzl,
founder of Zionist movement

About 800,000 Palestinians fled from areas annexed by Israel and became refugees in neighboring countries, thus creating the "Palestinian problem," which has troubled the region ever since. Approximately two-thirds of the 758,000–866,000 Jews who were expelled or fled from Arab lands after 1948 were absorbed and naturalized by the State of Israel. The departure of the European powers from direct control of the region, the establishment of Israel, and the increasing importance of the oil industry marked the creation of the modern Middle East. These developments led to a growing presence of the United States in Middle Eastern affairs.

The modern Middle East experienced genocide, ethnic cleansing, population displacement, and settler conflicts.

During the First World War, over a million Armenian children, adults, and older adults lost their lives in an event called the Armenian Genocide. Armenia has been divided for centuries, with ethnic Armenian pockets in many neighboring nations. Armenia has been a sovereign nation since the collapse of the Soviet Union, but most ethnic Armenians live in Turkey, Iran, Lebanon, Egypt, and other nations. In 1915, the Ottoman Empire expelled Christians living in their territory, including Armenians and other groups. They were forced on death marches into the Syrian Desert under armed guard and starved, raped and executed outright on the way. Estimates on the number of Armenians who perished in this event disagree, but they range from 800,000 to 1,500,000.

Armenian Genocide orphans

After the Holocaust, the world's surviving Jews decided it was time to have a nation of their own, which had been their compelling dream for two thousand years. The Levant was occupied and administered by the British. That nation's government refused to allow the creation of a Jewish state in that region, fearing (correctly, as it turned out) that doing so would destabilize the region. Although Palestine was administered by the British, many Jews did not believe that they were taking the role of defending them seriously. In 1920, Palestinian Jews had created the Haganah as a defense force against attacks from those Arabs who often attacked Jewish homes and settlements. The Haganah worked with the British during World War II, while other Jewish guerrilla groups, such as nationalistic Lehi, fought against them. Rival Jewish paramilitary groups, including Haganah, Lehi, and other smaller groups, united in 1945 to fight the British for a Jewish homeland.

In November 1947, the United Nations passed a proposal to partition Palestine into a Jewish state and an Arab state. This was accepted by the Jewish representatives but rejected by the Arab League and the Arab representatives from Palestine. The British mandate in Palestine was set to expire on May 15th, 1948. On December 1st, 1947, conflict broke out over the resolution as many Arabs attacked Jewish targets of all types. As the situation deteriorated into a civil war, a quarter of a million Arabs became refugees, leaving their homeland for their safety. This was the beginning of a long-term refugee crisis in the Middle East.

The independence of the Jewish republic was declared by its first president David Ben Gurion, on May 14th, 1948. The next day, when the British mandate expired, four neighboring Arab nations – Egypt, Syria, Jordan, and Iraq – attacked the Jews, setting off the Arab-Israeli war of 1948. With almost no heavy equipment, the Jews managed to defend against these four organized militaries for a full year until a cease-fire and tentative border were agreed upon in

1949. On May 11th, 1949, the nation of Israel was accepted as a member of the United Nations. About 700,000 additional Arab refugees were created during the Arab-Israeli war. The descendants of the refugees live in refugee camps, the Gaza strip, and the West Bank territory and are stateless at present. They now consider themselves a people with an identity – Palestinian Arabs – whose natural homeland is all of Palestine. The United Nations Relief and Works Agency administers the refugee camps. They estimate that, as of 2010, about 1.5 million Palestinian refugees live in displaced person camps in the neighboring Arab countries, and an additional 3.5 million live in the Gaza strip and West Bank.

The Palestinian refugee crisis is the central issue in the Levant conflict today. Arabs overwhelmingly believe that their land was taken by force and that they were forced off of it by the Jews. The Jewish opinion is that the area had been their historical homeland as well (Judaism and early Jewish settlement in Israel predate the existence of the Islamic religion by over a thousand years), therefore they had every right to establish a nation there, and that the Arabs were the original aggressors in 1948. The Jews also maintain that the Arabs left voluntarily and were rejected as refugees by Arab nations.

Palestine - Jaramana Refugee Camp, Damascus, Syria (1948)

A political solution has never been found, and guerilla groups, like Hamas and Hezbollah, have carried on intermittent insurgencies against Israel until the present. In 1977, American president Jimmy Carter brokered a peace agreement between Egypt and Israel, in which Egypt formally recognized Israel and agreed to observe peace with it. Egyptian president Anwar Sadat was later assassinated for this deal, but Egypt has never broken its word about maintaining the peace. Nor has Israel attacked Egypt since.

Pan-Arabism ideology pursued broad unification and briefly united Egypt and Syria.

Pan-Arabism is an ideology espousing the unification of the countries of North Africa and West Asia from the Atlantic Ocean to the Arabian Sea, an area referred to as the Arab world. It is closely connected to Arab nationalism, which asserts that Arabs constitute a single nation. Its popularity was at its height during the 1950s and 1960s. Advocates of pan-Arabism have often espoused socialist principles and strongly opposed Western political involvement in the Arab world. The movement also sought to protect Arab states from outside forces by forming alliances and, to a lesser extent, employing economic co-operation. The most prominent example of the application of this theory was the establishment of the United Arab Republic under the guidance of Gamal Abdel Nasser of Egypt. Nasser sought to establish a proto-socialist Arab state that would be non-aligned, though have strong socialist tendencies. The state only existed for a short while and only unified Egypt and Syria; however, this move showed strong support for left-wing principles of governance in the Middle East.

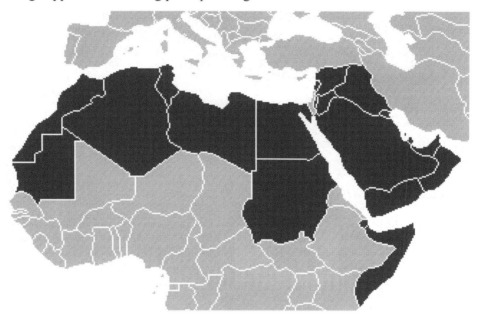

Nations of the Arab League

Islamic extremism surfaces.

Al-Qæda is a global militant Islamist organization founded by Osama bin Laden, Abdullah Azzam, and several others, at some point between August 1988 and late 1989. Its origins are traceable to Arab volunteers who fought against the Soviet invasion of Afghanistan in the 1980s. It operates as a network comprised of both a multinational, stateless army and an Islamist, extremist group. It has been designated as a terrorist group by the United Nations Security Council, the North Atlantic Treaty Organization (NATO), the European Union, the United States, Russia, India, and various other countries.

Al-Qaeda has mounted attacks on civilian and military targets in various countries, including the 1998 U.S. embassy bombings, the September 11 attacks, and the 2002 Bali bombings. Al-Qaeda ideologues envision a complete break from all foreign influence in

Muslim countries and the creation of a new worldwide Islamic caliphate. Al-Qaeda is also responsible for instigating sectarian violence among Muslims. Al-Qaeda leaders regard liberal Muslims, Shias, Sufis and other sects as apostates and have attacked their mosques and gatherings.

September 11 attack on the World Trade Center

Notes for active learning

Notes for active learning

South & Southeast Asia

Major historical events of the period:

1947:   India and Pakistan gain independence

1955–1975:   The Vietnam War

1963:   The "Buddhist Crisis" in Vietnam

1967:   The Association of Southeast Asian Nations is formed

1975:   Communist takeovers in Cambodia, Laos and Vietnam

PERIOD 4: Post-1900 C.E.

SOUTH AND SOUTHEAST ASIA

The UK recruited Indian Gurkhas for global deployments.

World War I was a global war, centered in Europe, that began on July 28, 1914, and lasted until November 11, 1918. It was one of the deadliest conflicts in history, paving the way for major political change, including revolutions in many of the nations involved. World War II was a global war that lasted from 1939 to 1945, though related conflicts began earlier. In a state of "total war," the major participants threw their entire economic, industrial, and scientific capabilities behind the war effort, erasing the distinction between civilian and military resources. It was the deadliest conflict in human history.

From the end of the Indian Rebellion of 1857 until the start of World War I, the Gurkha Regiments saw active service in Burma, Afghanistan, the Northeast frontier, and the Northwest frontiers of India, Malta, Malaya, China, and Tibet. Between 1901 and 1906, the Gurkha regiments were renumbered from the 1st to the 10th and re-designated as the Gurkha Rifles. In this time, the Brigade of Gurkhas, as the regiments came to be collectively known, was expanded to twenty battalions within the ten regiments.

During World War I, more than 200,000 Gurkhas served in the British Army, suffering approximately 20,000 casualties and receiving almost 2,000 gallantry awards. Following the end of the War, the Gurkhas were returned to India. During the inter-war years, they were largely kept away from the internal strife and urban conflicts of the sub-continent and instead were employed largely on the frontiers and in the hills, where fiercely independent tribesmen were a constant source of trouble. During World War II, there were also ten Gurkha regiments.

Gurkhas during First World War

Nationalist leaders in Asia and Africa challenged imperial rule.

Mohandas Gandhi (later Mahatma Gandhi) was the preeminent leader of the Indian independence movement in British-ruled India. Employing nonviolent civil disobedience, Gandhi led India to independence and inspired movements for civil rights and freedom across the world. Gandhi was born and raised in a Hindu merchant caste family in coastal Gujarat in Western India and trained as a lawyer at the Inner Temple in London. He first employed nonviolent civil disobedience as an expatriate lawyer in South Africa during the resident Indian community's struggle for civil rights.

Mahatma Gandhi, leader of the Indian independence movement

After Gandhi's return to India in 1915, he set about organizing peasants, farmers, and urban laborers to protest against excessive land-tax and discrimination. Assuming leadership of the Indian National Congress in 1921, Gandhi led nationwide campaigns to eradicate poverty, expand women's rights, build religious and ethnic amity, end untouchability (as a caste class) and, above all, to achieve "Swaraj," or self-rule.

Gandhi's vision of an independent India based on religious pluralism, however, was challenged in the early 1940s by new Muslim nationalism, which demanded a separate Muslim homeland be carved out of India. Eventually, in August 1947, Britain granted India independence, but the British Indian Empire was partitioned into two dominions: a majority-Hindu India and a Muslim Pakistan. Nathuram Godse, a Hindu nationalist, assassinated Gandhi on January 30, 1948, by firing three bullets into his chest at point-blank range. Indians widely describe Gandhi as the father of the nation, though the title has not been officially accorded to him by the Government of India. His birthday, October 2nd, is commemorated as Gandhi Jayanti, a national holiday, and worldwide as the International Day of Nonviolence.

Ho Chi Minh was a Vietnamese Communist revolutionary leader who was prime minister and president (1945–1969) of the Democratic Republic of Vietnam (North Vietnam). He was a key figure in the foundation of the Democratic Republic of Vietnam in 1945, as well as the People's Army of Vietnam and the Viet Cong during the Vietnam War. He led the Viet Minh independence movement from 1941 onward, establishing the Communist-ruled Democratic Republic of Vietnam in 1945 and defeating the French Union in 1954 at the battle of Dien Bien Phu. He officially stepped down from power in 1965 due to health problems but remained an inspiration for the Vietnamese fighting for his cause—a united, communist Vietnam—until his death. After the war, Saigon, the former capital of the Republic of Vietnam, was renamed Ho Chi Minh City.

The British Raj was dismantled, resulting in the creation of India and Pakistan.

Though Britain and the empire emerged victorious from the Second World War, the effects of the conflict were profound, both at home and abroad. Much of Europe – a continent that had dominated the world for several centuries – was in ruins and host to the armies of the United States and the Soviet Union, who now held the balance of global power. At the same time, anti-colonial movements were on the rise in European colonies. The change ultimately meant that the British Empire's days were numbered, and Britain adopted a policy of peaceful disengagement from its colonies once stable – non-Communist – governments were in place to transfer power to. This was in contrast to other European powers such as France and Portugal, who waged costly and, ultimately, unsuccessful wars to keep their empires intact.

The British Raj was the name given to the colonial rule of the British Empire in the Indian subcontinent between 1858 and 1947. The term can also refer to the period of dominion. India included areas directly administered by Britain, as well as the princely states ruled by individual rulers under the British Crown. The title "Empress of India" was officially created by Prime Minister Benjamin Disraeli for Queen Victoria in 1876. The system of governance had been instituted on June 28, 1858, when the rule of the British East India Company was transferred to the Crown in the person of Queen Victoria and lasted until 1947 when the British Indian Empire was partitioned into two sovereign dominion states: the Union of India and the Dominion of Pakistan. At the inception of the Raj in 1858, Lower Burma was already a part of British India; Upper Burma was added in 1886, and the resulting union was administered as an autonomous province until 1937, when it became a separate colony, gaining its independence in 1948.

Illustration of the official proclamation of
Queen Victoria as Empress of India

On August 14, 1947, the new Dominion of Pakistan (later the Islamic Republic of Pakistan) was established, with Muhammad Ali Jinnah sworn in as its first Governor-General in Karachi. The following day, August 15, 1947, the Union of India came into being with official ceremonies taking place in New Delhi and Jawaharlal Nehru, assuming the office of the prime minister.

Religious differences led to the founding of two states after Britain dismantles the Raj.

The founder of Pakistan, Muhammad Ali Jinnah, was a lawyer and politician. Born in Karachi and trained as a barrister at Lincoln's Inn in London, Jinnah rose to prominence in the Indian National Congress in the first two decades of the 20th century. He became a key leader in the All India Home Rule League and proposed a fourteen-point constitutional reform plan to safeguard the political rights of Muslims. In 1920, Jinnah resigned from the Congress when it agreed to follow a campaign of non-violent resistance, advocated by Gandhi. The Congress and the Muslim League could not reach a power-sharing formula for a united India, leading all parties to agree to separate independence for a predominately Hindu India and for a Muslim-majority state, to be called Pakistan. Jinnah died at age seventy-one in September of 1948, just over a year after Pakistan gained independence from the British Raj.

Muhammad Ali Jinnah,
Indian politician and lawyer

Populations relocated following the Partition of India.

Massive population exchanges occurred between the two newly formed states, India and Pakistan, in the months immediately following Partition. The population of undivided India in 1947 was approximately 390 million people, while after partition, there were 330 million people in India, 30 million people in West Pakistan, and 30 million people in East Pakistan (now Bangladesh). Once the state borders were established, about 14.5 million people crossed them in hopes of settling in the relative safety of their religious majority.

The 1951 Census of Pakistan identified the number of displaced persons in Pakistan at 7,226,600 – presumably all Muslims who had entered Pakistan from India. Similarly, the 1951 Census of India enumerated 7,295,870 displaced persons - apparently all Hindus and Sikhs who had moved to India from Pakistan immediately after the Partition. The two numbers add up to 14.5 million. Since both censuses were held about 3.6 years after the Partition, the enumeration included net population increase after the mass migration. Many Sikhs and Hindu Punjabis fled Western Punjab and settled in the Indian parts of Punjab and Delhi. Hindus fleeing from East Pakistan settled across Eastern India and Northeastern India, many ending up in neighboring Indian states such as West Bengal, Assam, and Tripura. Some migrants were sent to the Andaman Islands, where today Bengalis form the largest linguistic group.

Mahatma Gandhi set examples for future independence and social justice activism.

Mahatma Gandhi was a major political and spiritual leader of India, instrumental in the Indian independence movement. He was the pioneer of a brand of nonviolence, which he called *satyagraha*—translated literally as "truth force." This was the resistance of tyranny through civil disobedience that was not only nonviolent but also sought to change the heart of the opponent. During his thirty years of work (1917–1947) for the independence of his country from the British Raj, Gandhi led dozens of nonviolent campaigns, spent over seven years in prison and fasted nearly to his death on several occasions to obtain British compliance with a demand or to stop inter-communal violence. His efforts helped lead India to independence in 1947 and inspired movements for civil rights and freedom worldwide.

U.S. possession of the Philippines allowed steady immigration.

After the Spanish-American War in 1898, the Philippines became a colony of the United States. The United States established the Insular Government to rule the Philippines. After the end of the war, the Treaty of Manila established the independent Philippine Republic. Significant immigration to the United States began in the 1900s after the Spanish–American War, and the immigrants became United States nationals. Unlike other Asians, Filipinos, as U.S. nationals, were exempt from the immigration laws of the time. In December 1915, it was ruled that Filipinos be eligible for naturalization and citizenship. However, naturalization continued to remain difficult with documented cases of denied naturalization and de-naturalization occurring in the early 20th century.

Vietnamese fought colonial France and Japan to gain independence.

Vietnam was fully incorporated into the French Indochina colony (also comprising modern-day Laos and Cambodia) in the late 19th century, remaining a French possession for eighty-seven years. During World War II it was occupied by Japan. Japanese forces allowed the Viet Minh (the League for the Independence of Vietnam) and other nationalist groups to

Ho Chi Minh, President of the Democratic Republic of Vietnam

take over public buildings and weapons without resistance, which began the August Revolution of 1945. In September 1945, Ho Chi Minh read a proclamation during a public meeting in front of thousands of people, at what is now Ba Dinh Square in Ha Noi, announcing the birth of the Democratic Republic of Vietnam and the country's independence from France. War with France followed, lasting from December 1946 until August 1954. The disputed International Geneva Conference resulted in independence for Laos, Cambodia, and a Vietnam divided at the 17th parallel (Communists in control of North Vietnam and pro-Westerners in control of South Vietnam).

The newly created Republic of South Vietnam faced severe religious and political tensions.

The Republic of South Vietnam was founded by its first president, Ngo Dinh Diem, who was a member of the Catholic minority (most Vietnamese were Buddhist, but during a century of occupation by the Catholic French, many had converted to Catholicism for various reasons.) In 1963, Ngo faced a period called the "Buddhist Crisis," whereby his regime faced a protest by many Buddhists. He was accused of disproportionally supplying defensive weapons to Catholic communities to fight the communists and other policies which diminished Buddhism. In 1963, a Buddhist monk Thich Quang Duc expressed his protest in a public intersection of Saigon by setting himself on fire. Self-immolation has been practiced by many desperate people when they do not have the power to resist, in particular, by over a hundred people in Chinese-occupied Tibet in recent times.

Vietnam and Cambodia's chaotic and violent developments resulted in huge refugee numbers.

Following the communist takeovers in Vietnam, Cambodia, and Laos in 1975, about three million people attempted to escape in the subsequent decades. Massive daily influxes of refugees severely strained the resources of the receiving countries. The plight of the boat people became an international humanitarian crisis, and the United Nations High Commissioner for Refugees set up refugee camps in neighboring countries to process them.

Large numbers of Vietnamese became refugees after South Vietnam fell to the communist forces on April 30, 1975. Many tried to escape, some by boat, thus giving rise to the phrase "boat people." The Vietnamese refugees emigrated to Hong Kong, France, the United States, Canada, Australia, and other countries, creating sizable expatriate communities, notably in the United States. Since 1975, an estimated 1.4 million refugees from Vietnam and other Southeast Asian countries have been resettled in the United States. Most Asian countries were unwilling to accept refugees.

A side effect of the war in Vietnam was the destabilization of a neighboring nation of Cambodia (Kampuchea). Communist forces attempted to circumvent American, and ARVN (Army of the Republic of Vietnam) search and destroy forces by extending their covert supply line (referred to as the "Ho Chi Minh Trail" by Americans) through Laos and Cambodia. When this was discovered, President Johnson ordered the bombing of the trail in Laos and Cambodia. Meanwhile, the communists were working to create sympathetic groups within Cambodia, and the bombing of the Ho Chi Minh Trail helped them in getting local sympathy and recruits, especially after several Cambodian citizens were killed. A communist guerrilla group called the Khmer Rouge, which would become infamous for murder, was formed and gradually increased in size and relevance.

Khmer Rouge Administrative Zones for Democratic Kampuchea, 1975-78.

The Khmer Rouge fought the American-backed government in Cambodia until they successfully toppled it on April 17th, 1975, just days before the government of South Vietnam also fell to communists. For the next four years, the Khmer Rouge governed Cambodia brutally and murdered about thirty percent of its population – about two million people. Many were executed for having even the slightest association with western culture – even for being a school teacher or owning a car. Hundreds of thousands more were systematically starved to death, to maintain power through fear.

Eventually, the Khmer Rouge were driven out of power by the Vietnamese, but that campaign also created a new refugee crisis. The three phases of war precipitated a refugee crisis in Cambodia: the five-year-long civil war that brought the Khmer Rouge to power, during the Khmer Rouge period and the liberation by the Vietnamese. During each of these three periods, farming was severely disrupted, and local populations faced famine, hundreds of thousands fled to Thailand, and some were able to get to Australia. Today, millions of ethnic Khmer refugees and their descendants are living all over the world.

Southeast Asia is mostly united under the common ASEAN banner.

The Association of Southeast Asian Nations (ASEAN) is a political and economic organization of ten Southeast Asian countries. It was formed on August 8, 1967, by Indonesia, Malaysia, the Philippines, Singapore, and Thailand. Since then, membership has expanded to include Brunei, Cambodia, Laos, Myanmar (Burma), and Vietnam. Its aims include accelerating economic growth, social progress, sociocultural evolution among its members, protection of regional peace and stability, and opportunities for member countries to resolve differences peacefully.

Notes for active learning

Notes for active learning

East Asia

Major historical events of the period:

1910:	Japan annexes Korea
1912:	Qing Dynasty collapses in China
1927–1949:	The Chinese Civil War
1937:	Nanjing Massacre
1945:	Korea partitioned into North and South Korea
1959–1962:	The Great Chinese Famine
1989:	Tiananmen Square protests
1997:	Hong Kong is transferred back to China

PERIOD 4: Post-1900 C.E.

EAST ASIA

Qing Dynasty succeeded in preparing China for modernizations but failed to survive the ensuing political upheaval.

The Qing Empire (1644–1912) was the last great dynastic empire to rule China. Like most Chinese dynasties, the Qing Dynasty had powerful and long-reigning rulers at the beginning of the dynastic era, a period of prosperity in the beginning and middle of their dynastic era and natural disasters, rebellions, invasions and inept ruling courts at the end. For the last seventy-some years of the Qing dynasty, it was in decline. Symptomatic of this decline, reforms came slowly and with limited and sporadic government support. The Qing Restoration, which began around 1860, aimed to reinvigorate the Confucian state through administrative and tax reforms, as well as a practical application of Confucian principles in governance.

However, reforms soon acquired a life of their own. It became apparent early on that the adoption of one Western technological or diplomatic innovation would inevitably lead to the adoption of another. Modern guns and boats would require new military training, just as their manufacture would require machinists and engineers, and they, in turn, would demand support industries, such as coal mining and modern transportation infrastructure. By the end of the 19th century, some Chinese began to realize that, if they were to become a modern nation, their political system had to be seriously reformed and, should that fail, changed. The combined effect of modern commerce, industry, and education had led to major diversification and enrichment of Chinese elites who were poised for a greater say in politics. When their demands were not satisfied, they deserted the Qing Court, and the dynasty collapsed in 1912. Though all the efforts at reform and self-strengthening had failed, the Qing Dynasty had laid the foundation for modern China.

Japan pursued colonial ambitions in Asia, dwarfed European military strength in the region.

When the 20th century began, most of the world was someone else's colony. As Japan changed from Meiji Japan to a military dictatorship, its government developed imperial ambitions of its own. In 1910, Japan annexed the Korean peninsula and effectively enslaved all of its people. Britain and France had Asian colonies already but did not have substantial military forces there, as compared to the size of the Japanese army and navy. These two European powers underestimated the will and the military ability of the Japanese government to conquer its neighbors and drive the Europeans out of Asia. America administered the Philippines, Hawaii, and some smaller islands in the Pacific, but did not have imperial intentions or a military presence which matched that of Japan.

Japan committed crimes against humanity during World War II.

The Nanjing (formerly spelled Nanking) Massacre, was an episode of mass murder and mass rape by Japanese troops against the residents of Nanjing (the then capital of the Republic of China), which occurred during the Second Sino-Japanese War. The massacre occurred over six weeks, starting on December 13, 1937, the day that the Japanese captured Nanjing. During this period, soldiers of the Imperial Japanese Army murdered thousands of Chinese civilians, disarmed combatants, and perpetrated widespread rape and looting.

Victims of the Nanjing Massacre

Several key perpetrators were tried and found guilty at the International Military Tribunal for the Far East and the Nanjing War Crimes Tribunal and were executed. Since most Japanese military records on the killings were kept secret or destroyed shortly after Japan's surrender in 1945, historians have not been able to estimate the death toll of the massacre accurately. The International Military Tribunal for the Far East estimated in 1948 that over 200,000 Chinese were killed in the massacre and related incidents.

During World War Two, Imperial Japanese aggression resulted in the murder of an estimated fifteen to twenty million people, mostly civilians. The Japanese conducted bombing campaigns on cities that killed millions. Bombers made by the same Mitsubishi Company, which produces popular electronics today (Mitsubishi began as an engine manufacturer) were used as a tool to kill at least five million. The Japanese trained new bomber crews with target practice on Chinese population centers.

The Japanese military showed a callous disregard for civilian lives and was brutal with partisans and prisoners of war. "Division 731" was a biological warfare research unit in the Japanese military in China. Doctors assigned to the 731 conducted brutal pseudo-scientific experiments on prisoners of war and thousands of randomly selected Chinese civilians, often surgically opening their living bodies without anesthetic. The Japanese also came within days of implementing "Operation Sea Turtle" – the extermination of twenty thousand Jewish refugees living in the Japanese controlled Shanghai Ghetto, at the request of Hitler. Their surrender prevented this.

Asian nations reeling from wartime trauma develop along the contested ideologies of communism and western capitalism.

In East Asia, newly liberated nations took very different approaches to economic development. By 1945, most Asian nations had been occupied by the Japanese Empire for years. Many, including Japan itself, had been ruined by the war. Korea is an exceptional case study for comparison of economic policy, because it was divided between the opposing ideological camps, the Soviet and the Western, and because it had been virtually enslaved under Japanese statist domination for longer than any other Asian nation.

Atomic bombing of Nagasaki, Japan

In 1945, Korea was divided as part of an agreement between the victors – the Soviet Union on the one hand and America and its allies on the other. Both Koreas depended on foreign aid at first – North Korea, from the Soviet Union, South Korea, from the west. North Korea became a rigid communist nation with a dictator – Kim Il Sung – directly installed by Stalin. South Korea adopted a free market system and held its first democratic election in 1946. The economic philosophy of the North Korean dictatorship, personally developed by Kim Il Sung, was called "Ju Che," which translates roughly as "self-reliance." It is focused primarily on strengthening and developing the military, with all other economic needs being secondary to that. "Self-reliance," in practice, became absolute isolation from the rest of the world. North Korean citizens are not allowed any form of communication with the outside world, foreign products are completely banned, and travel is extremely restricted. Emigration is impossible, and escape is usually punished by forced labor, sometimes by execution. The evidence which has emerged from North Korea, as well as satellite reconnaissance of the country, shows an undeveloped nation that has endured a severe famine at least once in recent times.

In contrast, South Korea has developed the thirteenth largest economy in the world or thirtieth per capita. South Korean scholars claim that the "miracle of the Han River" occurred because of a strong emphasis on education, focusing on the development of high tech industries (chemicals, electronics, and scientific research) and, most of all, hard work. In contrast to North Korea, South Korea became a major trading nation.

Other Asian nations have pursued different paths to development as well. In the aftermath of the Second World War, Japan was occupied by the west, while China's communists won the civil war there and established a communist nation. In a move which was uncommon in prior geopolitical history, the United States did not annex or colonize defeated Japan, but rather implemented policy to remove the dictatorship from power, create a constitutional framework for democratic elections and freedom of the market and to disarm Japan, while allowing it a greatly reduced, though autonomous, Self Defense Force. Japan rebuilt its industries and its cities over the course of the next four decades, making international trade the main focus of its recovery. As a significantly industrialized nation in 1945, Japan could develop automobile and electronic industries, supplying the world with novel high-quality goods. The label "made in Japan" was carrying a reputation of quality, reliability, and state of the art technology until the early 1980s. Japan now has the 28th highest GDP per capita and the third-largest economy in the world (based on 2014 GDP).

Economically, China pivoted towards capitalism; agriculturally, the nation recovers from policy-caused famine.

After a long period of civil wars and conflicts with European powers, China's last imperial dynasty ended in 1912. The resulting republic was replaced, after another civil war (began in 1927), by the communist People's Republic in 1949. At the end of the 20th century, though still ruled by a communist party, China's economic system had adopted a semblance of capitalism, as part of the reform of the economic system by Deng Xiaoping. It was not capitalism per se since there was still a lot of restrictions imposed by the government, including limits on the number of foreign companies which could compete for business and on the ability to sell freely to whomever one wished to sell to. The Great Chinese Famine was a direct result of Maoist (communist) agricultural experiments and caused the deaths of tens of millions of Chinese peasants between 1959 and 1962. It is thought to be the largest famine in human history.

Deng Xiaoping, Chairman of the Chinese Communist Party,
with George H. W. Bush and Gerald Ford

China formulated the Great Leap Forward to close the distance towards industrialization and collectivization.

China's five-year plans were a series of social and economic development initiatives. The economy was shaped by the Chinese Communist Party (CCP) through the plenary sessions of the Central Committee and national congresses. The party played a leading role in establishing the foundations and principles of Chinese communism, mapping strategies for economic development, setting growth targets, and launching reforms. Planning was a key characteristic of centralized, communist economies, and one plan established for the entire country normally contained detailed economic development guidelines for all of its regions. To more accurately reflect China's transition from a Soviet-style planned economy to a socialist market economy, the name of its eleventh five-year program was changed to "guideline."

The Great Leap Forward was an economic and social campaign undertaken by the Communist Party of China (CPC) from 1958 to 1961. The campaign was led by Mao Zedong and aimed to rapidly transform the country from an agrarian economy into a socialist society via industrialization and collectivization. This campaign caused the Great Chinese Famine. One of the chief changes in the lives of rural Chinese as a result of the Great Leap Forward was the introduction of mandatory agricultural collectivization, which was introduced incrementally. Private farming was prohibited, and those engaged in it were labeled as counter-revolutionaries and persecuted. These restrictions were enforced through "public struggle sessions" and social pressure. Critics claimed the Great Leap Forward ended in catastrophe and resulted in tens of millions of deaths; however, supporters claimed the campaign did accelerate the industrialization of the state.

Tiananmen Square protest is crushed by the Chinese military.

The Tiananmen Square protests of 1989 in Beijing were student-led popular demonstrations that received broad support from city residents, exposing deep splits within China's political leadership. The protests were suppressed by leaders who ordered the military to enforce martial law in the country's capital. The crackdown they initiated on June 3–4 became known as the Tiananmen Square Massacre, or the June 4 Massacre, as troops with automatic weapons and tanks inflicted casualties on unarmed civilians trying to block the military's advance towards Tiananmen Square in the heart of Beijing, which students and other demonstrators had occupied for seven weeks. The number of civilian deaths has been estimated at anywhere between hundreds and thousands. The Chinese government condemned the protests as a counter-revolutionary riot and has largely prohibited discussion about and remembrance of the events.

Deng Xiaoping led Chinese efforts to reform the economy.

Deng Xiaoping was a Chinese revolutionary and statesman, the paramount leader of China from 1978 until his retirement in 1992. After Mao Zedong's death, Deng led his country through far-reaching market-economy reforms. Deng and Mao Zedong had a rivalry, particularly over agricultural policy, dating back to the early 1930s. As the party's Secretary-

General, Deng became instrumental in China's economic reconstruction following the Great Leap Forward in the early 1960s. His economic policies, however, were at odds with Mao's political ideologies. As a result, he was purged twice during the Cultural Revolution, but regained prominence in 1978 by outmaneuvering Mao's chosen successor, Hua Guofeng.

Hua Guofeng, Chinese leader

Inheriting a country fraught with social and institutional woes resulting from the Cultural Revolution and other political movements of the Mao era, Deng became the pre-eminent figure of the "second generation" of Chinese leadership. He is considered the "architect" of a new brand of socialist thinking, combining the Communist Party's socialist ideology with a pragmatic adoption of market economy-based practices. Deng opened China to foreign investment, the global market, and encouraged private competition. He is generally credited with developing China into one of the fastest-growing economies in the world for over thirty-five years and raising the standard of living of hundreds of millions of Chinese citizens. He was also a cold-blooded murderer, ordering his military to annihilate the populations of ethnic Vietnamese border villages who refused to accept Chinese rule.

Asian communism adopted socialist economic models.

In Asia, two of the states with socialist economies—the People's Republic of China and Vietnam—have experimented with a greater emphasis on market-based principles. These include the Chinese socialist market economy and the Vietnamese socialist-oriented market economy. They utilize state-owned corporate management models as opposed to modeling socialist enterprise on traditional management styles employed by government agencies. In China, living standards continued to improve rapidly despite the recession in the late-2000s, but centralized political control remained tight.

Though the authority of the state remained unchallenged under Doi Moi (economic reforms began in 1986), the government of Vietnam encouraged private ownership of farms and factories, economic deregulation and foreign investment, while maintaining control over strategic industries. The Vietnamese economy subsequently achieved strong growth in agricultural and industrial production, construction, exports, and foreign investment. However, these reforms have also caused a rise in nominal income inequality (which is different from injustice in pay related to actual productivity). Elsewhere in Asia, some elected socialist parties and communist parties remain prominent, particularly in India and Nepal. Other nations, such as North Korea and Laos, have rigidly retained command economies.

The popular Falun Gong spiritual movement was banned in China, followers persecuted.

Falun Gong or Falun Dafa is a Chinese spiritual practice that combines meditation and qigong exercises with a moral philosophy centered on the tenets of truthfulness, compassion, and forbearance. The practice emphasizes morality and the cultivation of virtue and identifies as a qigong practice of the Buddhist school, though its teachings also incorporate elements drawn from Taoist traditions. Through moral rectitude and the practice of meditation, practitioners of Falun Gong aspire to better health and, ultimately, spiritual enlightenment.

Falun Gong was first taught publicly in Northeast China in 1992 by Li Hongzhi. It emerged toward the end of China's "qigong boom"—a period that saw the proliferation of similar practices of meditation, slow-moving exercises, and regulated breathing. It differs from other qigong schools in its absence of fees or formal membership, lack of daily rituals of worship, its greater emphasis on morality, and the theological nature of its teachings. Western academics have described Falun Gong as a qigong discipline, a "spiritual movement," a "cultivation system" in the tradition of Chinese antiquity, or as a form of Chinese religion.

Works of Falun Gong are destroyed by communist Chinese government

In 1999, the Communist Party leadership in China initiated a nationwide crackdown and multifaceted propaganda campaign intended to eradicate the practice of Falun Gong. It blocked Internet access to websites that mention Falun Gong, and, in October 1999, it declared Falun Gong a "heretical organization" that threatened social stability. Human rights groups report that Falun Gong practitioners in China are subject to a wide range of human rights abuses: hundreds of thousands are estimated to have been imprisoned without trials, and practitioners in detention are subject to forced labor, psychological abuse, torture and other coercive methods of thought reform at the hands of Chinese authorities. As of 2009, at least 2,000 Falun Gong practitioners have died as a result of their abuse in state custody. In the years since the persecution began, Falun Gong practitioners have become active in advocating for greater human rights in China.

Notes for active learning

Notes for active learning

The Americas

Major historical events of the period:

1973–1990:   Chilean military dictatorship of Augusto Pinochet

1991:   Mescosur/Mercosul is established

1980:   First Quebec independence referendum

1995:   Second Quebec independence referendrum

2000s: Latin American "pink tide" results in the election of numerous left-leaning socialist heads of state

PERIOD 4: Post-1900 C.E.

THE AMERICAS

Socialism in Latin America experiences resurgence.

In Latin America, socialism was also adopted at the turn of the 21st century by Nicaraguan President Daniel Ortega, Bolivian President Evo Morales, and Ecuadorian president Rafael Correa, who refer to their political programs as socialist. "Pink tide" is a term currently being used in the media and elsewhere to describe Leftist ideology and politics.

U.S.-backed Chilean regime embarked on economic experimentation.

The military dictatorship of Chile was an authoritarian military government that ruled Chile between 1973 and 1990. Augusto José Ramón Pinochet was the dictator of Chile between 1973 and 1990 and Commander-in-Chief of the Chilean Army from 1973 to 1998. He came to power following a U.S.-backed coup d'état in 1973 that overthrew the elected socialist President Salvador Allende and ended civilian rule in Chile. The regime was strongly supported by the United States government, who viewed Chile as an experiment for the Chicago School of Economics, which would later inspire Reagan's economic policy. Under the influence of the free-market-oriented neoliberal "Chicago Boys," the military government of Pinochet implemented economic reforms, including currency stabilization, tariff cutting, opening Chile's markets to global trade, restricting labor unions, privatizing social security and the privatization of hundreds of state-controlled industries. These policies produced what has been referred to as the Miracle of Chile, as Chile was the best-performing economy in Latin America for most of the 1990s.

Pinochet meeting U.S. Secretary of State Henry Kissinger in 1976

South America adopted a shared customs union and trading bloc.

Mercosur or Mercosul is a sub-regional bloc that was created in 1991. Its full members are Argentina, Bolivia, Brazil, Paraguay, Uruguay, and Venezuela. Its associate countries are Chile, Peru, Colombia, and Ecuador. Observer countries are New Zealand and Mexico. Its purpose is to promote free trade and the fluid movement of goods, people, and currency. The official languages are Spanish, Portuguese, and Guarani. It has been updated, amended, and changed many times since. It is now a full customs union and a trading bloc. Mercosur and the Andean Community of Nations are customs unions that are components of a continuing process of South American integration connected to the Union of South American Nations.

The Quebec sovereignty movement fought Canadian federalism.

The Quebec sovereignty movement is a political movement advocating sovereignty for the Canadian province of Quebec. Several diverse political groups coalesced in the late 1960s to form the Parti Québécois, a provincial political party. Since 1968, the party has appealed for constitutional negotiations on the matter of provincial sovereignty, in addition to holding two provincial referendums on the matter. The first was in 1980, with the separatists being defeated. In 1995, after two failed attempts by the Mulroney government to secure Quebec's ratification of amendments to the constitution, the Parti Québécois held a second referendum.

2006 public celebration of Saint-Jean-Baptiste Day

The Quebec Liberal Party, Québec's other primary political party, as opposed to increasing political sovereignty for the province but has also historically been at odds, on occasion, with various Canadian federal governments. Thus, Quebec politics is effectively divided into two camps, which are principally opposed to the sovereignty issue. Quebec's sovereignty is politically opposed to the competing ideology of Canadian federalism.

Notes for active learning

Notes for active learning

IMAGE CREDITS

Period 1: Global Comparative

Lascaux cave paintings, A Painting of the Giant Deer from Lascaux. Aquitaine, France, Dordogne, Montignac. Wikimedia Commons

Paleolithic tools, "Paleolithic Tools from Newcomerstown and Amiens." *Popular Science Monthly 39* (1891). Wikimedia Commons

Bronze Age axes, Fabianski, F. *Essex Bronze Axes. Silesia Antigua 14,6,12.* Wikimedia Commons

The Nile River, Reis, Piri. "River Nile and Bulaq by Piri Reis." *Book of Navigation.* Wikimedia Commons

Egyptian king on his chariot, Wallis, Ernst. *Egyptian King on His Chariot: After a Mural in Thebes. Illustrerad Verldhistoria Utgifven Av E. Wallis. Band I.* Wikimedia Commons

Ancient Syrian water wheel pump for irrigation, Ancient Syrian Water Wheel Pump for Irrigation. Popular Science Monthly. Vol. 88. 1916. Wikimedia Commons

Emile Durkheim, economist, Emile Durkheim. c. 1917. *Marxists Internet Archive.* Wikimedia Commons

Terracotta jug from Mesopotamia, Jastrow. *Small Terracotta Jug, 3rd Century BC/CE. Found in Kish, Mesopotamia.* C. 3rd Century B.C. Terracotta. Louvre Museum: Department of Oriental Antiquities, Sully Wing, Ground Floor, Room 16, Paris. Wikimedia Commons

Ornate vessel of the Shang Dynasty, Vessel, China, Shang Dynasty, Bronze. Honolulu Academy of Arts, Honolulu.

Code of Hammurabi, Code of Hammurabi. Christian Theological Seminary. Christian Theological Seminary. Wikimedia Commons

Phoenician art depicting religious figure Baal, Baal with Thunder-bolt Stele. C. 1500–1200 B.C. Limestone. Louvre Museum: Department of Oriental Antiquities, Sully Wing, Ground Floor, Room 16, Paris.

Palace of Knossos, Jebulon. *Palace of Knossos, Crete, Greece.* Wikimedia Commons

Egyptian pyramid hieroglyphs, Unas Pyramidentexte. Brooklyn Museum Archives: Lantern Slide Collection. *Brooklyn Museum.* Brooklyn Museum. Wikimedia Commons

Homer, author of The Odyssey, Homer. 2nd Century B.C. Marble terminal bust. British Museum, London. Wikimedia Commons

Sitting Buddha temple, "Building, Ancient, Temple, Statue." Pixabay.

Colosseum, Pierer, Henry A. *Colosseum Roma.* 1891. *Universal Lexicon of the Present and Past.* 1891 Wikimedia Commons

Bust of Alexander the Great, Pederson, Gunnar Bach. *Alexander the Great.* Ny Carlsberg Glyptotek, Copenhagen, Denmark. Wikimedia Commons

Constantinople, Wolgemut, Michel, and Wilhelm Pleydenwurff. *Constantinople.* 1493. *The Nuremberg Chronicle.* Ed. Hartmann Schedel. *BORE Rare Books Digital Library.* Wikimedia Commons

People of the Silk Road, Per Honor et Gloria. People of the Silk Road, Dunhuang. c. 9th Century. Wikimedia Commons

Engraving of Cleopatra, Egyptian Pharaoh, De' Barbari, Jacopo. *Cleopatra.* c. 1509–1515. Engraving. Art Institute of Chicago: Clarence Buckingham Collection, Chicago. Wikimedia Commons

Tradesmen of the Tang dynasty, Merchants Tang Dynasty. c. 618–907. Cave painting. Absolute Museum, Phaidon. Wikimedia Commons

An Ab Anbar, a component of the Qanat, Dieulafoy, Jane. *Diolafoi Haj Kazem.* c. 19th Century. Sketch. Wikimedia Commons

Marcus Aurelius, Roman emperor, Yonge, Charlotte M. *Young Folks' History of Rome.* Boston: Estes & Lauriat; D. Lothrop, 1880. *Project Gutenberg.* Wikimedia Commons

Period 1: Europe

Engraving of Adam and Eve, Dürer, Albrecht. *Adam and Eve.* 1504. Engraving. The Morgan Library and Museum, New York. Wikimedia Commons

Christ on the cross with the Virgin and St. John, Dürer, Albrecht. *Christ on the Cross with the Virgin and St. John.* 1510. British Museum, London. Wikimedia Commons

Saint Peter's repentance, Seghers, Gerard. *The Repentance of St. Peter.* C1603–1651. Oil on canvas. Louvre Museum, Paris. Wikimedia Commons

Statue of the Greek god Apollo with Lyre and Griffin, Apollo with Lyre and Griffin. 1885. Wikimedia Commons

Socrates with his students, Greuter, Johann Friedrich. *Socrates and His Students.* 17th Century. *The Last Days of Socrates.* Kent Anderson, Ph.D., and Norm Freund, Ph.D. Wikimedia Commons

Aristotle, Greek philosopher, Ambrose, Tardieu. *Aristotle. Neuchatel Public and University Library.* Wikimedia Commons

Plato, Greek philosopher, Stanley, Thomas. *The History of Philosophy Containing the Lives, Opinions, Actions, and Discourses of the Philosophers of Every Sect. Illustrated with the Effigies of Divers of Them.* 1655. Print. Wikimedia Commons

The School of Athens by Raphael, Raphael. *The School of Athens.* 1509. Fresco. Stanza Della Segnatura, Palazzi Pontifici, Vatican, Rome. Wikimedia Commons

Frontispiece of The Iliad, Homer. *Iliad Frontispiece.* 1660. *The Iliad.* Trans. John Ogilby. 1660. Print. Wikimedia Commons

Pont du Gard, Baldus, Édouard. *Pont Du Gard Ca. 1860.* 1860. The Metropolitan Museum of Art, the Elisha Whittelsey Collection, The Elisha Whittelsey Fund, New York. Wikimedia Commons

Ancient Athens, James, Smillie, and Samuel F. B. Morse. *Ancient Athens.* c. 1872. Engraving of a painting by Morse. *Internet Archives.* Wikimedia Commons

Corinthian helmet, Greek, Corinthian Helmet. Late 7th Century BC. Princeton University Art Museum, Carl Otto Von Kienbusch, Jr. Memorial Collection, New Jersey. Wikimedia Commons

Drawing of Alexander the Great, Wallis, Ernst. *Alexander the Great.* 1875. *Illustrated World History.* Vol. 1. Print. Wikimedia Commons

Gaius Julius Caesar, Roman ruler, Gaius Julius Caesar. c. 100–144 B.C. National Archaeological Museum of Naples, Farnese Collection, Naples. *History of the World.* Ed. H. F. Helmolt. New York. 1902. Print. Engraving from the University of Texas Library Gallery. Wikimedia Commons

Solon, Athenian ruler, Bust of Solon. National Archaeological Museum of Naples: Farnese Collection, Naples. Wikimedia Commons

Coins of the Roman Republic, 1 Offense Coin. 211 B.C. *Antiqva.* Wikimedia Commons

Period 1: Africa

Section of the Papyrus of Ani manuscript showing Thoth's declaration to the Ennead. c. 1200 B.C. Wikimedia Commons

Statue of Queen Hatshepsut, Queen Hatshepsut with a cultic vessel. 18th Dynasty. c. 1475 B.C. Wikimedia Commons

The Great Hypostyle Hall at the Karnak Temple Complex, Blalonde. 18th Dynasty. Wikimedia Commons

Hannibal crossing the Alps on an elephant, Poussin, Nicolas. *Hannibal Crossing the Alps on an Elephant.* c. 1625–1626. Oil on canvas. Wikimedia

Final assault on Carthage during the Third Punic War, Jones Brothers. *Final Assault on Carthage: Third Punic War.* 146 B.C. New York Public Library, New York. Wikimedia Commons

Golden icon set in enamel and pearl, Morse with the Trinity, French. c. 1400–1410. Gold, enamel, and pearl. National Gallery of Art, Washington, D.C. Wikimedia Commons

Contemporary salt caravan using camels to traverse the Saharan Azalai route. Holger Reineccius. Wikimedia Commons

Period 1: Southwest Asia

Cuneiform, Jacobs, Joseph. *The Story of Geographical Discovery: How the World became Known.* 1854–1916 New York. D. Appleton. Wikimedia Commons

Phoenician colonies, Adrien-Hubert Brué. Wikimedia Commons

Sargon of Akkad, Mesopotamian ruler, Iraqi Directorate General of Antiquities. *Sargon of Akkad.* C. 2300 B.C. National Museum of Iraq, Baghdad. *Encyclopedia Britannica Online.* Wikimedia Commons

Hittite Chariot, Volz, Paul. *Hittite Chariot. The Biblical Antiquities.* Drawing from an Egyptian relief. Wikimedia Commons

Ancient ziggurat: the Tower of Babel, Laing, Samuel. *Tower of Babel.* 1892. *Human Origins.* Chapman and Hall Ld.; Richard Clay & Sons, Ld; London & Bungay, 1892. Wikimedia Commons

Ur-Nammu, king of the Third Dynasty, Stela of Ur-Nammu Detail. University of Pennsylvania Museum, Philadelphia. Wikimedia Commons

Moses with the Ten Commandments, Brockhaus and Efron. *Brockhaus and Efron Jewish Encyclopedia.* c. 1906. *The Jewish Encyclopedia of Brockhaus and Efron.* Wikimedia Commons

The Epic of Gilgamesh, Epic of Gilgamesh, Tablet 11: Story of the Flood. Neo-Assyrian clay tablet. British Museum, London. Wikimedia Commons

Abraham and the three angels, Doré, Gustave. *Abraham and the Three Angels.* 1866. *Doré English Bible.* Chicago: Belford-Clarke, 1891. Print. Wikimedia Commons

Darius the Great, Persian emperor, Flandin, Eugene, and Pascal Coste. *Voyage to Persia.* Ed. Gide and Baudry. Paris. 1851. Print. Wikimedia Commons

Ancient Phoenician coins, Cheyne, T. K., ed. *Encyclopaedia Biblica: A Critical Dictionary of the Literary, Political and Religious History, the Archaeology, Geography and Natural History of the Bible.* Vol. 3. New York: Macmillan, 1902. Print. Wikimedia Commons

Persian king and his charioteer, Wallis, Ernst. *Illustrerad Verldshistoria Utgifven.* Vol. 1. 1875. Wikimedia Commons

Crusaders attack Constantinople, Representation of Constantinople with Teh Palaiologan-era Flag of the Byzantine Empire. 1330. *La Conquête De Constantinople of Geoffroy De Villehardouin.* Venice. 1330. Wikimedia Commons

Art of the Indus River Valley civilization, Daderot. 2011. Wikimedia Commons

Period 1: South and Southeast Asia

Ceremonial Harappan vessel, Los Angeles County Museum of Art. c. 2600-2450 B.C.E. Wikimedia Commons

Map of the Ganges River Valley or "Plain," John Bartholomew and Sons, Edinburgh. "India: Orthographical Features" from *Imperial Gazetteer of India, Volume 26, Atlas* (Map Number 3) (1908). Wikimedia Commons

Brahmin priest painting his forehead with the marks of his caste, Brahmin Priest, in India, Painting His Forehead with the Red and White Marks of His Sect and Caste. c. 1900–1923. Frank and Frances Carpenter Collection, Library of Congress, Washington, DC. Wikimedia Commons

Face of the Buddha at Hong Hien, Cattell, J. McKeen, ed. *The Popular Science Monthly* 83 (1913). Print. Wikimedia Commons

Angkor Wat, Gsell, Emile. *The Earth and Its Peoples.* Tjeenk Willink & Son, 1906. *Project Gutenberg Literary Archive Foundation.* Wikimedia Commons

Coin representing Chandragupta II, Dinar of Chandragupta II. c. 376–414. Gold. Los Angeles County Museum of Art: South and Southeast Asian Art, Los Angeles. Wikimedia Commons

Stamp depicting a dhow, United Kingdom. Post Office. By the British Government. Wikimedia Commons

Period 1: East Asia

Marco Polo caravan traveling to India on the Silk Road, Atlas, Abraham Cresques Catalan. *The Caravan of Marco Polo Traveling to India.* 1375. Runners Seas, Poivre D'Arvor. Wikimedia Commons

Bronze tiger from the Shang Dynasty, Tiger from a Ding Cover, Shang Dynasty. C.1050 B.C. Bronze. Östasiatiska Museet, Stockholm, Sweden.

Dogū, Jomon Dogū Figurine. Musée Guimet à Paris, Paris. Wikimedia Commons

Statue of Confucius, "Confucius." Pixabay. Wikimedia Commons

Taoist Trio, Werner, E.T.C. *Myths and Legends of China.* Juliet Sutherland, Jeroen Hellingman, and Project Gutenberg, *Project Gutenberg.* Wikimedia Commons

Marble statue of the Buddha, The Historical Buddha. C 700–800 AD. Carved marble sculpture. Los Angeles County Museum of Art, Los Angeles. Wikimedia Commons

Liu Bang, Han emperor, Zhou, Shangguan. *Wan Hsiao Tang-Chu Chuang - Hua Chuan.* Print. Wikimedia Commons

Copyright © 2021 Sterling Test Prep.

Qin Shi Huang, Qin dynasty emperor, Yuan, Zhongyi. *China's Terracotta Army and the First Emperor's Mausoleum: the Art and Culture of Qin Shihuang's Underground Palace.* Paramus, New Jersey: Homa & Sekey Books, 2010. Wikimedia Commons

Vessel with a design of a Chinese Confucian Scholar, Sake Vessel with a Design of a Chinese Confucian Scholar (Tokkuri). c. 1700. Serviceware. Los Angeles County Museum of Art: Decorative Arts and Design, Los Angeles. Wikimedia Commons

Three brothers during the Yellow Turban Rebellion, A Qing Dynasty illustration of Liu Bei, Guan Yu, and Zhang Fei during the 184 Yellow Turban Rebellion in China. c. 184 C.E. The Scholars of Chenzhou. Wikimedia Commons

Period 1: The Americas

Olmec colossal head, Head, Olmec Culture. C. 11th–14th Century B.C. Carved volcanic stone. Honolulu Museum of Art, Honolulu. Wikimedia Commons

The San Lorenzo Monument 3, Maribel Ponce Ixba. Wikimedia Commons

Depiction of a messenger carrying a quipus. Wikimedia Commons

Pyramids in Teotihuacán, Mayer, Brantz. *Pyramids of St. Juan Teotihuacan-Western View. Mexico, as It Was and as It Is.* Philadelphia: G.B. Zieber, 1847. *Internet Archive.* Wikimedia Commons

Stucco Mayan glyphs, Kwamikagami. Wikimedia Commons

Period 2: Global Comparative

Astrolabe, Brockhaus, and Efron. *The Jewish Encyclopedia.* 1906. Wikimedia Commons

Compass, Davis, John. *The Seaman's Secrets.* London: Thomas Dawson, 1607. National Library of Canada. Wikimedia Commons

6th-century coins, Antique Coins, Metals. Arpajon-sur-Cère. *BNF Banque D'Images: Picture Collection.* Wikimedia Commons

Plague Altarpiece, Schaffner, Martin. *Two Wings of a Plague Altarpiece from the Augustinian Monastery Zu Den Wengen in Ulm.* c. 1513–1514. Germanisches Nationalmuseum, Nuremberg. Wikimedia Commons

St. Maruthas, Bishop of Martyropolis in Mesopotamia, Eastern Orthodox Catholicism, Saint Maruthas. 11th Century. Vatican Library, Rome. *Yandex.* Wikimedia Commons

French crossbowman, Auge, Claude, ed. *Larousse Illustrated Encyclopedia.* Pierre Larousse, 1898. Wikimedia Commons

Battle of Alexandria, Egypt, William of Tyre. *Battle of Alexandria.* 1173. *History of the Crusades.* Book XXI. Wikimedia Commons

Infection of smallpox from a 16th-century folio, Fields, Sherry (2008). *Pestilence and Headcolds: Encountering Illness in Colonial Mexico,* Gutenberg-e series, e-book edn. New York: Columbia University Press. Wikimedia Commons

Norman pirates in the 9th century, Luminais, Évareiste Vital. *Norman Pirates in the Ninth Century.* c. 9th Century. Oil on canvas. Museum Anne De Beaugeu, Moulins. Wikimedia Commons

Map of Constantinople (1422), Buondelmonti, Cristoforo. *Map of Constantinople.* 1422. National Library, Paris. Wikimedia Commons

Metal manufacturing guild, Schelhamer, Hans. *Mendel I.,* 1451. *House Book of Mendel Zwölfbrüderstiftung.* Vol. I. Nuremberg. Wikimedia Commons

Babylon, Van Heemskerck, Maerten. *Illustration of the Mythical Hanging Gardens of Babylon.* 16th Century. Wikimedia Commons

Period 2: Europe

Justinian I, Byzantine emperor, United States. Architect of the Capitol. U.S. House of Representatives. By Gaetano Cecere. Wikimedia Commons

Vikings, Die Gartenlaube (The Garden Arbor). Ernst Keil, 1879. Print. Wikimedia Commons

Marco Polo, Italian explorer, Edward R. Shaw: *Discoverers and Explorers.* New York/Cincinnati/Chicago: American Book Company, 1900. Project Gutenberg. Wikimedia Commons

Dance of Death: the Burgomaster and Death, The Burgomeister and Death, Showing Death with a Bladder-Pipe. c. 1488. Heidelberger Totentanz Galerie. *Heidelberger Totentanz.* Wikimedia Commons

Crusader, Mellin, and Gustaf Henrik. *Korsfarare.* 1850. British Library. *Den Skandinavska Nordens Historia.* Vol. 2. Wikimedia Commons

Edward III of England pays homage to Philip VI of France, Edward III, and Philip VI. 14th Century. Grandes Chroniques De France.*Maison St Claire.* Steven Proctor. Wikimedia Commons

Artwork from Mont Sainte-Odile, a convent in France, Alsace Mont Sainte-Odile. Mont Sainte Odile, Alsace, France. Wikimedia Commons

Period 2: Africa

Postcard of Djingereber Mosque in Timbuktu, Fortier, Edmond. *Fortier 372 Timbuktu Djingerber Mosque.* c. 1905–1906. *Dogon Images and Traditions.* Wikimedia Commons

Bantu migration pattern, Mark Dingemanse. *Bantu Expansion.* Wikimedia Commons

Ibn Battuta arrives in Egypt, Léon Benett. *Découverte de la terre.* 1878. Wikimedia Commons

Period 2: Southwest Asia

Khadīja bint Khuwaylid, wife of Mohammed, Rouillé, Guillaume. *Khadīja Bint Khuwaylid. Promptuarii Iconum Insigniorum.* 1553. Wikimedia Commons

An original One Thousand and One Nights manuscript, Danieliness. c. 13th century. Adlinor Collection. Wikimedia Commons

Jesus Christ as the Christian God, Doré, Gustave. *The Triumph of Christianity Over Paganism.* 1899. Wikimedia Commons

Muḥammad ibn Mūsā al-Khwārizmī, co-inventor of algebra, on a postage stamp, Yakiv Gluck. 1983. Wikimedia Commons

The provinces of the Abbasid Caliphate, Sykes, Percy Molesworth. "The Provinces of the Abbasid Caliphate, Showing the Chief High Roads." *A History of Persia.* 1921. Wikimedia Commons

Period 2: South and Southeast Asia

Map of Malay Peninsula, Ahoerstemeier. Wikimedia Commons

Sculpture of a person from the Brahmin class, Brahmin Ascetic, Eastern Java, Late Majapahit Period. c. 1294–1530. Limestone. Museum Für Indische Kunst, Berlin-Dahlem. Wikimedia Commons

People of the Tang Dynasty, A Palace Concert. c. 836–907. Ink and colors on silk. National Palace Museum, Formosa. Wikimedia Commons

Prambanan Shivaistic temple near Yogyakarta, Indonesia, Gunawan Kartapranata. 2010. Wikimedia Commons

Period 2: East Asia

Gaozong, emperor of China, Emperor Gaozong of Tang. 18th Century. *An 18th Century Album of Portraits of 86 Emperors of China, with Chinese Historical Notes.* Shelfmark: British Library. Wikimedia Commons

Representation of a Mongolian yurt, Kendall, Elizabeth Kimball. *A Wayfarer in China: Impressions of a Trip Across West China and Mongolia.* Boston and New York: Houghton Mifflin, 1913. Print. Wikimedia Commons

Genghis Khan, Mongolian emperor, United States. Department of Defense. American Forces Press Service. *United States Department of Defense.* By Jim Garamone. United States Government. Wikimedia Commons

Ögedei Khan, Ögedei Khan. 14th Century. National Palace Museum, Taipei. Wikimedia Commons

Shinto painting of the Buddha preaching the law, Hoyoku. *The Buddha Preaching the Law.* c. 984–989A.D. Ink and colors on silk. National Palace Museum, Taipei City. Wikimedia Commons

Papermaking in Ancient China, Mao Dynasty. *Making Paper.* Woodcut. Wikimedia Commons

Painting of the Polynesian Islands, Hodges, William. *View of the Islands of Otaha (Taaha) and Bola Bola (Bora Bora) with Part of the Island of Ulietea (Raiatea).* 1773. Oil on canvas. National Maritime Museum, Greenwich. Wikimedia Commons

Period 2: The Americas

Pre-contact Tenochtitlán, Wolfgang Sauber. 2008. Wikimedia Commons

Cahokia Monks Mound, McAdams, William. *Records of Ancient Races in the Mississippi Valley.* 1887. Wikimedia Commons

Incan road system, Koen Adams. 2015. Wikimedia Commons

Atahualpa, Fourteenth Inca, c.1750-1800. Brooklyn Museum. Wikimedia Commons

Modern Waru Waru, Bianco, Alfredo. *Waru Area Wrench - Perú.* c. 1988–1991. Perú. Wikimedia Commons

Period 3: Global Comparative

Harem, Ernst, Rudolf. *The Harem Bath.* 20th Century. Wikimedia Commons

Portuguese trading animals in Japan, the Columbian Exchange, Domi, Kano. *Barbarians from the South.* c. 1593–1600. Namban art. Wikimedia Commons

Peter the Great of Russia, Rambaud, Alfred. *History of Russia.* Vol. I. 1898. Wikimedia Commons

Titania from A Midsummer Night's Dream, Rackham, Arthur. *Titania Lying Asleep.* 1908. *A Midsummer Night's Dream.* By William Shakespeare. New York: Doubleday, Page, 1908. Wikimedia Commons

Factory of the American Hair Cloth Company, Industrial Revolution, Robert, Grieve. *Factory of the American Hair Cloth Co., Central Falls RI 1897. An Illustrated History of Pawtucket, Central Falls, and Vicinity.* 1897. Wikimedia Commons

Drawing of Eli Whitney's cotton gin, United States. Patent Office. *Textile Industry History.* Gary N. Mock. Wikimedia Commons

Hong Kong and Shanghai Banking Corporation, Wright, Arnold, and H. A. Cartwright, eds. *Twentieth Century Impressions of Hongkong, Shanghai, and Other Treaty Ports of China: Their History, People, Commerce, Industries, and Resources.* Lloyd's Greater Britain, 1908. *Internet Archive.* Wikimedia Commons

Fulton's design of the submarine, Fulton, Robert. *Submarine.* 1806. Engineering design in pencil, ink, and watercolor. Library of Congress: Prints and Photographs Division, Washington, D.C. Wikimedia Commons

Lenin at Putilov factory in May 1917, Brodsky, Isaak. *Lenin at Putilov Factory in May 1917.* 1929. The State Historical Museum, Moscow. *Independent Newspaper.* Wikimedia Commons

Chancellor Otto Von Bismarck, Von Lenbach, Franz. *The New International Encyclopedia,* V. 3, 1905. Wikimedia Commons

Children working in a textile mill, United States. National Child Labor Committee. Library of Congress: Prints and Photographs Division. *Ping News.* By Lewis Hine. Wikimedia Commons

President James Monroe, Stuart, Gilbert. *James Monroe.* c. 1755–1828. Library of Congress: Images of American Political History, Washington, D.C. Wikimedia Commons

President Andrew Jackson, Portrait Drawing of U.S. President Andrew Jackson. 1921. *Collier's New Encyclopedia.* Vol. 5. 1921. Wikimedia Commons

Herbert Spencer, Herbert Spencer. 19th Century. Smithsonian Institution Libraries: Dibner Library of History of Science and Technology. Wikimedia Commons

Jean-Jacques Rousseau, Library of General and Practical Knowledge, Vol. 5 (1905), French Literary History. Wikimedia Commons

Foreigners are killed during the Boxer Rebellion, 1900 Killing of Foreigners. 1861. British Library: Church Missionary Society Archives, London. *Lessing Images.* Wikimedia Commons

John Snow, Barker, Thomas Jones. *Portrait of John Snow.* c. 1815–1882. *UCLA Fielding School of Public Health.* UC Regents. Wikimedia Commons

Immigrant women, H. Arnold Barton, *A Folk Divided: Homeland Swedes and Swedish Americans, 1840–1940,* Uppsala: Acta Universitatis Upsaliensis, 1994. Wikimedia Commons

Period 3: Europe

Sebastian Cabot, Italian mapmaker and explorer, Hans Holbein the Younger; Rawle, Samuel. *Cabot.* 16th century. *National Maritime Museum.* London. Wikimedia Commons

Prince Henry the Navigator, Henry the Navigator. 17th Century. Line engraving. National Portrait Gallery, London. Wikimedia Commons

Willem de Vlamingh, Dutch explorer, Verkolje, Nicolaas, and Jan Verkolje. *Portrait of Willem De Vlamingh.* c. 1690–1700. Oil on canvas. Australian National Maritime Museum, Sydney. Wikimedia Commons

Martin Luther posts his 95 Theses, Pauwels, Ferdinand. *Luther Posting His 95 Theses in 1517.* 1872. *Flickr.* Wikimedia Commons

Desiderius Erasmus, German priest, Hans Holbein the Younger, *Hans Holbein le jeune: L'oeuvre du maitre.* Paris, Librairie Hachette & Cie. 1912. Wikimedia Commons

Leonardo da Vinci, Renaissance artist Leonardo Da Vinci. c.1864-1887. *Svenska Familj-Journalen.* 1864–1887. Wikimedia Commons

Miguel de Cervantes, author of Don Quixote, *The Hundred Greatest Men.* New York: D. Appleton & Company, 1885. Portrait Gallery, Perry-Castañeda Library, the University of Texas at Austin. Wikimedia Commons

Francis Drake, British pirate, Kraus, Hans P. *Portrait of Sir Francis Drake.* c. 1577–1580. Library of Congress: The Kraus Collection of Sir Francis Drake, Washington, D.C. Wikimedia Commons

Armed peasants of the German Peasants' War, German Peasants' War. 1525. Library of Congress, Washington, D.C. *Memmingen Articles of War.* Wikimedia Commons

Advertisement for James Watt & Co. pumping engines, Advertisement for James Watt & Co. Pumping Engines. Birmingham Museums Trust, 1895. Wikimedia Commons

Adam Smith, Scottish philosopher and theorist, Cadell and Davies, John Horsburgh, and R.C. Bell. *Profile of Adam Smith.* 1811. Etching. Harvard Business School: Vanderblue Collection, Cambridge. Wikimedia Commons

Montesquieu, philosopher of the French Enlightenment, Bayard, Emile. *Portrait of Montesquieu.* 1889. Engraving. *Album Du Centenaire.* By Augustin Challamel and Desire Lacroix. Ed. Jouvet & Cie. Paris: Magasin Pittoresque, 1889. Wikimedia Commons

John Locke, philosopher, and theorist of the Enlightenment, Sir Godfrey Kneller. *Portrait of John Locke.* 1697. Oil on canvas. Hermitage Museum: Collection of Sir Robert Walpole, Houghton Hall, St. Peters. Wikimedia Commons

Emperor Alexander II of Russia, Wormely. *Emperor Alexander II.* 1893. British Library: Mechanical Curator Collection, London. *Russia and Turkey in the Nineteenth Century.* By Mary Elizabeth Latimer. Wikimedia Commons

Napoleon Bonaparte, leader of the French Revolution, David, Jacques-Louis. *Napoleon Crossing the Alps.* 1800. Oil on canvas. Charlottenburg Palace, Berlin. Wikimedia Commons

Friedrich Engels (left), Lester, George. *Engels in 1868.* 1868. Wikimedia Commons

Karl Marx (right), Wunder, Friedrich Karl. *Karl Marx.* 1867. *Marxists Internet Archive.* Wikimedia Commons

Removal of peasants' vegetables during Holodomor, Holodomor Novo-Krasne Odessa November 1932. 1932. *TSDVR.* Wikimedia Commons

Elizabeth Cady Stanton, c. 1880. *Free School Press.* Wikimedia Commons

East and west shake hands at the laying of the last rail of the Union Pacific Railroad, Russell, Andrew J. *East and West Shaking Hands at the Laying of the Last Rail of the Union Pacific Railroad.* 1869. Yale University Libraries: Yale Collection of Western Americana, Beinecke Rare Book and Manuscript Library, New Haven. Wikimedia Commons

Slavery on an American sugar plantation, Bryant, William Cullen and Sydney Howard Gay. *A Popular History of the United States.* New York: Charles Scribners' Sons, 1881.

Period 3: Africa

Liverpool slave ship, Jackson, William. *A Liverpool Slave Ship.* Oil on canvas. National Museums Liverpool, BBC Paintings. Wikimedia Commons

French conquest of Algeria, Battle of Mazagran, Philippoteaux, Henri Felix Emmanuel. *Defense of Mazagran.* 1841.*Museums of France Portal Collections.* Ministry of Culture. Wikimedia Commons

The Battle of Majuba Hill in the First Boer War, Woodville, Richard Caton, Jr. *The Transvaal War, the Battle of Majuba Hill.* 1889. *London News.* London. Wikimedia Commons

Statue of Muhammad Ali of Egypt in Mansheya Square, Alexandria, Mansheya Square Alexandria. c. 1900–1919. *Yahoo.* Wikimedia Commons

Period 3: Southwest Asia

Abu Bakr, Muhammad's father-in-law, Turkish Artists. *Abu Bakr Stops Meccan Mob.* 16th Century. Wikimedia Commons

Mehmed II, Ottoman sultan, Mehmed II. University of Texas Library, Austin. Wikimedia Commons

Janissary, Weigel, Hans. *Janissary.* 1577. *Habitus Praecipuorum Populorum.* Trachtenbuch, 1577. Wikimedia Commons

Shah Abbas I of Iran, Custos, Dominicus. *Shah Abbas I.* c. 1560–1612. Engraving. Wikimedia Commons

Period 3: South and Southeast Asia

Guru Nanak, founder of Sikhism, Raja Ravi Varma. Wikimedia Commons

Dancing Mughal Women, Racinet, Auguste. *Le Costume Historique*, France. c. 1876–1888. Wikimedia Commons

The Mughal Empire in 1700, Gabagool. 2009. Wikimedia Commons

Boats Leaving for East India from the City of Veer in Zeeland (1601). 1601. *The Journey from Joris Van Spilbergen to Ceylon, Aceh, and Bantam.* Van Linschoten Society, 1933. Wikimedia Commons

British forces and their allies clash with mutineers, Chevalier Louis-William Desanges. c. 1859. Wikimedia Commons

The Battle of Manila Bay during the Spanish-American War. Wikimedia Commons

Period 3: East Asia

Zheng He's fleet, Zheng He Ships. 17th Century. *Ancient Chinese Explorers.* PBS. Wikimedia Commons

Yongle Emperor, Emperor Chengzu of the Ming Dynasty. c. 1368–1644. Ink and color on silk. National Palace Museum, Taibei. Wikimedia Commons

Manchu assault of Ningyuan, Bombs at Ningyuan. 1635. *Veritable Records of the Great Ancestor.* 1635. Wikimedia Commons

Tokugawa Masako, Portrait of Tokugawa Masako. Edo Period. Light Cloud Temple, Kyoto. *Japanese Hero Portrait Taizen MS.* Rekishi Dokuhon: Shin-Jinbutsuōrai-sha, 2007. Wikimedia Commons

Emperor Kangxi of the Qing dynasty, Kangxi Emperor. Netor Memorial. Netor. Wikimedia Commons

Prince Yamashina Kikumaro on the deck of a Japanese cruiser during the Russo-Japanese War, Joshikuni. *Prince Yamashina Kikumaro on Deck of Japanese Cruiser Yakumo, Russo-Japanese War.* 1905. *The Album, Japan, and Russia War.* Tokyo: Gusokuya, 1905. Wikimedia Commons

The Japanese royal family of 1904, including Emperor Matsuhito, The Japanese Royal Family in 1904. Library of Congress: Chronicling America: Historic American Newspapers, Washington, D.C. *The Tacoma Times.* Tacoma. 1904. Wikimedia Commons

Return of soldiers during the Opium Wars, Return of the Avengers. 1858. *Illustrated London News.* Canton. 1858. Wikimedia Commons

A scene from the Taiping Rebellion, Youru, Wu. *Regaining the Provincial Capital of Ruizhou.* 1886. *Battle of Qurman.* Wikimedia Commons

Period 3: The Americas

Francisco Pizarro, Spanish explorer, Pizarro. Photographic Archive of the University of Chile, Chile. Wikimedia Commons

Bernal Diaz del Castillo, Spanish historian and soldier, Garcia, Genaro. *Presumed Portrait of Spanish Conquistador Bernal Díaz Del Castillo.* 1904. Wikimedia Commons

Henry Hudson, British explorer, Edward R. Shaw*: Discoverers and Explorers.* New York/Cincinnati/Chicago: American Book Company, 1900. Project Gutenberg. Wikimedia Commons

Imaginary seaport painted at the height of mercantilism, Lorrain, Claude. *Seaport: Claude Lorrain.* 1638. Wikimedia Commons

The wedding of Pocahontas and John Rolfe, Spohni, Geo. *The Wedding of Pocahontas with John Rolfe.* c. 1867. Lithograph. Library of Congress Prints and Photographs Division, Washington, D.C. Wikimedia Commons

Slaves stacked like cargo during the Middle Passage, Description of a Slave Ship. 1789. Wood engraving. British Museum, London. Wikimedia Commons

Virgin of Guadalupe, Mayer, Brantz. *Mexico, as It Was and as It Is.* 3rd ed. Philadelphia: G.B. Zieber, 1847. *Internet Archive.* Wikimedia Commons

Cape Coast Castle, used as a collection and shipping enter of the Trans-Atlantic Slave Trade, Greenhill. *Cape Coast Castle in 1682.* 1682. *Denmark's History: The Colonies in Asia and Africa.* By Ole Feldbaek and Ole Justesen. Kobenhavn, 1980. Wikimedia Commons

European woman visiting a Mestizo woman for tea, Brandes, Jan. *Tea Business in a European House in Batavia.* 1779. Color drawing. Rijksmuseum, Amsterdam. Wikimedia Commons

Simón Bolívar, South American military leader, Simón Bolívar. c. 1890–1940. Library of Congress. Wikimedia Commons

Toussaint Louverture, leader of slave rebellion, Antoine Marie Thérèse Métral, Isaac Toussaint Louverture, *History of the French Expedition in Santo Domingo in the Consulate of Napoleon Bonaparte*, Paris, Fanjat aîné et Renouard, 1825. Wikimedia Commons

Period 4: Global Comparative

Pilot Neil Armstrong. The United States. National Aeronautics and Space Administration. Armstrong Flight Research Center. By U.S. Air Force. 1960. Wikimedia Commons

1920 Radio Station. 1920. Pittsburgh. *QST Magazine.* 1920. 32. Wikimedia Commons

Satellites in Earth Orbit. Solar Galaxy. The Soviet Union. Postal Service. By Office of the USSR. 1967. Wikimedia Commons

Poster of Red Cross nurse. The United States. U.S. Food Administration, Educational Division, Advertising Section. National Archives and Records Administration, College Park; Still Picture Records Section, Special Media Archives Services Division. c. 1917-1919. Wikimedia Commons

Alexander Fleming. The United States. Environmental Protection Agency. National Archives and Records Administration, College Park; Still Picture Records Section, Special Media Archives Services Division. 1973. Wikimedia Commons

Windpark. Hilger, F., 2006. St. Polten. Wikimedia Commons

Deforestation in Olympic National Timberland, Washington, due to drainage system. U.S. National Archives and Records Administration) [public domain]. Wikimedia Commons

Red Ribbon Hanging in the North Portico of the White House in Observation of World AIDS Day. Draper, Eric. 2007. White House, Washington, D.C. Wikimedia Commons

Birth Control Review, July 1919. By Margaret Sanger [public domain], via Wikimedia Commons.

President Franklin D. Roosevelt—1941. The United States. Associated Press. Library of Congress: Prints and Photographs Division: New World-Telegram and the Sun Newspaper Photograph Collection. 1940. Wikimedia Commons

Crane Removed Part of Wall Brandenburg Gate. The United States. U.S. Air Force. By F. Lee Corkran. 1989. Wikimedia Commons

Board of Governors - International Monetary Fund (IMF). The United States. International Monetary Fund. 1999. Wikimedia Commons

Flag of WHO. World Health Organization. 1948. Flag. Wikimedia Commons

President Bush, Canadian Prime Minister Brian Mulroney, and Mexican President Carlos Salinas Participate in the Initialing Ceremony of the North American Free Trade Agreement in San Antonio, Texas. Valdez, David. 1992. George Bush Library, College Station. *National Archives and Records Administration.* Wikimedia Commons

Sony Building, Tokyo, Japan. Carlson, Leonard V., 2005. Tokyo. Wikimedia Commons

John McConnell in Front of His Home Denver Colorado, the USA with His Earth Flag He Designed. Murray, Charles Michael. 2006. Courtesy of Endangered Planet, Laguna Beach, CA. Denver. Wikimedia Commons

Eleanor Roosevelt and Human Rights Declaration. 1949. Marist College FDR Library, Poughkeepsie. Wikimedia Commons

New World Alliance, 1980. Goldfarb, Gerald. 1980. *New Age Politics.* By Mark Satin. Wikimedia Commons

Forever England: A History of the National Side. Shaoul, Mark, and Tony Williamson. Stroud: Tempus, 2000. Print.

The Crimson Cross. Everett, George. 1920. *The Crimson Cross*. By N. Brewster Morse. Fanark Corporation. *Internet Archive*. Wikimedia Commons

Period 4: Europe

Einstein 1921 Portrait. Schmutzer, Ferdinand. 1921. *Bernisches Historisches Museum, Bern*. Musee D'Histoire De Berne. Wikimedia Commons

UN Charter Logo. United Nations. Digital image. 1945. Wikimedia Commons

Demonstration of Putilov Workers on the First Day of the February Revolution of 1917. 1917. State Museum of the Political History of Russia, St. Petersburg. Wikimedia Commons

Francisco Franco, in 1923. Government of Spain. 1923. Wikimedia Commons

Bill Clinton White House. The United States. Executive Office of the President of the United States. By David Scull. 1999. Wikimedia Commons

John Kenneth Galbraith, 1944. Dixon, Royden. c. 1944. Library of Congress, Washington, D.C. Wikimedia Commons

Margaret Thatcher, Former United Kingdom Prime Minister. Tikosko, Marion S., 1975. Library of Congress, Washington, D.C. *U.S. News & World Report*. Wikimedia Commons

Period 4: Africa

Starving girl during the Nigerian–Biafran War. The United States. Department of Health and Human Services. Centers for Disease Control and Prevention. *Public Health Image Library*. By Dr. Lyle Conrad. 1960s. Wikimedia Commons

European countries bring water to Rwandan refugees. The United States. United States Air Force. U.S. Army Africa Historical Image Archive. *SETAF History*. By Marv Krause. 1994. Wikimedia Commons

Nasser, Hussein, and Amer before Signing Egyptian-Jordanian Defense Pact. 1967. Bibliotheca Alexandrina, Alexandria. Wikimedia Commons

Julius Nyerere as Leader of the Legislative Council of Tanganyika. UK National Archives. c. 1958-1960. Wikimedia Commons

Period 4: Southwest Asia

Theodor Herzl. Pietzner, Carl. c. 1900. Wikimedia Commons

Armenian Genocide orphans, K. Polis. 1920. Wikimedia Commons

Palestine - Jaramana Refugee Camp, Damascus, Syria (1948). Public domain via Wikimedia Commons.

Nations of the Arab League, Karakizi. 2012. Wikimedia Commons

Statue of Liberty and WTC Fire. The United States. U.S. Federal Government. National Park Service. 2001. Wikimedia Commons

Period 4: South and Southeast Asia

Gurkhas in Campaigning Kit during First World War. c. 1914-1918. *Old Indian Photos: Historical Photographs of the Indian Subcontinent*. Wikimedia Commons

Gandhi Smiling. Life Magazine Photo Archive. 1946. Wikimedia Commons

Official Proclamation of Queen Victoria as Empress of India on the Steps of the Stock Exchange, London. 1876. The Bridgeman Art Library. *The Spanish and American Illustration*. Wikimedia Commons

Mohammed Ali Jinnah Smoking. c. 1947. *The Indian Express*. Wikimedia Commons

Ho Chi Minh, Indochinese Delegate to the French Communist Congress in Marseilles, 1921. News Agency Meurisse. 1921. National Library of France. Paris. Wikimedia Commons

Khmer Rouge Administrative Zones for Democratic Kampuchea, 1975-78. By Library of Congress. Federal Research Division. (Cambodia: a country study) [Public domain], via Wikimedia Commons

Period 4: East Asia

Victims of the Nanjing Massacre. Japan. Japanese Navy. Kisarazu Air Unit. By Itou Kaneo. 1937. Wikimedia Commons

Atomic Bombing of Nagasaki on August 9, 1945. The United States. U.S. Army. National Archives and Records Administration. By Charles Levy. 1945. Wikimedia Commons

Deng Xiaoping, George H. W. Bush, and Gerald Ford, 1975. Kennerly, David Hume. 1975. Gerald R. Ford Library Museum, Michigan. Executive Office of the President of the United States. Wikimedia Commons

Chinese Leader Hua Guofeng at a State Visit in Iran. Catherine Legrand, Jacques Legrand: Shah-i Iran. Creative Publishing International (farsi edition), Minnetonka, MN 1999. Wikimedia Commons

Works of Falun Gong Destroyed during the 1999 Crackdown in China. Mingui.org. 1999. *Clear Wisdom*. Wikimedia Commons

Period 4: The Americas

Pinochet meeting U.S. Secretary of State Henry Kissinger in 1976, Ministerio de Relaciones Exteriores de Chile. 1976. Wikimedia Commons

2006 public celebration of Saint-Jean-Baptiste Day, Francis Tremblay. 2006. Wikimedia Commons

Your purchase helps support global environmental causes

Sterling Test Prep is committed to protecting our planet by supporting environmental organizations for conservation, ecological research, and preservation of vital natural resources. A portion of our profits is donated to help these organizations continue their critical missions.

  The Ocean Conservancy advocates for a healthy ocean with sustainable solutions based on science and cleanup efforts.

 The Rainforest Trust saves critical lands for conservation through land purchases and protected area designations in over 16 countries.

PACIFIC WHALE FOUNDATION Pacific Whale Foundation saves whales from extinction and protects our oceans through science and advocacy.

We want to hear from you

Your feedback is important to us because we strive to provide the highest quality prep materials. Email us any comments or suggestions.

info@sterling–prep.com

Customer Satisfaction Guarantee
Contact us to resolve any issues to your satisfaction.

*We reply to all emails – **check your spam folder***

Thank you for choosing our products to achieve your educational goals!

SAT Subject Test prep books by Sterling Test Prep

- SAT Biology Practice Questions

- SAT Biology Review

- SAT Physics Practice Questions

- SAT Physics Review

- SAT Chemistry Practice Questions

- SAT Chemistry Review

- SAT U.S. History

AP prep books by Sterling Test Prep

- AP Biology Practice Questions
- AP Biology Review
- AP Chemistry Practice Questions
- AP Chemistry Review
- AP Physics 1 Practice Questions
- AP Physics 1 Review
- AP Physics 2 Practice Questions
- AP Physics 2 Review

- AP Environmental Science
- AP Human Geography
- AP Psychology
- AP U.S. History
- AP World History
- AP European History
- AP U.S. Government and Politics
- AP Comparative Government and Politics

To access the online SAT tests at a special pricing visit:
http://SAT.Sterling-Prep.com/bookowner.htm

Made in United States
Troutdale, OR
09/15/2023